DAYS *of* FIRE *and* GLORY

DAYS *of* FIRE *and* GLORY

The Rise and Fall of
a Charismatic Community

JULIA DUIN

CROSSLAND PRESS

2009

Published in the United States by
Crossland Press
P.O. Box 26290
Baltimore, MD 21210

ISBN-13: 978-0-9790279-7-0
ISBN-10: 0-9790279-7-7
Library of Congress Control Number: 2009932042

Book design by Sam Torode
Printed in the United States of America

*Dedicated to all those who delight
in the power of the Holy Spirit,
especially:*

*Carol Lee and Choppy Cusachs, who helped me
think through this book theologically;
Debbie Scott, who warned me of the window of opportunity;
Chris Hughes, who drove me across the country as I did interviews;
and Anita Higman, who never gave up.*

CONTENTS

Foreword

ENTECOSTAL fires that started burning in North America in 1900 swept into the mainline denominations and the Catholic Church in the 1960s, and from there into the Third World where Pentecostal and charismatic Christians are the fast-growing segment of the church. But the movement that begins in the fire and freedom of the Spirit sometimes leads to a surrender of freedom to an authoritarian leader, who manipulates believers for his own purposes.

Julia Duin gives us a look at this dynamism from the inside. Other communities have undergone similar convulsions. The Mother of God Community in Gaithersburg, Maryland, had many professional Washingtonians as members and had renowned theologians such as the Capuchin Father Thomas Weinandy as chaplains. But a core of leaders began to inculcate an extraordinary discipline into members of the community, which was joined by signing a covenant. Each member was responsible to a shepherd or guide or "buddy" who conveyed the discernment of the community to them, and this discernment extended to the decisions about where to live, where to work, and even whom to marry.

I was, during the early 1970s, on the fringe of this community. I knew Father Weinandy, with whom I have remained friends, and I also knew a leader of the charismatic prayer group at Catholic University. The leader, alas, was an active homosexual and eventually died of AIDS. A family that helped start the community set up businesses that employed community members. The family profited from these ventures legally, but perhaps not ethically. Community members had to give the leaders absolute loyalty and menial services, such as cleaning their bathrooms and walking their dogs.

Community members eventually asked Cardinal James Hickey to step in, and he warned the community that "no lay leader has a right to demand religious obedience from a fellow adult lay Catholic. We can help each other on the journey but we must all walk in freedom!" The community broke up in recriminations and divorces, and only a small group remains, now incorporated into the Archdiocese of Washington as a lay group.

Similar events destroyed other charismatic communities, such as the People of Praise in New Jersey and the Houston Episcopal parish that is the subject of this book. Americans are reputedly freedom-loving, but they sometimes surrender their freedom with alarming alacrity and ease. The hierarchy and canon law can serve as guards for freedom, by forbidding a too-quick or too-total surrender of the will to another person. Perhaps freedom of the type and level that Americans have is too great a burden for some adults, who seek to surrender the responsibility for every detail of their lives to the will of another, if that other can be seen as somehow conveying God's will.

Religious groups provide useful venues for pathological narcissists, who are charismatic in the psychological sense. These narcissists see themselves as the center of a world that is exciting and important, and others are attracted to this world. Narcissists like to manipulate, and some people wish to be controlled and to abandon responsibility for their lives. We will continue to see such narcissists exploiting Christian groups, and the story that Julia Duin tells in this book can serve as a caution and a warning for the future.

—LEON J. PODLES
author, *Sacrilege: Sexual Abuse in the Catholic Church*

Days of Fire and Glory

"Let that sink in. . . . This praise and adoration declaring who God is; His power and desire to save and then the confession, the experience of things that would separate us from God, that would entangle us, nigh overwhelm us and seem death-dealing and destructive and then he says, 'In my distress I called to the Lord, I cried to my God for help.' And that is the way out."

—Ladd Fields, July 13, 1990

9:45 a.m., September 22, 1989

"Write, therefore, what you have seen, what is now and what
will take place later."   —Revelation 1:19

I was seated in a gorgeous meadow overlooking the Sea of Galilee. Other
members of my tour group were wandering about the Mount of Beatitudes
but I needed some quiet. For about a year, the Almighty had been suggesting that I write about the Church of the Redeemer, the world-famous Episcopal
church I was attending in Houston's East End. The church's legendary personalities had made it a unique juxtaposition of Christian community and charismatic
power. And its story had already appeared in several books and on television.
But nothing had been written in at least a decade, and I sensed I was to tell the
whole story—whatever that was.

Peter the disciple had stepped out on this same lake with nothing but faith
to stand on. And that is all I would have. I knew I did not have the endurance
and strength to accomplish this awesome task. And the needed financial resources were daunting. Where was I going to find the time for such a massive
project? What if I did not finish; did not find a publisher or market; or got
stymied by the people at Redeemer itself? What if I lost friends over the writing
of this book? And where would I find the money to finance years of research?

And so I asked the Lord for the power to do it. And while gazing at that
lovely lake in the mid-morning Israeli sun, an impression sprang instantly to my
mind of Him saying, "You shall have it."

And so I began. The Redeemer was set up so that everyone adhered to a
strict line of authority. If the parish rector said a project was alright, then it was

assumed God was behind it. And so I sought out the three rectors who were in place during Redeemer's period of fame: Graham Pulkingham, Ladd Fields, and Jeff Schiffmayer. All had overseen the church during the 30-year period I was chronicling, which would end up being 1963–1993. Ladd was quick to give his approval, even agreeing to provide a letter on church stationery that I could send to 350 people scattered around the world. Stationed in a parish a two-hour drive away, Jeff said he would not oppose the book and wanted only minimal involvement with it. But the big fish was Graham, and so I flew to Pittsburgh. We spent five hours together on a cold November day. At first, he suggested I make the story into a novel. "No way," I said. "I am a journalist and the truth deserves telling."

He launched into a long discourse on community, saying the charismatic renewal was based upon the "principle of commonality." That is, God's power lay not only in spiritual gifts but in the community they sprang up in. Community was the fulcrum for everything: praise, worship, healing power, and supernatural events. This is how he interpreted Acts 2, the story of the birth of the powerful early church.

Then he paused. A book, he said, had enormous implications. He was not sure how much he could say; what pastoral confidences he might breach. He turned to me. If the book is neither an exposé nor a souped-up, glamorized rendition of earlier books on Redeemer, then what was it, he asked? What criteria would I use? If the criteria was sin—as in an exposé—he was not interested.

"Neither am I," I said.

Had I only known.

But, unsuspecting, I innocently told Graham that God had only directed me to write the thing. How and why was yet to be determined. Graham then posed a second challenge: did I not lack the theological depth and insight to write such a book? "If you are going to report," he said, "you will need to interpret and analyze."

The big unanswered question was where I'd find the time to write such a book. I had no grants or fellowships. I was working full-time as a religion reporter for the *Houston Chronicle*, one of the country's largest newspapers. Two years before, I'd written a short book on sexual purity. It had taken me every free weekend for seven months. This Redeemer book would take 10 times the time and energy, and my newspaper was not accustomed to granting year-long book sabbaticals.

Three months later, my employer suddenly fired me—with no explanation.

After I emerged from my tailspin, I realized that I now had several months in which to start this book before I left Houston to move to a seminary across the Ohio River from Graham's home. Here is where I would get the master's degree that would provide the theological underpinning I needed.

And so, a year later, in September 1990, I began showing up once a month at the manse of Graham and his wife, Betty Jane, to hear once again of what God had done at Redeemer. I was already driving about the country and putting significant money into long-distance calls to locate former members. I was digging into my theological studies three miles away across the river. The next two summers were spent camping out in Houston to interview more people.

I began to unearth not only the glories of Redeemer's history but also its terrible secrets. And then it was the summer of 1992, one of the coolest and rainiest on record in Pittsburgh. The night of August 10 was uncharacteristically hot and stuffy. I was sweltering in a non-air-conditioned second-floor apartment in Ambridge, a small town 20 miles north of Pittsburgh, making my way through a doctoral thesis on Redeemer for the University of Houston. At 9:30 p.m., the phone rang.

On the other end was Graham's familiar, clipped voice. Graham was an architect of a unique spiritual awakening begun in the 1960s in the United States that became one of the world's most potent religious forces. For 2,000 years, the Christian church had tried various ways of returning to the glory and power of the book of Acts, a time when Jesus's followers converted 3,000 people in a day and healed every ailment they ran across. Despite isolated revivals, Christianity never equaled the glorious achievements from those first years after Jesus's resurrection. Centuries of division and separation among Christians had taken their toll.

Then, inexplicably, a divine grace of mammoth proportions was poured out around the world on all Christian traditions. It was more radical than just another revival. It was a seismic shift in the nature of Christianity. The supernatural "gifts" of the Holy Spirit were reappearing, and the church seemingly was reawakening, Rip Van Winkle-like, from a 20-century slumber. People were combing through Scripture to find all sorts of coded references to an empowerment, a gift, a baptism in the Holy Spirit that the early church had known all about. How had this gotten lost through the centuries? Church of the Redeemer, positioned squarely in the beginning of this U.S. revival, uniquely contributed to the renewal's internationalization.

First, it was the coffeehouse in downtown Houston that Graham founded on the "hippie trail," linking the east coast and California and running through the southern states. It became the model for Christian coffeehouses around the country. Then, perhaps even more significant, it was the community—a network of 400 people living together, by the dozens, in homes, sharing salaries, preaching the Gospel, and transforming their low-income neighborhoods.

Then it was the music, primed by artists and musicians who drifted in from around the world, wedding guitars and drums to spirituality to create contemporary Christian songs that spread to churches everywhere. CBS' laudatory hour-long special on the church in 1972 was only one of the admiring bouquets tossed at Redeemer's feet.

Shortly after that, Graham moved to England in a bid to spread his influence to the seat of the Anglican Communion. In his absence, a cadre of elders started imposing draconian rules, and the spiritual freedom that had distinguished Redeemer's life quickly died. A top elder was caught in adultery, and the unrelated Jim Jones Guyana tragedy cast a pall over the entire notion of communal living. The households split up over a period of a few months and by the time Graham returned in 1980 to clean up the place, Redeemer was a spiritual ruin.

By then, the charismatic renewal had peaked across the rest of the country. But nowhere in the United States had it burned with such intensity as it had at Church of the Redeemer, where the New Testament repeated itself for a glamorous decade. People came there from all over the world, much like they did to the Azusa Street revival in the early 1900s to see the book of Acts in action, to experience the eternal, haunting quality of the music, to drink in the power and love of God.

When I first encountered Redeemer in 1986, mostly smoking embers were left of its original fire. It was the waning of an era. Times had changed, goals were reached, prophets had died. Traditions crept in, with bureaucracy replacing the Spirit. Leaders became set in their ways, and sin, I discovered, ruined this spiritual block party.

Redeemer was based on a movement that promised so much, but got easily corrupted. And yet, at its base, there was a shining reality that had set 120 people on fire on the first Pentecost. A generation of baby boomer Christians, converted and baptized in the Spirit during the 1960s and 1970s, could not deny this core experience. Just as a mind once stretched by a new idea can never go back to its original dimensions, so their spirits could never return to their previous levels. Any effort to do so ended in misery, for it was impossible to refold the gossamer wings and crawl back into the cocoon.

When I first met Graham, he was the most vibrant personality I had encountered in many years of reporting. His baptism in the Spirit had revealed to him an intimacy with God that, in the early years of his charismatic ministry, he shared with all his heart to thousands, if not millions. They too longed to drink from that same well.

Then a shadow arose. Only God knows the whole story, but what I found was the best story I could gather through years of shifting through church records, all of Graham's writings, dozens of tapes, and face-to-face interviews with 182 persons, including nine bishops, many clergy, and numerous hidden, humble people.

Graham was still on the other end of the line. I had not been able to finish my research because, at the core of my narrative was a deep secret involving him. I had to know what it was. Twice, when I had asked him about it, he had denied involvement in any impropriety. That July, I showed up at his office with the name of a man: Richard.

"Julia," he was saying over the phone, "I need to ask your forgiveness. You know the question you asked me about Richard? Well, there's truth in that. Richard is talking and I need not pretend."

I grabbed a note pad and began scribbling. Over the next half hour, he finally revealed his secret. Thirty years before, he had experienced God's love and power. Years later, he had allowed it to become power and desire, and now he was at the greatest crisis of his life, with the sand in his human hour glass fast running out.

I could see the beautiful edifice of this man's reputation shattering, thousands of sharp splinters landing in Pittsburgh, Houston, Colorado, England, and wherever people knew of the beauty that was once Graham's ministry at Redeemer. James Clark, the writer of the dissertation sitting on my lap, had called Redeemer "a unique and priceless laboratory" for the testing of the charismatic thesis. It was a laboratory like none other, with many spills, many broken laboratory dishes, and a few chemical explosions. And now here was a nuclear bomb.

Graham, I thought, *how could you?* There never was a beauty quite like Redeemer's. Those who have left there have never found anything quite like it elsewhere. The book of Acts really did come alive there, and for a few short years, Houston had been a glorious spiritual Camelot.

The power of the Holy Spirit had been like dawn, leaping over Houston, its powerful rays streaking across an azure Texas sky, its light turning a sea of skyscrapers into the bejeweled walls of a celestial city.

1963–1967

CHAPTER I

Pentecost

"When the day of Pentecost came, they were all together in one place. Suddenly a sound like the blowing of a violent wind came from heaven and filled the whole house where they were sitting. They saw what seemed to be tongues of fire that separated and came to rest on each of them. All of them were filled with the Holy Spirit and began to speak in other tongues as the Spirit enabled them."　　　—Acts 2:1-4

O N especially humid nights, a stellar cluster explodes on the Texas prairie. It is Houston; powerful, glittering, the city built by oil.

Just to the east of downtown are the trees, scattered about a neighborhood appropriately named Eastwood. The city's genteel residents settled it in the 1920s, planting graceful live oaks to shade the streets and block the heat. At night, their overhanging branches block out the moon and stars, creating shadows and silence except for a few blaring radios of Latino music. Those who venture into the neighborhood after dark drive past a gauntlet of bars, auto shops, a gas station, warehouses, junk yards, a tired-looking supermarket with a parking lot filled with trash, one *washateria*, a bakery that emits delicious odors, and the Maxwell House coffee factory a few blocks away, blazing with lights like the oil refineries to the east.

Getting there is simple. Take the interstate leading through downtown, then find the Cullen Street exit leading north from the University of Houston and follow that to Polk Street. Then make a right onto Polk, a badly lit road where several of the homes have stacks of trash and parked cars in the front yards. Eastwood is a barrio, meaning "neighborhood" in Spanish—it's also the flip way Anglos refer to a community overtaken by Mexicans. The second left is Eastwood

Street, which leads to a large gray stone church standing like a lonely monolith on a triangular plot where Dallas Avenue and Telephone Road intersect.

This is the Episcopal Church of the Redeemer. Enter through its glass doors. Curving around the inside front of the church and dominating the room is a huge, colorful, stunning mural. At the center is a compelling, life-sized, white-robed Jesus ascending in the clouds. His eyes follow you wherever you stand. He is clearly in charge.

Flanking him are 11 men of various races and occupations, dressed in World War II-era clothes, their gaze focused on the Lord. All their hats are off. Some are falling to their knees. Bordering everything are trees, sky, and stars painted on the walls, extending down the sides of the nave, as if the room is part of a forest.

In that church, there once was a priest. He arrived in the summer of 1963, his family unhappily trailing behind. People knew Graham Pulkingham as ambitious, cultured, and music-loving; a blond-haired 37-year-old clergyman with a slight paunch, fashionable liberal views, and a confident air of authority that people either hated or found irresistible. His professional life had been one stream of successes. Then he had moved his wife and children to an inner-city parish east of Houston, determined he was going to set the place right.

By the following August, he was shipwrecked on the shoals of Eastwood.

IT was the dead of summer and the appropriate time for a priest's family to leave on their annual four-week vacation. Thus, the Pulkinghams left for a lengthy stay in Burlington, North Carolina. Burlington was the peaceful oasis of the Carr family, whose eldest daughter, Betty Jane, had married Graham more than a decade before. The family hadn't been in Burlington more than a week when Graham, early in the morning, awoke feeling agitated. He sensed the Lord wanted to communicate with him, and sure enough, a familiar voice said, *"Go to New York."*

"When?" he wanted to know.

"Next Tuesday," the voice said.

"With what money?" Graham wondered aloud. He had five dollars in cash and a gasoline credit card.

"I can be trusted for that," the voice assured him. *"Do as I say."*

For months now, Graham had been waking up at odd hours of the night to focus on his new love, the Scriptures. Books he had never studied, much less read, came alive to him and words that were 2,000 years old spoke to his present situation. The night before he left for New York, he happened to turn to the book of Joel in the Old Testament. He read:

"Yet, even now," says the Lord, "return to me with all your heart, with fasting, with weeping and with mourning."

Repentance? Graham wondered. *Fasting?* He decided to fast on his way to New York, which would partly take care of both the food and money question. For the next few days, he reflected and wept over the passage, dimly recognizing that the verse was coming true in his own life. He remembered another verse, this one from John 12, about the kernel of wheat that falls to the ground, then bears much fruit. But first it must die.

"Lord," Graham prayed, "I don't know what kind of ministry or church it will be, but I know the kind I've experienced so far isn't any good. It's useless. Show me the way. I don't care what the consequences are. Please show me a new way."

By the time he arrived in the Big Apple, a desperate Graham was in his third day of fasting. No August rains cooled New York's broiling environs. Fleeing the simmering sidewalks, he took refuge in the cool interior of the majestic Trinity Episcopal Church on Wall Street. Weeping, he knelt behind the organ bench, hoping no one would discover him praying. He looked up to see the irate face of the church sexton.

"What are you doing here?" the man demanded.

"I'm praying."

"Well, get the hell out."

A	T the age of 32, David Wilkerson was already famous, in Christian circles, at least. Normally, his type, the son of pentecostal parents, would never have crossed paths with an Episcopal priest like Graham. He began humbly enough as the pastor of a small Pennsylvania church. Then one day in 1958, he happened to glance at *Life* magazine. The story was about the death of a crippled boy and his seven alleged murderers from the streets of New York City. Feeling compelled to reach these young killers with the Gospel, David drove to the courthouse where they were on trial. He tried contacting them inside the courtroom but was ejected by police. A photo of his arrest ended up on the front page of the *New York Daily News*, and when David took to the streets to seek gang members who were friends of the seven male defendants, they recognized him from the newspaper. Seeing him as a fellow victim of poor treatment by the cops, they were willing to listen to his preaching.

At the time, the problem of street gangs, racial warfare, and drug use was alien to most Americans, who wouldn't be caught dead in the shadier sections of New York. David, however, flourished there, that same year founding a ministry to drug addicts and alcoholics called Teen Challenge. But his method of helping them get off drugs was unorthodox. Not only were they told to go completely cold turkey, but they had to convert to Christianity and undergo an experience known as the "baptism in the Holy Spirit," during which participants were encouraged to seek the gift of speaking in tongues. David's new converts were actually staying off drugs, and many of them were going into the ministry themselves.

David Wilkerson's genius lay in something organized Christianity had not tried since the days of the apostles: applying pentecostal power to a glaring social problem. Beginning in the 1950s, street gangs were an unsolvable problem, as was vividly portrayed in the popular 1957 musical "West Side Story;" a Romeo and Juliet tale set against the backdrop of gang wars between poor whites and Puerto Ricans. David's biography, *The Cross and the Switchblade*, written by John and Elizabeth Sherrill, which had come out in the early 1960s, described how these addicts had been delivered, devoting two chapters to the baptism in the Spirit. The pentecostalism did not go down well with one denominational publisher, which threatened to withdraw a huge order for the book unless the offending chapters were withdrawn. The Sherrills refused, contending that the baptism was key to David's success.

It would defraud readers, they felt, not to describe how the Holy Spirit could break any drug habit. The book went on to sell millions of copies and eventually become a film starring Pat Boone. One of those copies landed in Graham's hands. Here was someone, Graham thought, who also wanted to help the poor and who, unlike Graham, had been given the power to do so. The pentecostal minister, who even spent his half-hour morning commute from Staten Island to Manhattan praying in tongues, seemed to have as direct a line to God as one could get.

When Graham described to David the mess he had caused in Houston, the two men clicked. Graham then confided a degrading secret: Married for more than a decade and the father of four children, he had sexual cravings for other men. Thoughts of sex with them would roar into his mind at the worst times, especially when he was preaching. He had hit nearly every rest area between North Carolina and New York, searching for male liaisons.

Horrified, David first instructed Graham to leave the ministry. But, if this were to happen, to whom would this pathetic man turn? David knew that Graham had taken many risks coming secretly, Nicodemus-like, to visit him. High society-style Episcopal priests rarely deigned to speak to lower-class pentecostals in those days, much less come asking for advice.

In a change of heart, David invited Graham to do street evangelism with him in Harlem the following night. That evening, they arrived in a neighborhood crowded with pushers and prostitutes, the sidewalks packed with people shooting up drugs, the dark side streets crowded with whispering mobs. Graham tagged alongside David and wept, then became totally undone when they entered someone's basement to find a group of boys twitching and shaking after having mainlined drugs.

My God, look at these pathetic creatures, he thought. The next thought was even worse: He, a minister of the Gospel, did not have the spiritual power to help these kids. The next day, Graham accompanied his host to upstate New York, stopping in Poughkeepsie at an old estate converted into a home for women fresh off the streets. As David talked with the mission director, Graham browsed among some books.

Suddenly David turned toward Graham. "I bear witness in my heart about you," he said. "Kneel down."

Graham did so, not knowing what to expect. David and the mission director crossed the room, placed their hands on Graham's head, and prayed over him in what sounded like strange, almost angelic languages. Graham's spirit lit up. He was being confronted with the most majestic presence and power he had ever known, and he staggered. This, he thought, must be what the New Testament meant by the "weight of glory." He first wondered what was being bestowed on him, and then he knew. "You shall receive power when the Holy Spirit comes upon you," Jesus had promised the disciples before Pentecost, and now, here it was.

Graham's soul lay surrendered and prostrate before the Third Person of the Trinity, who flooded him with love, and then, in one rush, swept him clean of sexual defilement. The degradation was gone. Graham, who had not guessed such deliverance was possible, bowed his head to the ground and convulsively sobbed.

"We can go now. The Baptizer's here," David announced to his friend. The two departed.

Sometime later, the presence departed as suddenly as He had come, and Graham, now at peace, stopped his weeping. He rose to his feet. So this was the baptism in the Spirit, he thought; this incredible power with the most gentle of Persons wrapping him in the tender embrace.

Thrilled by his experience, Graham headed back home.

CHAPTER 2

Trinity

"And the multitude of them that believed were of one heart and of one soul: neither said any of them that aught of the things which he possessed was his own; but they had all things in common.

"And with great power gave the apostles witness of the resurrection of the Lord Jesus: and great grace was upon them all."

—Acts 4:32-33 (KJV)

IN the early 1960s, Houston presented itself as having a glorious future. It was the Space City, with NASA headquarters on its southeastern flank and a presidential mandate to put a man on the moon before the Russians did. It had its own accent, chicken-fried steak, Mexican restaurants, king-sized cockroaches, instant millionaires, and glassed-in skyscrapers on a sprawling coastal plain. For nine years before statehood, Texas was a country—a short-lived republic proud of its distance and bigness compared to the rest of the country. It was extra proud of its warts, its rawness and a directness that admitted to no natural wonders, but dared you to complain about it.

Intersected by bayous, Houston was circumscribed by a highway loop and four major monstrous freeways that dominated and structured the flat landscape. Houston had no native beauty or natural vistas, such as mountains or bays, to soften its edges, and they would become even sharper with the addition of futuristic skyscrapers in the 1970s and 1980s. Houston was a city well-positioned for the second half of the 20th century. It was the epicenter of an explosion of confidence in the American way and in America's ability to pull off a moon landing in less than a decade. It had the leadership of President John F. Kennedy, whose own confidence inspired idealistic Americans to join the Peace

Corps, join in the space race, and embark on other long-term projects. All great civilizations require such energy, will, and creative power to sustain them in their ascendancies, and Houston was leading the way.

Not that Houston lacked creativity before all this. Its ultimate pre-Space Age showcase was the Shamrock Hotel, an extravagant building with 63 shades of green furnishings that opened with a gala debut on St. Patrick's Day, 1949. About 50,000 people turned out to see the 175 movie stars present. Its much-ballyhooed builder was a thoughtful man named Tom Tellepsen.

He was born Torjus, the son of Tellef the carpenter, on the first day of spring in 1888 in Tvedestrand, Norway. He emigrated to America in 1909, ending up in Houston, where he bought 160 acres for $800. After he returned to Norway in 1912 to marry a childhood sweetheart, the family settled in Eastwood, then a respectable neighborhood just east of downtown with neatly kept homes shaded by the spindly branches of live oaks. Torjus Americanized his name to Tom and began a construction and building business. In the late 1920s, he began building the Houston landmarks he became known for: Palmer Memorial Church on South Main Street; the chemistry building at Rice University; the Melrose Building; Children's Hospital; St. Luke's Hospital; the Medical Towers doctors' offices; and the Shamrock.

His most meaningful personal achievement never made the landmark list. During the Depression, Tom needed to keep his construction crews busy, so, as a project, he decided to build a community church called Church of the Redeemer in Eastwood, his favorite neighborhood. On the site of the original church, Tom built a much larger sanctuary and education building with one major oddity: Redeemer had no windows. Exceptionally large, with a seating capacity for about 1,000, it also had no stained glass.

The windowless space was designed partly to conserve on air-conditioning and to focus attention on the stunning mural of the Ascension behind the altar, painted by John Orth. The men flanking Jesus included a farmer, a sailor, a laborer holding a lunch box, an American Indian or Mexican, a vagabond, a minister, a cowboy, a black man, an oil man, a businessman, and a lawyer holding a briefcase. They were the 1940s version of the 11 disciples who saw Jesus ascend, and the bearded vagabond was Tom himself. Behind the male disciples were the indistinct faces of women. Tom had planned that as well: "It is the men," he said, "who mostly need religion." To everyone concerned, Redeemer was "Mr. Tom's church," and he was such good friends with its various rectors that he took them out to dinner after church almost every Sunday. That all stopped when the new rector arrived in 1963.

A year before the fateful trip to New York, Graham Pulkingham was no embracer of pentecostalism. *Time* magazine had just run an article about charismatic activity at Yale University, nicknaming its practitioners "Glosso Yalies," after *glossolalia*, the technical term for speaking in tongues. Graham had gotten wind of similar goings on among Episcopalians, but they were not his cup of tea. He disliked the religious enthusiasm of the sort he sometimes ran into with a prayer group at St. David's, the wealthy Austin parish where he was assistant rector. When his rector commented, "Graham, I don't know whether they have something I don't have, or something I don't want," Graham totally agreed.

One rainy spring day, he drove three hours from Austin for a talk with his confidante at the diocesan headquarters in Houston: Scott Field Bailey, a canon to John Hines, bishop of the Diocese of Texas. Graham was interested in leaving St. David's to head his own parish. After only a few moments of conversation, it was clear to Graham that Scott knew of no openings in parishes large enough to interest him. Then his confidante leaned forward.

"Graham, did you hear what happened to Bob Kemp?"

Graham had not. Scott went on to say that this seminary classmate of Graham's had been fired by Dr. Thomas Harris, rector of the Church of the Redeemer somewhere in Houston's East End. Tom Harris was of the old school, Scott said, a dyed-in-the-wool Anglo-Catholic who had created Redeemer as an island of Episcopal orthodoxy in a sea of liberalism. Tom Harris had isolated himself from the diocese, and the church was located in an increasingly rundown neighborhood three miles east of town.

I need to go see this church, Graham thought.

Thanking Scott, he left the building and steered his white 1958 Plymouth through the rain toward Eastwood. The area was a no-man's land of industrial complexes, warehouses, and gutted, burned-out apartments. Everywhere Graham looked, there were railroads and industrial switch tracks and more and more poverty. He finally found the church at 4411 Dallas Avenue, and as he drove by the rectory, he glimpsed Tom Harris staring wistfully out the door.

A voice inside Graham said, "You'll be the next rector of this church."

Graham thought the voice was crazy and turned his Plymouth in the direction of Austin.

S OON after Graham's conversation with Scott Bailey, Thomas Harris suffered a heart attack and prepared to retire. Graham became one of the three finalists for the position, so he and Betty Jane drove to Redeemer to conduct a service. Graham winced at the deplorable music. The air-conditioning was on full-tilt, the neon lighting was set at 40 percent full strength, and Graham could barely make out the hymnal. The service was sparsely attended.

Afterwards, a woman identifying herself as Grace Murray approached him. "The Holy Spirit has told me you're going to be the next rector of this parish," she informed him.

"Well, I hope He has the grace to tell me," Graham retorted, offended that this woman would claim to know the mind of God. Grace was not taken aback by his bluntness or his play on words. Involved in a pentecostal prayer group for eight years, she said she had prayed consistently for a Holy Spirit-filled man to head Redeemer. Though her friend, Wanda Plummer, categorized Graham as an "eyebrow-cocked, pipe-smoking Episcopal priest," Grace was sure he was the right man.

John and Edith Grimmet, long-time members at the church, were also looking Graham over. John, a no-frills blue-collar worker, was a foreman for Houston Power and Light. He had large workingman's hands, a muscled body, and a straightforward stare. John didn't trust his intellect much, but he had honed his spiritual instincts to a sharp edge.

Edith asked her husband what he thought of Graham.

"Well," said John, "he could lead you to the Lord or lead you in the opposite direction so you could believe you were there."

What nettled John was Graham's pipe smoking. Even worse was Betty Jane, who showed up in the parish hall clasping a cigarette in a cigarette holder. Betty was aghast at the whole situation. They had four children, including one still in diapers, and were living in a large, comfortable house in Austin. This was no time to uproot them, she thought. Austin was affluent and comfortable, with several pools and a huge public library nearby. Their eldest child, Bill, was happily attending St. Andrew's Episcopal School and taking cello lessons. Betty's younger sister, Nancy, had moved in with them to be of some support and to get a music degree at the University of Texas. Not only would Betty leave Nancy behind but Redeemer offered no yard, no parks, no family room, no play room, and mostly urchins for her offspring to play with. Under no circumstances, she told Graham later, would she take the children into that dingy rectory.

Betty became even more upset when she and Graham got a call from Bob Evans, the senior warden of the vestry. Vestries are uniquely Episcopal creations. They usually consist of 10 to 16 people who are the leadership core of a church; their mixture of business and spiritual leadership has the ultimate say over a parish. Its leader, called a senior warden, legally represents the will of the vestry.

The priest is the legal representative of the bishop—the very name "Episcopal" signifies a denomination governed by bishops.

"Well, Graham," Bob said, "we've considered all three and we want you to be our first choice."

When Graham told him of Betty's ultimatum, Evans said it was impossible to make structural changes in the rectory. Tom Tellepsen would not allow it.

Things remained at an impasse until the phone rang again. This time it was the bishop, John Hines. Bishop Hines was an old-timer in the diocese who believed that Texas's short experiment as a republic a century before had injected a streak of independence in its inhabitants. Texans didn't mind standing against the world and, thanks to its cotton factories and oil rigs, they had the financial resources to do it. And in his diocese was the bulk of the state's large, significant educational institutions: Baylor and Rice Universities, Texas A&M, the University of Texas, and several others.

That is why he placed chaplains on every campus he could. People often met the Episcopal Church for the first time while in college, and it was from these institutions that Hines drew most of his clergy. Graham enrolled at the University of Texas in Austin in 1950, and a year later, he came to the attention of Hines, who was stationed in Austin under Bishop Clinton Quin. Graham had appeared in Hines's office, saying he wanted to go into the ministry. The bishop looked at this platinum-haired, bright, congenial young man and liked him from the start. Besides, he needed students to sign up for the first class of the new Episcopal Seminary of the Southwest in Austin. Graham attended there two years, left to serve a stint in the U.S. Navy during the Korean War, then returned to graduate in 1956.

Graham's Navy experience had matured him, the bishop thought, though Graham had showed up in his office after graduation saying he didn't want to be a parish priest. "You'll do what I tell you to do," Bishop Hines replied, and sent him to two mission churches in Alta Loma and Hitchcock, both small towns near Galveston. Then he installed Graham as chaplain at the University of Texas Medical Branch in Galveston. In all three places, Graham had performed well, was diplomatic, and had worked hard. The churches had flourished under his direction. The bishop considered Graham to be brighter than most clergy even if there was an innate arrogance about the man that grated some of the other ministers. But the bishop wanted someone with gumption to head this East End parish. Redeemer was definitely on the decline, and unless someone with energy moved there, it was bound to die.

So Hines asked Graham to reconsider the Redeemer offer. Tom Tellepsen was a big contributor to the diocese, he said, and it would be unwise to give the parish to someone less qualified. Then Bob Evans called back. If Graham would change his mind, the vestry vote to accept him would be 7-5. It was not an encouraging mandate for a new rector. But the Pulkinghams gained one major concession: Tom Tellepsen agreed to add a playroom to the rectory. His bulldozers arrived the same day they moved in.

B ISHOP QUIN had pried out of Graham some of the particulars of the same secret Pulkingham would later share with David Wilkerson. They first talked in 1951, during Graham's interviews as a postulant for the diocese. Perhaps it was all just a quirk, or a fault of his upbringing, but Bishop Quin sent him to counseling and assumed it had gotten taken care of. But it had not. It had all started during his Depression-era childhood as the only son in an Irish-Catholic Canadian family with four daughters. The Protestant father, Bill, found his Catholic in-laws so overbearing that, for a few years, he moved his family from Hamilton, Ontario, to Alliance, Ohio, to escape them.

There, William Graham Pulkingham was born on Holy Cross Day, September 14, 1926. Then they moved back to Ontario. The child was devout, attended Mass daily, and was shunted off to parochial schools to serve as an acolyte and to be brought up by priests. His father ignored him and his mother devoted her attention to her daughters. Graham took to listening to classical music instead of playing sports, and by the time he was 12, he weighed 190 pounds, his eyes like slits in his fat face. He eventually slimmed down and, to his mother's infuriation, distanced himself from Catholicism in high school and college. Every good Catholic family was supposed to produce a priest or a nun, or both, whether this suited the children or not. And Graham, his mother decided, was priest material—he was the only surviving son after his twin brothers died before he was born. When Graham was 14, a priest asked him whether he wanted to be ordained. Sensing his mother was behind this, Graham refused. Infuriated, she simmered for years. While he was off at the University of Western Ontario, she considered him as good as dead. The next time he came home from vacation, he found his room rearranged, his clothes discarded, and his massive classical record collection given away.

Graham left Canada to pursue graduate studies in music, ending up at the University of Texas, where he discovered Episcopal liturgy and Betty Jane, who taught music there. They married a year later in 1951. At first, his mother had refused to attend the wedding or to let any of Graham's sisters come. When his father got wind of this, he put his foot down for the first time in years and went to his wife's adviser, the Catholic bishop of Hamilton.

"Choose one or the other," Bill Pulkingham said. "Either she goes to the wedding or I divorce her."

Thus, the family, plus an aunt, unwillingly came down from Canada to Betty's home in North Carolina. The night before the wedding, Graham's mother pulled Betty aside.

"You know my son has been called to be a priest," she said. "As soon as he comes to his senses, he'll have to put you away."

Years later, Graham would preach about the day his mother finally died and how they had found a dog-eared card under her pillow. It read: "Jesus, protect my wayward son in Your blood and draw him back to You." When he got to the part of the sermon where he identified himself as the "wayward son," he broke down and cried.

THE wayward son came to Redeemer in August 1963 armed with the same liberal Protestant framework with which most Episcopal seminaries had inculcated their students. His seminary had taught him about parish administration, how to use the Book of Common Prayer, a little bit of Episcopal politics, and a smattering of the various biblical theologies. He knew next to nothing about the Old Testament and had to use the index to find its various books. He did possess a social conscience, wanting to do something meaningful for the poor, and was typical of many Episcopal clergy of the time who believed they could change their worlds by sheer energy or good will. Unhappy about the plight of the disadvantaged and discriminated against, clergy were preoccupied with the city, and romanticized the inner city as a place where all kinds of people could be found and truly inclusive ministry could take place. Clergy were "enablers," fomenting community change, "doing" theology, getting involved in local politics and infiltrating community organizations. In time, the neglect of the spiritual would sap these clergy. The overwhelming fragmentation of the 1960s would discourage many of them, sending some to permanent cynicism, others to a maintenance mode, still others into theological liberalism, and a few to a new movement known as the charismatic renewal.

What broke Graham was Eastwood. The parish sat in the middle of a neighborhood that was an uneasy mix of Mexicans, blacks, and whites. Most of the latter were fleeing Eastwood for happier pastures in Houston's new western suburbs. Eastwood was a troubled 200-acre area in the East End, the city's industrial half. It was Houston's manufacturing section; its strong arms to unload the ships and barges in the nearby Ship Channel. Oil and chemicals were refined there and manufacturing plants abounded. The vast University of Houston central campus, which populated Eastwood with students, lay about a mile south of Redeemer. At certain hours of the day, the Maxwell House coffee plant on Harrisburg Boulevard on Eastwood's periphery filled the neighborhood with a burnt odor. A bread factory on Cullen Street made the neighborhood smell like a bakery. There were neat homes on some streets, but for the most part, lots in Eastwood were used as dump heaps. Obscenities were scribbled on abandoned houses. Second-rate merchandise, wilted produce, and cheap cuts of meat were sold in local stores. Many of the parents worked evening shifts and as a result, their children, some as young as eight years old, wandered the streets until 3 or 4 in the morning.

With the same energy as 10 social workers, Graham went to work, reaching out first to area teenagers. In the evenings, he would hit the streets. The residents' suffering became his suffering. Graham's middle-class lifestyle had never put him into contact with such people before. He obtained a copy of *The Cross and the Switchblade*, noticing how David Wilkerson had performed wonders with the drug addicts and gangs he worked with in Brooklyn. Graham planned to repeat that success in Houston.

He opened the parish hall and gym for basketball, and he had two pool tables and two ping pong tables transported to the unused third floor from the church basement. He staged supper dances for junior and senior high school youth and transformed the church into a community gathering spot for youth programs, Scout meetings, athletic events, and adult discussion groups. After the *Houston Chronicle* ran an article about Graham's plans to open the church to non-Episcopal use, the flood began in earnest.

One of the 12-year-olds so enticed was Ken "Kino" Langoria. The middle child of seven brothers and sisters, he lived just north of Eastwood. To escape his alcoholic father, who terrorized his children each night, Kino would hit the streets with his Mexican friends, ending up at Redeemer. Graham would welcome them, sometimes grabbing several of them at once and smothering them in a bear hug. At six feet tall and 220 pounds, he could quiet them down for a few seconds until they would glance up at Graham's eyes and wrestle themselves away. Sometimes, Kino saw Graham's eyes closed, and guessed that he was praying.

That same fall, a debate in St. Peter's Basilica in Rome would be linked to events unfolding in Eastwood. Opened by Pope John XXIII's prayer for "a new Pentecost," Vatican II had been percolating in Rome since the previous year. Now that the pope had died, Vatican II's outcome was anyone's guess. One of the Council's four moderators was the influential Belgian Cardinal Leo Josef Suenens, a church moderate. At issue were charisms, or gifts of the Holy Spirit. Cardinal Ernesto Ruffini of Palermo, a conservative, argued that the charisms were extraordinary graces given only to a few, such as priests, nuns, or monks. He objected to the mention of charisms in Vatican documents because they had almost completely ceased, he said. Cardinal Suenens, who had only been a cardinal for a year, felt that Ruffini's assertions could not go unchallenged. He gave a speech on Oct. 23, 1963, that forever engraved him in Vatican II annals for the verve and creativity of his remarks. Countering Ruffini, Suenens described how the Holy Spirit is given to all Christians and that He decides who gets which spiritual gifts. Suenens' view won the day.

Had the archbishop of Brussels not intervened, Vatican II might have quashed the very idea of charismatic gifts. Suenens had unwittingly set the stage for the explosive beginning of the Catholic charismatic renewal in 1967, a movement the cardinal had hardly foreseen in 1963. When it comes to movements of the Spirit, rarely are the theologians ahead of their time. This time they were.

CHAPTER 3

The Feast of
St. Mary Magdalene

"Mary Magdalene went to the disciples with the news: "I have seen the Lord!" And she told them that He had said these things to her."

—John 20:18

ETTY JANE was wondering how long her sanity would last. Ten-year-old Bill, who was a sensitive child to begin with, had stomach aches and cried every day before he left for Lantrip Elementary, which was across the street. Half of his classmates were Latinos who had been held back several grades because of their poor English. These days, he rarely spoke or ate, as if he was withdrawing from life for reasons of self-preservation.

Mary and Nathan were doing slightly better, but 11-month-old Jane would wake two or three times a night, crying whenever an ambulance or fire truck screeched by. It seemed as if they were miles away from people who watched the day's most popular movies (*Dr. Strangelove*, *Lawrence of Arabia*, and *Cleopatra*), or read its most influential books (like Rachel Carson's *Silent Spring*) or led otherwise normal lives.

Betty Jane spent a lot of time alone that fall, often receiving anonymous phone calls from people who suggested the Pulkinghams should not have come to the parish. Her husband was not of much help; he was traveling about the neighborhood at odd hours, ministering to God knows whom. All of life was one big malaise; President Kennedy had been shot, one day after touring Houston, and the whole nation was depressed.

To her, it was obvious that Graham's neighborhood experiment was failing and that none of the exciting liberal theology from seminary days was working. Neighborhood kids, many of them drunk, or high on airplane glue or marijuana, vandalized the church, sticking pool cues through the third floor ceiling, scrawling obscenities on the walls of the parish hall, and walking on the altar. As parishioners quickly began transferring out of Redeemer, the vestry unanimously voted to close the church doors to youth. Then Graham replaced the faltering neon lights in the nave with fluorescent lighting. The heightened lighting highlighted some minor faults in the mural that until then had been displayed in a romantic duskiness. The first Sunday the new lights were used, Tom Tellepsen entered, took one look at his beloved mural, then left, saying, "You have ruined my church." The next time he returned, it was for his own funeral in 1975.

But in early 1964, the Beatles had just arrived at the newly renamed Kennedy International Airport to perform at Shea Stadium and then sing before 73 million viewers of *The Ed Sullivan Show*. Graham and the church were plainly sinking fast. One-third of the 650-member parish had left the day Graham arrived. Others stayed at the parish a little longer as a courtesy to Tom Harris, but with Graham talking about "weird" topics such as serving the poor, they, too, decided to pull out.

Perhaps as a defense mechanism, Graham would assume an air of intellectual aloofness and self-importance that put off many people. In secret, he would seek refuge in a small chapel underneath the nave where he could sob brokenheartedly without any congregants discovering him. Lent, a penitential and somber liturgical season, had begun that month, but this was the worst Lent Graham had lived through. The church was in the same condition as when he had first come seven months before. Actually, it was worse, because of the vandalism and defacement that had resulted from his social experiment. When he wasn't weeping, he was railing at God for having brought him to Houston, only to have him fail.

One day, he was pacing back and forth in his office, trying to prepare a sermon, but berating himself for preaching a Gospel that was so obviously not working. Two words came to his mind: "Stop smoking."

What a stupid thought, he surmised.

But the two words returned with greater force. Annoyed, he wondered what a moralistic gesture like giving up smoking had to do with the world's great concerns of poverty and social justice. For three days, the words continued to haunt him, and then one night, while driving home from a prayer meeting, he impetuously threw his unfinished carton of cigarettes out the car window. At the same time, he asked God to heal him of his bleeding ulcers as well.

Another thought came: Read the third chapter of Matthew. He pulled up to the church and went to his office. Matthew 3 was a passage on repentance, finishing with John the Baptist's haunting promise: "I baptize you with water for repentance, but He who is coming after me is mightier than I, whose sandals I am not worthy to carry; He will baptize you with the Holy Spirit and with fire." Something was up, Graham knew, and it was with a new confidence that he flushed the rest of his cigarettes, antacids, barbiturates, and tranquilizers down the toilet and went to bed.

O N Maundy Thursday, a Methodist preacher showed up in Graham's life. Grover Newman had been converted at age nine as a Methodist in a rural community north of Houston called Cleveland. He discovered he had speaking ability and, by the age of 22, was preaching at five rural churches. He eventually came to Sunset United Methodist in Pasadena, a blue-collar community east of Houston made up mostly of oil refinery workers. He formed a prayer group with several men in the church that was drawn to the Scriptures and especially to passages about the Holy Spirit.

One of the men brought to a meeting some newspaper clippings about the "baptism in the Holy Spirit," the newest rage in Christian circles. They had just begun to pray when Grover felt a sensation he had never felt before. It was emotional and powerful. He felt bathed and loved and cleansed. The sensation was physically intense—ecstatic, even—and Grover half wondered if he was going to die of delight. The closest thing he could relate it to was an orgasm, yet this was not sexual.

I am discovering the key to life's depths, Grover thought, and the Old Testament passage of the prophet Elijah giving his spirit to his disciple Elisha came to mind. "Lord," Grover prayed, "give me a double portion of your Spirit."

His prayer group got wind of the news that Dennis Bennett, a famous charismatic Episcopal priest from Seattle, was in town. Dennis had encountered some charismatics at his former parish in Van Nuys, California, had prayed to be baptized in the Spirit, and ended up, to his surprise, praying in tongues. He announced this fact the following April 3 at a Palm Sunday service. His parishioners reacted so violently that he resigned on the spot, but once the media got wind of the story, Dennis found himself on TV, being asked to demonstrate what the gift of tongues sounded like. His April 1960 ejection from St. Mark's Episcopal Church in Van Nuys was the unofficial beginning of the charismatic movement. Everyone knew that pentecostals had been using all these strange spiritual gifts for years, but this was the first time the media had found a real live clergyman from a mainline denomination who admitted to the experience. Four years later, after relocating to a Seattle parish, Bennett was speaking at St. John the Divine Episcopal Church in River Oaks, an exclusive Houston suburb. Grover went to listen to Bennett, who patiently explained how one could learn to pray in tongues, mainly by asking God for the gift. Tongues, he instructed, could be a gift of exquisite beauty that should attract, not repel. Normally, the ability accompanied one's baptism in the Spirit—if not immediately, at least within a few days or weeks—and happened with a combination of faith and guts. One would simply babble nonsensical syllables until things clicked, a "prayer language" arrived, and the recipient sensed he or she was communicating mysteries to God in a language they did not know. Grover scoffed at the idea until he found himself doing the tongues speaking himself.

A Redeemer parishioner invited Grover to Redeemer's Maundy Thursday service and Grover sought Graham out afterwards. They talked until 2 a.m. about this new strand of pentecostalism that was entering the historic denominations. Graham was still repelled by it all.

Betty Masquelette, a laywoman at St. John the Divine, had received her baptism in the Spirit at Bennett's hands. She was friends with Tom and Doris Sumners—he was the rector of St. John the Divine. One day, Doris invited Betty Masquelette to lunch with a new couple in town: Betty Jane and Graham Pulkingham. Graham, Betty thought, seemed musical, stiff, and pompous. Betty Jane was attractive and quiet. Redeemer was the dregs, so the grapevine went, and Betty wondered how this odd couple would survive its coming ruin.

Graham continued his sojourns in the chapel that, as the weeks progressed, turned into a running debate between him and God. He moaned that he had done all he could, yet God had let him down. He was glimpsing visions of Redeemer as something totally other than the social service provider he had tried to create.

Then, one night in the chapel, the Lord informed him, *"If you will turn it over to Me, I will establish a church that will be a light to the denominational churches of America."*

How would he do that? Graham's ministry would have to drastically change, maybe die. Perhaps he had misheard the Lord. Another night, he sat down in frustration and said, "Lord, you said the gates of hell would not prevail against the church. Well, the gates of the church aren't prevailing against hell."

A voice responded, *"You've been sent in My name, with My authority."*

"Yes," Graham retorted, "but not to take Your place."

"In a sense, you have been sent to take My place," came the response. *"You must love with*

My love, suffer with My suffering, forgive with My forgiveness in the places where I send you; and I'll enable you then to pray effectually with My faith and to do miracles with My power."

So, Graham concluded, Redeemer would become charismatic. Not only would the gifts of the Holy Spirit operate, but Graham would receive an authority he had never before possessed. He could almost see it. It would not be an ecclesiastical authority given him by the Episcopal Church, but it would be an authority over evil, given him by Jesus Himself. Graham had never experienced such power; it was almost beyond his imagining that such gifts would be given out in the 20th century. Yet, here they were for the taking, and he wanted them.

"You've seen the needy lives around you: diseased, bound, suffering and tormented by sin," the voice continued. *"You've asked Me to open their blind eyes and deaf ears and to soften their hardened hearts. I'll do it, all of it, and at your hands. I'm offering you grace enough for that. But grace of this kind is costly, not free like the grace I give for yourself. It's free for them, but if you continue to serve Me in the needs of these people, in one way or another I'll require your life at their hands."*

"But how?" he asked into the still chapel air.

"By My Spirit," was the reply.

B Y the time her newly Spirit-baptized husband arrived back from New York, Betty Jane was getting frantic. Having some real doubts about Graham's stability and the future of their marriage, she planned to tell him when he returned from New York that she and the children would stay in Burlington until he became more stable. She confided her troubles to her mother, Bey Carr, who took Graham's side.

"Betty," she said to her daughter, "I want you to consider two things. First, Graham's the Lord's anointed, my dear. Don't touch him. And remember, he's your husband. You need to do as he says."

Betty acquiesced. Then, and at intervals for decades to come, she would feel the bitterness of what it meant to keep her marriage vows. It had been such a long haul. Born just before the Great Depression to a lawyer and his wife, she was an only child for eight years, until a brother was born. Then her sister Nancy arrived in 1940. Betty had loved music since she was tiny and would try conducting an imaginary orchestra. She also loved harmonies and would teach various parts of a song to her family. Betty was baptized at age 11 at a Methodist church, at which time her mother sat her down to make sure her blonde-haired daughter was giving her life to the Lord.

She majored in music in college, then got a job at the University of Texas School of Fine Arts, though she had never been west of the Mississippi River.

Arriving in Austin, she agreed to direct the choir at All Saints, the Episcopal chapel at UT. One of the baritones in the choir was a man with perfectly combed blond hair. Betty took a closer look. This man was certainly no corn pone, East Texas twanger; he was more like a Greek god, she thought. He was so immaculately dressed, he almost seemed like a dandy. Graham was struck by the regal young woman directing the choir and surmised that since she was a teacher, she was probably too old for him. Actually, she was two years his junior. He liked her because she had class and was not ditzy like some other women he knew.

Fourteen years and four children later, Betty was steamed. It's not fair, she told God. It's not fair that you tell him all these special secrets, and when to come and when to go, and which Bible verses to read. You never do that for me. What's so special about him? I reckon you just do these sorts of things for ministers. Is that it? What about the children and me? Do we just live off the crumbs?

Her only answer was a sudden impression of a single verse, Ephesians 3:15: "Of whom the whole family in heaven and earth is named."

She was annoyed and bewildered. What could this mean? Then the words "the whole family" leapt off the page. Of course. The whole Pulkingham family would be involved in whatever happened with her husband.

Betty Jane was not prepared for the first agenda item on this family plan: her smoking. After she and Graham returned to Houston, he got her to read *The Cross and the Switchblade*. She plaintively asked God why such miraculous events could not happen in Houston as well.

"How can you be so sure that I can deliver them of their addiction when you will not let me deliver you of yours?" came the answer. Why, there it was, the still small voice that Betty had known but ignored for years, not realizing whose it was. For several weeks, she wavered back and forth, then asked for a miraculous sign to prove that God's power would work for her. That night, as she slept, Graham awoke and felt directed to pray for his wife. He laid his hands on her, drowsily prayed, then dropped off to sleep. The next day, she was astonished to find that the two dozen warts on her hands had disappeared. Her faith blossomed and she dropped smoking altogether.

That fall, she became pregnant with their fifth child, an event of some anguish because of a degenerative disc in her lower spine. Doctors had warned her to stop having children because of the pressure pregnancy put on her back. Struggling with chronic pain, she had been learning to trust the Lord in a new way since that momentous August. So why had He allowed her to get pregnant with another child? Not long after that, she and her family drove to Grace

Chapel, a small pentecostal Chinese-American church in north Houston where the worship was disarmingly simple and quiet. The music seemed simplistic to her trained ear, but she was touched by the tenderness of the worship and the unaffectedness with which the people sang.

During an interlude, one of the men stood up. Since early that day, he announced, God had given him a picture of someone's spinal cord that was "like new." As soon as the service ended, Betty was at the front of the church where the elders were praying for people and claiming her back was healed. The next morning, usually the time of day when her back was most sore, she felt no pain at all. Soon after that, she was baptized in the Spirit at Grace Chapel in a way most appropriate for her. While some women prayed over her, Betty opened her mouth to sing. Instead of a song in English, out came a melody of surpassing beauty in a language she did not know.

T HE enlisting of Graham on the side of the nascent charismatic renewal was a strategic development of great import. Here was a man who had undergone a major personal transformation, going from troubled parish priest to prophet. He had tremendous personal magnetism and a liberal social conscience—not the pentecostal "type" at all—and his wife's musical talents perfectly counterbalanced his prophetic gifts. His natural arrogance would stand him in good stead in the face of considerable opposition. But this time, Graham was not depending only on the sheer force of his personality. He was counting on an authority and power that had not been there before, minus the degradation that had haunted him for more than two decades. The problems in the neighborhood were just as overwhelming, but the newly Spirit-anointed Graham had a purpose and assurance he had previously lacked. This time, he knew God would back him up.

Graham's foray into the miraculous was not long in coming. One Sunday morning, he was giving out Communion wafers at the altar rail when he noticed a woman uncomfortably kneeling on one knee. Her other foot was broken, as evidenced by the crutches leaning against the altar rail. Here was his Rubicon: Would God heal this woman through him? All those dialogues in the chapel had come to this point. Walking over to the woman, he laid a hand on her shoulder, briefly prayed for her healing, then went on giving out wafers. The woman got up, hesitantly took one step, then another on her wounded foot, then raced down the aisle, half running, half skipping while the congregation's eyes were fixated on her crutches, abandoned at the altar rail.

Word spread among Episcopal clergy that Graham had gone off the deep end. It didn't help that Graham spoke at an Episcopal layman's retreat in the Texas coastal city of Baytown that fall, going into detail about traveling to New York and being prayed over by David Wilkerson. Not only that, but Graham had tactlessly mentioned how, a few weeks later, he had begun praying in tongues. His listeners knew that this was totally outside their realm. After Graham finished, everyone sat there stunned, until a man from St. John the Divine began singing the Doxology.

Graham's reception by other clergy was not much better, with one exception. Al Rountree was an Episcopal priest at St. Timothy's near Hobby Airport in southeast Houston and a closet charismatic. When he heard Graham speak to clergy about what had happened to him in New York, Al was astounded. With that sophisticated group, one just didn't get up and talk about emotions or experiences of God. Most of the clergy scoffed, but Al wept and later approached Graham and embraced him, saying, "Brother, something like this has happened to me."

Most of the clergy avoided Graham. At a diocesan convention, Graham was on his way to the men's room, when he nearly collided with a seminary classmate. The hapless classmate faltered a moment, then whispered theatrically, "Dahling, say something to me in tongues!" Another priestly friend, who had been the best man at Graham's wedding, drove from Austin to plead with Graham to undergo psychiatric care. The man's godchild and Graham's eldest son, Bill, prayed that the man be filled with the Spirit.

Graham had another test of his sanity that fall when he encountered Bob Eckert, a friend from Graham's days as chaplain at the University of Texas Medical Branch in Galveston. Bob had been in med school then and he and his wife Nancy had built their dream house in nearby Alta Loma with "his" and "her" carports plus a partnership in a liquor store. For the sake of upward mobility, they had joined the Episcopal Church. Anxious to show off his plush lifestyle and his four sons, Bob invited the Pulkinghams to dinner. At first, Graham put him off, knowing that one of the first signs of schizophrenia was a dramatic personality change. He feared facing Bob, who, as a doctor, would not hesitate to tell Graham that he had lost his sanity. After all, Bob's main memory of Graham was of him with a cup of coffee in one hand, a cigarette in the other, and an ulcer tablet at the ready.

Finally, the Pulkinghams were coaxed into coming down to Alta Loma for the evening. Ever the gracious host, Bob invited Graham to be the first to tell what he'd been up to. Two hours later, Graham was still talking about the prior fruitlessness of life at Redeemer, his encounter with the Holy Spirit, and the miraculous events that followed. Graham snuck a glance at Bob to see his reaction. The 34-year-old doctor had tears running down his face.

This is what I want, Bob was thinking to himself, *that relationship Graham has with God. I want God to be number one in my life—no, that's not it. God wants to be my whole life. But this will cost me everything.*

The next day, Bob was visited by Bertha, a catatonic schizophrenic threatening to kill her two children. A mischievous idea occurred to him. He wrote out a prescription slip with the address of the church on it and gave it to Bertha. A little while later, Graham called. Why, he asked, had this "lovely, vivacious lady" come to Redeemer? Apparently, she had been delivered of her troubles en route. The next day, Bob sent another hopeless psychotic case up to Redeemer. He was transfixed when he heard that the woman had been healed by Graham's prayers. Something was definitely going on at that church.

Within a few days, Bob and Nancy visited Redeemer, looking over the place and listening to a new preacher who was teaching at the church. He was Earle Frid, an elder at Grace Chapel. Earle offered to teach a class on Tuesday nights, "on one condition," he said. "That I be free to teach exactly what the Bible says, whether the Episcopal Church agrees or not."

Graham agreed. One night, Earle brought up the topic of the Holy Spirit, so they trooped over to the chapel, where Graham and Earle prayed over everyone. Although Bob and Nancy felt nothing different, Bob began to pray for his patients. Sometimes he would only say, "God bless you," and that person would be healed. Bob and Nancy began holding Bible studies and testimony meetings at their home. These turned into weekends of renewal, which were like charismatic house parties. Earle, Bob, or Graham would teach. They would also go to Sunday night prayer meetings at Grace Chapel. One night, Bob asked the elders there to pray for him to receive the gift of tongues. When nothing happened and he was clearly struggling, Graham called over his 10-year-old daughter, Mary, who placed her hand on Bob's knee and immediately began to pray in the Spirit. Bob opened his eyes, but instead of seeing Mary, he saw Jesus hanging on a cross, gazing at him with eyes that said, "I understand." Bob was in agony. Up-and-coming doctors shouldn't be making fools of themselves. He started to say, "I'm sorry" to the figure on the cross, but suddenly found himself speaking with the gift he had sought.

One of the couples drawn to the Eckerts' renewal weekends was Jerry and Esther Barker, he from a family of Galveston lawyers. Quiet and well-mannered, he wore the black-rimmed glasses that were popular with men in the 1960s. He had met Graham at the laymen's retreat in Baytown. He, too, was hungry for the

Holy Spirit. Esther had been hospitalized in 1963 for mental problems and was still depressed, addicted to weight-reducing pills and unable to speak rationally. She would sometimes hide out in her room for days at a time. Jerry was desperate. They had five children, ages 6 to mid-teens, and they needed a functioning mother. One night, just after learning she would have to be institutionalized, Jerry was walking home, extremely downcast. "What," he asked the sky, "am I going to do?"

"Lord," he continued, "I don't know what I can do about all this, and yet I do know. I know there is nothing I can do. I know the situation is hopeless and I can't bear the pressure much longer." Just after he mentally turned over his problems to the Lord, he felt, without any warning, a strong sense of the Lord's presence and power. His knees buckled and he almost fell.

"*I will heal Esther and she will come back home,*" the Almighty informed him. Jerry rushed home to tell his children of his experience and, sure enough, Esther came home two months later. The healing affected Jerry's business as well. He noticed himself sailing through the preparation of his court cases like never before. He then caught wind of charismatic events around the diocese, so when he met Graham a year later, the two men compared notes about their experiences. The one difference was that Graham had spoken in tongues and Jerry had not.

"Have you ever asked the Lord for it?" Graham asked.

Jerry admitted he had not. It almost seemed too simple. He put in the request that night while driving home and words sprang to his lips right away. It went on for some time and when he paused, he got an interpretation of what he had said. It was one of the most endearing messages he had heard in his life. He was sobbing so hard, he could barely drive the car.

At the men's prayer group at Sunset United Methodist, the same vibrant presence that filled Grover also astonished Ladd Fields, an instrument engineer from Oklahoma. One night, Ladd awoke, awash in God's presence. It was the same presence that had startled the men's group, only this time, Ladd felt personally immersed in adoration, as if the Lord was making love to him. He wanted to burst with joy. Soon afterwards, he sought out a pentecostal men's meeting of the sort springing up around Houston at the time. Meeting attendees prayed for him to speak in tongues. Ladd did so, wryly thinking he sounded like a tobacco auctioneer. Finally, the men laughingly placed him in a corner until he quieted down.

Ladd began taking high school students from Sunset to Grace Chapel, but had to stop when parents complained of their children turning pentecostal. He heard of Redeemer through Grover, and he was awakened in the middle of the night by the words, "Go to the Church of the Redeemer," ringing in his ears. He and his wife June went, but the Episcopal rituals confused them. People genuflected before approaching the altar, women wore lace veils and gloves, the priest said Communion with his back to the congregation, and the liturgy called for constant standing, then kneeling. Yet, the Fields couple still felt they were in the right place and conferred with Graham, who responded, "Well, I don't know what all the Lord's doing, but he's doing something."

Then Ladd started getting insightful words—"prophetic utterances," people called them—most of which were passages from Scripture. The gift of prophecy, he knew, showed up in the Old and New Testaments. What he didn't know much about was its 20th-century equivalent. Ladd was once leading a board of stewards meeting at Sunset when Grover blurted out a message in tongues. Ladd jumped in with the interpretation. This added fuel to the fire at Sunset as Ladd gradually began to realize his days as a Methodist were over.

CHAPTER 4

The Feast of
the Transfiguration

"After six days, Jesus took Peter, James and John with him and led them up a high mountain, where they were all alone. There he was transfigured before them."   —Mark 9:1–2

B Y January 1965, the Houston Episcopal Diocese had a new bishop, Milton Richardson. Elected presiding bishop, Hines had moved to New York. Richardson privately contacted senior warden Bob Evans to ask if Graham had gone insane.

"I don't think so," Bob replied, "but I think he's had a religious conversion into this charismatic thing. If you think that's crazy, then he is."

For Graham was speaking publicly of "repenting of being an Episcopal priest." He was not breaking his ordination vows or any canon law—he still believed in the creeds of the church and what the Book of Common Prayer said—but he wanted no part of the traditionalism, emptiness, and professionalism that, in his view, plagued many clergy. He had given up drinking as well as smoking cigarettes, but when he went to a deanery meeting of priests, he tried to fit in by taking two sips of wine. He got drunk. *"You don't have to drink,"* the Lord told him. *"You don't have to keep up the image. Just obey me."*

In January 1965, a Redeemer member approached Graham with a prophecy about the church: "I have chosen and called you to be a pastor of my pastors." Mulling over this, Graham went to the chapel to pray, turning to the second chapter of Ezekiel.

"Son of man," it said, "stand up on your feet and I will speak to you. Son of man, I send you to the people of Israel, to a nation of rebels, who have rebelled against me to this very day. The people also are impudent and stubborn: I send you to them; and you shall say to them, 'Thus says the Lord God.' And whether they hear or refuse to hear (for they are a rebellious house) they will know there has been a prophet among them. . . "

A wind blew through the still chapel and, wrapped with a sense of God's presence as tremendous as he had ever felt, he felt compelled to stand up. So *this* was his calling; toward his own kind, the "rebellious house" of the Episcopal Church. Somehow, through Redeemer, the Episcopal Church would be renewed in pentecostal power. Not too many months before, he had been as rebellious as any of them. He read into the third chapter: "For you are not sent to a people of foreign speech and a hard language, but to the house of Israel," said verse five. This was no easy matter, for pentecostal friends were urging Graham to interpret the Revelation passages on Babylon about "coming out from among them" to mean he should leave the Episcopal Church.

Later, a preacher from Mar Thoma Church in India came to preach. A picturesque man in long white robes, he was accustomed to speaking to thousands without a microphone. For 90 minutes, he harangued them, saying Redeemer should "come out from among them." Graham held his peace and afterward, even as the speaker was praying in the chapel, the Indian preacher began to prophesy, his words reversing everything he had said before: "Stay where you are," he said. "I have chosen you to be a miracle witness. I will raise up a church that will be a witness to the denominational churches of America." It was almost word for word what Graham had heard previously in the chapel.

Despite its high calling, Redeemer had no idea how to be a light to the Episcopal Church. One of the most stalwart denominations of the 1950s, the Episcopal Church was teetering on the edge of chaos. At the center of the whirlwind was one Bishop James Pike of San Francisco, who, besides setting up commissions debunking glossolalia, publicly questioned the divinity of Christ, the Trinity, and Christian standards of sexual morality. The Episcopal House of Bishops would fail to reprimand him for this in 1965, despite a petition for a heresy trial submitted by 14 Arizona clergy. The bishops' moral failure in not punishing this, or in not disciplining the four dissident bishops who illegally ordained the first female priests later in 1974, would set an irreparable precedent for the Episcopal Church. The Pike incident showed bishops that their peers would not punish error.

Adding to the confusion was British Bishop J.A.T. Robinson's 1960 book *Honest to God*, which declared Christian theology to be myth. In 1966, the

Episcopal Church had 3.6 million members, but would henceforth suffer decades of unbroken losses and shed one-third of its adherents. One of the few forces that would help retain membership would be the Episcopal charismatic renewal, made up of priests like Dennis Bennett and Graham Pulkingham, who refused to leave the denomination (though Bennett was forced to resign from St. Mark's). Graham had one advantage over Dennis; he was one of the few Episcopal priests in that era to keep his parish. Most charismatic priests he knew were being fired or their church was splitting over this new movement.

A few churches watched the movement from a distance. That Lent, Graham was invited to preach to the conservative, staid Grace Episcopal Church in Galveston. It was the first such invitation he had received since news of his charismatic beliefs had leaked out. He had no sooner begun talking than his listeners realized they were in for some mighty different spiritual fare. The congregation was mesmerized by his testimony, and three-quarters of them remained afterwards to watch the action as Graham invited people forward to the altar rail for healing.

A young woman came out of a pew on crutches, her ankle as big as a football. She hobbled forward in obvious pain. She leaned her crutches against the altar rail and waited for Graham, flanked by Bob Eckert and Jerry Barker, to pray for her. As Bob started to pray, Jerry wondered how they were going to pull this one off, especially since this was his home parish. Then, Graham looked down. The ankle had shrunk to normal size.

"There's no need to say anything more, Bob," the priest told his friend. "She's healed." Graham instructed the woman to return to her seat and, as she did so, it was clear she was no longer in pain. She also left her crutches at the altar rail. The congregation gasped and began to whisper. That night, a number of them decided to commit their lives to Christ. Jerry closed the deal by inviting a small crowd to his home to be baptized in the Spirit.

This second crutches-left-at-the-altar-rail miracle boosted Graham's confidence that he had indeed been given spiritual power. Miracles had a way of silencing the opposition, such as the one involving John Grimmet's mother-in-law. John and Edith were also baptized in the Spirit at Grace Chapel, but her mother was dead set against the new goings-on at Redeemer. Then one Sunday, just at the end of the service, the mother-in-law dropped to the floor. There was quite a flurry as people rushed to her side to pray. As the medics were taking her body out the door, Bob informed Graham that as far as he could tell, she had died of a heart attack. The ambulance was not more than a block from the hospital when the mother-in-law sat bolt upright and demanded to know where she was. The emergency room found nothing wrong with her and as of that day, her complaining about the church ceased.

T HE spring of 1965 crept into Houston, delivering as close a foretaste of heaven as Texas seasons can. Bluebonnets were splashed along the high-ways like oil slicks of blue on grassy seas. Floral riots of blossoming, dainty white Mexican plum trees, lavender wisteria vines, pansies, azaleas of varying hues of red, pink, purple and white, plus dogwood, monkey grass, Texas moun-tain laurel with its purple blossoms, pink-orange and white tulips and blue and white hyacinths were everywhere.

The Houston Astrodome opened that April with President Lyndon Johnson attending an exhibition game between the Astros and the New York Mets. Starting that Easter, a tightly knit group of 31 persons, including Bob Eckert, John Grimmet, Ladd Fields, Graham, and Jerry Barker, began meeting daily at the church to pray and worship. The usual starting time was 5:30 a.m.; partici-pation required an enormous commitment for those who worked full-time. For John and Ladd, even getting there involved a 20-minute commute. For Jerry and Bob, it took 45 minutes. Three single women also came, including Betty's sister, Nancy, who had moved to Houston. In the evenings and on Saturdays and Sundays, the spouses and the children joined them for another time of prayer. These gatherings were wellsprings of spiritual power. It seemed as if practically every time they prayed for something in the morning, that prayer was answered in some glorious fashion by nightfall. One of the earlier tests came that summer, when the second Pulkingham son, 6-year-old Nathan, hurt his knee while playing. He came wailing into the house. Graham and Betty prayed for him, then were about ready to call Bob Eckert for an X-ray when Nathan asked, pointedly, "Didn't we ask Jesus to heal it?"

Well, yes, his parents said, but Dr. Eckert still needed to check it.

"No, He healed it. We don't have to do any more," Nathan insisted. Days passed and although it seemed plain Nathan had a broken kneecap, he insisted Jesus would heal it. He refused to have the knee bandaged up or to take pain-killers. His parents were in turmoil. Bey Carr, who was visiting, scolded Betty and Graham for letting the knee go untended. One night, during evening prayers in the chapel, Graham glanced over to see how Nathan was doing, and was startled to see the child's eyes closed, his hands lifted and his face tilted upward. He was quietly praying in tongues for the first time.

A few days later, his distracted parents were about to take him to a doctor when Graham was interrupted by the Lord. *'Which would you rather—that he have a crippled leg or a crippled faith?'* the voice asked. By the next evening, the knee was normal and the boy was without pain. That episode got Graham's attention. This charismatic movement was birthing all sorts of healing ministries, all of which were making extravagant claims. But Graham decided that from then on, he would not claim a healing, or pray for it, unless the sick person was convinced God wanted it.

The scattered elders soon grew tired of their lengthy commutes. Bob Eckert believed he should be an evangelist and give up his medical practice, sell his lovely home and move to walking distance of the church. He ended up at a two-bedroom apartment on Eastwood at Clay, near the ship channel, and found an opening on the staff of Parkview Clinic, a small independent health clinic that mainly tended to Mexicans. The position paid next to nothing, but the place was loaded with people with desperate spiritual as well as physical needs, many of whom Bob referred to Redeemer.

The move was a shock to the Eckert children. The nearby Jackson Junior High School was rife with gangs, and the oldest Eckert son, Rob Jr., joined one. Hubcaps began disappearing from cars, and one day, the Eckerts awoke to find their car missing. They called the police, not to punish the person who had stolen the car, but to give the thief the title and keys as well. Bob figured that they should literally obey Matthew 5:40, which said if someone steals your tunic, give them your cloak as well, and apply it to cars. Bob put a literal spin on other Bible verses, which released a spiritual power he had never experienced. After they forsook the crowded apartment for a house on McKinney Street, the Eckerts discovered some Mexican boys stealing materials out of their garage. Nancy baked them a chocolate cake, found the boys' house and gave it to them, figuring that if someone does her harm, the Bible says to love them aggressively back. The boys never stole from them again.

The Barkers also moved to Houston that June with the one piece of moving equipment they could scrounge up: an open truck on which they placed their antique furniture and a baby grand piano. As they reached LaMarque, about one-third of the way to Houston, they got caught in a downpour.

"Let's ask the Lord to part the cloud like the Red Sea and to take us through dry all the way," Jerry told his children as the skies opened up. Groaning, they drove the rest of the way to Eastwood, then dashed to the back of the truck, expecting to find a load of ruined furniture. The inside of the truck was as dry as a bone, even though water was still running off the cab. Years later, Jerry would remember the summer of 1965 as a time of spiritual intoxication. Anything they asked from God, they got. They had no sooner moved to Houston than three

41

men, perhaps one step above street people, came to live with them. However one categorized them, they could not make it on their own and would revert to their former condition if they returned to old friends. Moving in with a Redeemer family helped stabilize them. It was a kindhearted reaction to a sad situation. Little did these community pioneers know they were starting a Christian trend.

Ladd let his three daughters spend the summer of 1965 in Eastwood, and in the fall moved his family into the neighborhood, purchasing a house on Polk Street. June Fields had reservations about moving to Eastwood, but kept them to herself in view of her husband's and daughters' enthusiasm. The move cost them in more ways than one, for at the end of that year, when Redeemer came up short on its annual assessment to the diocese, Ladd and June made up the difference out of their life savings. By this time, Ladd had become known as the resident prophet. Hearing him was like listening to a loud, powerful wave. He would get so caught up in the moment that, as he prayed over people, he would shake. One day, Ladd felt a hand laid on his arm.

"Ladd," said Graham, "do you have to shake?"

"No, no," was his response.

"Good. Then quit it, will you?"

The Grimmets left a home in South Houston to move to Eastwood, giving away a boat, a tractor and trailer, and their children's favorite TV set. John Grimmet had lost interest in life's luxuries and felt his family needed to learn the same lesson. However, his children did not quite perceive Redeemer as such a pearl of great price that they must sell everything to get it. His son Robert was soon in prison and naturally, he blamed his father and the upheaval of the move. "Daddy, if you hadn't given away everything, I wouldn't be where I am now," he complained.

But John was not looking back. He was now part of a circle of five elders who roughly fit the prescription in Ephesians 4:11 of the five-fold ministry of apostle, prophet, evangelist, pastor, and teacher. There was no question that Graham was the apostle, Ladd was a prophet, Bob an evangelist, Jerry a teacher, and John a pastor. They frequently interchanged these duties, but the genius of those early days is that five strong-willed men pooled their talents and balanced each other out, creating an exceptionally healthy church. What Redeemer had was power, a youthful, fiery masculinity that was irresistible to all who visited.

That summer, the little community witnessed its first marriage. The bride, Susan Bassett, was 28 years old and a high school Spanish teacher. She and Gordon Abbott had been at Redeemer only since January, but what had impressed Susan was that every visitor was received as if he or she had been sent from the Spirit of God, and so all would be listened to. Friends of theirs, a couple named Ralph and Sue Neal, came to inspect Redeemer about the same time. Ralph, who had known Bob Eckert before he went to medical school and had already been baptized in the Spirit there, coaxed Sue to come hear Graham speak. "That's the most arrogant man I've ever heard," she told Ralph afterwards, but they soon bought a house near the church. Having given away many of their possessions, many Redeemer members were low-income people. The one thing they were expected to be extravagant with was their time, which was to be spent either at the church or with their households.

Fresh into their marriage, Susan and Gordon Abbott were assigned to head a household for some of the newly arrived street people. Susan was overwhelmed, and spent much of the next two years crying, trying to cope with the marginal people who wandered about her church and home like walking flaws. One woman who lived with them had no idea how to clean a house. Others insisted that Susan be constantly present to help them, like the mother some never had. When their demands intruded into the time she set aside for Sunday afternoon naps, Susan reached her breaking point. She could not get away from these people, but she could not live with them, either.

"You've got a yardstick in yourself that grows as you do," the Lord informed Susan one day. *"You'll never attain perfection, so you might as well snap that yardstick in half."* After that, Susan dropped her high expectations of herself and found the others' shortcomings easier to bear.

Graham seemed to sail through this time, acting as the central role model. He abounded in spiritual gifts, and people wanted to copy him. He had an uncanny ability to perceive the truth about a person and say it. This bluntness sometimes got him into trouble while at the same time, people lined up to imitate him. At times, even Graham put his will at the disposal of the others, meaning that either they would move together on a certain matter or they would not move at all. In the long run, it was a slower but paradoxically faster way, and vastly more effective in reining in the desires and energies of the entire group. Graham was realizing that in giving up his dream for social justice, he would get it back in a vastly transformed manner. People were doing the kinds of radical things with their time and money that he had always hoped for, but this time, spiritual power was involved and explosions would happen.

HAVING hired Graham two years before, senior warden Bob Evans was indifferent about meeting-time prayers, healings, and speaking in tongues, but he was nettled by prophecies and "words of knowledge" he thought too banal to have come from the creator of the universe. Yet, Evans thought, Graham was preaching legitimate truth from the pulpit. Graham might be responsible for getting people's emotions keyed up, but he was not responsible for some of their excesses.

Still, the new arrivals, led by their rector, made it clear that charismatic gifts and born-again experience were becoming mandatory at Redeemer. So, as traditionalist parishioners left in puzzlement or disgust, the church grew shorter and shorter on money. Sunday morning attendance had slipped below 200, and the remaining members joked about the church's "backdoor revival." Al Rountree had been bounced out of his parish because of his charismatic activities, and the vestry had agreed in December 1965 to take him on at $7,000 a year. Graham invited Al to move to a house owned by the church, but had no idea where his salary would come from. Then one day, he received a phone call from a lawyer settling an estate for an old Eastwood family still on Redeemer's books. The lawyer informed Graham that the deceased family member had left the church seven shares of insurance stock worth $1,000 a share.

It scandalized the old-timers that the Pulkinghams had all these needy, broken people moving into the rectory with them and living hand to mouth alongside them. Graham's solution to many people's problems seemed simplistic. "Come live with me," he would say, as if people could be healed by the sheer goodness of what was happening at the church. Worse still, the Pulkinghams had to cash in their life insurance policies and children's trust funds to afford these guests. Finally, Graham asked the vestry to take him off salary and put the money and his benefits into a ministry fund that all persons on his growing staff could dip into. From then on, everyone on staff got equal pay.

All this was too much for the old-timers, who began planning ways to impeach him. By 1966, membership was beginning to pick up again, but the church's new senior warden opposed Graham. He visited Bishop Richardson with his concerns, but Richardson put him off by informing the senior warden that he had to get a majority of the vestry to agree to eject Graham before the bishop would act. The way to do this was through the vestry, a major sticking point. It had 12 members, with one vacancy, and Ladd Fields, the runner-up in the most recent vestry election, was due to come on. The vestry was slowly getting stacked with charismatics, and the senior warden knew that Ladd was in Graham's court. With Ladd, Graham would have five vestrymen on his side. Three were opposed to Graham and four were on the fence. Thus, a vestry vote on whether to allow Ladd onto the board would prove pivotal.

One day, Graham was driving around downtown when he received the strongest impression he should visit Richardson. Parish priests do not normally visit their bishops unless summoned, but Graham could not get the idea out of his mind. If there was a parking place available, he told God, he would drop by. Sure enough, there was a space near the diocesan entrance, and a few minutes later, he was in Richardson's office. Richardson mentioned the senior warden's visit, then in his broad Georgia accent asked,

"Do you have moah or less money in the offering plates this yeah than last yeah?"

More money, Graham responded.

"Do you have moah or less peopuh in yoah services this yeah than last yeah?"

More people, Graham responded.

"Do you still use the prayah book?"

"Yes," said Graham.

"Quite frankly, Fathah Pulkingham," Richardson said, "I don't know what all yoah doin' out there, and if ah deed know, ah might nawt approve, but since you seem to have a successful parish, you have mah blessing."

At a vestry breakfast the next Saturday, one of the "on-the-fence" vestrymen began to weep. When Bob Eckert stood behind him and placed a hand on his shoulder, the man began to sob over his sweet roll and coffee.

"I've been an Episcopalian all my life. I've served on vestries on big churches and little churches. But you," he said, looking at Graham, "have something I don't have and I want it." They prayed for him to be baptized in the Spirit on the spot.

The next Monday night, the vestry met to decide how to bring on the 12th person. There was a motion to allow the vestry to disregard the parish vote selecting Ladd and choose someone else. Five voted for the process that would bring in Ladd and five voted against it. Realizing that someone had not voted, Graham called for a second vote. The eleventh vote belonged to Carl Appelberg, an anti-Graham vestryman whose wife, Helen, had been baptized in the Spirit at Redeemer. "I tried to raise my hand twice," said Carl, who was as white as a sheet, "but something kept my arm pinned to my side and I couldn't move it."

His abstention defeated the motion, allowing Ladd to come onto the vestry. From this point on, charismatics would be in the majority. The senior warden stood, admitted to what he had been planning, then said, "I don't belong in this church or this congregation," and left.

CHAPTER 5

Holy Cross Day

"And then shall appear the sign of the Son of man in heaven: and then shall all the tribes of the earth mourn, and they shall see the Son of man coming in the clouds of heaven with power and great glory."
—Matthew 24:30 (KJV)

ARLY in the spring of 1966, 21-year-old Bill Farra, a law student and church organist, began attending church. Shirley, his wife of a few months, was dying of leukemia. She was not responding to prayers for healing. Graham sympathized with the lonely law student, and Bill liked Graham's strong, peaceful personality and pragmatic theology on healing. One week, Graham gave Bill an embrace, saying the Lord had given him a special love for him. The parish fasted one weekend for Shirley's recovery. One day, Graham called Bill into his office, saying he had gotten a mysterious call from a woman in St. Louis. Kathleen Thomerson had played the organ at Redeemer and gotten baptized in the Spirit the previous summer. Not knowing anything about Bill, she had called Graham to say she'd sensed through prayer that they were fasting about some important matter. She too had been praying, she said, but God had been giving her verses about being glorified by death. Could this apply to someone in the parish? she asked. And, she added, the Lord had given her the name Shirley. Was there such a person at Redeemer?

Bill realized his wife's days were numbered, and Graham sat beside him and held him while he wept. But other friends, counseling the couple to believe in God's ability to heal Shirley, urged him to take her off all medication and to bring her home. But she only worsened, and finally Bill took her back to the hospital, where she could at least be comfortable while she waited to die. One

47

Wednesday in late May, the first day of his law school exams, she slipped into a coma. By that afternoon, she was gone. Three weeks later, at Graham's invitation, Bill moved into Redeemer's rectory with the Pulkinghams to put his shattered life back together.

Another visitor who would drastically affect Redeemer arrived in February 1966. Michael Harper had been a 31-year-old curate at All Souls Church, Langham Place, in London when he was baptized in the Spirit in 1962. All Souls, a strictly evangelical British institution, did not take well to the charismatic element that followed Harper to the church, especially the speaking in tongues, healing, miracles, and prophetic gifts.

By 1964, Harper had left All Souls to set up a new charismatic British organization called Fountain Trust. He was a brilliant writer whose work soon led to the founding of a charismatic magazine, *Renewal*. Graham struck Michael as an intense, imposing man one could rightly be in awe of. He seemed forthright on where he thought this neo-pentecostal movement was headed. He wanted no part of its more airy-fairy details, and he didn't want a glossolalia club. Most American charismatics Michael had met were supremely individualistic, so Graham was a refreshing change. Not only did Graham have a vision for the church, but for the inner-city church. Michael took notes for a possible article and returned for a church supper and prayer meeting, where he spoke some encouraging words to the gathering. The parishioners took their British visitor's arrival as God's endorsement that they were on the right track. Michael, in turn, was entranced by the sense of power there.

Suddenly, said a woman, "The Lord has given me a Scripture. The words are very strange. The words are going around in my head, and I simply can't get rid of them."

"Never mind," said Graham. "Let's hear them."

"They're from Leviticus," she said, "Thou shalt not uncover thy sister's nakedness.'"

No one stirred, so it fell to Graham to interpret what the Spirit of God was saying. So much was happening that did not need to be broadcast yet, he thought. The final conclusion had not arrived; things were potentially confused and difficult.

"I reckon God is saying something here about our church," said Graham slowly. "God is saying that we are not to seek or allow any publicity for the moment. This is a work of God which should not be uncovered. We have a reporter here," and he turned toward their visitor, smiling. "These words refer to you, Michael."

CHANGE was in the air that spring. The Mamas and the Papas' ethereal harmonies were filling the airwaves with beguiling songs about California, Walt Disney had died and women were beginning to wear miniskirts. Color TV was becoming the rage, just in time to showcase a war that was heating up in southeast Asia. A few months later, Bishop Pike, who by then had become quite notorious for his statements of unbelief, resigned. A culture of atheism was forming, typified by *Time* magazine's April 8, 1966, cover story that asked, "Is God Dead?" Because of writers like Samuel Beckett (*Waiting for Godot*), existentialism was enormously popular on college campuses and society was restless. Simon and Garfunkel's "Sounds of Silence" portrayed loneliness and alienation in a decade that *Time* was calling a "December for religion."

Meanwhile, Graham and Earle had split over leadership differences and the coterie of five elders—the priest, the lawyer, the doctor, the engineer, and the lineman— were completely in charge. Often, Ladd would offer a prophecy, Bob would convey an evangelistic message, Jerry would teach, Graham would have an apostolic message, and John would claim a gift of faith to the point where, in the name of Christ, he would command bees not to sting him because he had dominion over them. John could be beyond believing sometimes. It was not beneath him to polish the other men's shoes when they met as elders. His words were profundities, gorgeously appropriate, and even conversation-stoppers. Possessed of a deep humility, he was always praying.

Headed by this quintet, the church got a very balanced meal. Cars, houses, and possessions changed hands many times as the other members copied what they saw the leaders doing. "The Holy Spirit," Bob Eckert would say, "has to be careful of what He reveals to us because that's what we'll do." One authenticating sign was the flood of poor people showing up at the church. The ones who were there just for handouts left soonafter discovering they would have to live in a household. Others stayed and Redeemer became prophetic in its poverty, for it was obvious that if something other than white, middle-class people were hanging about the church, the Holy Spirit had to be doing something there.

Mentally disturbed people, including a governor's wife from a nearby state, showed up and six women, working two to a shift, assisted her for several weeks until she was healed. Most people would be prayed with, had evil spirits cast out of them and were then invited to live with church members so their minds could be rebuilt by Scripture.

A widow at the church, Essie Ringo, caught the Eckerts' attention. Her husband had died and she had 22 adopted children, plus an invalid mother to care for in a three-bedroom bungalow. The Eckerts had 14 women, their four boys, and themselves crammed into a six-bedroom house on McKinney. Sure enough, Nancy and Bob began to hear the Lord directing them to "give" their home to Essie, furniture and all. They did not move out; they planned to walk out, relocating to another, smaller dwelling that had only a stove and a refrigerator. Three days before the move, they got a call from a church member, Polly Sumner. She had just taken in a roommate, Polly said. Could the roommate store all her furniture at the Eckerts' house?

It was one thing to read the Scriptures; it was another thing to act them out. Those who pay a cheap price get a cheap product; the Redeemerites were paying heavily and getting priceless spiritual power in return. These Christians wanted to excel, not merely qualify in heaven's stakes, and Graham had little patience with those who traveled across Houston to be part of them but would not pay the full price.

"There are many in this fellowship who are withholding themselves from daily fellowship—and you're grieving the Lord," he scolded them one evening as they cooled off in one of the church basement rooms. "He wants to glorify himself in you but can't until all the thorns and twigs and underbrush are taken out. And the only way it's going to come out is for you to put yourself in contact with other human beings long enough to bring this stuff to the surface."

The true test of the love of Christ, he added, would be how they handled their personal confrontations day by day. Sometimes, Graham got a taste of his own medicine, as when Ralph Neal, a prophetic soul, would confront Graham on any teachings that were off. After praying together, Graham would eventually admit that Ralph was right.

O N September 14, 1966, Bette Graham, a flamboyant TV script writer with an epileptic 6-year-old son, entered Graham's office. She was psychotic, schizophrenic, depressed, suicidal—and desperate. Before relatives brought her to the church, asking for someone, anyone to pray over her before she was committed to a mental hospital, she had just tried to kill herself again. She walked into Graham's office, lit a cigarette, and blew the smoke into his face.

She had unwittingly arrived at the most opportune time. Bob Eckert and Graham had spent considerable time discussing whether deliverance, the kind that involved demons and exorcism, really existed in the 1960s. It was a New Testament doctrine they were not familiar with and, wishing to know the mind of God on the matter, asked for a sign to occur on Graham's 40th birthday, which was Holy Cross Day.

Now here was Bette Graham.

"I know you don't approve of smoking," she said.

"It's not whether or not I approve of smoking," he replied, "but when the Lord fills your life, you won't smoke anymore."

After some conversation, "I've never known a person prouder than you, except myself," Graham said, before asking her if she wanted to receive Christ. Several hours later, after prayers for salvation, baptism in the Spirit, deliverance and healing, Bette left Graham's office feeling as though a celestial vacuum cleaner had emptied her of sin, then filled her with power. Her psychotic episodes did not reoccur. She moved into the Eckerts' home that day and gave away all she owned except for two dresses. She gave the church her Corvette, which Graham gave to Bill Farra. A few months later, at Grace Chapel, she was introducing herself to the guest speaker, Costa Deir, when he abruptly asked if she had an epileptic son. She had never mentioned Troy, nor, to her knowledge, had Deir ever seen the boy. The speaker prayed for Troy, Bette threw out his medication, and the seizures ceased. What astonished Bette was how at Redeemer, such a miraculous feat was considered normal.

By this time, Redeemer was surpassing Grace Chapel as the model, the front-runner, the pioneer for fledgling charismatic churches in east Texas. It was also a pilot project for liberal evangelicals for whom the dominant Southern Baptist culture was forbidding. Not that Redeemer was liberal; Graham spent months preaching on Genesis, sounding like any other biblical literalist. His theology was almost unrecognizable from what it had been pre-1964. But Graham had a larger vision for the renewal of Redeemer, one that went beyond the personal and private, because God, he felt, was not as interested in the individual Christian as He was in the church being corporately faithful. The sum of the parts was greater than the whole at Redeemer, where people were committed to sharing their lives fully.

This bowled over Grady and Janice Manley, a pentecostal couple who lived nearby on McKinney Street. He was an Assemblies of God pastor who taught at a local Bible college. She came from a family of pentecostal pioneers. Spiritual gifts were old hat to them. What got their attention was Graham's preaching on the corporate nature of the body of Christ and on practical ways people could love each other. This had been totally left out of any pentecostal teachings they had ever heard. These Episcopalians, they thought, had more life than their own pentecostal churches, which was strange: The average Episcopalian was no champion of biblical orthodoxy or even literacy. Most were genteel liberals, barely knowing the layout of the New Testament and knowing nothing about how the

Old Testament was structured. If anything, Episcopalians were known to play fast and loose with the Bible.

Graham, the Manleys agreed, was different. He was always captivating, and his testimony about his experiences in New York was positively radiant. In all his years of ministry, Grady had never heard anyone as profound as Graham, nor heard anyone explain Scripture as powerfully as he did. The priest was captivating, as was his testimony. They were also impressed with how Graham curtailed certain pentecostal practices, such as clapping or cheering during services, and liked how he regulated spiritual gifts by reminding people it was possible to prophesy without screaming the message. After several prophecies had been given, Graham would ask an elder to summarize their theme. Sometimes, the elder would gently criticize anyone who had prophesied out of line.

Graham was forging the character of the church, setting a foundation of biblical teachings and emphasizing the spiritual power which results from the time individuals spent with the Lord. He even went so far as to say God could be ministered to only by Spirit-baptized persons. One August evening, two years after his visit to New York, he asked how many spoke in tongues. About 90 percent of those attending raised their hands. When he asked how many prayed in tongues at least a half hour a day, he was disappointed to see only a dozen raise their hands. That percentage, he said, needed to go up. By the mid-1960s, it was obvious the phenomenal spread of the charismatic movement could not be explained apart from this gift. For most people, it was their entry into renewal, and a step of faith that God used to leverage His power into their lives and help people fall in love with Him for the first time. Graham understood this. He often woke up at 3 or 4 a.m. to find himself praying in tongues in his sleep. He'd tell stories about waking up that morning, wondering why he felt so refreshed, then realize he'd also been singing in the Spirit while he slept.

Graham needed every ounce of empowerment he could get. He was constantly bailing youths out of jail. One of them was Kino Langoria, who ended up in Graham's office, being handed a copy of *The Cross and the Switchblade*. During study hall, Kino read it all the way through and was surprised to see there were kids like him in New York City. Kino was friends with Larry, a Vietnam vet whom Graham had also helped. Larry had various satanic tatoos on him: Skulls, crossbones, and the devil. When Larry stole a bulky bronze altar cross from the church, the two tried to unload it on friends or pawn shops, but no one would take it.

"Larry," Kino said, "we need to take that cross back. You don't go jacking with the man upstairs. We're messing with the church."

But Larry shrugged and laughed off the suggestion. They went to one-eyed Pat, a female fence who could deal with the most nettlesome stolen goods. Pat had a patch over her glass eye, wore a rosary around her neck, and lived on Clay Street near the church. It was late in the evening when they arrived and Kino waited outside the apartment. After a long time, Pat led a stunned Larry out the door. Trying to catch her breath, Pat informed Ken that when Larry set down the cross, he lifted off the ground. Then, after he fell to the floor, she threw her rosary over him. Larry was now rubbing his skin, crying that his tattoos were on fire and whimpering about returning the cross to the church.

"Wherever you got that cross, take it back and get it out of my house," ordered Pat. Kino went inside and retrieved it. He then drove up to the rectory, plunked the cross on the doorstep, rang the doorbell, and took off.

I N 1967, two events happened, each at least 1,000 miles from Houston, that would dramatically affect Church of the Redeemer. The Episcopal General Convention came to Seattle and one of its more far-reaching actions that summer was to vote in a missionary bishop for Guatemala. They chose a cleric who was working in Costa Rica, who already knew Spanish, who had grown up in Houston, and who was married with five children. He was a serious-looking man with black hair, thick black-rimmed glasses, and the commanding yet reassuring bass voice of the radio disk jockey he had been in Houston in the 1940s. His name was William Frey and he was 37.

Earlier that year, an event happened near Pittsburgh that would forever change the Roman Catholic Church. It had begun as the brainchild of a group of brilliant, intense, young Roman Catholic intellectuals attracted to Cursillo— a three-day retreat that combined lectures, music, and prayer for an unusually powerful way of presenting their faith in 20th-century terms. One of the intellectuals was Steve Clark, an owlish-looking man who converted to Catholicism in 1960 while studying intellectual history at Yale. He lived a monastic life, and had a knack for systematizing religious thought, thanks to his graduate studies in philosophy and his year as a Fulbright student studying theology in Germany.

Another of the intellectuals was Ralph Martin, a philosophy major with luminous blue eyes and sideburns who specialized in Nietzsche. He had tossed aside his Catholic upbringing as an undergraduate, and became the University of Notre Dame's resident atheist. The first time he met Stephen Clark, they argued over Christianity. Ralph's atheistic sojourn ended while experiencing a dramatic conversion during a Cursillo weekend, and he was preparing to begin a philosophy doctorate at Princeton.

The two young men spent the summer of 1965 together at a monastery in Elmira, New York, during which time they both concluded God was calling them to leave graduate school for full-time Christian work. They resigned their fellowships at Yale and Princeton, gave away all their possessions, including Steve's huge library, and most of their clothes. By August, everything they owned fit in one large army pack. They had 87 cents between them, but salaried positions at a student parish at Michigan State University awaited them in the fall. They had also been hired for positions on the National Secretariat of the Cursillo.

Meanwhile, a mutual friend was undergoing some profound changes. Ralph Kiefer, a lay theologian who taught at Duquesne University in Pittsburgh, was meeting with William Storey, a fellow professor at Duquesne. Both were devouring *The Cross and the Switchblade*, which led to their baptism in the Spirit. The book had been recommended to them by Ralph Martin and Steve Clark. Kiefer and Storey began looking for opportunities to share with others what had happened to them. Their big chance came during a weekend retreat February 17-19, 1967, at a retreat center in the woods north of Pittsburgh called the Ark and the Dove. The 30 students gathered were from the conservative, traditional Catholic campus fraternity Chi Rho—not exactly obvious candidates for the world's first Catholic charismatic prayer meeting.

The professors assigned the students to read *The Cross and the Switchblade*, plus the first four chapters of Acts. David Wilkerson's miracle-laced testimony of God's power affecting hardened drug addicts, combined with the Bible's description of the early church's first giddy months after Pentecost, had the desired effect. Thoroughly prepped, students were more than willing to hear the testimony of a charismatic Episcopal lay woman, who came for a few hours the morning of Saturday the 18th. Some of the students thought it odd to hear teaching from a Protestant, but they were impressed with what she had to say about salvation. Some wondered if they needed to reaffirm their own vows to follow Christ. Like Episcopalians, Catholics considered their water baptism as infants as the way one becomes a Christian. This woman's testimony of an added commitment to Christ that accomplished far more than the baptismal rite stirred their souls.

That afternoon, a broken water pump was mysteriously fixed after students prayed for it. A birthday party had been planned that night, but students were unenthused about attending. Instead, they felt drawn to a small upstairs chapel, where they felt overwhelmed by the presence of God. Several students were so overcome, they fell to the floor. The Catholic Church had never told them about this.

The delighted professors laid hands on some of them, to be filled with the Holy Spirit, and several students spoke in tongues. Others prophesied or wept. They stayed in the chapel until 5 a.m., worshipping. For the first time, many of them were experiencing their faith, feeling the emotions they had read about in Wilkerson's book. Returning to campus, they caused much consternation among students by urging this experience on their friends. Duquesne faculty members simply did not know how to handle it and the guidance center began working overtime.

Notre Dame was much more hospitable toward this new movement. In early March, William Storey visited South Bend to apply for a faculty position. He was also spreading the news about Duquesne to as many Notre Dame students and faculty as possible. Some of them asked to be prayed over for the baptism in the Spirit, but most of the Catholics felt befuddled about a few details. One of them knew of Ray Bullard, the president of the South Bend branch of the Full Gospel Businessmen's Fellowship International and gave him a call. Could they come to his house to talk? they asked.

Bullard assented, then sank into shock. Just what was he, a blue collar pentecostal, going to do with all these Catholic intellectuals? He got on the phone to muster reinforcements. When nine Catholics arrived the evening of March 13, they were met by a house full of pentecostal ministers and their wives from around the state of Indiana. The evening's discussion topic ended in a tussle over speaking in tongues. The Catholics believed they had already been baptized in the Spirit; the pentecostals said they needed tongues as evidence. Finally, the Catholics assented to letting the pentecostals pray over them. The two groups lined up on opposite sides of Bullard's basement. The pentecostal ministers walked forward, arms outstretched, praying in tongues. Before they were halfway across the room, the Catholics were also praying in the Spirit. One of the pentecostal ministers added some comic relief to the evening by going around to each Catholic in the room with a tape recorder and microphone.

Meanwhile, Steve Clark and Ralph Martin had also heard about the Duquesne weekend and, making their way to Pittsburgh, they too were filled with the Spirit. Returning to Michigan State, they began talking up the experience. After that, things began moving quickly, as 90 students, priests, and Cursillo leaders from East Lansing, South Bend, and Cleveland met in April for a conference at Notre Dame. The media dubbed them "Catholic Pentecostals," and the Catholic press wrote up the conference in sensational terms, which only helped swell the numbers at Notre Dame prayer meetings. That summer, 3,000 priests, nuns, seminarians, and lay people came to the annual summer sessions at Notre Dame, many of them visiting charismatic prayer meetings on the sly. As these people returned to their homes, they spread the word about renewal. Something of great spiritual import was obviously happening but no one knew quite what. But hadn't Pope John XXIII prayed for a "new Pentecost" before Vatican II? Future Notre Dame summer conferences would show that, mathematically, the renewal was reproducing itself several times each year. One hundred fifty attended the 1968 conference, 450 came in 1969, 1,300 came in 1970, 4,500 came in 1971, almost 12,000 came in 1972 and 20,000 showed up in 1973.

None of this came without some cost. Because of their charismatic involvements, Martin and Clark were fired from their positions at Michigan State, but they bounced back by landing jobs assisting the Catholic chaplain at the University of Michigan at Ann Arbor. They were joined by two Notre Dame graduates, Gerry Rauch, and Jim Cavnar. The four men rented an apartment in the middle of downtown Ann Arbor, where they held prayer meetings. Pretty soon, the crowds forced them to meet in the Catholic student center, then in a local parish hall. With the Catholic connection in place, the fires of Pentecost now could spread in earnest.

1968–1974

CHAPTER 6

The Feast of St. Matthew

"Then Jesus came to them and said, 'All authority in heaven and on earth has been given to me. Therefore, go and make disciples of all nations, baptizing them in the name of the Father and of the Son and of the Holy Spirit.' " — Matthew 28:19

R EDEEMER'S story was mapped not just in earthly time but in an eternal time frame—what the Greeks call *kairos*. The Episcopal liturgical year mirrors this. After the red flames of Pentecost comes Trinity, colored green for living things, stretching like a belt through six summer and autumn months filled with the days of the saints: Matthew, St. Michael the Archangel, Saints Luke, James, Simon, Jude and, finally, All Saints.

In this *kairos*, each season has its color and timing; the universal time from which God views the world outside of earthly confines. The world runs on chronological time, and its concerns are temporal; the church runs on *kairos* time, and its concerns are eternal. Trinity is the sole church season based on a doctrine of God's makeup. God is one, yet there are three who are God. He is the Father, who cannot be seen by mortals until the day the veil lifts and all shall see Him as He is. He is the Son, appearing in *chronos*, or Earth's time, for 33 years, who was equal to God. And He is the Holy Spirit, always present in Christians, whose burst of activity in the mid-20th century tipped world Christianity toward pentecostal power.

Based in eternity, the Three are united yet distinct in a way that beings in space and time cannot fathom. We who live in time, who say that one thing cannot simultaneously be another, cannot understand He who is outside of time. They are co-equal. They are co-eternal. The Triune God is three in one. Three equals one. One is three. Three is the complete number, and Earth is the third planet from the sun. When the heavens open and the Earth ceases its orbit, then chronos shall be no more.

IT was a warm evening at a Maryland campground and the Pulkingham household was getting ready for bed. This was no ordinary nuclear family, for the household included Betty, the five children, Nancy Carr, Bill Farra, and Nancy's friend, Arabella Miner. Arabella was a medical editor at M.D. Anderson's world-famous cancer hospital in Houston. She could intellectualize things, and make concepts understandable. A few years later, she would help Graham write his first book.

Graham had been ministering almost non-stop for three years and was taking the summer of 1967 off, partly to see how well the church could do without him. They had been on the road two months, visiting the World's Fair in Montreal and dimly noticing that the whole world seemed to be in an uproar over a six-day war in which Israel defeated several neighboring Arab states. Jerusalem was in Jewish hands 19 years into the existence of the state of Israel. Fifty thousand people were demonstrating against the Vietnam War at the Lincoln Memorial in Washington. China had detonated its first hydrogen bomb, and the Beatles were singing, "All You Need is Love."

Graham was about ready to turn in that evening when he noticed Bill had disappeared into the shadows. Graham waited up for him and, when Bill returned to the campsite at midnight, asked him where he had been.

"Sightseeing," Bill said.

"Seeing what?" Graham asked.

"Sights." Bill was obviously upset, so the two men sat down by the campfire while Graham pried the truth out of him. It turned out that Bill felt quite hemmed in by all the people and was not sure he wanted this intimacy. This astonished Graham. Didn't Bill know how invaluable he was? he asked. Didn't he know how much he meant to him? Didn't Bill know that he was like the younger brother Graham never had? That night, the two men made a pact that as long as they ministered together, they would never part.

Graham began to include Bill in counseling sessions and take him along on ministry visits. Once they went to a hospital to visit a dying woman, who told them she had dreamed about Bill.

"God has great things for you," she said to the young man. "Stay with him," indicating Graham. Graham was struck by this. God, he thought, had singled out Bill to do something special at Redeemer. Somehow, the Lord was making him responsible for Bill, and Graham wasn't going to neglect him—no, not for anything in the world.

B Y October, attendance at the main Sunday morning service had gone over the 300-person milestone. Graham's absence had not affected Redeemer adversely as long as Jerry Barker doubled as part-time pastor while managing his law practice. Al Rountree performed the priestly functions. Friday night meetings were already attracting people outside the parish, including some clergy who snuck in by wearing civilian clothing. They would sit through the worship and teaching, then head to the downstairs chapel to be baptized in the Spirit. Redeemer was one of the few places in Houston considered neutral territory between the pentecostals and the mainstream church, and the Episcopalians were seen as midway between Roman Catholicism and the Protestant fundamentalists. Jerry Barker had a pentecostal friend, also a lawyer, who would come to sit in the chapel and weep.

"I've been a pentecostal all my life," he told Jerry, "and I've never seen God move like this with such power."

Marie Marzullo, a transplant to Redeemer from New York's Greenwich Village, also sensed tremendous power. She swore she once heard the sound of angels' wings during a service, which unnerved her. When her father, a New York longshoreman, visited the church, he broke down and cried. He and his wife told Marie that during a service, they saw Jesus come out of the mural and toward them. No one thought him strange for saying this; such sightings were considered par for the course at Redeemer.

Bob and Mary Ella Evans's college-age daughter Carol Lee began eating dinner once a week at the Pulkinghams and listening to talk about the baptism in the Spirit. The crowds had gotten too big for the chapel, so prayers for the baptism were moved upstairs to the church sanctuary. One Friday night, she felt compelled to sit in the front row, but when the leaders invited people to come to the altar rail for prayer, she was too terrified to move. "Lord, if you want me to have this, you'll have to come get me," she prayed. Then she felt Graham's hand on hers.

"Carol Lee, the Lord wants you to be baptized in the Spirit," he said kindly, taking her by the hand and leading her to the rail. After they had prayed for her to speak in tongues, and she had, Carol Lee looked out on a new vista of spiritual power. By the time she got home, she was radiant and grinning instead of her usually reclusive self, making her parents wonder even more about changes at the church.

Graham had an unerring instinct when it came to knowing what other people should do. Ed Baggett was a thoughtful, sensitive student from Cornell University who joined Redeemer and was obviously leadership material. Once, Ed was kneeling in church during a Friday night service when Graham approached him to say, "I think the Lord is telling you to come up here behind the altar rail and pray with people."

"Well," said Ed, "I'll pray about it and see if the Lord tells me to do so."

"Maybe He just did," Graham responded and marched back up behind the rail.

Like Carol Lee and Ed, more and more college students were coming to Redeemer, many from around the country. Most would abruptly decide the Lord wanted them in Houston, and effectuate a transfer from whatever university they were attending at the time. Some of them, such as Bob Burlingame, moved in with the elders. Bob was a graduate of Rice University, a classy, tree-lined, academically rigorous campus several miles south of Redeemer. He belonged to a prayer group of charismatic Church of Christ students at Rice, through which he met Jon Wilkes, a member of Jerry Barker's household. Jon invited Bob to live with the Barkers and take some of his meals at the church, along with other single people. Bob was in awe of Graham, whom everyone regarded as a mouthpiece of God. It was evident that Graham thought so, too; he was always sure he was right, Bob noticed.

Bob joined forces with John Grimmet on the maintenance crew, which had the sole task of cleaning the vast building. John had valiantly quit his foreman's job at Houston Light & Power, giving up all rights to retirement benefits, so he could be a sexton at the church after Graham had fired the first two sextons. Learning that John intended to leave HL&P to work full-time at the church, Bob Evans, a vice president at HL&P as well as Redeemer's senior warden, called him into his office to make sure John knew what he was doing. He offered John a year's leave of absence so he could think things over.

"I'm not trying anything out," John told him, "and I don't want to leave any bridges for me to cross back over."

Once at the church, John relaxed and took long meal breaks until he felt an inner rebuke. *This is My house. I sit on the commodes. I walk on the floors. And I want them clean,* the Lord informed him. Thus the maintenance crew was driven by John's conscience and stamina. The crowds were getting larger and Redeemer was becoming more active than ever. Prayer times were at 6 and 9 a.m., followed by "Bible sharing" at 10 a.m. and Bible study at 11. At the Bible sharing, participants were expected to share biblical insights garnered from private daily prayer with God. It grew to be a powerful ministry by virtue of its simplicity and democratic set-up—everyone's insights from the Lord were listened to and respected.

Everyone was hungry for anything biblical. *The Light*, a 12-page church newsletter, faithfully reproduced segments of Graham's teachings, which were heavily laced with biblical passages and allusions. By 1968, four years after Graham's power encounter in New York, the baptism in the Spirit was very much a part of the fabric at Redeemer. Graham made it clear that those who had not been baptized in the Spirit should not expect to grow in their wisdom and knowledge of God. Thus, everyone eventually made it to the chapel or the altar rail to be prayed over. Graham was impossible to refuse; there was a starkness and a purity about his words, a directness and confidence that felt prophetic. On the last page, *The Light* always printed an unsigned testimony by a parishioner, anonymous to keep with Redeemer's egalitarian policy that everyone, whether elder or peon, was one in Christ. During sermons, Graham called everyone to the most intense commitment possible, even telling them they should be prepared to reside in the nearby Hispanic and black neighborhoods, living exactly as they lived and maybe poorer, for they would be expected to give away their possessions to their neighbors. Their attitude toward their brothers in Christ, he said, was the same as one has for a child; to put aside all rights to proper sleep, privacy, individuality, quiet, and peace for the sake of the child. Graham termed this attitude as "laying down your life" for that person, which essentially meant they lowered their natural boundaries out of love for other Christians.

This was the 1960s, a short time of innocence when thousands of American youth were making their way to San Francisco—a time when it was natural for everyone to hitchhike, or pick up hitchhikers, and when life's possibilities seemed limitless. Yet, people began to wonder how far this would go. Obviously, Graham and the elders seemed to be laying down their lives for others. John Grimmet surely had, in laying down his job. With this sort of all-out commitment, there seemed no limit to where this type of Christianity could go. Most Christians were ineffective because they were not willing to die for what they believed. This group was.

O NE day in the spring of 1968, a call came into the church office. Just the night before, Bob Eckert had informed Graham that the Lord would bring another priest to Redeemer—someone young and single, with a high-church background. The next morning, a priest named Jeff Schiffmayer showed up. Jeff had graduated four years previous from the high citadel of Anglo-Catholicism: Nashotah House seminary in Wisconsin. He had spent the last few years in Malawi as a chaplain at a boarding school for village children and was entranced by African village-style community. Jeff would have stayed in Africa forever, but his bishop wanted him to spend several years in an average parish. Redeemer was hardly an average parish, but Jeff got wind of community at Redeemer and called Graham, who invited him to visit for five days.

He was billeted at McKinney House, a smelly, run-down place inhabited by five other college-age men who neither made their beds nor aimed well at the toilets. *I don't ask for much,* Jeff thought, *but almost worse were people's habits of saying, "The Lord told me this" and "The Lord told me that." Worst of all was how people endlessly hugged each other.*

They don't need a seminarian, Jeff thought, *when all these people have a direct line to the Lord.*

He began planning a way to leave on the fourth day of his visit. As he searched for a phone to call a taxi, he stopped for a few seconds on the sidewalk outside the church to give God one last chance to protest. Sure enough, the Lord did.

"What do you think is the most important thing about Me?" the voice asked.

"Your love," Jeff replied.

"And now that you've found this in a community of people, you're going to run from it?" the voice said. *"Do you remember the parable of the seed that grew secretly?"* Jeff wasn't sure he did, but he said yes.

"Well," said the Lord, *"you're my little seed that I want to plant among these people."*

Oh my God, Jeff thought.

"Do you know what happens when a seed grows in the ground?" the voice continued.

"Its walls get decomposed, and I'll be destroyed," Jeff answered.

"You won't be destroyed," the Lord assured him. *"The part of you that mixes with the ground is what I want to have happen with you at this church."*

Jeff turned on his heels and walked back into the church, where he was greeted by two ushers who hugged him. Jeff flinched, silently begging the Lord for help. In an instant, something broke inside him, and Jeff fell, weeping on the neck of Wayne Hightower, the larger of the two ushers. Simultaneously, a picture of his father flashed into his mind. After that experience, Jeff was like a child, always wanting to hug and to be hugged.

He went on staff with Graham and Al Rountree, lived at McKinney House, and celebrated his first Eucharist there on June 12 at a Wednesday morning service. Twelve people came. He fit in. When Graham began traveling a year later, Jeff was promoted to associate rector and married Sylvia Sumner, Polly's daughter.

Jeff was not the only person bowled over by the ushers, Redeemer's spiritual advance team. Everyone who entered the church's front glass doors got a hug from an usher, whether they wanted one or not. The idea was to melt people's resistance to the Lord. Wayne Hightower was a quintessential usher and resident of the Lone Star State. Gruff, robust, beefy, blue-eyed, and sun-tanned, he was through-and-through Texan to the point where he pronounced San Antonio "San Antone." Wayne had found Redeemer in 1966, when all kinds of people, including prostitutes and the emotionally disturbed, were seeking help from the church. Graham was teaching Genesis, and Wayne had never heard such a clear sermon. One week, when Wayne's wife Sarah got sick, he called Graham, who said, "I knew you'd be calling me. I've been waiting on your call."

Wayne asked for an appointment, thinking he would not get to see Graham for at least a week. Graham asked him to come at 2:30 that very afternoon. When Wayne arrived, Graham explained to him how Redeemer would be like a New Testament church. He was hooked, and both Hightowers joined.

Now the crowds had found their way to Redeemer and Wayne was helping lead the corps of ushers, who saw their job as part bouncer and part spiritual calling. Sometimes, they would lead obviously distraught people down to the chapel to pray. Other times, they would be busy throwing hecklers out. When a man charged into the church to try to kidnap his ex-wife, five ushers tackled him, and the melée went crashing through the glass doors. Another time, a man walked into the vestibule, pulled out a cocked .38 revolver, and threatened to walk into the church.

"Over my dead body," usher Gordon Abbott said. The two eyeballed each other and the man finally walked off. Once, a man walked into the church with a trumpet. After the ushers relieved him of that, he tried to stand up and interrupt Graham's sermon. John Grimmet commanded him to shut up in the name of Jesus and the man tried to answer back, but no sounds came out of his mouth. It was said there was so much spiritual power present at the service, people reacted like a spark put to gunpowder: They fainted, threw up, and had seizures or fits, and the ushers would gamely carry them out to a quieter spot.

Graham encouraged the release of pentecostal power, reasoning that any excesses would take care of themselves. Thanks to the ushers and the sheer force of Graham's presence in the pulpit, they always did. Graham was a man of strong statements, Carol Lee thought, and a strong and persuasive personality who usually got what he wanted. He developed strong relationships in the same way he preached—with no holds barred. He drew people in, then shared his soul with them. He was a brilliant therapist who could listen between the lines, and who most times could discern the truth of a matter. Everything he did was done with such enormous energy and vigor that people found him impossible to resist. He had a personality that overwhelmed, and he was utterly confident he was not only hearing directly from the Almighty, but had a mandate to put whatever he heard into practice in the growing church. A certain degree of authoritarianism goes with the territory when a leader gets his directions from God, and Redeemer was doing well under Graham's leadership, no doubt about that.

After the conversation at the Maryland campground, Graham decided to partner with Bill in performing various functions. This went unquestioned, though it subtly upset the delicate balance among the five elders. Being close to Graham's age, Ladd, Bob, John, and Jerry could challenge him if need be. Three of them had known him before his baptism in the Spirit. They were men's men and to be part of their group was like being a fighter pilot asked to join the squadron. Yet, here was Bill, 19 years younger than Graham, fresh from the death of a spouse, malleable, and willing to please. The equation did not add up.

As Graham sought to heal Bill's depression following Shirley's death, they were together constantly, often sitting close to each other and throwing their arms about each other. Sharp-witted Carol Lee noticed this, as well as when the rest of the parish began to copy Bill and Graham's relationship. People began to hug each other, not in a mindless sort of way, but with deeply felt, frontal-style hugs that communicated a willingness to touch and be touched. After all, this was the way Graham did it. These hugs were absolutely genuine. Whole households would sit in the pews, their arms linked around each other.

Bob Eckert especially was left in the lurch by the Graham-Bill arrangement. Mentally and physically Graham's equal, he was more capable than his four fellow vestrymen of reining in Graham when need be. As the evangelist, Bob had a blunt Baptist way of doing things that netted souls and simplified terms. Bob saw the individual believer, or a group clustered around a teacher, as central. The only real authority was the local congregation.

Graham saw the church as a central corporate body, with the real authority belonging to the bishop. Neither Graham nor Bob would budge on their idea of the church. The dynamic tension between the two added zest and spark to Redeemer, prompting Bob Evans to tell Bob Eckert, "I bet if you all stop loving each other, this will fall apart." The doctor agreed. There was no way to maintain the explosion that was Redeemer unless a five-part harmony was sung at the top.

The rest of them sensed that Bob and Graham were on the cutting edge with the Lord, and if you wanted to be close to the Lord, you stayed near them.

Such philosophical differences might have ironed themselves out, but Graham's decision to start appearing with Bill as a team at out-of-town speaking engagements threw things off kilter. To have Redeemer's most significant personalities absent for long periods of time did not feel right and caused all the vestry relationships to change. The profoundness of the elders' relationship began to diminish, but the spiritual dangers were so subtle that only a year or two later did the elders realize how much they were drifting apart. By then, Graham was out of town more, often traveling with Bill, and it was too late to change things. The tide had already gone out. Never again would Graham be as accountable to anyone as he had been to the other four elders.

CHAPTER 7

The Feast of St. Michael and All Angels

"And then there was war in heaven. Michael and his angels fought against the dragon and the dragon and his angels fought back But he was not strong enough, and they lost their place in heaven."

—Revelation 12:7–8

A car pulled up to a ramshackle house on North Main Street across Buffalo Bayou and just north of the glitter of downtown Houston. Out piled Graham, Betty, Arabella, Bill, and Nancy and up they walked to the building, knocking on the door. The owner ushered them into a dimly lit hallway.

Betty regarded the two-story frame house at 1517 Main with horror. Graham, who was always two steps ahead of everyone else, had wanted to locate a household in the middle of Houston's hippie district, where winos frequently hung out at the nearby train tracks. But surely, she thought, he could not mean *this*. Jerry Barker had first spotted the house, which was caked with dirt. There were gaping holes in the ceiling and floor and peeling plaster everywhere.

Suddenly, Arabella cried out: "Graham! Look!" To their left was a parlor with a large bay window and window seat. "It's just like the one in my dream," she explained. "It was this very room."

Betty dimly remembered when Arabella had shared with her a dream about one of the women at church playing the guitar in some mysterious room near a window. Betty was far from enthused. Hadn't Graham any idea, she wondered, how hard it would be to transport her now six children, ages 15 to a few months, to this mess and make it livable? Arabella may have had a vision of the house's future, but to Betty, it was more like a vision out of lower hell. Main Street was extremely busy, choked with coal dust and diesel fumes from all the cars and trucks. A trucking company behind the house had a loading dock where freight was noisily moved throughout the early morning hours.

Nevertheless, the family moved in, and for 10 months repaired and remodeled the house as best they could. At first, there were no chairs, so people sat on carpet remnants. It was so cold there in the winter that some of the people kept their coats on when they slept. More people joined the household until there were at least two dozen residents. Some were either getting off drugs, or were schizophrenic or depressed, such as Carolyn Shaver, a traumatized woman from West Virginia. Carolyn would not speak above a whisper when she first arrived, but she was quite taken with Graham who upon meeting her, embraced her and laid her head on his chest like the father she never had. Carolyn was put to work picking out edible fruit pieces from a pile of days-old fruit donated by Jamails Food Market. Because few in the household worked, money was so tight that members lived on old fruit, hamburger with rice, regular milk mixed with dry milk to make it stretch, and one egg per person per week.

Their freezer was so tiny that there was room for only two ice cube trays. Each resident received two ice cubes a day in a town where scorching temperatures were the norm eight months out of the year.

Graham and Betty's youthful housemates had a culture of their own. They greeted visitors with a "bless you" and a hug. They were trained not to be frivolous in conversation and to say what they meant. People prayed at the drop of a hat, trying to take to heart, as much as possible, the Apostle Paul's admonition to "pray without ceasing."

Next to the house was an old garage that, with lots of willing hands, was renovated into a coffeehouse, from which a team of young evangelists departed to evangelize at nearby Allen's Landing. Allen's Landing, a grassy area where the Allen Brothers, the founders of Houston, had landed 132 years before, had become quite the hangout for hippies. The warehouse district just across the bridge was a conglomeration of head shops and boutiques. At night, the place came alive for blocks, all the way to Market Square behind the *Houston Chronicle* building. Thousands of people packed the area, known as Houston's Haight Ashbury, filling the district's shops and coffeehouses until midnight, which was when the police swept through and kicked out everyone under 18. It was a light, innocent time of free love, free speech, and free drugs.

Words like "far out," "groovy," "flower power," "mellow," "trip," "be-in," "cool," "uptight," "outasight," and "peace" were the shibboleths of the age, and

Houston, with its warm evenings during most of the year, was a perfect spot to mellow out. People could wander about the Landing and engage in conversations with total strangers at what was, in effect, a massive block party. The area was filled with runaways, many of them teenage girls, along with drug dealers and sidewalk musicians. Coffeehouses and performers were everywhere. Every available space was filled with psychedelic head shops, for, as the saying went, you were down there to "sell, buy, score, or deal."

In June 1969, the church sent a team of 11 youth to New York City to train in street evangelism under David Wilkerson's Teen Challenge workers, learn how to use music in a public setting, give testimonies, and pass out tracts. Returning to Houston, they crammed the Main Street house for a meeting to decide the name of their new venture. They sang a few songs and discussed a few possibilities, but nothing seemed to click.

Betty Jane cradled baby David on the street outside their house, which was set in front of a tunnel. As she thought of the cars streaming out of the darkness, she murmured half to herself, "The way out."

Bill Farra turned to look at her.

"The way in," he said. And that was it. The Way In coffeehouse opened July 4, 1969, the same summer that 400,000 people gathered at a farm in upstate New York in what would be known as Woodstock. Two weeks later, two Americans would land on the moon for the first time. The coffeehouse's opening did not get nearly the same amount of media coverage as those two other events, but it was a stroke of genius, and it became Redeemer's most successful foray into the surrounding culture. It rapidly found itself on the Jesus freak map of places to visit—Houston not only was a southern crossroads on the way to California, but it had a Space Age vitality that was on everyone's lips. After all, the word "Houston" had been the first word out of the astronauts' mouths upon landing on the moon.

Spurred by movies such as *Easy Rider*, the country was full of young people on the road, wandering from place to place with little else but a backpack, and the coffeehouse was a natural gathering spot. Coffeehouse visitors were treated to an evening of evangelistic songs, poetry readings, skits, and dances. During musical breaks, one could drink Cokes on used cable spools outside. It was not the only Christian coffeehouse in the area, but it was artier and less of a hard sell than others. Soon, 400 persons were showing up each night and, to accommodate everyone, the musicians were doing five separate 45-minute sets.

Romance would have been natural in such a setting, but Graham forbade any "he-ing and she-ing" at the Main Street house because, he ordered, attendees were to be focused on God instead of each other. This rule made for a disciplined core group of about 20 young adults who brought forth Redeemer's springtime of creativity. New songs were being composed and tried out weekly in the coffeehouse. Chief among the composers was Mimi Armstrong, a former Fulbright scholar in music who had studied at the New England Conservatory in Boston. In her early 30s, she was a voice teacher at Carleton College in Minnesota when her older sister, Kathleen Thomerson, the substitute organist at Redeemer, enthusiastically told her of this new church. A lively and energetic personality, Mimi visited Redeemer for two summers and was so wooed by the lifestyle that she quit her teaching position at Carleton to move to Houston.

Artists and musicians are often the first to click in with a revival, because they are irresistibly attracted to the spiritual. That's why a group of newly converted music majors from Sam Houston State University in Huntsville, 75 miles north of Houston, heard of the Way In. After some of them were baptized in the Spirit at the coffeehouse, they asked Grover's advice on how to start a prayer group on campus. Grover advised them to not always close their eyes during worship. "Worship is horizontal as well as vertical," he told Wiley Beveridge, a flute and piano major who belonged to the group.

Sure enough, when members of the prayer group kept their eyes open and engaged each other in worship, the result was indescribably powerful. They began their own coffeehouse in Huntsville, which they called the Open Door, and listened to tapes by Florida pastor Bob Mumford on discipleship and those by Graham on community and leadership. Two of the young community leaders, James Von Minden and Don McLane, began a household and promised lifelong commitment to this community. Communes were the rage in the hippie culture, and households like these fit in perfectly with the popular culture.

Victor Wilson, a backslidden Southern Baptist from Kilgore, Texas, was hanging around Allen's Landing one evening when he encountered two Way In evangelists, Jeff Cothran and Martha Keys. It was a warm summer night, and here were these two normal-looking people inviting people to some coffeehouse.

Jeff was 21, tall and lanky, and had a great sense of humor. He needed it for all the sexual torment he was living through. Jeff had been baptized in the Spirit during the winter of 1966, hoping desperately that it would deliver him from the homosexual cravings he had felt all his life. He was not delivered and, two years later, he met a college classmate who told him about Redeemer. Maybe *this* would bring the deliverance he sought, he thought. When he arrived the next June, just before the coffeehouse opened, Jeff became part of the evangelistic teams who strolled around Allen's Landing, inviting the lounging hippies to visit their no-cover-charge coffeehouse a half-mile up the road.

Unaware of Jeff's sexual identity struggle, Victor Wilson was impressed with the two evangelists, for, to him, they were unlike most Christians who tried to witness. Often, Victor would get stoned, then go down to the Landing to argue with whatever Christian witnessing teams he found there. He had made the rounds of all the Christian coffeehouses, and he could confound recent converts with trick Bible questions learned from his days in Sunday school. The Way In people stood out in how they didn't argue, but instead invited people to come and see worship at their coffeehouse.

When Victor arrived, he found a remodeled garage with a piano, stage, lighting, microphones, and Christian graffiti written on the walls. There were two dozen or so visitors, all of them seated on the floor in their bellbottom pants, paisley shirts, and various hot pink, chartreuse, orange, or brown outfits. All the women had long hair. All the men had shaggy hair with sideburns. Omnipresent were beads, peace symbol necklaces, head bands, long skirts, pale lipstick and circlet-shaped necklaces, patent leather, high-heeled boots with mini-skirts, wide lapels on men's jackets, fishnet stockings, halter tops, headbands, sandals, long vests, beaded vests or suede vests with fringes. When dressed up, the men sported wide, garish ties and checkered pants, the women long skirts.

Victor hobnobbed, noticing that at the Way In, they at least tried to learn your name and get to know you. Nearly everyone there was college age, and although it wasn't totally hip, it was not as square as some of the other coffeehouses run by Baptist Student Union types. In watching them pray, Victor noticed they were really praying, really worshipping. He prayed, too, and got a mental image of himself at the edge of a cliff with the sun setting. "Step out," the Lord urged him, and he did. That night, he and a visiting Catholic seminarian were baptized in the Spirit, after which he moved into a household with a newly married couple: Jon and Sylvia Wilkes.

SEVERAL hundred students stood around at the anti-war rally at the University of Houston central campus holding signs like "Hell no, we won't go." Protest music filled the air. Emceeing the demonstration was a long-haired man with a gravelly voice, wearing sun glasses and beads, and holding a guitar. This was Mikel Kennedy, leader of the war protest movement at the University of Houston, leader of the Students for a Democratic Society, and an LSD addict. The grandson of a Southern Baptist preacher, Mikel was in full rebellion against his upbringing.

His anti-war days got cut short when he overdosed and nearly died, ending up at his parents' home to recuperate. Having just discovered Redeemer and been baptized in the Spirit there, his parents invited Graham and Bill Farra to help. When Mikel briefly regained consciousness, he looked up to see a priest sitting on his bed. There was something genuine, confident, and kind about the man, who invited him to Redeemer and life in McKinney House, which was filled with all sorts of odd people in various stages of drug use and mental capabilities.

Mikel groped his way toward God as he struggled with his penchant for drugs. One Friday night, he went to the altar rail. Earle Frid laid his hands on him, then directed him to pray in tongues. After that evening, Mikel felt a new power he had not experienced before in resisting drugs. Mikel's musical background, hippie attire and experience leading anti-war rallies made him a natural at emceeing at the Way In.

One day, a handsome Dominican priest from St. Louis, Francis MacNutt, visited the coffeehouse and sat up all night to tell Mikel about the charismatic scene in the U.S. There was actually a charismatic circuit, Francis informed him. First, you went to Duquesne in Pittsburgh to solve any intellectual problems about the renewal. Then you visited Word of God, Ralph Martin's and Steve Clark's growing Catholic charismatic community in Ann Arbor, for the baptism. Then you went to Redeemer in Houston to find out how to integrate it all.

Mikel was intrigued enough to want to visit Word of God, whose reputation was spreading as fast as Redeemer's. After the charismatic Catholics at Notre Dame invited Graham to speak at their third annual conference in 1969, things began picking up between Word of God and Redeemer. The next year, Mikel and Grover Newman flew to Ann Arbor for a month. Their hosts were Steve, Ralph, and Jim Cavnar, three of the four single male founders of Word of God. Jim was a guitarist. He had been ready to graduate from Notre Dame when the renewal arrived there and that summer, he gravitated to Ann Arbor along with Clark, Martin and Gerry Rauch, the fourth founding member. That fall during a prayer meeting, Jim suddenly received a prophecy. "The work you have begun in Michigan will continue and spread to many other states," the Lord said through him. "I will raise up spiritual sons and daughters armed for My work. A shining cross of My body . . . will be raised up among you. I will send people to you from all across the nation to receive a message from you that they will take back."

In 1970, the young charismatic Catholics founded Word of God. The title came from another prophecy—this one from Bruce Yocum, the community's leading prophet.

"I . . . call you the Word of God, because you are My word now to the whole face of the earth," it said. "I am going to pour out upon you a spirit of power, grandeur, and glory so that all who see you will know that I am God, and that I am among you."

Grover and Mikel's arrival fit well with these prophecies, although the Word of God men knew they had things to learn from Redeemer as well. While Jim taught Mikel how to lead worship with a guitar, Mikel passed along songs from the Way In's singing group, The Keyhole. By 1970, the Keyhole had already cut their first record and was forming a non-profit corporation, The Fishermen. Redeemer and Word of God worked out an agreement whereby they could use each other's songs without having to pay licensing fees. The only unsettling thing about their visit was one prayer meeting in which someone prophesied that God would "decimate" Redeemer. The group decided the interpretation meant that people would be sent out of Redeemer.

Word of God leaders then made their way to Texas where they were greatly impressed with the way people there loved each other. Word of God was good at organizing and getting things done, and they would end up being major system-atizers of community and charismatic renewal. But the Redeemer people knew how to love and lay down their lives for each other, how to make community a life-transforming event, which impressed the Michigan visitors no end. Word of God people got the idea of extended-family households, which were mainly singles living with Redeemer families, from Redeemer. They saw how families like the Barkers had taken on a reformed alcoholic and five men, including one dressed in rags and calling himself John the Baptist. This man had multiple personalities, which church leaders figured were evil spirits. After they prayed over him, the man went on maintenance crew, attended Bible studies, and later got well, becoming a missionary. However, placing a handful of sick people in a household of teenagers and a mother with a history of mental illness was overkill, decided Jerry's eldest son, Owen. When he flunked out of college after 18 months, Owen first thought he was stupid. He then realized that the pres-ence of five mentally ill people in his home was not helping his study habits.

These marginal people made things harder when Redeemer experimented in community economics in the spring and summer of 1969 by forming the "Redeemer Ministering Community." Sixteen households with 120 people were set aside as the "ministers" at Redeemer and everything they had was to be shared. The RMC looked good on paper—it was a tax-exempt organization whose salaries and belongings were shared and its money centrally handled. But the administrative part was a nightmare, even with Gordon Abbott as full-time business administrator. Banks refused to finance cars and houses that belonged to the RMC because they wanted an individual to be responsible for the bills. Also, the needy people who had moved into households and who had never seen a dentist in their lives were racking up thousands of dollars in dental bills. The RMC eventually dissolved and finances were handled by household. Thus, households varied greatly in their financial set-up. Some households had more wage earners and a luxurious existence; others, mostly of students or the unemployed, barely squeaked by.

Household life could be both heady and hellish, or a spiritual frat party. The genius of the idea was the households' geographic closeness to the church. Most households were walking distance from Redeemer and each other, which made living in a household a bonding experience and transformed the neighborhood as well. One was always waving to folks walking by on the sidewalk. Redeemer saw a varied batch of charismatics at every economic level moving in, including a number of clergy. Just about anyone who showed up on Redeemer's doorstep and wanted to become part of a household could do so. But, as Graham toured the country, he would talk up Redeemer's healing properties and parishes would send their basket cases to Redeemer. Several Redeemer households were overwhelmed with mentally sick people arriving from around the country.

Eventually, the church appointed two household administrators to assess what households needed in terms of wage earners, which people were spiritually or mentally sick, which ones weren't, those who would work with children, and those who would work at the church. It was all supposed to balance out somehow, but the way it usually worked is that whole households would switch residents every six months or so. The worst hit were single people who got transferred from household to household like so much baggage, as many of the married people owned their property and could not be shifted about as easily. Household members jokingly called such moves "fruit basket turnovers." In addition, if you did not like your current household, there was a good chance you would soon get transferred to another.

WITHIN a year, the coffeehouse was enlarged to three times its size to seat 200. Ed Baggett was put in charge, the Pulkinghams moved out to much nicer quarters on North MacGregor Way near the University of Houston and the Wilkes took over leadership of their former household. During the summer of 1970, Houston hosted the General Convention of the Episcopal Church at the Albert Thomas Convention Center downtown, the timing of which could not have been more convenient. The convention attracted Episcopalians from around the country who were on the lookout for whatever was new and different. Accordingly, Mikel staffed a booth at the convention center with Way In albums and books. He placed a tape recorder before him with earphones, and over him hung a sign, "Ever Heard Glossolalia?" On the tape were Redeemerites singing in the Spirit, with a message and interpretation by Earle Frid. Then Mikel would hand curiosity-seekers maps to the coffeehouse, which was open every night that week. On the second night of the convention, Jeff Schiffmayer, resplendent in rainbow-colored robes, celebrated an outdoor Eucharist outside the convention center. Clergy, bishops, and lay delegates flooded the Way In, many of them to be prayed over for the baptism in the Spirit.

One of the Way In visitors was Raymond Davis, rector of Truro Episcopal Church, a large, conservative parish in Fairfax, Virginia. Restless from the all-day meetings at the convention, he slipped off to Redeemer's exhibit. Graham, who was standing there, invited Davis to a noon service at the church. Davis was impressed with its informality and with how Graham dealt with parishioners, treating them courteously and even asking the sexton for forgiveness for being irritable that morning. That November, Derek Prince, a British born pentecostal leader living in South Florida, spoke at Truro and offered to pray over the rector. Davis spoke in tongues and, wishing to learn more about this movement, invited Graham to visit the parish the following February. Graham made quite a splash and, during later visits, brought a team to introduce music from The Keyhole. But Graham could be slightly testy, Davis noticed. When one woman in his congregation bellowed from the back, "We can't hear you!" Graham retorted with, "Well, move up to the front!"

The one critical eye was that of Davis's assistant, Stephen Noll, a recent seminary graduate from the Episcopal Church Divinity School of the Pacific in Berkeley. Stephen had just been baptized in the Spirit at a parish in nearby Corte Madera, and the Redeemer folk seemed so self-enclosed, he thought, such an entity unto themselves. Who was calling *them* into account? An even greater warning signal was Graham's rhetoric about the family. Graham spent a lot of time talking about the nuclear family being dead and community becoming the norm. Graham, a 1960s liberal and social activist, *would* think that, Stephen thought, but would it fly in Fairfax? It seemed that Graham's baptism in the Spirit empowered what he had already been about, which was ministry to the poor. But had it really changed Graham's agenda? Stephen put aside his doubts for a while, and he and his wife, Peggy, and their five children ended up briefly opening their household to outsiders. But the idea never caught on in northern Virginia's far-flung suburbs, and he ended up routing Truro's energies into small group Bible studies.

Graham was, in fact, developing a radical idea of the family. He would preach that everyone was brothers in Christ, a "brother in Christ" being a theological category, by which Jesus was the elder brother and all other Christians were younger brothers. A "sister in Christ" was somehow a lesser category, so Graham, to the amusement of many of his listeners, would refer to his wife as his "brother" in Christ, which put her on the same footing as himself and Jesus. If the greatest relationship in Christianity were brothers in Christ, then Graham could love Betty more as his brother than as his wife, or so the reasoning went. Graham's view was so egalitarian that he believed he had no business preferring his wife over another brother or sister. This is how he rationalized leaving his wife and family to minister to others. All, he felt, had an equal call on his life. He described this scenario at one of his conferences.

"Something happens that draws you together with other people where you're filled with the Spirit and that gets in the way of family life," he said. Then, running his words together for a breathless, hurried effect, "Suddenly, the relationship that you had to your wife and to your children and all the lovely plans you had for taking that weekend off and going to such and such a place and having a holiday and having the privacy of your own time and suddenly there are people who need help, so they are living in your back bedroom and they're screaming half the night and you don't know what to do with them, and you can't get rid of them at holiday time and so you spend half your holiday time tending to some poor soul who needs help and suddenly your wife is right at your throat, you know. You're getting the picture?"

His audience laughed, as this was a familiar scenario to them, and it was Graham's life. Then came the zinger. Graham described how a 20th-century marriage would have never happened in Old Testament times when the father was *really* the head of his immediate family and an extended family and whoever else might desire his services.

"It would be unthinkable," he repeated, "that a man would sacrifice his calling to be the father of the family in preference to his relationship to his wife. Never! But," he concluded reproachfully, "that happens to us."

Any wives seated there could not fail to get the message. His was a philosophy that would radically influence most Redeemer marriages, since Graham never got around to teaching where being one in Christ stopped and being one in marriage began. Couples never learned how to be married; instead, people were taught that exclusive relationships were wrong. The only thing that could be exclusive was, as Graham would put it, "what happens between the sheets."

CHAPTER 8

The Feast of St. Francis

"After they prayed, the place where they were meeting was shaken. And they were all filled with the Holy Spirit and spoke the word of God boldly."   —Acts 4:31

IT was 2 a.m. and four men sat in a hotel room in Ft. Lauderdale. All four were charismatic leaders who had just ministered at a conference that had ended hours before. But these men were not sleeping. Word had reached them of a friend's immorality. What particularly concerned them was his similarity to them. Like "Frank," they all were itinerant evangelists, accountable to no one, spending many lonely hours on the road, receiving more flattery than was good for them.

"Not one of us is immune to the deception which trapped Frank," mused Charles Simpson, a Southern Baptist minister from Mobile, Alabama. "I want you to know," he added, leaning forward, "that, like Frank, I've been close to going over the edge. Only by the grace of God have I been spared; not because I'm better than he is. Through his problem, I believe God is showing us how vulnerable we all are."

The four men looked at each other and each admitted to a battery of temptations and fears that beset them.

"It's spiritual warfare we're in," said Derek Prince, the British pentecostal scholar and one-time philosophy fellow at King's College, Cambridge. Even then, he was researching a book on spiritual warfare and fasting.

"The devil's tactics are always to pick us off one by one," Prince said. "He waits for the right moment, then strikes us at the weakest point in our defenses. Do you realize how many men with ministries of real power have disappeared from the Christian scene in the past few years?" He listed several names of prominent ministers they all knew.

"It seems to me," Prince concluded, "that in every case these men made one fatal mistake: They failed to submit themselves to the body of Christ. They all tried to go it alone."

Nodding assent was Don Basham, a Disciples of Christ minister, a talented author who would describe this scene in a later book, *Deliver Us from Evil.* The fourth participant, Bible teacher Bob Mumford, broke in to say he thought he had the solution to their problem.

"For years, I've longed to join my ministry to those of other men I could trust," he said. "I've come to know you three. I've seen the fruits of your ministries all across this nation. I'd like to be a part of what God is doing, in and through each of you."

Then and there, the quartet agreed to be accountable to each other in praying, correcting, supporting, and encouraging the other three. Mumford and Simpson were the most extroverted of the quartet. Basham was a specialist in deliverance ministry. Along with the immorality problem, they were also concerned with the lack of decent teaching in the charismatic renewal. The Holy Spirit was doing something unprecedented in New Testament times among Christians, and there was no body of teaching to handle it. Perhaps, they thought, it was up to them to provide it.

Their mutual agreement of accountability would be a watershed in the charismatic renewal. The four would pool their resources and knowledge to create a powerhouse of charismatic teaching. In 1968, they founded the Holy Spirit Teaching Mission in Ft. Lauderdale, which published a magazine, *New Wine*, free to all who requested it. The ministry would eventually take on a new name, Christian Growth Ministries, and a fifth member, Canadian pentecostal Ern Baxter. Edited by Basham, the magazine began pumping out articles on prayer groups, Spirit baptism, and speaking in tongues. As the renewal matured, the magazine broadened to topics like ecumenical unity and deliverance and issues of authority, discipline, and community. The Ft. Lauderdale teachers began to minister more as a team. One place they visited was a church in Midland, Texas, where they met an oil engineer, Jim Clowe, and his former airline stewardess wife, Jane.

Jim had bushy eyebrows, a restless charm, and a refreshing bluntness about him. Jane was vivacious, talkative, and attractive. Both had been baptized in the Spirit in 1967 when Graham, Earle, Bob, and Jerry had spoken at their Episcopal church in Lafayette, Louisiana. En route to moving to Midland, they spent the night in a Redeemer household on the way. It was beastly hot, with no air-conditioning and large mosquitoes flying about. After slapping at mosquitoes all night, Jim decided he was not cut out for community.

Still, he and his wife kept up their contacts with Redeemer and Earle would sometimes come out to Midland to teach. That, plus teachings from Ft. Lauderdale and cassette tapes by pentecostal pioneer David duPlessis, gave them an informal schooling in the Bible and of the new concepts coming out of Ft. Lauderdale. Some of the Ft. Lauderdale teachers were preaching a "come out from among them" message about leaving the godless institutional church. Then these teachers had to come up with some way to pastor all those persons they had "called out." Thus was born the shepherding and discipleship movement, where new converts would have an older Christian or "shepherd" discipling them. These shepherds would answer to overshepherds, who would answer to the Ft. Lauderdale teachers, who were to be accountable to each other. It sounded right, and thousands of charismatics were buying into this spiritual pyramid scheme. It fascinated Jim Clowe to no end. At one point, he traveled to Ft. Lauderdale to discuss the tension between fundamentalism and liturgy with Derek Prince.

The Clowes and their five children spent Holy Week of 1970 at Redeemer, and were much more impressed than their unfortunate visit of two years before. Jeff Schiffmayer announced from the pulpit that the church had 35–50 out-of-town guests that weekend. Redeemer prided itself on its ability to house all its guests to give them a taste of community. Jeff asked for a show of hands of how many of its members were sleeping on the floor. No hands were raised.

"I tell you," said Jeff, "until we're all sleeping on the floor, we don't have enough guests."

Jim was awed. He had never heard anyone talk like that. But then again, this was Redeemer, where breathless commitment and sacrificial living was the common currency. Small wonder that, 18 months later, when his company transferred him to Houston, he was delighted. They bought a seven-bedroom home at 4402 Bell for $27,500, sold their 4,500-square-foot home in Midland, and gave away the dollar difference.

Also at Redeemer that Holy Week was a Roman Catholic couple, Paul and Mary Felton, with their five children. Paul was tall and slim, with luminous eyes and a monkish, contemplative manner. Once an Episcopal priest, he had converted to Catholicism but now felt he was being drawn back "home" fourteen and a half years later. They had encountered the Fishermen at Word of God and were impressed enough to follow them back to Redeemer. Paul gave up his job teaching on peace and justice issues at St. Louis University and moved his family to Houston. The church gave them a house so dilapidated that Earle Frid joked the Lord would return before it was remodeled. To top it all off, the church then asked them if they could take on seven people as guests. Paul, who had a doctorate in religious studies, thought the way Redeemerites used Scripture was naive and literalistic, but he couldn't deny the power of the faith they drew from the Bibles they carried around.

That same spring, a depressed woman named Ruth Newell came to explore Redeemer. As she approached the door, a priest came out, who, she thought, had the face of Christ.

"I've had the most wonderful hour with Jesus," the priest told her. That was Jeff Schiffmayer. Ruth was stunned. No priest had ever said to her that he had seen or heard from Jesus. She entered a room where a Bible study was being held. The atmosphere was electrifying and the people there also talked about Jesus as if He was a real person. She felt herself to be in another dimension. She began spending blocks of time at the church and noticed certain spooky happenings, like the time during a noonday Eucharist when she heard ethereal voices from some enormous height above singing in some mysterious language. *Were those angels?* she wondered.

Another newcomer was Taft Metcalf, a software engineer working for Lockheed in Clear Lake near NASA. Although a lifelong Methodist and a church organist, he considered himself a reluctant agnostic. A friend took him to a Friday night service and his first impression was how ordinary everyone looked. Then they swung into "Alleluia, Sing to Jesus," a popular renewal hymn. He began to choke up, then realized it was not proper for an agnostic to cry in church. The friend wanted to go down to the chapel to be prayed for the baptism in the Spirit. Taft and the friend's wife tagged along and sat in a back pew. After the friend was prayed for, everyone present began to sing in the Spirit, which impressed the musician in Taft. Then they had an altar call for salvation and for some undefinable reason, Taft went forward. Bob Hansen, a new assistant priest at Redeemer who was presiding that night, warned them they were signing their "death warrant," then led them in a prayer for salvation. Taft arrived home at 2 a.m. and crawled into bed, grinning.

"Did you get saved?" his wife, Peggy, asked.

"Yes," he said.

"You've got to be kidding."

The next Friday night, Taft returned to be baptized in the Spirit. They put two questions to him: Did he know he was a son of God? Did he know who his pastor was? The first question pertained to his qualification to be empowered for service; the reasoning for the latter was that baptism in the Spirit opened you further to the spiritual world, making it all the more necessary to be under some pastoral authority. After they prayed for him, he felt a sensation of heat. He began singing in the Spirit, then stopped when he realized what he was doing. Clearly, something had happened.

Redeemer's fervor deeply impressed Camp Huntington, a scruffy 28-year-old who stopped by Redeemer on his way to catch a freighter overseas. He had just come from Israel, where he had worked in a copper mine and on a kibbutz, then became a Christian through a woman who witnessed to him at the Garden Tomb. He showed up with long hair, a beard, and an old leather jacket with an American flag on it. Graham was preaching that Friday night and the man sure had power, Camp thought. He even had the gall to gently rebuke some of the congregation members by name, and to Camp's amazement, they lapped it up. The freighter got delayed a week, so Camp stayed, amazed by how much the cross was preached at Redeemer and that, paradoxically, the cross—an instrument of death—brought so much life to the church. Their whole lifestyle was sacrifice, which created tremendous spiritual power. This was obviously a group of people who were going somewhere, and doing it all together. The freighter got delayed another week and Camp began thinking about staying. He prayed with one of the community members, and that night had four vivid dreams about staying. After that, the freighter did not stand a chance.

Soon after, Camp was living at the North Main house and given the twice-weekly job of driving to a dairy 20 miles north of Houston to pick up 70 gallons of milk. Far from being monotonous, he realized the task was loaded with meaning, as everything was around there. Everyone was contributing to this spiritual Camelot, where tons of people were meeting the Lord, getting healed, and receiving the Holy Spirit and where good dreams really were coming true. No matter how mundane the daily tasks, such as carting milk halfway across Houston, the worship on Friday nights and at the coffeehouse made everything worthwhile. People were really living, or at least trying to live, the Gospel, and the suffering and sacrifice involved in that made for powerful, no-compromise preaching. It was commonplace to walk into the middle of a conversation between two people doggedly trying to hash out their differences, and to know they would not leave that room until they had done so. Households were structured so you could not avoid each other. "You can't hide in a blender," was the saying, and people assumed it was more important to heal a relationship or solve a conflict than get a particular task done. It was a most inefficient way of doing things, but instead of hidden agendas and buried hatchets, feelings were brought into the open and dealt with. Those in the households felt secure and loved by each other, which helped them to meet newcomers with a winsome and artless sort of affection that was impossible to reject.

B Y the fall of 1970, Redeemer's Friday night services were attracting 500 people, outstripping Sunday morning attendance. Friday nights were the major drawing card for visitors who felt compelled to attend their own churches on Sunday mornings. An average Friday night would include six or seven testimonies, an extremely powerful form of witness. Testimonies built trust in God and people were reminded that the devil was being put to flight by the power of believers' testimonies. A generation of Catholic priests and nuns from around east Texas were baptized in the Spirit there, including two Irish nuns, Kathleen Smith and Bernice O'Keefe, who lived at the Villa de Matel, a retreat center two miles east of Redeemer.

There were charismatic stirrings in other churches besides Redeemer, but because of the leanings of their rectors, the flames were never lit. Thomas Sumners, rector of St. John the Divine, remained quiet about his experience with the Holy Spirit. His parish was one of Houston's moneyed Episcopal watering holes, where there was no desperation akin to what Graham had faced in 1964. St. John's was in a prime Houston suburb, it was wealthy and well-behaved, the church of Houston's new money. It could—and did—survive without the renewal. In 1974, Sumners turned the church over to a new rector from San Antonio, a former Air Force captain and West Point graduate-turned-priest named Maurice "Ben" Benitez.

Both Benitez and the rector of another popular Episcopal church, Claxton Monro, shared the same suspicion about the renewal's most volatile element—speaking in tongues. Monro welcomed people associated with the renewal at St. Stephen's Episcopal in the trendy Montrose district with the stipulation there be no messages in tongues. His parish was already doing well, thanks to a lay witnessing movement that Monro helped pioneer in the 1950s. The sheer embarrassment of spiritual gifts limited these otherwise successful men in ways that Graham did not allow himself to be limited.

Redeemer attracted people like Chris Caros, a communications major at the University of Houston who arrived near the end of 1970. A self-described hellion and the child of Greek immigrants, he came from a power background. His father owned the largest chain of liquor stores in Texas, and his uncle ran a Democratic party machine in Louisiana. At one point, Chris contemplated joining the Mafia, as everything he did was done out of hatred. He was not used to kindness from anyone, which is why he was surprised when a girl walked up to him one day on campus and handed him half of a cheese sandwich.

Some time later, he met some Redeemerites on campus and, through them, finally visited the church. The moment he touched the property, a serenity hit him and the world seemed to melt away. He entered the packed service, looked at the mural of Jesus and the disciples, and was converted. For months afterwards, he wept every time he saw it.

Then, one day, a girl approached him in the sanctuary. "I am the girl who handed you the cheese sandwich," she said, "and the Lord told me to pray for you. And I have been praying for you for a year and a half."

Campuses were the most fertile grounds for evangelism because that was where the numbers were. The babyboom generation, which was 50 percent larger than its predecessor, was hitting college. From 1940–1960, the 14–24 year-old cohort was about 24 million. In the 1960s, it swelled to 40 million. This was the generation of the Vietnam War, the assassinations, the revolution in rock music, the end of prayer and Bible reading in schools, and a sharp rise in sex outside of marriage. The world was one of moral ambiguity, where the old rules no longer held, and where so many people were breaking those rules with impunity. Psychedelic drugs and rock music pervaded everything, and it was unusual to find someone who had not smoked marijuana at least once. The Beatles began writing about LSD trips and took to hanging around an Indian guru.

The ravaging '60s created a social climate conducive to religious experience of any kind. Cults, as well as groups that would later become cults, were booming. It was the day of the folk mass, the rock opera *Jesus Christ Superstar*, and Beatle George Harrison's "My Sweet Lord." The Jesus movement made the cover of the June 21, 1971, issue of *Time* magazine. Contemporary Christian music was taking off, pioneered by a long-haired blond musician called Larry Norman who sang about the end times in his song, "I Wish We'd All Been Ready." Christian groups called Love Song, Bethlehem, Mustard Seed Faith, and The Liberated Wailing Wall were cutting albums. Christian coffee houses were springing up in church basements and cheap rented spaces for the millions wasted by the drug culture and looking for alternatives.

Only those with vision and faith reached out to those hippies, who would form the base of a vast spiritual awakening. The name for these converted hippies, "Jesus freaks," may have been coined in the summer of 1968, when 41-year-old Chuck Smith, pastor of Calvary Chapel in Costa Mesa, baptized 50 long-haired converts in the surf. Beach-side baptisms became a regular occurrence after Monday night Bible studies at the church, reaching such numbers (1,200 was the one-time record) that reporters came by to investigate. *Look* magazine photographer Jack Cheetham went hunting for the Jesus movement in the spring of 1970. He and his wife, Betty, attended services at the charismatic Melodyland Christian Center in Anaheim, where they heard testimonies of deliverance from drugs.

"I think you found your Jesus movement," Betty whispered as Jack snapped photos.

Meanwhile, *Look* reporter Brian Vachon was attending a Calvary Chapel beach baptism where he encountered Rene, a shivering but radiant young woman who had just emerged from the water. Three weeks earlier, she told him, she had wandered, stoned and scared, into a Christian drug-help center.

"But on that day," she continued, "I asked Jesus to come into my heart and He's been with me ever since."

"But how long is it going to last?" Vachon asked.

"It's going to last forever. There isn't anything else."

"You look very beautiful," said Vachon, somewhat at a loss for words.

"You see the Lord in me," she said.

"You also look very cold."

"I'm not at all. I'm just filled with the Holy Spirit."

"And you also look a little stoned."

"I *am* stoned. I'm stoned on Jesus. Only it's far better than being stoned. Drugs are a downer. This is the most incredible up in the world. I feel like I'm floating all the time with Jesus."

"They say Jesus is coming back soon," said Vachon, lamely.

"Yes, He will come back very soon. And He will take the people who have accepted Him as their personal Savior. They will be raptured."

"What's raptured?"

"That's when Jesus comes to His people, and He takes them, no matter what they're doing at the moment. He takes them with Him right into heaven."

"How many people will this happen to?"

"All the people who've accepted Jesus into their hearts."

"What about the people in India, China, and Africa who've never heard about Jesus? Do they get left out?"

"It'll be OK. God's a fair guy. And how about you? Have you accepted Christ as your personal savior?"

Cheetham's pictures of grungy hippies praising God in the February 1971 issue brought other media running. *Time* followed with its cover story in June about a colorful, daring, and brash movement resplendent with faddish buttons, posters, Christian wristwatches, even a "Jesus cheer." "If it's a fad," evangelist Billy Graham said, "I welcome it." Jesus, he added, was naturally popular with the youth because of His history of associating with radicals, subversives, prostitutes, and street people. *Time*'s cover portrayed Him as a pop-art, purple-hued hippie with long hair, beard, robe, and sandals, with the habit of sneaking off alone to desert places.

CBS-TV got into the act in 1970, when it began work on a special on the Jesus people. A producer contacted the church about including Redeemer in an overview about the Jesus people but, upon arriving in Houston, was so awed by the church that the network decided to devote the entire program, which it called "Following the Spirit," to Redeemer. It included sweeping views of the congregation singing in the Spirit, Graham at his desk, Mimi singing, and cameos by some of the households. The show was powerful and compelling, airing on Pentecost Sunday, 1971. At the time, Graham was writing his first book, *Gathered for Power*, and Michael Harper was finally writing his book about Redeemer, *A New Way of Living*. To top it all off, the widely read *Guideposts* magazine would choose Redeemer as its "Church of the Year" in 1972. Redeemer was now a fixture on the charismatic map, and floods of visitors were arriving.

B OB ECKERT's life had gotten complicated because of Redeemer's most sophisticated form of social outreach—a medical clinic in Houston's Fourth Ward, a ghetto sandwiched between downtown and Montrose. The Fourth Ward was an eight-by-10-block area that was exceptionally poor. Houston was divided into four wards and, in the mid-19th century, governed by aldermen. Some of the names had stuck. By this time, Bob's practice at the Parkview Clinic had boomed because of his habit of picking up the tab for some of his poorest patients, and his penchant for treating patients the same way he would treat members of his own family. A man of unquenchable faith, Bob paraphrased the Lord as saying that whoever came into the clinic would be handpicked by Him, and that Bob would treat them accordingly.

So when Al Rountree told church leaders about a pocket of poverty he had found in the Fourth Ward, Bob was reluctant to change a good thing. Yet, he and his son, Rob, looked over the area and located an empty storefront to serve as a clinic. The owner agreed to rent it for very little money and, on the morning it opened, they had one desk and a dining room table plus a janitor with a broom, a receptionist without a chair, and Bob with his black bag. Four patients came that day, and Bob had everything he needed to treat them in his bag. A mother came by to ask whether they did immunizations. They had no refrigerator, said Bob, and hence did no immunizations. But tomorrow they would.

The next day, someone contributed a refrigerator and Bob got some immunizations from the Parkview Clinic. Within two weeks, there were nurses volunteering each of the five days the clinic was open to the mostly poor, black, Hispanic, and hippie types who came. Although originally named the Kennedy Brothers Clinic, after the slain president and his brother, when it opened in 1968, it soon was renamed the Fourth Ward Clinic. Eventually, various hospitals and doctors' clinics began to contribute supplies and furniture, and the clinic grew to 65-75 full-time employees and 30 or so part-time workers. They relocated to an empty supermarket and became quite professional, with triage nurses, its own lab, a dentist, optometrist, physical therapists, a psychiatric nurse, several nurse practitioners and social workers, as well as a pharmacy, free clothing and a food cupboard. A sign in the waiting room read that this was a private clinic and patients would not get billed, but the clinic received no government help and staff salaries depended on what patients paid. The four full-time doctors worked for nothing and the rest of the staff got what was left over after the bills were paid.

Every morning, the staff met for worship, sharing, and Bible study. It was obvious that the group's spiritual resources was the secret factor to overcoming the area's depression and the crushing load of 2,500 patient visits a month. It was not a rule that workers had to be Christians, but many were. An amazing camaraderie among professions grew there that was not typical of the medical profession in Texas in the early 1970s. No pictures of Jesus or crosses hung in the clinic and some of its strongest supporters were Jews. The Weingartens, a Jewish family, set them up in the supermarket building after the president of the Harris County Medical Society wrote a flattering editorial about Eckert. This impressed Ed Wulfe, who headed Weingarten Realty, which owned the empty supermarket. Learning of Bob's interest in the building, Wulfe asked him where he would get the money to remodel it into a clinic.

"Mr. Wulfe," Bob responded, quoting Psalm 50:10, "my Father is a rancher and He owns all the cattle on a thousand hills."

"Dr. Eckert," Wulfe said, "I'll see what we can do." The Weingartens ended up doing the exterior remodeling themselves.

There were days when Bob and three assisting physicians would process 125–150 patients, whereas the average clinic with 10 times the number of doctors would process 50–70. Bob was balancing two jobs, working six hours a week at another doctor's office to pay his own bills, then coming to the clinic.

Meanwhile, the Eckert household was assuming hotel-like proportions. Bob's invitations to down-and-outs whom he would meet at the clinic, plus his family's willingness to take on troubled boys from the Harris County Probation Department, drove up their household total to 25 at one point. Finally, the church supplied a cook to relieve Nancy, who by now had five sons. The cook was 400-pound, bearded Ray Toni, trained in restaurant cooking and able to feed household members on 11 cents a meal.

There were tensions, though. With his larger-than-life, supremely confident, fearless persona, Bob gave the impression he could see right through anyone, and was a compelling personality in his own right. He was a full-time elder, a full-time doctor, and three out of four weekends a month, he was out speaking.

One visitor to the Eckert household was Charles Meisgeier, a college professor who wanted to experience community during the summer of 1970. Room was so scarce that for three months he slept on the couch and kept his belongings in a coat closet. Meisgeier was a charismatic Presbyterian at the University of Texas in Austin who was responsible for leading many Presbyterian ministers and students into the baptism in the Spirit. Meisgeier had come to the renewal through Dennis Bennett, and was amazed to discover that one of the places renewal had taken over an entire church was just a three-hour drive southeast of him. He was impressed with the work households did with people in the Jesus movement and how counselors would stay up all night with a person. Clearly, households were the center of gravity at Redeemer. What concerned him was the church's tendency to place a few powerful individuals in leadership and allow the rest of the people to remain like children. In Redeemer's culture, the leaders were interested in a blend, not in one person standing out. All the subordinates simply accepted everything coming from leadership because God was supposed to be speaking through the leaders. Rarely were subordinates allowed to graduate from households as fully functioning people.

Meisgeier realized that some of the household heads were incapable as leaders, plus they were carrying their own dysfunctions into household life. As a result, the lead individual's pathology became part of the household's pathology. The worst cases involved the household leaders who believed in strict control. Meisgeier was horrified to find out that a household member could not go out to eat with someone without asking permission, which was not always granted.

He also noticed that Graham called elders' meetings every night, beginning no earlier than 10 p.m., meaning that the man of the house was out until the wee hours of the morning and was supposed to function on only a few hours of sleep. This went on night after night. Redeemer, he decided, was a mixture of very wonderful, powerful things and very sick things. However, he figured, they would be addressed in due time. Redeemer's leaders were too smart to let things get too weird.

As Bill was doing ministry with Graham, not only were the other four elders left out in the cold, but so was Betty Jane. During their sabbatical from Redeemer, Betty Jane had her hands full with Martha, who was then two, plus their four other children. Then David was born in 1968. In what spare time she had, she directed the choir. Graham and Betty did not have the concept of a team ministry; she did her thing and he did his, increasingly with Bill as a teammate. Graham's drive was to meet people's needs himself, which is why he would stay up until midnight counseling people. Years later, he would say that he and Betty were still involved in a mindless marriage, meaning that the woman falls in line behind her husband in whatever he wants to do. The husband could put on a show of listening to her, but they both knew the outcome was whatever he decided. It never occurred to him that Betty would not follow him. One day, Graham was startled to watch Bill and Mary imitate him and Betty Jane. Bill would preach and Mary would sit and listen. One day, Mary got fed up.

"I get so tired of holding babies and saying 'Amen,'" she said. After he stopped laughing, Graham began thinking.

One day, Betty was in the rectory and something inside her blew. The true, full story never came out as to why she put her left fist through the kitchen window. Was it out of sheer frustration, or bitterness and anger? Rumors circulated that she had tried to end it all right there. It was a clash between the demands of having six children and wanting a husband around to help out, yet at the same time having to share her husband with everyone else. She was terrified. So much was being asked of her. She was a lonely, desperate, deserted wife managing a household of 30 persons while her husband was helping lead a worldwide renewal movement.

Her one comfort was the presence of an old friend in the household, Virginia Withey, a flamboyant personality and prototypical Texas woman: independent, resourceful, and willing to buck tradition to try something new. Betty also had nannies, but they did not have the same responsibilities as a mother, and they certainly were no substitute for husbands. The arrangement was bound to affect the children negatively, which was especially ironic. Graham had felt abandoned by his parents at an early age. Now he was contributing to the same scenario with his own children.

No doubt it was the same struggle that Ed Baggett saw one day when he walked into the chapel and saw Betty kneeling there, in the throes of agony before the Lord. Then she arose and went to lead choir practice, with no light at all in her eyes.

CHAPTER 9

The Feast of St. Luke
the Evangelist

"God sets the lonely in families."   —Psalm 68:6

ELIEF came, but not the sort Betty expected. It arrived in the person
of George and Leslie Mims. Leslie had been a child piano prodigy,
playing "Mendelssohn's Concerto in D" at age 9 with the Jacksonville
Symphony Orchestra. She met George at Baylor University in Waco, Texas,
where he was getting his BA in music. The two moved to New York, where he
got a master's in music from Union Theological Seminary and she studied piano
under Rosina Lhevine, Van Cliburn's instructor, at the Julliard School of Music.
One Tuesday evening in the spring of 1969, George attended a candlelight
service in the chapel. The intense worship, the singing, and the hugging of
fellow congregants appealed to George, and so he began asking questions. "Do
you know our anointed shepherd?" one of the women asked him in response, so
George made an appointment to see Graham.

Graham waxed eloquent on how he had received the baptism in the Spirit.
George returned on a Friday night with his wife, only to listen to a visiting British
preacher fairly scream out the sermon. While the couple cringed, Graham said
nothing until after the sermon, when he asked the congregation, "What is the
Lord saying?" which was his way of correcting the speaker. George and Leslie
decided they liked the music, though it was a bit on the simple side, much like
what George had learned during his Southern Baptist childhood. When they
showed up at a choir rehearsal, Betty asked them to take over the music while the
bulk of the choir went to New York for two weeks to prepare for a coffeehouse
opening.

Just before the coffeehouse opened, Graham asked George how much an organist/choirmaster cost.

"Well, for you, nothing," George said, and Graham hired him for almost that. They got $300 per month plus their telephone and an apartment for them and their baby daughter. The RMC was still in effect then, George learned to his dismay, which meant the hours were long and the salaries abysmally low—in the $17,000–$20,000 range. It was never spelled out just how he and Betty Jane would share choir directing duties. George's style reflected the ultra-professionalism of New York City, with excruciating attention to detail. Trained on the viola, he thought more like an orchestral musician than an organist, and his goal was to create a palate of sound not centered on a keyboard or a choir. He soon formed a group of musicians around him who composed to their hearts' content and tried out their compositions during noon Eucharists and Friday night services. Creative people attracted other creative people, and Redeemer fast became a drawing card for musical types around the Houston area.

George had his quirks as well. A perfectionist, he did not set limits on himself, nor did he limit how hard he drove others to meet his standards. The vagueness of George's job description would resolve itself when the Pulkinghams moved from Houston three years later, but no one planned on what would happen if they ever returned.

George's first task that summer of 1969 was to direct the choir in singing Fauré's *Requiem*. He set aside Tuesday nights as a time to teach church members how to sing together, a feat most congregations do not master. Everyone paired off, faced each other, then mimicked the other person's movements. Then they would do the same thing, this time with their voice. This was George's way of teaching people to synchronize with each other. Then the pairs would form threesomes and foursomes and repeat these steps. Thus, George taught the congregation to begin *thinking* in parts. Then he taught parts: basses first, followed by tenors, altos, then sopranos singing the melody. If he began with the melody, it set a pattern in the minds of the non-sopranos and the song would not get off the ground. Thus, George laid the ground work for what would be the indescribable sound of congregational singing at Redeemer. Because people were willing to blend with each other, there was a unity to it that overwhelmed visitors. That was one more ingredient in the stunning health of Redeemer's charismatic worship—it had an authenticity that did not push or force but wooed.

Things went well with George for about six months. Then Graham met with him and Leslie and a few others to tell him he was not submitted enough to Betty to allow the anointing to pass from her to him.

"You never mentioned anything about anointing," George said to Graham. Also at issue was that Leslie had not gone through the required initiation of being baptized in the Spirit, which was expected of worship leaders. George had done so, but Leslie balked, not feeling she really understood it and wanting to wait until the time was right for her. When people made an issue of it, she quit the choir. It did not help that Leslie, from a spiritual standpoint, felt vastly inferior to Betty Jane and Mimi, and being scolded like this made her feel like she had been caught doing something awful.

After the meeting, Leslie sat and cried. Oddly enough, no one offered to spend time with her to explain things until she understood. Leslie did not want something concocted; she wanted God to intervene. She was a pragmatic woman who saw through a lot of things and who decided to fight for her integrity and that of her family, especially when, a few years later, her marriage nearly hit the shoals. She had no stomach for spiritual imitations.

Later, she did go through the required initiation, but at the bottom of her dilemma was an issue that troubled the whole renewal. How was this baptism to be conveyed? The apostles never reported a problem with laying hands on people and having them prophesy or speak in tongues right away. The early pentecostals believed you had to tarry for the baptism, even if the wait took days. When it arrived, the signs had to be unmistakable. Early pentecostal writers talked about gushings of joy, power, visions and more. One had to speak in tongues, or the baptism didn't "take."

The charismatics short-circuited this process by saying the baptism could be received by faith and it did not matter if senses of power or anointing were not forthcoming. Such feelings were supposed to arrive eventually. Meanwhile, everyone was still expected to speak in tongues, or at least make a stab at it. For some, this worked splendidly. But for others, it was grossly humiliating, and the sensation of power or anointing never did arrive. Unlike salvation, which was a step made in faith, baptism in the Spirit, by its nature, was experiential. People could not take an experience "on faith;" they either experienced something or they did not. If the Holy Spirit had not done the work, the person involved knew it, and no amount of convincing was going to change things.

During this era, the same principle was being applied in prayers for healing. The sick were told to "claim" their healing, whether or not they felt healed. Those failing to experience that power would often not stick with the charismatic movement. They lost confidence in the movement especially when they saw "healings" that were not real, or if they felt duped into speaking in what they decided was not the gift of tongues. Either they blamed themselves for being spiritual failures or began to wonder if there was a lie at the root of it all.

Graham eventually urged Leslie to rejoin the choir and the Mimses promised they would get with the program more. But Leslie's confidence was shaken to the core, and it took her five years to get up the courage to play the piano for a service, and even longer to lead worship.

Mikel Kennedy married in 1970, choosing Ladd's middle daughter, Carol, 18, as his wife. She wore a short skirt at her Sunday morning wedding, due to Graham's insistence that Christ, not the bride, be the center of the ceremony. Twenty years later, she would mourn that she listened to him instead of holding out for the traditional long white gown she had really wanted.

Two University of Houston honors students, Carl Wheeler and Max Dyer, walked in on that April 12 wedding. They had tried transcendental meditation, and now they were curious about Redeemer. First, they got hugged by the enormous ushers. Then, in the middle of the service, more people hugged them during the "kiss of peace." The place was filled with barefoot, long-haired college students who had invited Carl to the coffeehouse, then to a meeting in Graham's home, where he was baptized in the Spirit, spoke in tongues and told Max about it. Max, a cello major with dark brown hair, deep-set eyes, and a beard, looked like a modern-day Jesus in hippie clothing. He began attending music sessions at the coffeehouse, and time seemed to stand still during the sultry evenings. The songs had a liquidity to them that spread anointing. The musicians didn't really care how they looked or sounded; God was present and everyone knew it.

Like Word of God situated near the University of Michigan, Redeemer had the advantage of being close to large student populations at several universities. Redeemer had such energy that one would gladly give up career and schooling for it, although at the time, men were strongly advised to stay in college to avoid the draft. The five elders were exalted by the congregation, Max thought, and he particularly liked to hang around Graham, who was all too glad to be an elder to another "younger."

Seekers like Max and Carl swelled the number of people living in Redeemer households to more than 350, which was about one-third of the 1,400-member church. It was a numbing amount of people to pastor. Word of God was growing even faster. By September 1972, the charismatic Catholic community had 420 persons living in households. For governing purposes, the huge community was split into 12 districts, each with one coordinator who oversaw a team of 10 men (called "servants") and 10 women (called "handmaids") who provided pastoral care. Eventually, 250 persons and 25 coordinators were involved in governing the community.

Word of God had come up with a mode of entry into their community that Redeemer badly needed. Called the "Life in the Spirit" seminar, it was developed in 1970 as a way of teaching about conversion and baptism in the Spirit in seven easy lessons. No more were people forced to accept Christ and pray in tongues in one fell swoop. Instead, they were allowed to feel their way gradually into the renewal, and by the fifth week, most were ready to be baptized in the Spirit. In fact, no one was admitted to community membership without this experience. Thus, everyone was inculcated with the same basic understanding and vision of the house. The mandatory seminar avoided the spiritual sloppiness that plagued other communities by giving would-be members a taste of the real thing and some basic theology.

Small wonder that Word of God blossomed into the country's largest community with 3,000 adults and children. With their constant networking with each other, Catholic charismatics were better at coming up with the big picture. Graham preferred the company of Catholics, who he felt understood the corporate nature of what he was doing. He endorsed the fledgling Catholic charismatic magazine *New Covenant* as a publication that agreed with the aims of Redeemer and the Fishermen, to the point the Redeemer even decided not to begin its own publication because *New Covenant* was already doing the job.

Bob Burlingame's new wife Norma came into the movement by attending a Catholic charismatic conference at the University of Notre Dame, then visiting Redeemer. Her first stop was at the coffeehouse, where she met Bill and Graham.

"Is this biblically based?" she asked Graham. His answer was vague, but Norma, who had studied at Fuller Seminary, was convinced it was based on the Bible. When she walked into her first Friday night meeting, she thought, *The kingdom has come and this is it.*

Redeemer *was* a dream come true, and central to that was Graham, a mixture of havoc and creativity. You didn't even need to be in church to know he was in town. There was an electricity in the air. Graham was moving in the gifts of the Spirit, especially the gift of knowledge, which he'd use as often as possible. Some of his judgments seemed made by the seat of his pants, but much of what he said hit home with unerring accuracy. People tried to imitate that, and it was common for household members newly baptized-in-the-Spirit to be given, after a few months, counseling responsibilities over suicidal or divorced people. The method of helping them was often praying in tongues, then shooting from the hip. You believed that whatever you said, the Lord was in it. The possibility that the Lord might grow tired of dispensing the required wisdom was never discussed.

GRAHAM and Betty Jane ended up moving out of the Way In and into vastly more comfortable quarters in University Oaks, a suburb adjacent to Eastwood. It was New Year's Eve at their new home and Bette Graham was there, in terrible pain from a horrific accident outside the coffeehouse. The last thing she knew, she had been on the busy street outside the Way In, helping police investigate an accident. A truck came roaring up, ramming her into a car, crushing her pelvis, and driving her left leg bone into her abdominal cavity. Mikel Kennedy followed the ambulance to the hospital and somehow scared up $40 to get her admitted. She was put in traction and doctors predicted she'd never walk again—her left leg was now several inches shorter than her right leg.

Witnessing all this was Cathleen Gillis, a coffeehouse newcomer who had spent four years living in a convent and loved working among the poor. She had met a Catholic seminarian who told her he'd gone to Allen's Landing so he could commit suicide by jumping off the bridge into the bayou. Instead, a team from the coffeehouse found him and moved him into a household.

More curious than anything else, Cathleen had dropped by the coffeehouse, only to see Bette's accident. At the hospital, she saw Bette in traction and holding court with a room full of fascinating people from the church. One evening, Cathleen was leaving the hospital room to have a smoke when Bette informed her that God didn't want her to smoke again. Ignoring her, Cathleen went downstairs and went through three cartons, trying to light a cigarette. They all tasted foul to her. When she showed up at Bette's room the next day, Bette said, "God did it, didn't He?"

Bette was incapacitated for four months. On New Year's Eve, a Catholic priest friend of hers came to visit and debate with Graham about whether miracles still happen. Bette was still on crutches and her doctor had told her to expect another 18 months on them. Meanwhile her muscles had atrophied.

After some conversation, the priest, who was a theology professor, said, "Look, I believe in miracles, but not the way you believe in them. I wish you'd stop talking about that. It's making me very uncomfortable." Graham turned to Bette.

"Why aren't you saying anything about this?" he grumped. "You of all people are always yakking about healing and miracles."

"For the first time in all these months, I'm in so much pain, I can't think of anything other than myself," Bette replied. "I really need you guys to pray for me."

They ignored her at first. Finally, Graham gathered a group around her and prayed she would be content in her current state. That was it. A half hour later, Bette got up to go to the bathroom, taking her crutches with her. Once in the bathroom, she found she could walk perfectly. She shot out of the bathroom and back into the den, where a small riot ensued. Of the 40-some people in the house that night, only Graham and Bill Farra did not urge her to get back on her crutches. The next day, as she tried to get out of bed, she groaned from the pain. Graham heard her.

"Bette Graham," he called out from downstairs, "doubt will try to tell you that you cannot walk this morning. But Bill and I saw it and we believe that as you take that first step of faith, you'll find you can walk."

She did walk, although the pain persisted for a month. When she saw her orthopedist, he blurted out, "My God, a miracle."

Seeing all this, Cathleen joined the community, ending up in the Pulkingham household where she was appointed part-time nanny to the younger children. Betty and Graham were often gone, and Cathleen found herself raising the children more than she thought was good for them. Graham did not call or write when he was on trips. The two oldest children, Bill and Mary, bore the brunt of community living, she thought. They did not dare invite their friends home from school because of all the strange people living in their house. Obviously, they were unhappy children.

Jane Clowe noticed this, too. One night, she was sitting on the steps of the coffeehouse talking with Mary.

"It was nice having your father out with us in Midland," said Jane, trying to start a conversation.

"Yes," the girl flashed, "it would be nice to have him here, too." Jane detected hate in Mary's voice. Having her mother around was not enough.

About the time Bill graduated from high school in the spring of 1971, Graham noticed how depressed his eldest son looked. He asked Bill what he wanted as a graduation present.

"To get as far away from you as I can," Bill replied sullenly. His father had never come to his Little League games in Austin; years later, Graham would neglect Bill's law school graduation as well.

Now, the elder Graham had an idea: There were people in New Zealand who wanted to know about renewal and who craved more of Graham's time than he could give. He had thought of loaning Bill Farra to them for a few months. So that fall, Bill flew to Auckland. With him went Bill Pulkingham, flying to the other side of the globe, and about as far away from his father as he could get.

Graham went into mourning over the loss of Bill Farra, his closest friend, then cast about for replacements, one of whom was an intense, brown-eyed young man with curly brown hair named Tim Whipple. Having left home at the age of 15, Tim was looking for a family and wound up as a youth minister at Dennis Bennett's church, St. Luke's, in Seattle. Tim had been part of a seven-man band at a 1970 renewal conference in Michigan where Graham was teaching on community. Tim was fascinated, and even more so when Graham approached the band, saying, "I think God wants me to talk to you boys." The next day in their hotel room, Graham brought in Bill and taught from the Bible. Six months later when Graham was in Seattle, he looked Tim up. Six months after that, Graham returned to Seattle, where he called Tim early on a Sunday morning. "I think God wants you to come with me," he said. Shocked, Tim said he'd have to pray.

"I'll call you in 10 minutes," Graham replied and hung up. Tim accompanied Graham to speaking engagements up and down the west coast. He ended up at Redeemer, where Tim saw the church taking broken people like himself and placing them in families. Like Graham, Dennis was on the road most of the time. Graham emphasized community—the horizontal. Dennis emphasized relationship to God—the vertical. But St. Luke's was more evangelistic and teaching-oriented. The same message got repeated every Friday night as people would come to Seattle from around the world to be baptized in the Spirit. Dennis was down-to-earth, practical, and an excellent teacher. His anecdotes tended to stick in your memory and the man was brilliant. You had to be, in order to lead this movement.

ONE day before leaving for New Zealand, Bill Farra told other elders the Lord had given him a verse from Isaiah about the walls of the city coming down and the Lord being the residents' only protection. This puzzled everyone. Within three hours of the meeting, though, Jeff got three phone calls from reporters wanting to do stories on the church. Then Betty Jane had had a dream of Redeemer looking like a movie theater on a Saturday morning after a Friday night service: Popcorn boxes, cups and candy wrappers were everywhere. Its message: The coming crowds would trash the place.

On Christmas Eve 1971, a bus with white and blue lettering stating "Jesus Christ is the same yesterday, today, and forever" pulled up to the church. In it was the Symphony of Souls, a troupe of converted hippies from Greenwich Village. Previously they were braless and barefoot, studying I-Ching, Tibetan Buddhism, yoga, and other Eastern philosophies. Their mass conversion began with 18-year-old Ruth Gordon, who begged God, if He existed, to show her the truth. One night Ruth, who was raised Jewish, ran out into the rain, wishing she was dead. In desperation, she called out, "Jesus Christ, Son of God, have mercy on me."

Instantly, she felt flooded with peace, and she ran back to the loft she shared with a dozen of her friends, crying, "I'm saved. I'm saved."

Eventually, they all converted, giving away everything they owned, buying a bus and knapsacks and, because most of them were musicians, formed their own group. The men cut their long hair and wore white shirts and plain workpants. The women gave up make-up and adopted long skirts, scarves, and white blouses. They set off around the country in June and landed at Redeemer just before its Christmas Eve service. They made a dramatic entrance, dressed in their formal habits of long sleeved robes and veils and parading down the aisle. Several Symphony members promptly moved into Redeemer households.

Plenty of other odd visitors came by. Seventeen-year-old Bonnie Ramirez was living in an orphanage in Dallas when she found her way to a prayer meeting. The daughter of an Indian mother and Mexican father, she was a lost child whose early life was the stuff of horror films. One of her first memories was being sexually molested at age 6. To deal with such experiences as an aunt performing illegal abortions that required Bonnie's help, she developed multiple personalities. Her mother, who was involved with voodoo, beat her and swore Bonnie would become a prostitute like her. But Bonnie knew she was destined to become something better. Life improved slightly when the state removed her from her mother at age 11, only to place her in various orphanages and a foster home. One night, at a prayer meeting, she accepted Christ and at the same time struck up a friendship with another teenager, Donna Hollis, while the two smoked dope outside. When the duo arrived at Redeemer, it didn't take long for church leaders to know they needed help. Jeff Schiffmayer discovered Donna standing disconsolately by a window on the church's top floor. Not wanting her to jump out, he questioned her and learned she was deeply depressed. Twenty-four hours later, she was in a household.

Bonnie's arrival was more dramatic. Involved in the occult since childhood, she knew Redeemer was a dangerous place for the likes of her. When she went inside in search of Donna, she was intercepted by four men. "Your power is stronger than my power," she told them, but it took six men to cart her into the rectory. After she hit one of the men with a two-by-four, they performed a deliverance on the spot. Bonnie passed out.

Bonnie and Donna were assigned to Ralph and Sue Neal's household in University Oaks, the pleasant, tree-lined community near the University of Houston campus. It and Ann and Darrell Wafer's household were frequent depositories for troubled young people, and thus were known as "deliverance households." The Neals hated that designation and instead called their 3,400-square foot home a "healing household," but they had at least four people there who should have been institutionalized. Unlike many households, they gave members allowances and protected their weaker members from overzealous church members who tried to minister to them. When Bonnie moved in, little did the Neals know they were signing up for a multi-year commitment. Aware of her suicidal tendencies, the household gave Bonnie a 24-hour guard. Everywhere she went, including the bathroom, she was accompanied by one of the 12 women living in the house. Bonnie was a handful. She'd claim to hear voices, impulsively throw belongings out of her window, put her fist through the glass, then run to the nearby bayou. Nevertheless, she was enrolled in high school and put on the church maintenance team, a training ground and discipleship course for persons getting off drugs. Church leaders figured that anyone, even an emotional zombie, could be put to work pushing a broom around the parish hall.

Because their charges had no inner resources, deliverance households acted as a bodyguard to fight off spiritual attacks and repel drug pushers, who would visit households looking for their former prey. Loving the disturbed people as intensely as their abusers had abused them was the operating theory, which sometimes meant attaching themselves to a deliveree 24 hours a day. After preliminary anger, the troubled woman would learn to trust her household and, it was hoped, would eventually learn to trust God and relate to Him. Households were set up to minister to five to seven women at a time. Ann Wafer headed the deliverance ministry at her household. She had three female assistants, including Carol Lee Evans, working under her. Many people got healed, but some, like schizophrenics, were out of their league. Redeemer's only frame of reference was spiritual, not psychological.

When one young woman, Kathleen Crow, joined the Wafer household, it didn't take her long to size up promotion possibilities. First, she realized, you had to move in. Then you became a minister. Then you became a support. If you were a main support, you quit your job and worked at the church. Then you became a household head, then an elder. By that point, you were up by 6 a.m. for household prayer and rarely in bed before midnight because, the joke went, God rarely spoke before then. A lot of the meals were low in protein and high in carbohydrates. No one was allowed to go anywhere alone; as part of a training process, you always had to go places in twos. The community became your total identity.

Nor could you make decisions. When she assented to being part of a play being performed at the church, she was reamed by her household for not having asked Ann and Darrell's permission. Some of these things made her feel uneasy. After all, cults, too, would not allow members to be alone, fed people little protein, and allowed people little sleep.

Every so often, there were true shining moments. Jeanette Harrington, the Wafers' housekeeper, went to the coffeehouse stoned out of her mind, only to find herself miraculously straight as soon as she walked in. She was impressed by the power she felt there—allusions to a mysterious "baptism in the Spirit," and the abundant speaking in tongues she had overheard. Jeanette was involved in witchcraft, avidly read Edgar Cayce, and knew true spiritual power when she saw it. Shortly after encountering the Christians at the coffeehouse, she attended a party where a warlock spoke in tongues while laying a curse on someone. The demonic counterfeit terrified her. The next day, she broke her ties with her witchcraft friends and was baptized in September 1970.

Not long after that, Jeanette was setting forks on the Wafer dining room table. Suddenly everything changed. The forks in her hands became liquid gold, encrusted with emeralds and diamonds. She saw two men in white setting place cards at place settings and discussing who should sit where. Jeanette went to get the knives and began setting them. They, too, turned into gold- and jewel-encrusted tableware. The two men were still nearby, setting place cards. It was like listening in on a phone call with the wires crossed, and Jeanette realized the angels were setting place cards at a future heavenly banquet. This went on for 20 minutes as Jeanette watched. That night at dinner, she recounted her vision to an awed household. Finally, Ann said, "I've seen them, too."

"Household" for a lot of people was like chemotherapy; you appreciated what it did, but you didn't care for the side effects. Some people were more equal than others. Jeff Cothran noticed that Graham could go out and buy lunch, but Jeff was limited to baloney sandwiches. But, he learned, you didn't question what Graham did. If you did, you just weren't hearing the Lord, though you would, sooner or later. Jeff had a wit about him that was unbearably funny and kept community life liveable. It was Jeff who renamed the households' powdered milk "white beverage" to make it sound classier. It was Jeff who came up with the dances. What kept him and a lot of people going was the stupendous nature of the worship. Somehow, community life and worship at Redeemer fused into a single fabric, and because everyone felt less fragmented, they healed faster—except for Jeff.

After several months at Redeemer, it was obvious he would not be healed of homosexuality. It did not help that the men with whom he shared a bedroom walked around naked a lot. Three other men in his University Oaks household were also gay, but Jeff was the only one who talked about it. Although he sometimes picked up a quick trick in a public restroom, he would mourn, weep, confess his transgression, and be forgiven by his housemates. Redeemer had not thought out much about how God dealt with heterosexuality, much less homosexuality. Things were kept at such an emotional high pitch in the households that many of the sexual needs people formerly took care of physically instead got taken care of emotionally. Household members were expected to channel their sexual impulses into their emotions. At one point, Jeff's household head disappointedly stated that a lot of the men had been masturbating recently, "and that says a lot about our life together."

But the church did not encourage marriage because everything, including romance and marriage, had to include the community. Norma Burlingame noticed that not only were their marriages to be non-exclusive, but their relationships with God were to be non-exclusive as well. Every day at sharing sessions, you had to report what God had said to you that day. Everyone was expected to hear a word from the Lord. Not surprisingly, this was very powerful.

Jon and Sylvia Wilkes noticed how everything at Redeemer seemed to conflict with normal marriages. After the Pulkinghams moved out, they were the ones appointed to head up the Way In, and they had next to no privacy. People would barge into their bedroom— the Wilkes did not lock their doors— while they were making love. It was thought unchristian and exclusive to bar others from your activities. Yes, things were so intimate at Redeemer that everyone knew everyone else's problems. Jon was in the choir that was grouped in the back of the altar facing the congregation, a George Mims innovation. Week after week, he'd watch people come forward to receive Communion, to receive from God no matter what state they were in, and some of those states were pretty messy. It was intimately personal and intimately corporate.

One day, he realized the quality he saw in people's faces. It was nobility. It took a certain nobility to come forward as a statement of faith that Christ's workmanship was in progress and no one was about to give up on themselves. In a lot of churches, Communion was often a fashion show, but at Redeemer, it was an act of worship. Jon would see John and Edith Grimmet come forward and know what they were going through with their eldest son Robert, who was either in prison or in trouble, or Betty Jane, who was obviously so deserted and lonely. But they all still came up to receive Communion so they could keep on keeping on.

CHAPTER 10

The Feast of St. James, the First Bishop of Jerusalem

"I saw none of the other apostles; only James, the Lord's brother."
—Galatians 1:19

SHE stood outside of the house in University Oaks one evening, a dark-haired, lonely University of Houston student who loved to take walks in the neighborhood. She heard, inside this house, the loveliest singing she had heard in a long time, and Diane Andrew, a mezzo-soprano, knew good music when she heard it.

Then out popped one of the men, Gary Miles, who noticed her wistful expression. He asked if she would like to sing with them soon at the nearby Hermann Park. Diane was too surprised to say no. She later learned that Betty Jane, who was listening in on the conversation, had been informed by the Lord that Diane would someday move in with them.

That day came in the summer of 1970, when Diane joined 33 people living at the North Main house. Household living was so excruciating that Diane took her frustrations out on her music, coming up with her best compositions during her most intense times of pain. One song that had unusual power was "I am a rock," a melancholic piece that had God crooning to His depressed servant. She and Max Dyer performed it for her music theory class, which asked for two encores. Some of the students wept and the Jewish professor was visibly moved. When she performed it at a Keyhole retreat, everyone cried. Pain, as horrible as it was, especially when induced by community living, was the wellspring of her creativity.

The high level of creativity that burst forth out of Redeemer in the early '70s came mostly from single people like Diane. Instead of being allowed to date, they were directed to put their energies into ministry outlets like the coffeehouse. Normally, the mixing of several dozen hormonally active college students in one household would create raised eyebrows during the libertine '70s, but in truth, their sexual energy was sublimated into the arts, music, dance, and drama. Singles were kept so busy and so tired that they did not have time to think of jumping into bed with each other.

As Christian communities began springing up across the country, many of them copied the system in place at Redeemer, where a courting couple was rarely left alone. The best they could hope for was light kissing on the lips, hugs, and handholding. Sometimes, even kisses were forbidden. It seemed like a throwback to the Puritans, but the rules on courtship held down overt competition for partners and minimized break-ups and reversals that could traumatize a whole household. Romantically attracted persons had to decide whether or not to be a public couple and, if so, they got engaged and quickly married to cut back on sexual temptation. At Redeemer and many other communities, romantic relationships were brokered by one's household head. It was a cumbersome arrangement, but at least it reduced the chances of rejection or unreciprocated love. The man was expected to initiate the relationship through his household head. That person broached the woman's household head, who would then run it by the woman. If she said no, that ended it right there. Either household head also had the power to nip the romance in the bud. Only the more determined couples made it through that gauntlet.

One of them was Ed Baggett, who married fellow Keyhole member Francine in 1971, only to notice how little support his new marriage received. Within the community there was a false sense that marriages would work out somehow even though both spouses were 100 percent involved in ministry.

Ed didn't have the nerve to suggest moving out of the community so they could find themselves as a couple. There was no concept of being on a ministering team with one's wife, because that was not how Graham operated. In fact, married couples were often split up on ministry visits, and no one thought anything of it. It was as if married people were expected to act like singles, while singles were treated like neutered beings.

Nevertheless, marriage was the handiest ticket out of household and on to better things. For those who never married, household was like going to high school and never graduating. The way headship was set up at Redeemer, one simply did not leave without the blessing of the household heads, and the household heads only let you go if you were getting married. The married at least got a room to themselves while singles bunked up to six to a chamber. Often, just being married and owning a house was enough to persuade the church to give couples leadership as household heads.

Marriages were expected to follow Graham's example of laying "family relationships on the altar." Using Arabella, one of his single housemates, as an example, he would preach that everyone must chiefly relate as brothers and sisters in the Lord. The notion was patterned after a passage in Mark 3:31-35, when Jesus says all who do his will are his brothers, sisters, and mothers.

"If you want to go through one of the biggest struggles in your life, open up your family to include other people as first-class citizens," he began one day. "Now I know lots of people who say, 'Oh, brother we've done that for years; we have all these crippled children in our home.' That's a different matter, because I usually find that when people open up their homes, the husband-wife relationship is still the inviolable relationship. And every other relationship is second to that. That is to say—and I'll say it in the most inflammatory way I can so you get the picture of what we went through—if at 11 o'clock at night my wife's needs were raised and at the same time Arabella's needs were raised, whose needs do I attend to at that moment?"

His audience was silent. The husband-wife relationship, he continued, is quite accustomed to be exclusive, in-grown, and not interfered with by outside influences, including their children. Besides, "The loneliest period of a single person's day is between 10 o'clock at night and two in the morning—and that's just all there is to it," he said. "That's also the time husbands and wives anticipate being alone together. Can you see the problems that were raised?"

In a conservative church culture that practically worshipped marriage, Graham's assertion that singles deserved to have their needs met, too, was way ahead of his time. Yet, life in community was like climbing a mountain without a summit. Originally intended as a temporary stopping-off place to live in order to receive ministry, it had now become an end in itself. Plus, there was no end to the commitment being asked of the people in community. Sometimes the results were grand, as when leaders stayed up until 4 a.m. with a troubled member, or loaned their car to the singles for a three-week vacation, or fasted quietly and prayerfully for people under their care, or came up with hundreds of dollars when someone had to go to the hospital during a crisis. When community worked right, the results were outstanding.

ELAINE HOLWAY was 22 and on her way to becoming an opera singer when she moved into a household as a way to combat her depression. She was made a nanny and housekeeper, typical assignments for single women, whether they had a talent for it or not. Nannies did the child care in some of the immense households to either aid mothers of small children or in some cases substitute for them if the mothers were church leaders. Often these mothers were busy doing "ministry" at Redeemer while nannies raised their children and cleaned their homes. Because single women were not assumed to have a ministry, and the church did not consider staying home with one's children enough of a ministry in itself, nannies were given a job with all the responsibilities of motherhood, but without any of the benefits. Even a gifted artist like Cathleen Gillis was put to work taking care of the Pulkingham children, meaning she had to craft designs for Graham's books and church publications in her spare time. As for the men, they had to take at least 12 hours of college classes to avoid getting drafted for the Vietnam War, so they were not asked to drop out of school, as many of the women were.

Elaine's household limited her dating to one night a week. On other nights, she was instructed not to leave the house except for a church function. Nannies were often encouraged not to date or marry, and their lives were circumscribed by the household schedules. Elaine had formerly loved taking long walks alone, but household life forbade that. Most single women had to report their whereabouts at all times, whereas the single men were free to come and go as they wished. Single women, even the divorced and widowed, also rarely got personal money for various things whereas the single men, at least those working at the clinic, got a $50 a month stipend. This arrangement suited some of the younger women, who needed a safe place to be while trying to get off drugs or straighten out their lives. But it harmed others, especially those who put their education and careers on hold for years and never regained the lost time. Elaine's elders forbade her to attend music school to further train her voice, fearing that she might lose "anointing" if she had professional advice.

Elaine gamely accepted these orders and agreed to ironing duty, which she also hated. She had but one dress and a pair of dress pants to her name, while household heads, she noticed, were buying themselves luxurious items. Finally she was given $80, whereupon she bought a bunch of clothes that fell apart. Such things incensed Redeemer's single members, who were the mighty pool of labor that enabled Redeemer to wield so much spiritual influence.

The singles were instrumental in pulling off a massive project: renovating Lantrip Elementary across the street from Redeemer. Built by Tom Tellepsen

during World War I, the school had gone downhill, especially when desegrega-
tion in 1971 brought busing into the picture and forced an unhappy marriage
of Hispanic, white and black students. Parish children were traumatized at the
school and began getting into fights, reflecting the troubled, violent, over-
crowded nature of the neighborhood. Things were so bad that even the teachers
were advising parents to remove their kids. Feeling somewhat responsible for
Lantrip, the church took it on as a challenge and decided to claim the school for
Christ, beginning with a multi-day parish fast. Soon after that, the principal told
Jeff Schiffmayer the Houston Independent School District had chosen Lantrip
as a test case for a new program that brought neighborhood volunteers into
local schools. Could Jeff produce those volunteers?

Jeff hit the phones and within a half-hour, the priest had 17 church members
ready to go over to the church as classroom, recess, and bus monitors. Others were
full-time teachers in other Houston schools who agreed to volunteer at Lantrip
while their households supported them. The bus monitors took guitars on board
to teach the children songs so they would not fight. One of the bus drivers,
accustomed to delivering children to their bus stops with bloody noses and torn
clothing, was so overcome by the difference the guitarist made on his bus that he
burst into tears, crying out, "What's going on here? What is happening?"

At one point, school officials were unhappy with their janitor, a Redeemer
member who had a degree in psychology. Thinking he would leave his post as
soon as a better job came along, they gave him two weeks to do an impossible
task: bringing the school up to code. The dilapidated school had not met that
standard in decades. The janitor begged church elders to intervene on his behalf.
Redeemer responded by sending 75 people during a two-week stretch to strip
and wax floors, trim trees, put plants in classrooms, install flower beds and a
small garden, scrape gum off desk bottoms, and otherwise wash, mop, scrub,
and paint the place. When the teachers returned that fall, they wept. Eventually,
12 Redeemer members were hired to work there, and they continued to transform the place.

There seemed to be nothing the households could not do once they applied
their energies to it. Susan Abbott had gotten used to living in a church household, and ran hers like a well-ordered ship. In the spring of 1972, a social
worker named Ivis Good moved in. Ivis was dating Dick Bird, 34, a divorced
engineer employed at a phosphate plant. They liked the church and approached
Jeff after a Friday night service to suggest they exchange marriage vows at
Redeemer. He just looked at them. Then they met with some of the newer
elders: Grover Newman, Bob Hansen, and Bill's older brother John Farra, a

lawyer. The trio explained it was not Redeemer policy to marry couples they did not know. The requirement, they said, was to spend time around the parish and build relationships. This exasperated Dick, but Ivis decided to go along. She was assigned to live with the Abbotts.

Thirteen people lived in that household, and the first rule Ivis ran up against was that singles were not supposed to date because their first commitment was to their household. Secondly, the household needed another wage earner, so Ivis kept her job. She would turn over her entire salary to the household; they would give her back $5 a day. There was so little protein in the meals that people would grab for bits of tuna in the casseroles. Her household lived on $800 a month, $500 of which was her salary. Ivis noted with some amusement that per capita, her household lived on less money than the people she was counseling as a caseworker. She had not lived there long when she shyly mentioned to Susan that she needed more than she was being fed because she was hypoglycemic.

"You'd better be healed," Susan retorted, "because we can't afford to feed you six meals a day." To Ivis's amazement, her low blood sugar never bothered her after that. But other things did, such as the never-ending meetings. Ivis, who worked all day, would end up babysitting the household children in the evenings so that the other adults, especially Susan, an inveterate meeting-goer, could attend meetings at the church. Meetings would go until 3 or 4 a.m. and sometimes the attendees would put in all-nighters, come home, eat breakfast, and depart for another day's work. Then everyone would nod off at the supper table. The idea behind it all was to walk in faith that the Lord would restore their energy.

Finally, Dick and Ivis were allowed to marry. To their surprise, his divorce, which they thought would be a real sticking point, was never brought up. This was possibly because some of the elders themselves had been divorced before coming to Redeemer, but it seemed like a subtle compromise to them. Advice given them on sexual matters consisted of one session of Jeff saying, "Don't hop on and hop off." Considering all the waiting they had done, the counseling was anticlimactic.

What was important to the leaders was that the wedding be performed as part of a family function at the church. This meant it had to take place on Sunday morning, and woven into the rest of the service. This also meant that Ivis's sister could not be a bridesmaid in the service because she was not a born-again Christian—only a member of the household of faith should take part in the ceremony. Ivis gave into that without a whimper, and asked her aggrieved sister to step out of the ceremony.

One thousand persons attended the wedding, which was held on a Sunday morning in May. It was the first church wedding to include a liturgical dance. Bishop Richardson had appointed Redeemer as an experimental parish, meaning it could try to implement liturgical innovations. The reception was in the Mims's backyard, and everything from the catering and cooking to the decorations were gifts of the households. It had rained the night before the wedding, so that morning, George got members of his household to climb up in the trees to shake the water off the leaves, because he did not want guests to get dripped on. Ivis learned an important lesson that day: Unless you were in a household, no one really knew you. But if you were a household member, people laid down their lives for you.

MANY of the gracious Victorian homes in Evanston, Illinois, came with porch swings, the sort that are delightful to swing on while watching the neighborhood. And that suburb, just north of Chicago, had become thoroughly integrated by the time Graham Pulkingham came in 1971 to explain how the growing Mennonite community there could experience the power of the Holy Spirit.

Graham's travels by now had taken on whirlwind proportions. But this visit to Evanston was epic in scope. Writing about it 16 years later, Reba chroniclers Dave and Neta Jackson called Graham's one-day stint there in late 1971 "the visitation," the same wording one would use for a bishop. That essentially is what Graham was to churches and fellowships across the country. He had a way of speaking with unquestioned authority, as if he were 100 percent sure the Lord was speaking through him. Reba Place was wary of the charismatic movement but interested in Graham, who seemed, like them, to be reserved, yet who spoke in tongues and presided over a church with a community life far more intense than Reba's.

Graham's theology on the baptism in the Spirit was evolving. He now said baptism was not given so much to individuals as to the church. He got this from Acts 2, he said, but there was a difference: The New Testament said the gifts were given for *the sake of* the church, but they were still given to individuals. Graham turned this around because, he reasoned, the gifts of the Spirit were usable only in community.

Graham's visit electrified Reba Place, particularly his assertion that, after he had prayed over them, they had all been baptized in the Spirit as a community. All they needed to do was act on what they already had. The next year, well over a dozen Reba Place members made pilgrimages to Redeemer and, upon their return, set up a system of elders and households patterned after what they had seen in Texas. Consistent with their pacifist Mennonite beliefs, they dedicated themselves to a simple lifestyle where everyone got a clothing and spending allowance of $21 per month. Households typically ordered cheese in bulk and consumed 60 dozen eggs a month. Anything that could be made from scratch, even hamburger buns, was, and chicken was considered a luxury meat.

Dave and Neta Jackson visited Redeemer in the summer of 1972, as one of a dozen communities they were researching for a book. They were immediately repulsed by the strictness they encountered at their host household, led by Bob Hansen. As they listened to conversations about the church, they were struck by how people seemed overly preoccupied with submission, authority, and leadership. The second night of their stay, there was a blow-up between Hansen and Dave Jackson, after which Hansen took Jackson to a marathon Redeemer elders' meeting to show him how authority worked there. Sure enough, Dave was impressed with the mutual submission and respect he witnessed.

What also amazed Dave was the amount of time the elders spent going over every detail of their Friday and Sunday worship services, discussing until 2 a.m. the songs, the prophecies given, the teachings, and so on. These meetings were Redeemer's main outreach and more than 1,000 people typically showed up each time, hence the elders' concern that everything go right. Dave also realized that with the massive amount of problem people and new Christians Redeemer was taking on, it needed a strong authority system to give these people guidance until they matured. No doubt the place was a tremendously healing place to be and there was plenty of on-site supervision to make sure people got healed.

But what disturbed him was the lack of a servant mindset in Bob Hansen and the other elders he observed. He figured it was not a long journey from the current mindset to a religious dictatorship where leaders compelled submission rather than eliciting it, as Jesus did. After the Jacksons dined at the Pulkingham home in University Oaks, they began to think many Redeemer households lived too luxuriously, with flashy clothes, wall-to-wall carpeting, exquisite draperies, fine furniture, and expensive cars.

At an elders meeting, when Graham had brought up his wish to move to the more spacious and well-to-do University Oaks household, he received no consensus. Most of the elders, except for George Mims, Graham, and Bill Farra, had left for the evening. Bill asked Graham what he was going to do with the house.

"I'm going to buy it," said Graham. Listening in, George wondered if all the rhetoric about unity and shared leadership was a facade to allow Graham to do as he pleased. It certainly looked like it. What else of supposedly supernatural origin at Redeemer, he wondered, had been manipulated by human control panels?

George Mims had thrown himself into life at Redeemer with much intensity. When it came time for Leslie to have their third daughter, George did not accompany her to the hospital because he was expected to be at the Sunday service. Leslie had gone into labor early that morning, but when it had dragged on, she went to the hospital alone, she thought, to finish the job. Instead, the child had her umbilical cord twisted around her neck. After seven hours of labor, doctors were ready to do a C-section, but the baby dropped and Sarah was born without surgery. Leslie fumed, realizing that George had not been present at the near-death of their child and that Redeemer's values were such that its gorgeous worship service was more important to George than their baby.

No one learned a lesson from that incident. A few years later, Jeff Schiffmayer's wife, Sylvia, also went into labor on a Sunday morning and he stayed at the church to lead the service, only learning about the birth of his son when the phone atop the organ rang in the middle of the service.

Commitment was everything at Redeemer, and George's choir was the most committed and disciplined unit there. Its 85 members sat in three different parts of the church, pastored and prayed for each other, and served as voice coaches to less talented members. George would give lessons on dictation, music theory, and music history. A member simply was not late to, or miss, a service or practice unless deathly ill. Those who slipped up were asked if they were *really* committed to the choir. Diane Andrew was one of the star singers. One Christmas, she managed to sing solos while fighting off laryngitis. Her voice was at the service of the community, she thought, and she had no right to withhold it. Just after the holiday, she took part as the choir recorded a new album, "Christ Among Us," which entailed Redeemer's biggest effort to date to sing high-quality classics. Her participation in one of George's marathon recording sessions ruined her voice for six months.

The choir had a rule that members could not skip out of the Christmas Eve service to go home to family. Instead, the family they worshipped with on Christmas Eve was Redeemer as Christmas Eve was a principal emotional high point for the community and everyone was expected to be there. Those who balked were asked who *really* was their family. This worked well for persons whose natural families attended Redeemer or whose relatives lived nearby. But it damaged those people, most of them single, whose families were out of state and who were expected to miss the holidays with their next of kin year after year. This policy applied across the board at Redeemer, since households did not believe in spending money to send members home for Christmas. The natural family got shunted aside, causing much bitterness on both sides, since the people who enforced the rules tended to have their families living with them in Houston.

Bill Farra's family, including his older brother, John, followed him into the church. John joined in 1971 with his fun-loving wife, Margo. Underneath her open, welcoming, light-hearted exterior was a lifetime of pain. Born illegitimate, Margo was adopted when she was 17 days old. Her parents adopted a sister a few years later, once leaving them both alone in the house for a few hours. The terrified child never forgot that incident. Her father would tease her but not love her, at least not as she wanted to be loved. Then she married John and together they discovered community through this new church Bill had gotten so much out of. Margo, who had always wanted a family, bore four children. She suspected early that her marriage might not make it through the kids' growing years.

"When John and I joined this lifestyle," she would say years later, "he was made an elder at Church of the Redeemer. That came about five minutes after he joined the church. And I was in suburbia. . . it was so hard. I remember getting down on my knees and asking, "Should I stay married to John?" And the Lord said, "That's the wrong question. The question is: What would you do with what I am asking of you?"

No doubt about it, life was meant to be hard. In January 1972, Marisa Simon, Margo's niece and the 7-month-old daughter of Bill and John's sister Pat, choked to death in her homemade cloth sleeping bag. Soon after she died, Graham gave a Friday night teaching on unanswered prayer, attended by some of the medics who had attended Marisa. It was Redeemer's first major trauma, and Pat's marriage, which produced two more daughters, never recovered. Eventually, she and her husband Curt divorced. Children were not supposed to die during this magical time of renewal; they were supposed to be healed.

But as physical healings declined at Redeemer, inner healing became the rage. In January 1972, an inner healing conference, featuring Michael and Jeanne Harper as speakers, was hosted by Redeemer after Graham, at the Harpers' invitation, had visited England in 1971 to attend a Fountain Trust conference. Everyone was into "healing of the memories," and Graham's every other word seemed to be "hallelujah" or "praise the Lord." A new psychiatrist at the church, Jim Stringham, spoke about listening to one's subconscious.

A few months later on Mother's Day, Mary Ella Evans came back to visit Redeemer at the invitation of her daughter. The changes in the church were so immense—all that singing in tongues, the Prayers of the People, and the inter-cessory part of the liturgy seemed to go on and on. Mary Ella felt like a hypocrite, pretending she was comfortable while feeling totally out of place. The next day, she had lunch with Carol Lee and wept all over her. She was losing her baby daughter to something she did not even understand.

Carol Lee was fortunate, compared to another single woman living in a University Oaks household. That woman stayed at home one day to take care of one of the community children while the others went to Bible sharing at the church. She was recovering from a nervous breakdown and perhaps was not thinking too coherently when she heard someone at the door. When she an-swered it, two men said they needed to use the phone. Once inside, they perceived she was alone, put a gun to her head, dragged her into one of the bedrooms, and raped her. She was 21. Community members took her to a doctor, but no evidence of the crime was collected and no police investigation requested. Later, she was brought into a counseling session with five elders, only one of them female.

"Have you ever admitted saying you enjoyed it?" one of the elders asked her. She was also instructed to say nothing about it except to the pastors. After all, if it was passed off as her fault, people would neither panic nor move out of the community. The woman tried to put the crime out of her mind, and not until she moved out of community and went into therapy eight years later did the incident haunt her again.

Other women intuited things to come. One day in the spring of 1972, Pat Beall, a theater major at the University of Houston who was living with the Eckerts, was reading her Bible. James 5:7-8 struck her with great force. It read: "Be patient, then, brothers, until the Lord's coming. See how the farmer waits for the land to yield its valuable crop and how patient he is for the autumn and spring rains. You, too, be patient and stand firm, because the Lord's coming is near."

"Well, Lord, what is this?" she asked.

"This is not for now; this is for another renewal in 15 or 20 years," He replied. That shocked her. What better renewal could happen years in the future? She sensed that whatever that was, it would be massive, like one vast wave engulfing the whole world. Twenty years later, in the spring of 1992, she would stand in front of the Redeemer congregation and read those same words.

Other forces were at work that spring of 1972. Thousands of miles away, in Grahamstown, South Africa, Anglican Bishop Bill Burnett entered his chapel at just past noon on March 12. He had been a bishop 15 years, spending much of that time trying to teach and convince fellow South Africans that apartheid was not consistent with the Gospel. He was frustrated. Results from his politicking had been meager. He knew it, and he knew he was out of ideas on what to do next. He felt as if he was to yield his life to Lord, but he didn't know why.

"Lord," Burnett prayed, "I don't know why I'm here, I don't know what you want, I've got nothing to give you. I've got nothing you could possibly want."

It was now 12:15 p.m. and Burnett, feeling both despised and something he was not, suddenly felt swept up into something, he did not know what or who— it was the Lord, he realized, full of power, full of love. Bill knew instantly he was the beloved son of the Father in Jesus. He was so overwhelmed, he sank prostrate on the floor. *So, this is what it was all about. He was to be a living sacrifice.* What he loved he also resisted, but the heavens had been rent asunder, Jacob's ladder was a reality, and he was climbing it. He would know what Jacob had only dreamt about, and thus his deepest longings would be fulfilled. For him, it was icing on the cake that he was also praying in tongues for the first time.

Nine months later, the bishop of Singapore, Ban It Chiu, was attending an international Christian conference in Bangkok when an Anglican Indian priest from Fiji gave him Dennis Bennett's *Nine O'Clock in the Morning.* Initially skeptical and repelled by the idea of spiritual gifts, Chiu read through the book in one morning, then offhandedly prayed that the Lord would grant him His Holy Spirit as He had given Him to Dennis Bennett. He then dozed off. When he awoke, he felt the air electric with the presence of God. Chiu burst into praise and thanks in English, then Chinese, and then, to his surprise, in a language he didn't know. Summoning his Anglican friend from Fiji, he told him about his experience. The Indian summoned a Mexican pentecostal bishop and an American pentecostal minister, who cross-examined Chiu, heard him pray in tongues, and assured him that he had indeed been baptized in the Spirit.

B Y the summer of 1972, the message being preached at church was to stay with the community at all costs. During one hot and sticky renewal weekend in August, Graham spoke on Philippians 2, explaining that the way to be like Jesus was to live a common life with other Christians. The first two verses of the chapter, he said, meant that Christians should have "a common soul, a common personality, a common life, a common heart" in spite of the fact that Paul does not mention the word "common" in either verse.

"I can't possibly be like Jesus Christ in my own personality and humanity now," Graham explained. "I live in a sinful body in a sinful world. If anyone comes and tells you that you individually and personally can stand up and be like Jesus Christ at this moment, they are dead wrong. In your spiritual life, you can be like Jesus Christ," he continued. "You can in spirit be the son of God. You can have a new spirit within you.

"But that new spirit is the spirit of Christ shared by all of us who are in Christ," he said. "It's not my spirit. It's the spirit of Christ that we share. . . in that I give my life, body, soul, and spirit to share a common life with you. Then the spirit of Christ dwells in that common life and somehow that common life comes alive to be the Son of God."

The novel idea of Jesus as being the same thing as community life didn't attract any immediate comment from the congregation, so Graham continued. Receiving the gifts of the Spirit is dependent on living in community, he added, meaning that, "People who are not given to a common life will not receive these ministering gifts."

Moving on to verse six, he pointed out that Jesus became a man "to show us the path to being gods, if I may say it that way. And the path to our being gods is in the corporate community of the body of Christ. . . not in our individual professions of faith."

Here was the push to not leave community, and who would, considering that one was certainly less of a Christian when not in community? Then he delivered the punch line.

"To put your whole life in the community means to. . . lose control of your whole life," he said. "Your life is no longer your own; it is the possession of the community."

Noticing the startled reaction of his listeners, he teased, "How many of you think it would be kind of scary to be in that kind of community? Be honest. Put your hands up!"

He scanned the crowd. "All right. Of those who put your hands up, how many always want to do what the Lord wants you to do? OK. Is the Lord the love of your life? Yes. Is He the Lord of communities? Then there's nothing to be afraid of, is there?"

They all laughed.

"Right?" he said. "Because you always want to do what He wants you to do and He's only going to tell you what He wants you to do in and through the communities, so you're safe. There's nothing to be afraid of."

Noticing that the congregation did not seem all that convinced, he flipped to I John 4.

"When you give your life to the Lord and trust Him, He requires that you trust your brother 100 percent. . . Now, something in us says, 'Now look, brother, I can trust the Lord, but I don't know if I can trust you.'

"But those who cannot love the brother they see cannot claim to love the God they cannot see," he said before flipping to Ephesians 5.

"He tells us to submit ourselves one to another as to the Lord," Graham read from the 21st verse. "Does that mean we submit ourselves to our brother to the extent that we can trust him? Is that what it means? No. What does it mean? It means I can trust the Lord in my brother. But you know, I don't have control over the Lord in my brother, do I? So that's a scary place to be."

It was a scary place, especially because the system expected the followers to hear the Lord in their leaders but did not require the leaders to trust their followers. A few weeks later, at another renewal weekend, Jeff spoke about to whom God had given authority to make the real decisions at Redeemer.

"The fullness of Christ's anointing rests on our leadership that has really laid down everything to the point where God will give His gift, the gift of the ministry of Christ, to that small group," he explained. "Everything that is going to happen is going to flow out of that group of leaders. And all that is necessary is that, as you come into the body of Christ, be open to whatever that direction says. That's the Lord. . . People need to be free to trust the leadership enough and know that whatever the leaders ask of them, they can do and know that that is the leading of the Lord Jesus Christ in that leadership."

Thus were Redeemer leaders carefully laying the foundation for their authority. If God was going to speak or act, they reasoned, He would do so through them and only through them. This cut off any effective dissent from below, for if any of the troops protested, it meant they were not trusting the Lord enough.

CHAPTER 11

The Feast of Saints
Simon and Jude

"But you, dear friends, build yourselves up in your most holy faith and
pray in the Holy Spirit."   —Jude 20

ON September 5, 1972, Graham packed his family into a Dodge Sports-
man van and headed northeast on Houston's spaghetti-bowl freeway
system. Ten people were inside. The other members of the household
were making their way east via another route, with the plan to rendezvous in Ft.
Lauderdale. The Pulkinghams had not spent much time in Florida since the
1950s, when they were stationed with the Navy in Key West, but this time, they
were not in Florida to stay. They were moving to England.

Graham was a pioneer, not a settler, and Redeemer by this time was ploughed
and furrowed ground. Redeemer, he thought, was too identified with him.
Redeemer's foundation had been well-laid and people were mostly asking him
maintenance questions rather than foundational questions. Instead of consulting the Lord, they would consult him.

He himself wanted something more, and saw England as the center of the
Anglican ethos. Graham was anxious to prove his charismatic experiment during
a three-to-five-year span in the most influential spot possible. Thus, when he
met Cuthbert Bardsley, the bishop of Coventry, on one of his trips, Graham saw
his opportunity. When Bardsley asked him about his future, Graham informed
him that the Holy Spirit had told him he would be working in England and in
Bardsley's diocese. Graham was obviously angling for something and Bardsley,
not willing to say no to the Holy Spirit, invited him a year later. Bardsley's

invitation was worth its weight in gold. Graham could defend his move by saying a bishop had invited him.

That left Graham with one more obstacle—transporting a large number of people to England. In late 1971, while he was speaking in Vancouver, British Columbia, a woman informed him that her deceased husband had been president of Icelandic Airlines. If he needed to get to Europe, she told him, she could arrange for some discount fares. When Graham returned to Houston, Jeff Schiffmayer informed him that Bette Graham had come up with the oddest vision: a desk calendar opened to Feb. 23 with the number 27 by it. Jeff seemed to think Bette was daffy, but Graham could not dismiss it. He knew it had something to do with England. He recontacted the woman in Vancouver, who came through with a good group rate. It was decided that Graham's entire 16-member household would go with him because the airline was willing to bill only $2,000 for 16 people, if they could catch the flight out of Ft. Lauderdale.

Once at Coventry in Great Britain, the advance team decided it needed 10 more people to round out a performing team. Ten more Redeemerites came, but it took them several months to get discount tickets. Meanwhile, Bill Pulkingham called England from New Zealand.

"I want to come home now, Dad," he said.

"But . . . where is home?"

Bill and the team of 10 flew in from different parts of the world on the same day, February 23.

THE advance team was Redeemer's cream of the crop. Redeemer had developed a class structure of two groups: The gifted (musicians, dancers, actors, actresses, and poets) and the non-gifted. According to the rumors, the gifted were clustered in the better households and sometimes got preferential treatment. Rarely did they spend much time on something as plebeian as the maintenance crew. Jon and Sylvia Wilkes were part of the advance team, for Graham was where the action was, Jon reasoned, and now that Jon was part of the traveling Fisherman team, it was only natural that he should go overseas. Besides, Graham concocted some informal and vague relationship by which he ceded leadership at Redeemer to Jeff. Jon surmised the church would crater under Jeff and he did not want to stick around Houston to watch that happen. Redeemer had a tiger by the tail and Graham could hardly handle it, much less Jeff. No, thought Jon, it's best to exit in a blaze of glory now.

Just before Graham left, there was a big plea for money with which to send him and the others off. Everyone dug deep into their pockets. Jane Trigg, a lonely

Rice University student who had lived with Graham at 1517 N. Main, gave them $500 from an inheritance fund. Years later, she realized she had never been thanked. That was sort of the way things were at Redeemer. Everyone was supposed to be "in submission" to their leaders, which involved sitting through agonizing criticism sessions with one's household, where you were expected to meekly receive any criticism your housemates dished out. Yet, when she once tried correcting a female elder, the woman snapped back, "You don't have a ministry of correction over me!" And there was no getting out of the system. Once, when Jane Trigg tried to reach Jeff Schiffmayer through the church switchboard, the operator said she had to go through her household head to talk to him.

What also stymied her were the re-baptisms beginning the summer of 1969, which were contrary to Episcopal theology that one's baptism as an infant was good enough in the eyes of God. Graham had allowed the re-baptisms as a way of rededicating one's life to the Lord, and in those days, re-baptism of the born-again was definitely the rage. They would have river baptisms on Pentecost Sunday, and even Graham was re-baptized. Afterwards, he would refer to it as "the waters of regeneration closing over my nose." However, all the baptism and re-baptism in the world didn't cure Jane's depression, and no one seemed to recognize it for what it was. She was told to pray and believe, and that things would improve.

Her brother, Wilson, was three years older than she and was also living in community at Redeemer. Wilson, who would later become an Episcopal priest, was more theologically astute and at first a great admirer of the self-assured, urbane Graham, who had "discovered" him at Carleton, the same Minnesota college at which Mimi had taught, and invited to Houston. Wilson, who had worked for Eugene McCarthy's presidential campaign in 1968, was frustrated with political dead-ends and willing to try Redeemer.

He found a place where everyone was reading Watchman Nee, a Chinese Christian who, prior to his death in 1972, wrote a stack of books on living the perfect Christian life. His books were the fashion in the Jesus Movement, where everyone was trying to live the way Nee recommended. Nee had a semi-gnostic view of human nature, which he saw as a triple-decker sandwich of body, soul, and spirit. The spirit was in tune with God, but the body and soul were evil. At Redeemer, this meant that, after a while, you were mature enough in Christ for sin to be unreal and you were perfect, or at least approaching perfection. There was never a question of the elders being wrong or off base. Sin was somewhere else, but not in them. If anyone felt sick, they were not to admit to such a weakness. Sex was also part of your flesh, and you were supposed to be spiritual enough to be above all. Wilson heard one of the leaders remarking that the only reason he said the General Confession in the Episcopal Prayer Book was to be in solidarity with everyone else, for he had not sinned lately.

Graham sometimes had nutty ideas, Wilson thought, but fundamentally he was sane enough to see when things were going off the edge. He had a sense of proportion, an internal monitor to balance things out. But Graham was gone most of the time in the early 1970s and then he moved to England. Thus, Redeemer slowly began to go awry.

The central reason for the change was Jeff, who was associate rector by 1972. Jeff knew he was in way over his head, in spite of the fact that he had the support of the elders, who then made him acting rector. Officially, Graham would be rector in absentia for the next three years as a way of staying canonically resident in Texas until he knew whether or not the English experiment was a go. Also, Jeff had not decided on whether to return to Africa so Graham left the reins of the colossal parish in Jeff's hands until he made up his mind. It was an arrangement that benefited Graham but emasculated Jeff's authority, for he knew that, at any time, Graham could sweep in from overseas and reverse his decisions.

Graham never did so, perhaps because Jeff did not dare deviate from what Graham had set in motion. The quality of a man's work is determined by the quality of his successor, and the best Jeff could do was to maintain. A secure leader will replace himself with an equally strong successor, but Graham was unwilling to pass on the mantle yet. He was likewise unwilling to entrust the parish to Jeff and let it change into something Graham had no part in. The two men could not have been more different. Graham was theological and authoritative; Jeff was touchy-feely and a lightweight. While it rarely occurred to Graham that he might be wrong, Jeff was loving and anxious to listen, counsel, and please. He was not one to literally apply the Bible to hard situations such as divorce, especially if the result was harsh.

"There are laws, seemingly, laid down in the Scriptures about marriage," Jeff said during one renewal weekend. "Yet, Jesus Himself pointed out that God allowed exceptions because the law, when you related that law to men. . . was a crushing burden to them. . . God loved this world so much that He gave His only begotten Son to die on the cross for the world so He sure was not going to go splat with His word to condemn and to cripple and to crush and to stifle people's lives, which is how I hear some people use quotations about marriage. There's no legalism in this life. . . There are all these canon laws about marriage. God is not bound by law. If God is bound by anything, He is bound by love and we need to be bound by love, not law also."

Thus, those who wanted to hear what God's Word was on a particular situation could not always expect it from Jeff.

The way Graham saw it, Jeff's weaknesses would be offset by the strengths of supporting elders. After all, hadn't Jeff done fine leading the church in 1971 and 1972 when Graham had been gone so much on speaking engagements? The diocese would not interfere, either, for as long as the church paid its bills, which it did and on time, it was left alone. Communities stay healthier if the bishop gets involved, but none of the Texas bishops seemed curious enough about Redeemer. Most parishioners considered Graham's trip to England as a kind of long business trip, without much more effect on the parish than Graham's previous jaunts. Jerry Barker privately worried how the parish would do without Graham, but Graham said all the elders needed to do is get out of the way. So they did.

T HE founding elders' exodus from Redeemer began when John Grimmet started volunteering as a chaplain in the Harris County jail. He noticed that when prisoners got released, they had nowhere to go. "They're as lost as a goose in a storm," he would say, and at first he brought them to his own household. Meanwhile, some church members had been building a lodge on land the Eckerts owned in Nixon, in chicken ranch country 150 miles west of Houston. There was no running water, nor toilets and electricity, and everyone lived in trailers or A-frames draped in plastic. No former convicts ever came to the lodge, but the Nixon ranch ended up as a place for potential juvenile delinquents, mostly community kids. Adults living at the ranch worked at nearby chicken farms, loading frozen chickens onto trucks to support the ranch ministry. People with troubled marriages also came to the ranch, stayed a while, and left with their marriages healed. The church closed down the ranch in 1973, though the Grimmets were never told why. It never occurred to them to ask. Because he had to make a living, John began learning the watchmaking business. His days as a mover and shaker at Redeemer were over.

Likewise, Jerry Barker looked for somewhere else to put his energies. While traveling to his Fourth Ward law office, he noticed a derelict house on Baldwin Street that he thought would be ideal as an outreach to the white hippie culture. The place was filled with old tires and tin cans, and the only water source was a spigot in the back yard. Several men moved in, including Jerry, his sons Owen and Conway, and John Grimmet's son, Johnny. It was February, freezing, and the fireplace furnished the only heat. They cooked on camping burners with kerosene lights. In the middle of the night, the police broke in to see who was there and Jerry had to produce a copy of the lease to show they were legitimate. Druggies soon heard of the place, and dozens of them would show up for the free food and sharing of testimonies. At least 30 of them became Christians and were placed in other households. Years later, Jerry would look back and wonder how he ever found the energy to stay up, night after night, to counsel and pray with people while continuing as an effective attorney day by day. There was always enough success, including conversions, to keep things exciting, and the sheer energy there kept him from being wrung out.

After a year at Baldwin House, the Barkers helped found Wilson House in the middle of the blackest section of the Fourth Ward. One couple who came to join them were Charles and Gloria High, he a top competitive pianist who left it all to preach the Gospel in the Fourth Ward and teach music at Texas Southern University. Four times a week after dinner, Charles would play the piano and sing, and the surrounding homes would empty out as neighbors packed the place. After an hour, Jerry would teach. He had never before felt such anointing on his preaching, and he never would again. It was an odd combination: The black pianist and the white Galveston lawyer preaching truths in the simplest terms to poor black day-laborers. Jerry's household would spend Sundays visiting the neighborhood black churches, and Jerry detected something he had never noticed before: a deep rage in the black culture.

Seven months later, Redeemer received a letter from the inner city Church of the Messiah in Detroit. Messiah was half-black, half-white, and led by a black pastor, Ron Spann, who, he said, needed someone from Redeemer to tell him what to do. By this time, Redeemer was finding that community could be manufactured and duplicated in a fashion, so they sent the Barkers to Detroit to help out. Jerry left with the understanding that other elders would replace him at Wilson and Baldwin houses and their ministries would continue. But Jerry's presence and knowledge were a hard act to follow, and when Redeemer sent Charles and Gloria to Detroit to help the Barkers out, the Wilson House experiment folded. When Baldwin, too, folded after a year, Jerry realized that for anything to happen long-term, one had to stay years in a place, not just a few months.

Up in Detroit, the Barkers and Highs tried to recreate Redeemer's experiment. It was one of Redeemer's more successful transplants, and the community formed there lasted some years. It was especially a boon to Spann, who was struggling with his homosexuality. For him, community was enormously healing, and a place where he could confess his struggles. Twenty years later, he would write a gripping article about how Redeemer's experiment at Church of the Messiah helped him recover dignity and hope so he did not have to buy into the assumptions of the predominantly white gay movement.

The Barkers subsequently asked the Neals to move to Detroit to maintain a community household while they were on the road speaking at conferences. The Neals happily obliged, for Redeemer had become less of a pleasure for them. Ralph was either working or attending late-night elders meeting. As senior warden, he was not allowed to miss one, so he was managing only about three hours of sleep a night. The elders' meetings were becoming power wars, and Ralph was often too tired to resist the dominant personalities there. With Graham not present, it was a free-for-all as to who got their way.

The Neals stayed only three months in Detroit. They were told that a flower shop Ralph had started had been ordered closed by John Farra, who was ascending to the top of the eldership ladder. The unsold merchandise was just left in the closed shop. They returned to Houston, only to find they were barricaded out of their own home and that household members were told not to talk with them. For the next three months, until they regained their property, they lived out of their station wagon. A lot of their furniture had been taken or sold, and large debts run up by the flower shop business. Furious at what had happened, they left the church for several years.

Bob Eckert was increasingly involved with the clinic, which had been transferred to the oversight of St. Matthew's, a charismatic Episcopal church across town, to work in partnership with Redeemer. Meanwhile, the church was getting calls from many parishes asking Redeemer to send them someone to help, or to at least be a seed presence to begin something new that was more of the Spirit. And Redeemer often did, in the form of traveling music teams, speakers, or groups of Redeemerites who moved to churches in Detroit, England, Rhode Island, Hawaii, and New Zealand to help start community there. Redeemer was breaking new ground on a major sociological trend and everyone else wanted to know how it was done.

And there were plenty of bodies to send out. More than 150 families had moved from the suburbs to Eastwood, and the time was ripe to spin off satellites as Redeemer was getting saturated. Many more people were knocking at the door than could be let in, and the constant use of Redeemer's stock phrase, "Come and live with us and you will know us," was resulting in quite an influx. Several hundred visitors from 30 countries were coming as well. Most people would be brought in at the bottom rung and assigned to clean toilets, mop floors, or help out at the bookstore. This effectively equalized everyone and was a powerful test to ensure that one was there for pure motives. It was a powerful socialization technique, along with the constant embraces and exhortations to share your life with the hosts ("Why are you here?" "What is the Lord doing in your life?"). To most who came, it was totally disarming.

By 1971, Redeemer counted more than 1,400 active participants, maybe one-half of whom were confirmed Episcopalians and one-third of whom lived in community. This was almost a 1,000 percent growth in eight years. Total weekly attendance at parish services and activities averaged 2,200 persons, or more than 150 percent of those on the membership rolls. It seemed time to start reproducing.

St. Peter's Episcopal Church in Narragansett was one that requested Redeemer's help. In the fall of 1973, Ladd left for Rhode Island, taking with him his family and household members like Jane Trigg and David Lenzo to help boost renewal. Jane gave up her senior year at Rice University to go. Such a sacrifice seemed like nothing in light of the great things lying ahead.

Thus, junior elders such as Grover, John Farra, and Ed Baggett found themselves running the show at Redeemer along with Jeff. This time around, it was tougher going. The original five elders had had several years to weave their lives together in obscurity and iron out their differences. The church's resulting fruitfulness arose from the grace of the early days, plus lots of hard work. The newest crop of elders had no such leeway, and life slowly became less charismatic and more bureaucratic.

T HE airport at Guatemala City was a concrete bunker where people entering it could cluster about a balcony overlooking those who were departing. They had plenty to look at on October 3, 1971, as Bill Frey, the Episcopal bishop of Guatemala, his wife, and five children left at gunpoint.

His wife, Barbara, had gotten the orders that they were to leave the country in three days. Bill had been elsewhere in the country ministering to some of the 3,000 souls who considered themselves Anglicans in that mountainous, largely Catholic country. Now the Freys were all together and scared. Bill remembered his arrival in that country in 1967. Soldiers had stood on every street corner with helmets, machine guns, and heavy bullet belts straight out of a Nazi film festival. Then he began hearing rumors about killings and disappearances, and found himself presiding at the funerals of some of those *desaparecidos*.

Then there was the time when he heard that one of his leading church members would be killed. Frey visited the military to protest. He was ushered into the office of a lower echelon officer, who conducted the conversation with a loaded gun on his desk. The officer sounded cooperative, but the church member was later murdered anyway. Unbowed, the bishop helped create a commission to investigate the killings. One day, his children came home from school, weeping, because they had heard in school that their father would be killed for his peacemaking efforts.

He ended up not being assassinated, but he was expelled with 72 hours notice. Adversity tends to reveal true friendships and it was enlightening to see who showed up at the airport to say good-bye and who stayed away. Then there was the officer who kept a machine gun trained on them until they boarded the plane. Yes, it was a thrilling Grade B movie all the way.

They ended up in Fayetteville, Arkansas, where Bill had a job as Episcopal chaplain to the University of Arkansas. Their 17-year-old son, Paul, who had been smoking dope daily, plus experimenting with other drugs for several years, went to hear David Wilkerson preach against drugs. Paul was turned off by Wilkerson's fire and brimstone preaching. But a few weeks later, he attended an Episcopal prayer group where his parents were baptized in the Spirit. They gave up smoking and hard liquor, which freaked out Paul, who knew that if they stopped smoking, they would smell his dope. One night, he returned to the prayer group with his mother and was impressed with its willingness to accept his long hair and hippie demeanor. As the group prayed over him, he saw himself being pulled underwater by black, slimy hands. "Satan, let go of this child!" ordered the prayer group leader, and Paul saw flaming white hands grab his arms and pull upwards. A tug of war ensued, and he managed to jerk himself free. He repented of his involvement in the occult and with drugs, and accepted the Lord, and that night began devouring his Bible.

Meanwhile, his father was enjoying the freedom that came from nixing his nightly mixture of alcohol and sleeping pills. Soon after counseling a woman, then praying over her, he experienced a feeling of power. On his way from that appointment, he felt so joyful, he began singing hymns in his car. That, both naturally and gracefully, became singing in tongues. *So this was it,* he thought. *One only needed to pray in such a language for a few seconds to perceive the amazing, subtle, and quick mind of the Lord.*

Though the news seeped out that he was now a neo-pentecostal, which is what baptized Catholics and mainline Protestants were being called at the time, Bill Frey, in the summer of 1972, was unanimously elected bishop of Colorado on the fourth ballot. This made him one of the celebrity guests at a gathering of 300 Episcopal clergy at St. Matthew's Cathedral in Dallas the following February. It was a first-ever meeting of Episcopal charismatics. Graham, having just moved to England, was missing, but all the other Episcopal luminaries were there, including Dennis Bennett and retired U.S. Army General Ralph Haines. Even David duPlessis made an appearance, to offer Texas-style, down-home advice to the conferees. "Don't imitate Pentecostalism," he told them. "Be Episcopalian." The testimonies were full of references to speaking in tongues, the dangers of charismania and, if they were fortunate, the overflowing pews and offering plates that could result if their congregations went charismatic. However, there were also war stories of parishes that had fired their priests over the issue. Priests would bump into buddies they had known in seminary—guys who they never thought would go charismatic—and wonderingly asked, "You?? Not *you!*"

The summer of 1973, the Freys visited Houston. Bill had heard Redeemer alternately praised and condemned. Some people were saying it was the best thing that ever happened; others were saying it was the death of the church. The first night they arrived, the bishop's prayer was interrupted.

"Take off your miter and become as a little child," the Lord said. *"Take off your shoes; this is holy ground."*

Out of the blue, Jeff Schiffmayer asked Paul to come live at Redeemer. The entrance requirements included being interviewed by four elders and confessing one's sins. Paul moved into Park House, where he shared a room with six other men who, in their spare time, created Captain Charismatic, a cartoon character with a plastic smile, hands that raised automatically, and built-in abilities to speak 20 languages and attend six prayer meetings per night. He was faster than a screaming pentecostal, more powerful than 10 burly agnostics, and able to leap to vast conclusions from a single page of text.

CHAPTER 12

Thanksgiving

"I have not stopped giving thanks for you, remembering you in my
prayers."   —Ephesians 1:16

IT was July of 1973 and Fountain Trust was gearing up for its second
international charismatic conference at Nottingham University. It was a
gala six-day affair, with many speakers and a theme of "Gathered for
Power," the title of Graham's first book. A dozen more Redeemer musicians and
artists were flown over for an event that essentially starred the Fishermen and
Graham. They wowed the audience with dance and drama—the first time such
things had ever been done at a charismatic conference. Graham was given high
profile, and he rose to the occasion, preaching on "Glory in the Church" in front
of 1,500 people. He was at the height of his powers and flush with the success
of Redeemer. The Nottingham conference established Redeemer as renewal's
hottest trend, and the Fishermen received an avalanche of invitations after the
conference. One of the team members had a vision of a plane flying into
England over dozens of campfires. The plane crashed, all the fires joined, and
the whole island went up in flames. It was about that time they changed their
name. An English cleric, unable to remember the name Fishermen, had introduced them as "those . . . those young . . . Fisherfolk," and the name stuck.

Betty Pulkingham had not been in England two months when Edward
England, religion editor of the respectable British publisher Hodder & Stoughton,
asked her and Jeanne Harper to co-edit a songbook. The new book sold amaz-
ingly well and Celebration Services, Yeldall, Ltd. was formed as a corporation. A
year later, it was changed to Celebration Services, International, Ltd. with music
recordings as its main line. This provided legal income for the Americans, who

were not allowed to hold work permits or get regular jobs in Britain.

The Americans needed all the encouragement they could get, for the situation at Coventry was not working out well. Even Graham was calling it a "minor disaster of a sort," considering all the clashes there were with the vicar and his wife. The arrival of 27 Americans had strained the parish's resources to the breaking point. When eight more decided to stay in England after the Nottingham conference, things really bogged down and bickering broke out. Though the vicar had wanted renewal to happen, and the Americans more than met his expectations, they created several headaches. At first, the Fisherfolk were ignorant of the protocol of a British parish and made some blunders. They soon found they had presumed more of an interest in Jesus than actually existed there. Plus, four to five Americans were squeezed into each room at the tiny house they were assigned to and meals were served in the garage.

They had almost no money to pay for their food and they prayed about what to do. One of the women in the community saw in her mind's eye the loaves and fishes story from the Gospels and began pestering other community members about it. Every time they sat down for a meal or a meeting, she'd pipe up about the loaves and the fishes until everyone grew weary of it. One day, a British visitor came to one of their Thursday night meetings.

"I feel impressed that we should read about the loaves and the fishes," he volunteered. Stunned, the community began to ponder what this could mean. There was mention that each of them had left nest eggs back in the States, to use starting the day of their return: bank accounts, stocks, bonds, and other forms of savings. That, they decided, were the "loaves and fishes" they needed to cash in, then and there. They acted out the prophecy, gathering a sum of about $15,000, which got them through that first difficult year.

One day, Virginia Withey and Betty Jane were driving along a British country road, bewailing their lack of room. "We need a convent," Virginia was saying when they saw a man in a cassock walking along the road. Stopping, they discovered he was Benedict Reed, the prior of Three Rivers Abbey in Michigan and an old friend. He mentioned a dirty, unused convent his Benedictine order wanted to lease: Yeldall Manor, a 40-bedroom place east of Reading. Dust was everywhere, the throw rugs were filthy, the hardwood floors had not been washed or waxed in years, and the grounds were overgrown. But it was available for lease from the monks of nearby Nashdom Abbey for one pound a year plus upkeep, a deal the Fisherfolk could not pass up. They suddenly left Coventry, much to the displeasure of the bishop. Bardsley was having doubts about the community's effectiveness, and this abrupt leave-taking confirmed them. So many people joined them at Yeldall that the Fisherfolk acquired another piece of property, called the Thatched House, in the nearby village of Wargrave. Eventually, more than 100 people lived on the two estates, supporting three Fisherfolk teams who traveled about England giving charismatic concerts at various cathedrals.

Meanwhile, the Barkers' visit at Detroit had gone so well that the Church of the Messiah could stand on its own and Jerry felt he had done all he could. They had begun racially mixed households, and a few prominent people had joined their community. Charles and Gloria High were well-accepted, and Charles even composed a special Mass for the church. But Esther Barker was reverting to her pre-Redeemer instability, and the Barkers moved to a Catholic rectory in Providence to help a group of charismatic priests. He briefly left her in Providence while he tried to set up a household at a Catholic parish in Detroit, but Esther's condition was deteriorating and they eventually returned to Houston. Esther was given into the hands of Jim and Charlotte Stringham for counseling, and Jerry knocked about the church, helping in the Fisherfolk office but feeling like the Ghost of Christmas Past. He was old leadership now, and he felt as if he no longer belonged. On one of Graham and Bill's return trips to Houston taken as a last-ditch effort to help his wife, Jerry begged to come to England for more counseling.

E VERY so often, Graham would fly back to the United States and Redeemer, sometimes to give a teaching and other times to furtively slip in to see a few people. Each time he breezed through, he would attract more Redeemerites to follow him to some far off locale to help staff one of his communities. The most gifted and brightest people always caught his eye, and usually they would consent to go. The man had a presence and authority about him that was nearly impossible to resist. The idea was that when Graham spoke, you were hearing the Lord, and the Lord did not always ask twice. The whole thing became a standing joke, and people took to calling Graham the "International Harvester." But his skimming the community cream off the top of its leadership had an effect. The coffeehouse closed in October 1973, partly because so much of the core group had been shipped to England. It was like producing a play, then removing all the lead actors.

General Convention time rolled around again and, this time, Redeemerites were headed for Louisville, armed with thousands of glossy brochures to advertise their competence in providing corporate renewal. Dozens of Redeemerites, including members of the Keyhole, traveled to Louisville to perform in burgundy polyester plaid jackets and gray slacks and stay in camper-trailers in a KOA outside of town. It was miserably wet and rainy the whole time, and Sylvia Schiffmayer and a new member of her household, Joyce Rogers, cooked for this huge group. Joyce liked living in the elite Schiffmayer household. Everything, including food and furniture, was better and classier at the Schiffmayers, and the residents there were usually not subject to fruit basket turnover moves, as was the rest of the community.

As the rector, Jeff could always bend the rules a little. Because it was top of the line, all the bishops stayed there, as did Graham during his visits. They enjoyed an unheard-of luxury, all on $28 per person a month. Sylvia was one of the best economists Redeemer had. She was also a real person, known to fall asleep at household meetings, and not often talking or relating much. She didn't want invalids as members of her household, so instead of turning over their paychecks, she insisted that members open a checking account and make out a check. *Yes*, thought Joyce, *once Sylvia and Jeff wanted you in, you were in.* Joyce was a nanny for the Schiffmayer children and helped Sylvia cook fabulous gourmet dinners, complete with home-baked bread and wine, for a never-ending stream of nightly visitors. One year, they had more than 300 such guests.

One of them was Bob Woodson, an Alabama deputy to the Louisville convention. The lone member of his delegation to support women's ordination, Bob followed the Keyhole everywhere and plied Ladd and Gordon Abbott with questions. Next, he contacted Jeff about his desire to come to Redeemer.

"You know, Bob," said Jeff, "if the Lord is calling you to Houston, if you don't quit dragging your feet in the mud, you'll never get there."

Bob passed that message onto his wife, Eileen, whom everyone called Topsy. That November, they moved to Houston with no idea where Bob would find work. They plunked their three teenagers into their new Eastwood home, sending one to Jackson Junior High, where he got held up daily for his lunch money. Bob, a large, beefy man with blond hair who reeked of human kindness, eventually found a job and volunteered to head the Redeemer yard crew in his spare time. One day he was cutting grass at the rectory when a young man from the University of Houston roared up on a motorcycle. His name was Wally Braud.

"Are you Graham Pulkingham?" Wally asked.

Another guest arrived in Houston in a slightly more secretive fashion. Cardinal Suenens had gotten word of Redeemer. The prelate made repeated trips to the States in the early 1970s, obviously enraptured with the charismatic movement unfolding so rapidly among the Catholic charismatic communities in the Midwest U.S. *In Spiritu Sancto* ("in the Holy Spirit") had been his personal motto since 1945. By 1973, he admitted to being baptized in the Spirit and to have spoken in tongues.

"Something is happening in America, some new sign of hope, some star in the darkness," he told a group of 600 people in Milwaukee that March. That same month, he visited Word of God.

"Why God should have chosen Ann Arbor and Houston, I do not know," he told them. "In Paradise, I will ask Him about this surprise." When the white-haired, dignified cardinal and his entourage first visited Redeemer, it was very cloak-and-dagger. It was not to be publicized that a Catholic cardinal had come to learn something from the Episcopalians. Suenens came incognito to a Friday night meeting, then met with the elders. It was a secret visit, or as secret as any visit could be with the top echelon of Redeemer's leadership packed into the same room as these austere Catholics. Suenens brought priests, secretaries, and two nuns with him, both of whom had been baptized in the Spirit at Word of God. With the help of translators, the Catholics asked: "Why did you come together? How? What is the glue that holds you together?" Various elders tried to explain Redeemer in theological and sociological terms. Suenens listened graciously. Finally, it grew quiet and John Grimmet stood up.

"May I say something?" he asked. "Cardinal," he began, "I want to tell you what really happened at Redeemer. The Spirit of God brought a bunch of us together and we fell in love. Like a bunch of schoolgirls, we all fell in love with each other. After work, I used to want to go home and have a beer. But now I want to meet with my brothers and sisters in Christ." As he went on and on, the nuns fought back tears. Even Suenens blinked. Everyone was undone by the simplicity and truth of John's statements.

THESE were the salad days for the charismatic renewal. People were dropping by Redeemer by the hundreds and reporters were writing stories. At all hours, the church was filled with international visitors and volunteers, most of them college-age with long hair, sandals, and the hippie attire of the day. The place was packed with the Holy Spirit and power radiated from the walls. By the end of 1974, attendance on Friday nights and Sunday mornings was regularly in the 700s and 800s. When these standing-room-only crowds worshipped, the atmosphere was electric.

When charismatic author Robert Frost showed up for a weekend of renewal in October 1974, 1,183 people crammed their way into Redeemer on Friday night. Redeemer's yearly attendance total of all people at all services had long since shot through the roof, almost quadrupling from 38,434 in 1970 to

143,528 in 1974. Even on an awkward day like Thanksgiving, 478 would come out to worship. The weekday noon services were drawing 80-90 people. Word had gone around the world. Between 1974 and 1976, Redeemer would play host to 1,800 visitors from 46 states and 30 countries, many of them drawn by the church's powerful music.

It was, as some said, the book of Acts in living color. Redeemer was the epicenter of an explosion of confidence and faith in God as people believed He was more than willing to direct, guide, and back them if they risked great things. It was around that time that a troubled couple from nearby Conroe—he a mechanical engineer and she a psychotherapist—visited Redeemer. It was one week before their divorce would be finalized. The sheer spiritual energy of a Friday night service bowled over Billy and Jennifer Crain.

"What's written in the New Testament is real," Billy thought as the worship poured over him. "Miracles can happen and people can live together."

They came back again and again, receiving counseling and slowly putting their marriage back together again. He would end up joining the staff at Redeemer. They and other visitors discovered a set of stock Redeemer phrases, such as "the Lord's provisions" (which meant wearing only blue jeans and eating vegetables no one had ever heard of from the co-op), "Who is your pastor?" or "Who has the 'no' in your life?" or "Hearing the Lord in your brother" or "I don't hear the Lord in that." There was even a Redeemer lilt to people's speech patterns; a considered, deliberate way of speaking that the leaders used and many people copied.

Charlotte and Jim Stringham were brought on board at Graham's request to help with the enormous counseling load. They were an ideal couple who ministered as professionals, one of the few the church allowed in. He was a psychiatrist and she was a nurse, and it was not long after they arrived in 1972 that they were seeing 50 people a week, often at all hours. Exposed to the secrets only they were privy to, they began sensing that something was very wrong at Redeemer. People were not admitting that their sin was really sin. At one Friday night meeting, when he spoke on sin, Jim had everyone write down what sin was besetting them and offer it to the Lord.

One of his listeners, a young man named Jeff Wilson, wrote nothing down. There was nothing he felt he had done wrong, or he felt forgiven for it. Not for another 12 years would Jeff realize the depths of his sin. Until then, he would pray and prophesy with the best of them. And he knew that a lot of the people were just like him. They played the songs, sang the songs, *wrote* the songs. They were lifting their hands and saying the words, but at some deep level they did not understand. Redeemer was unquestionably a power church, but something valuable was getting lost amidst the power. Redeemer, Jeff Schiffmayer would say, was like a merry-go-round. No matter how desperately you wanted to ride, you had to be moving pretty fast to jump on. And those who moved slowly got thrown off.

Still, the Redeemer's effect was so enticing that inquirers simply tried again and again to become part of the place. One charismatic Texas A&M student visitor found himself at odds with his fiancée over the church's virtues. Steve Capper, a tall, blue-eyed, sandy-haired fellow who was fairly new to the renewal, dropped by with his girlfriend, Karen. She fell in love with the households; he thought the leaders were heavy-handed and tended to expend too much energy on needy or parasitic members. There were way too many unhealthy people in the households, though he admired the sacrificial living and the gorgeous liturgy at the church. He had never heard such singing in the Spirit. Nor had he encountered ushers with such a penchant for enormous hugs.

Steve thought Jeff's sermons were nondescript, and indeed it was true—the teachings were not Redemeer's strong point if Graham was not preaching. The most solid teachings happened during the renewal weekends, but apart from those, the older members got less and less spiritual food. After Earle left the teaching circle, many basic Bible doctrines were assumed or not taught at all, which meant people were not well versed in many biblical facts. If the popular question at Redeemer was, "What is the Lord saying to you today?", that transferred authority from the Bible to whatever one felt God was saying. It was an important difference.

There were other subtle shifts. Norma Burlingame, the woman who had asked Graham if community was theologically correct, began to have second thoughts. Within a year or two after Graham had left, baptism in the Spirit and spiritual gifts didn't seem to make a difference to anyone she knew; in fact, neither seemed to be a present reality for them. She had no idea if those in her household spoke in tongues, because that simply was not seen as essential to their life together. No one had ever put the question to her, either. Instead, people were schooled in community, and most teachings were related in some way to it. The Bible, she noticed, was being used to shore up community, and in the process, charismatic renewal was getting de-emphasized. Although a number of charismatic speakers keynoted Redeemer's renewal weekends, the church did not consider itself part of the charismatic mainstream. Some of this stemmed from Graham's disgust with where the renewal was going. The emphasis on speaking in tongues and spiritual gifts had turned him off early, causing him to align himself with the most stable, experienced Christians possible, and they were not always the charismatics.

Thus, there was a lot of assumed charismatic and evangelistic activity at Redeemer. Many of the people arriving after 1972 had not received the same caliber of training in basic Christianity as their predecessors had. Unlike at Grace Chapel, people were not mentored in the simple art of praying for other people, and what apprenticeship system had existed broke down as leaders were transferred to other communities. The coffeehouse had once been a place for simple beginner teachings on conversion and baptism in the Spirit, but once it was shut down in 1973, there was nothing to replace it.

IN December 1973, a charismatic Episcopal priest from Miami found himself seated in the home of one of the Ft. Lauderdale Five. Philip Weeks was rector of Holy Comforter Church in Miami and intensely interested in the latest charismatic happenings. And things were sure happening in Ft. Lauderdale. The next day, the leader told him, 400 "shepherds" from Dade and Broward counties would meet for the first time. Philip went to that meeting, and was astonished to find that some of the shepherds were all of 19 years old.

You can always predict what the Holy Spirit will be saying to the church in the next year by attending a Ft. Lauderdale shepherds conference, Philip Weeks thought ruefully. These people exercised tremendous influence; in fact, they were like a charismatic Vatican. Philip had learned the hard way that one cannot commandeer the Holy Spirit. He had tried to do that after visiting Church of the Redeemer in Houston in 1970 and being bowled over by what he saw, including the tall, young, blond man in charge of one of the street ministries, who informed Philip he was willing to die for his faith. With hopes of founding a Miami Redeemer, he returned to Florida to try to reproduce Redeemer there. It did not take at all. No, you cannot duplicate the Holy Spirit, he thought. God is not creating a Howard Johnson chain of churches.

Domestically, the charismatic renewal's penetration of the church was occurring at a relentless pace, as many believers were finding references, in code as it were, to the baptism in the Spirit in Scripture. After having had the experience, it was impossible to read books like Acts and Corinthians in the same way, and many wondered how they could have missed something so obvious to the New Testament writers.

The renewal was becoming a force with which to reckon overseas as well.

In response, evangelicals like Michael Harper's old boss, John R.W. Stott, wrote a book, *The Baptism and Fullness of the Holy Spirit*, that counteracted the new charismatic theology, downplayed tongues, and questioned whether the baptism in the Spirit was a valid "second experience" following conversion. What made things more confusing was that for some people, especially Catholics, the baptism in the Spirit *was* their conversion. It grew increasingly harder to sort out the theological threads on exactly what the baptism was supposed to be: feelings of power, or solely speaking in tongues? There were people like Graham who experienced the power of the Spirit a month before he spoke in tongues; others felt very little or no power, but they spoke in tongues right away.

Graham linked all spiritual power to living in community, an attitude that greatly irked his fellow clergy friends. At a charismatic Episcopal leaders conference in Cincinnati in 1974, Graham alienated the renewal's core leadership forever. Like a teacher lecturing a crowd of ignorant school boys, he preached that the local church was the place where rocky relationships are worked out. If his listeners were not at peace in their parishes, he said, they had no business being on the road as public speakers.

This unwelcome advice came during a time when most clergy were at odds with their vestries or parishes or fighting for their lives as priests. Some of them took his remarks to infer that they should be living in community if they were truly spiritual. Even Bill Frey, who was there, was put off.

"We circled each other like suspicious dogs," Frey would remember later. Humility was not Graham's greatest asset, and he had a way of talking down to people. After that conference, the Episcopal Charismatic Fellowship board decided never to have him speak again. They thought him caustic, he ordered people about, and he landed too hard on the people there, most of whom were new to renewal. Graham had been at it 10 years. That same year, Graham had a blow-out with Stephen Clark and Ralph Martin over women in leadership, and now they, too, had decided not to invite him to their conferences. Thinking he had burned his bridges in the United States, and that Redeemer seemed to be doing fine without him, he decided it might be time to put permanent roots down in England.

That June, 30,000 people attended the Eighth Annual Conference on the Charismatic Renewal in the Catholic Church at the Notre Dame football stadium. Members of the Fourth Ward Clinic got to go and speak about their work. It rained nearly the whole weekend, but that did not stop the musicians, in borrowed jackets and raincoats, from singing and swaying to the music, their arms wrapped around each other. Cardinal Suenens celebrated Mass the next night, preceded by a procession of 700 white-clad priests who wound their way from the north side of the stadium. The altar stood on the 40-yard line and candles were lit from an altar flame and carried out to the crowd. Soon, 30,000 points of light were bobbing. It rained the next morning as well until finally Francis MacNutt called on the 30,000 to pray the rain would stop, which it did.

That same summer, the Stringhams approached the elders about a root of evil at Redeemer that they guessed had to do with sexual sin. Like Achan, the Israelite whose theft of sacred things during the time of Joshua brought sin and judgment into the entire nation, someone at Redeemer was corrupting the entire mix. It was not clear who this was. The elders did not receive this information well; the Stringhams were told they were being judgmental and should stop counseling. Eighteen months later, the Stringhams tried again to meet with the elders. This time, they were forbidden to teach or work at Redeemer. Sadly, they phased themselves out of the church and moved to Reba Place.

They may have been the first people to see that the fruit was still visible but the root had died. Chris Caros may have been the second. It was 1974, two years after a popular song called "American Pie" talked about "the day the music died." He and a friend named Walter were at a service where, according to a prophecy given, Redeemerites would be spread to the four winds, just as the fall leaves are blown about. Everyone clapped, thinking this meant evangelism.

But Chris turned to Walter and said, "This signals the death of Redeemer." And Walter said, "You're right."

1975–1979

CHAPTER 13

Advent

"The land is full of adulterers; because of the curse the land lies parched and the pastures in the desert are withered. The prophets follow an evil course and use their power unjustly.

"Both prophet and priest are godless; even in my temple I find their wickedness, declares the Lord.

"Therefore their path will become slippery; they will be banished to darkness and there they will fall. I will bring disaster on them in the year they are punished, declares the Lord.

". . . And among the prophets of Jerusalem I have seen something horrible: They commit adultery and live a lie. . ."

—Jeremiah 23:10–12, 14a

O N May 19, 1975, an extraordinary event took place in St. Peter's Basilica in Rome. Ten thousand charismatic Catholics from 50 countries stood rapt, gazing at the 700 priests surrounding Cardinal Suenens. Suenens was granted the immense honor of celebrating Mass from the magnificent central altar ordinarily reserved for the pope alone. People wept as they heard centuries-old Latin chants *and* charismatic songs less than a decade old. Then, casting aside all restraints, they filled the cavernous space with otherworldly melodies in the Spirit. Topping off the day was the appearance of Pope Paul VI, who gave an encouraging message in French, then summoned all the bishops in attendance to bestow their apostolic blessing on the assembly.

But the prophecies given that day had a foreboding air to them.

"Because I love you," one said, "I want to show you what I am doing in the world today. I want to prepare you for what is to come. Days of darkness are coming on the world, days of tribulation. . . Buildings that are now standing will not be standing. Supports that are there for My people now will not be there. I want you to be prepared, My people, to know only Me and to cleave to Me and to have Me in a way deeper than ever before. I will lead you into the desert. . . I will strip you of everything that you are depending on now, so you depend just on Me. A time of darkness is coming on the world, but a time of glory is coming for my church, a time of glory is coming for my people . . ."

It continued on, warning of an unprecedented time of evangelism in the midst of enormous upheaval, marked by the collapse of law and order and Western society. Other prophecies, along the same lines, were delivered. Everyone was excited, expectant, half-afraid of where the ax would fall, when would the hardships commence, and glad they were on the cutting edge of it all. But some remembered a similar, albeit more dramatic prophecy, given in August 1973 by David Wilkerson to charismatic Lutherans in Minneapolis, proclaiming an economic recession, worldwide famine, a tremendous rise in pornography, a major American earthquake, and intense persecution from the Roman Catholic Church against its own charismatics. Yet, here was Pope Paul VI embracing the charismatics.

People awaited the fulfillment of those 1975 prophecies for five, 10, and then 15 years. Thirty years later, most of them have yet to happen. How long do people wait for such words to come true? Or, as others feared, had the prophecies, given in the anointed atmosphere of St. Peter's, been false?

T HE Swedish sky was like a brilliant blue pool in which a radiant sun swam. Max Dyer was one of the Fisherfolk basking in the northern sun as Ed Baggett opened a letter from Francine. It was devastating news: Francine had written to say she was leaving him. Ed had gone to England in 1974 along with the Barkers, leaving Francine behind to finish her degree at the University of Houston, after which she would join him. Now she never would.

Tears streamed down Ed's face; his eyes were like broken glass, Max thought. Francine had visited Ed once, for seven days, then returned to the States. And now this. Contemplating his shattered marriage, Ed later realized that neither the community nor its leaders had ever encouraged him to return to the States to find out what was delaying Francine. Graham's position, he realized, was that he had laid down his own life for the sake of the ministry and Betty Jane had stayed with him. Others had to come to the same crossroads to find out where their commitment lay, and if it meant the loss of a wife, so be it.

Other marriages were also falling by the wayside. Darrell and Ann Wafer were splitting up as were Jerry and Esther Barker. Within a year of moving to England, Esther had left Jerry to return to the States. He would fly back to Texas in October 1975 to make peace with her, only to be served divorce papers soon after arriving in the country. A few months later, Esther would remarry, leaving Jerry to return to England, a morose and grief-stricken man. A 36-year-old school teacher named Alison Allan took pity on the brokenhearted man and began to talk to him. One of the Fisherfolk's British followers, she had so upset her family when she moved into community that her mother wrote her out of her will. After that jolt, Alison met Margo Farra and asked her advice on community living.

"Buy all the nice clothes you can now because you won't get anything decent once you move in," Margo replied. With that encouraging word, Alison joined the community, which a few days later left Yeldall to split three ways: Part of the group remaining at the Thatched House, part of them moving to Post Green, an English estate in Dorset, and the rest moving to Cumbrae, an island off the Scotland coast, due west of Glasgow. Graham had been asked to be provost of the Cathedral of the Isles there, and he had begun the job in March. This forced him to finally resign the rectorship of Redeemer, as he could not head up two parishes at once. The vestry unanimously voted Jeff in as rector but gave him no ceremony officially marking the transfer.

Already there were tensions between Graham and the old church he had renewed. When he came back to Redeemer that February to speak at a Friday night meeting, he blasted the parish for becoming inbred and perfectionist. Its real obligation, he reminded everyone, was to the neighborhood. When Graham was later informed by a few of the leaders that he was no longer welcome at Redeemer unless invited, grief swept through the Scottish community.

The advance party at Cumbrae had been Cathleen Gillis, now married to an Episcopal priest named Bob Morris. They arrived with their newborn daughter, Clare, plus another female community member. The housing at Cumbrae was as wretched as Yeldall's had been: musty, cold rooms, old stone buildings with no heat, no washing machine or dryer. They had to dry the diapers in front of the fireplaces, which took them three days to learn to light correctly. The buildings had received little care for at least 50 years, and the first thing community members had to do was winterize them. Scotland weather would make for rigorous living. Rooms without fireplaces were heated by a radiator, which did little to dispel the clammy cold wind that seeped through the windows. Worse still, the cathedral had no heat at all. Cathedral quarters were divided into a North and a South College, both built in 1851.

Cumbrae was a time for hunkering down, for making a living, for performing less and living more. One of the community members had a vision of the
Lord saying, "Take the stars out of your eyes," which the community took to
mean that glitzy members had become too performance-oriented. And it was
true: The men wore corduroy suits, the women Laura Ashley-style dresses.
Because it was a "clean act," the invitations to perform were pouring in. So there
they had landed, an island of American Episcopalians surrounded by an ocean
of Presbyterian Scots.

Filled with grazing sheep, the island gave a whole new meaning to isolation.
To get there from Glasgow required an unwieldy combination of train, ferry,
and bus rides. Fortunately, the cathedral was only a few hundred feet from the
water and a five-minute walk from the tiny commercial district of Millport.
One entered the cathedral grounds through a large, red stone arch with a black
oak door, then walked 100 feet through the woods to a large Gothic-style stone
edifice. A walk up several stone steps to the narthex revealed a tiny church with
marvelous acoustics.

There was precedent for what the community hoped to do. After all, many
Celtic saints such as Columba and Aidan had their missionary centers on
islands. But relating to the islanders was hard, despite helping to start a bakery in
Millport that sold breads, cakes, scones, tea bread, and Scottish morning rolls.
Bill Pulkingham and his new wife Margi managed this enterprise, which helped
convince the Scots that the newcomers were not freeloaders. Margi was tiny and
blonde and bore an amazing resemblance to Mary, the second Pulkingham
daughter. Pert and curious, she was an artist and a dancer who once had thought
of becoming a nun. Redeemer had fulfilled her desire for a religious vocation,
and she could now be among the large family she had always wanted. She had
come to the Nottingham conference expecting to stay six weeks. She would end
up staying 10 years in Britain, beginning with a stint as nanny to the younger
Pulkingham children. She adored being with the Pulkingham family, so when
she and Bill joined the international team, she knew she had found permanent
entree to this incredible family.

R EDEEMER hit its highest Sunday attendance figure in 1975 when 1,220
persons crammed their way into the March 30 Easter service. In an era
before megachurches, Redeemer was drawing 900 to 1,000 people to its Friday
and Sunday services, as people could not get enough of this renewal. That year,
a new elder came on board at Redeemer. Jack Minor, an administrator for the
Social Security Administration, and his wife Delores transferred to Redeemer in

1970 from a more traditional parish. "I've found something absolutely compelling," he told his priest before leaving.

Jack knew almost from the beginning that he wanted to be an elder or at least associate with the likes of Bob Eckert, Jerry Barker, Grover Newman, and Graham. He realized there were ways to rise up in the pecking order, and the first step was to buy a house near the church. That done, the next step was to form a household and accept whomever the administrators chose to send their way. The first two people sent to the household proved to be disasters, but the Minors hung in there, believing that good times were soon to come. And they did; a musician named Brian Howard, Max Dyer, and an artistic young woman named Ruth Wieting moved in.

Next, Jack took on the task of Scoutmaster to the Redeemer Boy Scout troop, a natural choice because of his two sons. This backseat kind of ministry convinced others of his requisite humility while waiting to be called on for greater things. By the mid-1970s, it was clear he was the kind of leadership material the church wanted: someone with a successful business background who was easy to get along with and had the needed charismatic credentials.

Rarely were elders raised up from the formerly needy. Instead, they were usually successful, married businessmen. As in most churches, Redeemer had a class system based on one's musical or dancing gifts or who you were in the world, which is why new members who were trained ballerinas, architects, or musicians, or were from well-to-do families ended up better than those with no credentials. Upon arriving at Redeemer, everyone was directed to lay aside their talents, but eventually they took them up again and the cream did rise to the top.

When Jack quit his job in June and became the church administrator, he found himself organizing a half-million-dollar business. The church's income was $250,000, and money from 40 households provided another $250,000. Redeemer was also supporting Graham at $20,000 a year. Close to 75 people were working full-time at the church as clergy, bookstore employees, members of the maintenance and remodeling crews, child care workers, the music ministry, administrators, clerks at the resale shop, and the Hispanic and neighborhood ministries. Plus, there was the church-owned camp at Giddings and counselors counseling all day and into the night. It reminded Jack of a cross between a military operation and a Roman circus.

Lastly, the elders themselves were traveling and speaking around the country. Jack could see a split forming, for Bob Eckert and Jim Clowe were more of the fundamentalist variety; Graham, Jeff, a new priest named George Moses, and Jack himself were more of the easier-going Anglican type, and less literalist about the

Bible. The latter trio was more interested in community and, increasingly, that's what most of the teachings were about. Jack discerned that Bob and Jim were fighting a losing battle to make Redeemer look more non-denominational. Jim especially was heavier into the charismatic end of things, even as spiritual gifts at the church were slowly fading from public view. Although Bob had phased out of Redeemer by then, Jim's influence was so strong that it took the other three elders—George, Jeff and Jack—to function as counterweights.

The four elders could exercise enormous power over the parish and, as a small example, it was they who dictated how everyone should fast every Lent. It was different each year. One Lent, people had to stick with soup and bread; another time, they were to abstain from coffee—a Lenten sacrifice that caused some to suffer violent headaches. The fourth elder, George Moses, was Bob Morris's classmate at General Seminary who did his diaconate at Redeemer. His ordination to the priesthood in 1973 automatically propelled him into leadership, and by 1975, along with the other elders, he had assumed a heavy counseling load. Community had a way of bringing problems to the fore. Households were a safe environment where people felt for the first time in their lives that they had a support group on which they could unload all of their personal problems.

Thus, the waiting line for free counseling at the church was practically endless. Even as a deacon, George was seeing 20-30 counselees a week. Moreover, most of the counselors, he noticed, had no training at all in psychology and were reduced to giving out the seat-of-the-pants advice along with prayer and a few Scriptural passages. Success was hit and miss. Other counselors took to being dictatorial, telling people what to do instead of seeking out what the Lord was telling them to do. People assumed the Holy Spirit was guiding their counseling. But what if He was not? Not knowing the answer to that question, George was quietly becoming more cynical and disheartened with the system and his role in it.

Moreover, the sheen of protection that had encircled Redeemer for a decade had melted. Several area robberies took place that year, particularly at the church itself, where at one point, the staff surprised robbers with guns. The robbers who did not get caught relieved the church of thousands of dollars in silver Communion sets and office equipment until the parish switched to using pottery chalices. John Grimmet was heard to remark that the anointing had left Redeemer, and that everyone was sitting ducks for whatever crime came next.

But what had caused that anointing to lift? The four elders got a hint of the enormity of the problem on the first night of an elders retreat. Just when they were beginning to relax over dinner, Jim dropped a bomb. He was having an affair, he blurted out; in fact, he had had affairs with two of the female counselors, one of whom, Marilyn Mazak, headed a huge household. Shocked by the news, the other elders called Grover, who was in Colorado, and begged him to come back to Houston as fast as possible. Grover hopped on the first plane available and the quintet met at a motel on Interstate-45 to decide Jim's future.

"Kick this man out," Jack told them, amidst all the weeping and recriminations. But Grover persuaded them to forgive Jim and to get him to repent and behave himself. Meanwhile, Jim was promising he would not get sexually involved with other women again. The elders found some Scripture to warrant letting Jim off the hook, but overlooked a caution from I Timothy 5:19-20 that orders elders who sin to be rebuked publicly as a warning to others. The elders set up a strict surveillance system with Jim, cut back his co-counseling with one of the women to six hours a week, and built safeguards into the system so he would not have the chance to commit adultery again.

CHAPTER 14

The Feast of St. Andrew

"My beloved hath a vineyard in a very fruitful hill:
And he fenced it and gathered out the stones thereof,
and planted it with the choicest vine,
and built a tower in the midst of it,
and also made out a wine-press therein:
and he looked that it should bring forth grapes,
    and it brought forth wild grapes. . .
What could have been done more to my vineyard,
    that I have not done it?
wherefore, when I looked that it should bring forth grapes,
    brought forth wild grapes?
And now go to; I will tell you what I will do in my vineyard:
I will take away the hedge thereof, and it shall be eaten up;
    and break down the wall thereof, and it shall be trodden down:
And I will lay it waste. . ."
                —Isaiah 5:1–6a (KJV)

THAT October, Reid Wightman, a sensitive young man who kept copious notes in his diary, moved into household. It was around that time that the above passage from the beginning of Isaiah 5, in which God destroys His wayward vineyard, was read in church. It was optimistically interpreted to mean that Redeemer was breaking down its own protective walls to reach out to the neighborhood.

Reid was brought up by his grandparents and never saw his real father until the age of 13. His stepfather beat him and Reid retaliated by getting involved in obsessive emotional relationships with men. By the time he began attending

Oral Roberts University, he was extremely confused sexually. He set up his own campus still, where he made wine and dallied in sexual activity in ORU dorms. During his freshman year in Russian class, a group of students prayed over him to be baptized in the Spirit. After he mumbled something, a fellow student shouted, "Hallelujah, it's French!" and they let him go. Fortunately, the chaplain in Reid's dorm took him under his wing that night and prayed over him in a far more relaxed fashion. Reid began to weep and the chaplain asked him why.

"I've never felt more loved and more guilty in my whole life," Reid admitted.

"That's it," the chaplain responded. "Other people will tell you about gifts, but the real relationship with the Holy Spirit is about confession of sin and about repentance."

Reid did not change overnight. Although he got engaged in the spring of 1975, he was not just sleeping with various men, but living on Camel cigarettes and gin. He then informed the Lord he wanted no part of Him, so the Lord left him alone until one frightened moment in August when Reid was close to suicide. He was six-foot-two and weighed 135 pounds; his cheeks were sunken and his ribs stuck out.

"I'm here," the Lord told him. *"Go to Redeemer."*

"Somehow I got the feeling my stay at Redeemer would be no picnic," Reid wrote in his diary after his third day there, "but I never thought the party would be over so fast." He was in a 24-person household that lived on three paychecks. Everyone there either needed to be ministered to or was on the remodeling crew. Reid was suffering from severe withdrawal from gin and cigarettes, and his problems were so obvious that he was moved to the Hightowers, a much smaller household, for closer supervision. The burly and hyper-masculine Wayne Hightower soon became the father Reid never had.

Reid began attending counseling sessions for healing, only to be told that his homosexuality was merely an indication of other things wrong in his life. Though his behavior might change, the counselor said, he would always be gay. Upset by this point of view, Wayne pulled Reid out of counseling and got him a job painting houses with another church member. As time went on, Reid was healed by simply being with others in community.

Reid's problems went unnoticed by most Redeemerites, who were far more involved in another fruit basket turnover at the church. Ever since Graham had left for England, the Fishermen/Fisherfolk had become a stronger entity at Redeemer—indeed, it was a business in its own right. They had lawyers and accountants to handle the contracts and royalties generated by the rising stack of music books and records flowing from the creativity of Betty Jane and the musicians. Letters by the thousands, many of them with requests for visits by a Fisherfolk team, poured into the third-floor office, draining the church of valuable resources, some thought. Jim Clowe was no fan of the group, and he was not sorry to hear they planned to leave and establish a separate ministry in Waxahatchie, Texas. If the traveling teams wanted their own base of operations, that would get them out of Redeemer's hair, he thought.

Then when Graham moved to Scotland, lots of personnel were suddenly needed to staff three Communities of Celebration in Britain. The Waxahatchie plans fell through and Graham was forced to humble himself at the feet of Bishop Frey. Frey had invited the community to live in his diocese, but Graham had rebuffed him after the disastrous Episcopal clergy meeting the year before in Cincinnati. This time, however, Graham had to beg the bishop for help. Bill Frey was willing to forgive and forget, but Graham, he had determined, needed some oversight. And he sure wasn't going to give the man canonical residency, either.

"You wouldn't obey me anyway," Frey told Graham. "You're your own bishop."

The bishop had come up with an offer for the Redeemerites. For $1 a year, Grace Church, a parish in Colorado Springs, would rent them 100 acres of a summer church camp 8,500 feet high in the mountains. It was in a small town called Woodland Park, 18 miles west of the Springs. Shaped like a backwards California, the acreage was all timberland except the acre containing several structures for a summer church camp. This was to be their new home. The new tenants merely needed to modernize and winterize the place.

These negotiations took place nearly at the last minute, and the 53 Redeemerites did not find out their destination until the day before they moved. Things were a bit frantic at the Friday night service, where it was said, "We don't know where we're going, but we're going to get on the 610 Loop [the beltway surrounding Houston] and drive around it until God tells us where to go."

By the next morning, all had been finalized. Splitting into two groups, the vanguard left that Sunday morning. After a 1,000 mile drive, they arrived at the starkest of lodgings, with bare light bulbs, concrete floors, and group showers. This being early September, they had to winterize everything fast, before the snows came. Fortunately, two of the men, Marty Pearsall and Brian Howard, knew something about remodeling. Those who were not putting up sheetrock or insulation were laying carpet or cutting firewood, the main source of heat for the winter. What made things even crazier were the six cars they had inherited, each with over 200,000 miles on them, including a "prayermobile" whose key did not turn in the lock until you prayed over it. One night, they decided they had had enough of remodeling and decorated one of the cabins for a wine and cheese party. A blizzard came in that evening, blowing out the candles because of huge cracks in the walls. The next morning, some of them awoke with an inch of snow on their beds.

The move to Colorado was the final step in the depleting of Redeemer's leadership, and a fatal miscalculation few grasped at the time. The logic for the move was that a group gone 50 percent of the time could not be a vital part of any parish; thus, the group needed its own base of operations. Earlier, Darrell Wafer had warned Graham that he had to choose between the Fishermen and Redeemer. "You can't have both," Darrell warned. "If you choose the Fishermen, you'll destroy the parish."

Sure enough, once the Fishermen, renamed the Fisherfolk, left, the parish seemed to lose its purpose. The concern for worldwide church renewal and the need to subject everything to renewal had moved to Colorado, and no one had any idea what to do for an encore. Predictably, Redeemer elders would hear a call from God to return to the neighborhood. There was little else left for them to do, and no other great vision had emerged.

But the makeup of the new Colorado community was wrong. The old monastics knew that to establish a new group, a pie-shaped piece had to be cut from the old group. This included a few leaders, a few more cream-of-the-crop youngers, a base of regular types, and a few basket cases. But the Fisherfolk were not asking for anyone's advice, much less consulting tradition, and thus they established communities of mostly arty people—the select, the invited, the wanted.

The new community had a Fisherfolk traveling team that included Mary Sukys and Marty Pearsall, whose courtship had originated at Redeemer. Once they joined the Fisherfolk team, they had to promise they would pursue no romantic relationships for two years. This put them in quite a quandary, especially Marty, who had been engaged to another woman, red-headed Kathleen Crow, while still in Houston. He and Kathleen went to the church, expecting to set a wedding date, but were confronted by six elders. One of the elders, they were told, "has a check about this relationship." From then on, they could relate only in "ministry." Kathleen went into shock; because the elders supposedly could hear God better, the couple had no recourse. Now allowed to see each other only in the company of a third person, she and Marty drifted apart. One day, Kathleen saw Marty, with Mary, walking toward her, and a vision of the two of them in wedding clothes flashed across her terrified mind.

By the time Marty and Mary got to Colorado, their romance was cooking and the couple begged elders to let them marry—to no avail until Mary heard that two members of the international teams, including Graham's son Bill, had been allowed to wed. Mary complained directly to Graham, who intervened to allow the marriage. Graham was like that—freer than many of the elders and more trusting that people could know what was best for themselves. He rarely relied on rules because he had the unique position of being able to make or break them, no questions asked.

Even after they were married, the Pearsalls' relationship was scrutinized, with one of the elders chastising them for kissing in the back of the team bus. Because they were supposed to be relating as equals, it was a point of pride for the Fisherfolk when onlookers could not determine which of them was the married couple. Life as newlyweds was tough in a household of 24, headed by John and Margo, whose own marriage was not reputed to be the finest. Mary felt John was authoritarian and, because he was a lawyer, had a superior command of the English language and could easily defeat other community members in an argument. One of John's first blow-ups was with Paul Patton, a Redeemer elder who had moved to Colorado with the Fisherfolk.

Paul, a distant relative of famed World War II General George Patton, had run his Redeemer household on Clay Street with the same military efficiency. Sweets were rarely allowed, and one member who came home with some jellybeans had them taken away. Bread had to be broken into four pieces at meals, and the budget allowed 50 cents per person per meal. Individual 15-minute stints in the bathroom began at 4 a.m. If time ran short, then four people simultaneously used the same bathroom: two at the sink, one on the john, and one standing in the bathtub waiting for the john. Household morning prayers were from 5:30 a.m. to 6. No newspapers, magazines, or TV were allowed in the house, as people had to relate to each other rather than hiding behind newsprint. Rules were strictly enforced in a seven-bedroom, three-bathroom household that held anywhere from 15-23 persons. It was a healing/deliverance household for people on drugs, homosexuals, and couples with marriage problems.

Paul was executive vice president of the Fisherfolk and president of a related company, Net Productions. Soon after he followed the Fisherfolk to Colorado, it was decided that the Fisherfolk assets, including all the music copyrights, would be transferred to Scotland, leaving Paul without a job. About the same time, John and Margo arrived from Britain but instead of being forced to take time off to mend their failing marriage, the Farras became leaders at Woodland Park. John was strong, smart, and articulate, and not the sort of person to be demoted to the rank and file, the other elders thought. It was hoped he could be tamed by serving with a team of leaders. But John was not going to be tamed by anyone and it was not long before the Pattons and the Farras collided. The community informed the Pattons they were to leave within 24 hours, and that other community members would not be allowed to talk with them. They were given a pickup truck, $1,000 and all the household goods they could load into it. They drove off in a blizzard on New Year's Eve. The pickup soon broke down, which ate up the $1,000 and Paul, his wife Suzie and their son lived on potato chips and crackers until they could reach a friend's home in another state.

The rest of the team somehow made it intact through two years on the road, but then people began dropping out in 1977, beginning with Jeff Cothran. On Holy Saturday, the day before Easter, he announced he was leaving community and the celibate life. He was tired, he said, of the years of hard work in trying not to be gay.

"The only thing I hadn't tried in all these years was doing what I wanted to openly," he wrote a friend. "When (a friend) had talked with me about my double life three years ago, I had tried with all I had to make it succeed, and it hadn't happened, so instead of putting my money where my mouth was, I decided to put my mouth where my money was and go from there. Whether or not it's the right decision, I don't know; what I do know is that it's the real decision, the one that has motivated my actions for a long time."

He left for Boston, where he hooked up with another former Redeemerite who had "come out." Another person, then another, left, too, thoroughly disenchanted with the dynamics of community, especially the tension and the frayed nerves. Community discussions would be filled with wrangling over things like whether one household should have jam on their toast if the other households could not afford jam, and other contentious issues on how to stay in lockstep. They all ate the same things, got their clothes from the same places, and drove the same six Hondas.

Some members fled to a much looser, more gracious community set up by Bill and Barbara Frey. Here at last was sanity, family and serenity. The Freys had been so impressed by what they had seen at Redeemer in 1973 that they formed a cluster of households in Denver. By 1975, they had 15 persons living with them. One night after Christmas, they invited the entire Woodland Park community to spend the night. Seventy-six people somehow crammed themselves inside the Freys' 26-room Victorian home. The Freys' philosophy of community was radically different from Redeemer's. Unlike Betty and Graham, the Freys considered their marriage the primary relationship in the community. Community should strengthen marriages, they believed, and their particular community existed to support his ministry as bishop. Because the bishop is typically isolated from parish life, the community was Bill's parish and extended family and, he hoped, the people who would speak the truth to him.

With other communities springing up like mushrooms around the country, it came as no surprise that a group calling itself the Community of Communities formed in 1975. These 13 communities were the vanguard of the evangelical left. Three of them were located in Michigan, two in Colorado, two in Ohio, others in Montana, Berkeley, and Philadelphia; Redeemer in Houston, Post Green in England, and one named Sojourners in Washington, D.C. Most of them had been influenced, to a greater or lesser extent, by Graham. They were all mainly concerned with peace and justice issues, working and living with the poor, communal living, and political activism. Some of the Redeemer elders were suspicious about the group, sensing that Graham would work his way into some sort of position as bishop over them. "Graham," the elders told him, "we have a bishop. It's Richardson."

Some of the communities exchanged mailing lists. The Fisherfolk received a listing of Sojourners subscribers, to whom they sent a copy of their products and music, plus an explanation of their history. One of their letters went to a mailbox at Lewis and Clark College in Portland, Oregon, belonging to a college freshman from Washington state who was planning to be a newspaper reporter. She avidly read all about the Fisherfolk, who combined in themselves all the elements that fascinated her: charismatic renewal, the Episcopal Church, and community. She dropped them a line, asking to be put on their mailing list.

M EANWHILE, the charismatic renewal was showing signs of severe internal stress. That August, a who's who of 30 charismatic leaders met in Minneapolis for a showdown with the Ft. Lauderdale Five. One of the detractors was Pat Robertson, the founder of the Christian Broadcasting Network, who had discovered that some of the operators manning CBN's counseling phones were spreading the shepherding doctrine. Typically, a counselor would ask a caller, "Who are you submitted to?" when all the caller wanted was prayer. Sometimes the counselors would refuse to pray for the caller unless the caller was submitted to a shepherd.

When word of this reached Robertson, he went into the stratosphere, then shot off a staff memo calling discipleship "a charismatic dictatorship." Next, he banned all teachings by the Ft. Lauderdale Five from his 54 radio and TV outlets. "Why," Robertson reportedly said at the August meeting, "do charismatics always have to take simple Bible truths and push them to such ridiculous extremes that they become unbalanced and heretical?"

Any church historian familiar with the writings of 18th-century American preacher Jonathan Edwards could have told him that the moment a renewal shows promise, Satan mounts a counterattack. If the enemy cannot destroy a renewal, he will derail and disorient it by inserting counterweights to deceive those genuinely seeking salvation and to discredit the revival. One such counter-weight is extremism. Those entering the shepherding movement came in with a pure intent, as most were new to Christianity and wanted some hands-on training. Shepherding was based on the theory that a committed relationship between two persons, with the "sheep" submitted to the "shepherd" was the biblical pattern for Christian maturity. The sheep got direction from the shep-herd in every aspect of life: Who to marry, who to shun, how to dress, what news publications to read, and how to manage one's finances. Even the follower's sex life was open to inspection. The shepherd, in turn, submitted to another spiritual elder and so on up the chain of submissions to the top tier of five Ft. Lauderdale leaders. The theory behind it all was that the shepherd would chip away at the raw material of the sheep, attempting to create a disciple patterned after the biblical model.

However, most shepherds had nowhere near the wisdom Jesus used in training His disciples and, as a result, shepherds often bullied their sheep rather than laying down their lives for them. Sheep were sometimes expected to provide services, such as housecleaning, cooking, and babysitting to "honor" their shep-herd. Tithing to one's shepherd was also common, and if the sheep belonged to a church, that meant a double-tithe. If the sheep could not afford that, the shepherd got first rights to the money, which irked pastors who saw church revenues filtered off into the shepherds' wallets.

What kept the system afloat across the country was the belief that shep-herds, or elders as Redeemer termed them, were nearly perfect. As late as 1974, Graham was speaking about this during guest appearances at Redeemer. Wan-dering far beyond the strictures of the balanced shepherding concepts in I Timothy, Graham was a genius at reaching the outermost boundaries of ortho-doxy. He would say outrageous things, but then, if called on the carpet, would scoot back into theological correctness.

Elders, Graham said during one sermon, are "those whose lives are abso-lutely perfect in Christ, without a single flaw, who are absolutely, uncondition-ally, totally committed to live the life of the Father and who in fact do it publicly, openly, powerfully, and who, by the exemplary fashion of their life and the wisdom of their teachings, command every member of the community to follow their example, and will not countenance anything that is compromise. They are perfect, without any flaws whatsoever."

He went on to give a job description.

"An elder," he said, "is a commanding person. Nevertheless, he must not be standoffish or stuffy. He must be yielded to people's needs . . . An elder is perfect in his ways, whose life is a full revelation of the Father. No man ever gets to be that way under his own strength. The only way a man gets to be that way is relating his life to a man who is like that, so that he is a participant of the grace of the person to whom he relates."

This is what Jesus did with His disciples, Graham insisted. At the heart of the family was not the husband and wife, he said. Instead, the really important relationship in the family was father-son.

"Which is to say," Graham explained, "the father imparts all of his life, all of his grace, all of his authority, all of his inheritance to the obedient sons that are his. He imparts it to them. They walk in his life. They walk in all he is and has. That's the *important* relationship; it's the only concept of the family that you'll read about in the New Testament or the Old Testament."

Seeing that no one contradicted this amazing assertion, Graham went on to describe the notion of a family centered on a husband and wife as "not Christian" and "an idolatrous institution." Western civilization has idolized the male-female relationship, he pointed out, whereas biblically, the family was so much more than that. It was an extended family centered on the father figure who has laid his life down for others.

If the husband-wife relationship is not the center of the family, someone asked, what good is it?

"The relationship between the husband and wife in the extended natural family is," Graham teased, "are you ready? It's primarily sexual." To the Old Testament Jew, the woman was a sexual creature whose sole function was to produce sons, he explained. The wife, it seemed, was there only to meet certain needs and to help propagate the species, but she was not to be part of the top relationship in the man's life. That was reserved for the husband's elder.

By relating to an elder, Graham promised that "you'll learn that perfection; that you'll work out the sin in your life, you'll work out the fear, the doubt, the inadequacy, the self-rejection, the ignorance, the confusion, you'll work all of that out in your life in deep fellowship with elders, and with an elder who'll reflect the fullness of Christ's grace to you and mediate that perfection to you."

Listening to this, Jack Minor knew something was very wrong, but he couldn't put his finger on why. After all, the community was as righteous as you could expect from a conglomeration of several hundred hormonally active young adults and their leaders. There was no smoking, no drinking that he knew of, precious little TV, no divorces, and 100 percent attendance at most church services. At least people were trying to live the life. One thing about perfectionism; it may be a heresy, he thought, but it at least gave people something to shoot for. And the elders were supposed to be the most perfect of all.

"We were real powerful—the four of us," he would remember years later. "We had hundreds of singles looking to us for direction and married people looking to us to solve their marital problems. We had to keep the action going. You wanted an exciting ministry to keep people's minds off how hard they were working. Other than that, it would have been drudgery."

Elders felt they had to continually remind people, especially those postponing marriages and colleges for the sake of Redeemer, and especially those in households forced to tithe 20 percent of their income, that they were part of a great movement. The problem was, both Jack and Jim were hearing stories that Graham was living high on the hog, eating at expensive restaurants and staying at plush hotels thanks to private credit cards supplied by benefactors, and that, while on the road, he required huge financial commitments from his followers. Those in Scotland were noticing how Graham got to frequently fly back to the States for his medical treatments while they had to make do with whatever was available in Glasgow.

No one could question any of this because Graham had long since taught that God delegates all authority through a chain of command, beginning with the elders. Therefore, to question authority was to rebel against God. The popular author Watchman Nee taught along a similar vein, including the idea that Christians should obey their authority, *right or wrong*, because God does not hold individuals culpable for wrong decisions; He holds their authority responsible. Moreover, one's authority, or elder, would have a revelation from God about their subordinate, which overrode anything God said to the subordinate. Nee also originated the idea of "covering," which meant that Christians needed to be "covered" in an obedient relationship with someone else. This was widely picked up and taught in the shepherding movement; married women especially were told they had to be "covered" by their husbands. It was thought that women who made decisions without their husbands' covering could be influenced by Satan.

Nee taught that those who disagreed with their leaders disobeyed God. Thus, even when leaders went far beyond biblical mandates in controlling followers' lives in non-doctrinal and non-moral matters, the followers were to obey them without question. Eventually, such a system of beliefs, buttressed by Scripture, would go a long way toward souring a whole generation of young Christians against authority.

In the fall of 1975, the elders approved a research proposal by Jim Clark, a doctoral student at the University of Houston, who wanted to do his dissertation on Redeemer. By then, academics were noticing the burgeoning charismatic movement and wanting a piece of the action. Clark was assigned to live in several households over the course of a year. He found a $1.2 million system structured like a small village whose economy was based on wages and the estimated value of services provided by dozens of volunteers in 32 households. The parish roll in 1976 listed 986 members, he noted, one-third of whom were in households. Over them were 57 leader-elders and four official elders. He began questioning the group of 57 about their habits and learned that the community was exceedingly isolated. Two or three elders might visit a friend outside the community only once or twice a year, and more than half seldom or ever visited their relatives. Half the elders never watched TV, and seldom went to the movies. However, most did read a daily newspaper. Households had three persons for every car and a typical household numbered nine to 12 persons. Leaders were typically white, young, married, and well-educated.

When Clark polled elders on qualities they valued in a person, they listed forgiving, loving, honest, responsible and obedient—all characteristics of a communal life. Last on their list were characteristics of an individualistic, rational way of life: independent, intellectual, ambitious, polite, and logical. Whenever Clark was introduced to someone in community, the person would identify himself or herself as a member of a certain household, almost as if they had acquired a new last name. Households tended to attend all events, whether it was the movies or a parish picnic, as a single unit, and thus its members learned to think as a group. Households automatically defined a person's niche in the parish. They also illustrated that freedom and community were opposites, and you had to choose one or the other.

Clark noted how everything, no matter how random the event, was attributed to God. He was once assigned to do some work in the resale shop and given a clump of keys with which to unlock one of the doors. For 10 minutes, he tried everything on the chain at least several times until he became convinced he was missing the right key. He went through the keys one last time, jiggling each to see if the door would pop open. Suddenly, one of the keys worked and the door opened.

Later, the elder in charge of the resale stopped by and asked how he had opened the door. Clark told of his lengthy attempts, concluding he had finally gotten lucky by finding the right key. A look of friendly concern came over the elder's face.

"No, Jim," she said, "the Lord did it. There was probably a reason for it happening just as it did."

Luck and randomness were alien concepts in this elder's life, and Jim realized that what he considered as impersonal cause and effect was the "work of the Lord" in the sacred air at Redeemer. Things clicked more into place once he began attending the elaborately planned Sunday services. Anywhere from 100-150 priests, singers, dancers, musicians, artists, writers, printers, ushers, and childcare workers pooled their energies every week to produce several services, culminating with the Sunday morning Eucharist. Sunday, he realized, was the emotional high point for the parish. George Mims knew how to craft a service that would peak in a spontaneous moment of ecstasy—most often, the whole congregation erupted into singing in the Spirit—that was beyond anything Clark had ever experienced. Obviously, worship was the reinforcement that kept everyone going.

One Sunday, one of the elders was speaking on love, a common theme at Redeemer. The message was that the Lord wanted everyone to live and love with abandon, trusting Him to work out the details. Thus, don't worry about the future, but instead take risks and live recklessly. About 800 people were packed into the church and as the sermon ended, a slow rhythmic clapping began. People began to rise and the clapping increased in tempo. Finally, the whole congregation was standing and the intensity was growing; the elder giving the sermon turned to walk toward the choir. Just as he reached the front of the congregation, he turned to face the risen Christ in the mural and broke out into a dance. The assembly exploded into applause, shouts of joy, songs, and finally, as if time was suspended, everyone became silent. Never had Clark, the sociologist, seen anything to compare with the sense of unity and power he experienced that morning.

Around the country, charismatics were definitely in the driver's seat. In mid-1976, an alliance of the Catholic charismatic communities met in South Bend, Indiana, home of the People of Praise community. About 3,000 persons came to hear about being a people separated for God's purposes.

"In order to be able to hear Me, you simply must be willing to give up everything," one prophecy began. "My plan cannot succeed through a mixture of your desires and My word to you. You must give up everything. I know what this means to you. For those of you who are young, it means laying down before

Me the choices for your very life. For those who are older, it means laying before Me the entire life that you have built up over the years. . . If you do not wish to give up everything, then I ask you now, as your loving Father, to withdraw from this people that I am drawing together. Your brothers and sisters will continue to love you. I will love you nonetheless. But I am at work to gather and to consolidate a people who are totally committed to My purpose. . . Those who give up all for Me shall lead the richer life."

The message was clear. It was all or nothing. Either get with the program by joining a community or get out. Community was a natural fit for charismatics. Just being baptized in the Spirit enrolled one in the community of shared experience. And if the renewal waned, so would community; you could not share life together if you were not sure the person next to you was charismatic.

One of those in the movement's driver's seat was Steve Clark (no relation to Jim Clark), who was then compiling a 732-page book, *Man and Woman in Christ*, which defined sex roles among Christians. Women should not have authority, Clark wrote, because they were more open to spiritual influences, both good and bad, than men. Although women find it easier to embrace faith, it was Eve who was deceived, not Adam. Thus, men's ability to resist deception made them more capable of governing a community. He produced sociological data showing that men bond with each other to govern while women are more oriented toward the home and children. Thus, he reasoned, women form less stable groupings with other women and respond better to male authority than female authority.

Also, he urged, the sexes should be separated at an early age. Men were primarily responsible for the upbringing of their sons, and women responsible for bringing up their daughters. Clark added that the father-daughter relationship should be strong enough to give the daughter an experience of her father's love during formative years, but he wrote nothing at all about the mother-son relationship.

The never-married Clark was especially concerned that men not be feminized through over-exposure to women. When members of the burgeoning Word of God began to apply his teachings, women were told not to wear pants, and men not to wear pink. Men were not allowed to do the dishes, change diapers, or be at their wife's side during childbirth. To drive the point home further, beginning in 1976, women were to wear veil-like head coverings, symbolizing submission, to community meetings, while men wore mantles, symbolizing headship. The 2,000-year-old custom of veiling women at Christian gatherings was light years from the braless and mini-skirted look so popular then.

Sixteen years later, the *Detroit Free Press* would run a photo of a community meeting in a gym decorated with banners. Shown were several dozen people, including the community orchestra. The men had white cloth stoles draped about their shoulders and the women wore long skirts with white cloths that covered their heads and fell to their waists. As several men with sideburns and wide ties wandered about, one woman adjusted her veil while another stood off to the side talking with what looked like an elder. Her veil was clenched in her hands.

CHAPTER 15

The Feast of St. Clement

"Brothers and sisters, we must have faith. We are engaged in the contest of the living God and are being trained by the present life in order to win laurels in the life to come."
—from St. Clement's Second Letter to the Corinthians

S o many spiritually and mentally ill people were coming to Redeemer for healing that 13 full-time and 15–20 part-time counselors were on duty at the church. Lead counselors were the four elders and some women, among them Marilyn Mazak, a mother of six.

Married at the age of 18, Marilyn was a country girl who fell in love with a former Air Force enlisted man. Marilyn and Bob moved to Redeemer on faith, buying, as she called it, an "ole yucky house" on Walker Street before he had a job. Marilyn didn't like Redeemer, but she was much enamored of the Pulkingham household and Graham's caring manner. Her own household boomed to 22 people, including 10 children. Her 4½-year-old son, Paul, composed "Jesus is a Friend of Mine," which became a classic at Redeemer. Soon, the Mazaks began to fit in. After a few years, Marilyn was asked to come onto the pastoral counseling staff, which she loved, taking to counseling like a duck to water. While other people took care of her children and cleaned her home, Marilyn would handle six to ten counseling appointments a day, learning the ropes from Jim Clowe.

Jim was a natural at counseling and its half-sister, deliverance, which began to be practiced around 1976. Lots of ideas were floating around charismatic Christianity about exorcism and deliverance, especially after the release of the movie *The Exorcist* a few years earlier. Redeemer deliverances involved lengthy sessions where the counselee enumerated all sins, past and present. Then people were badgered with Scripture and song so that if any demon were present, it would want to exit. Sometimes people found themselves "delivered" of personality traits. Before long, it became clear that something was terribly amiss with the whole idea. Sessions could be lengthy and brutal, with the deliverers questioning whether that person really knew the Lord. After such a degrading session, anyone could slink away wondering if he or she truly was saved.

Perhaps the person most damaged by this was Clare Sears, the first wife of Don Sears, the head of administration and purchasing at Exxon. Beginning in 1972, Don had become so entranced with Redeemer that they sold their nice home at a loss in Houston's ritzy Memorial section to move to Eastwood. He also gave up a job transfer to New Jersey, which resulted in his demotion. However, no sacrifice was too much for Redeemer, or almost no sacrifice. The deliverance ministry wrecked Clare, who was excommunicated from the church. In 1978, after becoming increasingly schizophrenic and depressed, Clare committed suicide.

One night after a men's meeting at the church, Redeemer business manager Gene Antill was walking down the sidewalk when a six-pack of beer cans hit his foot. He looked over to see a friend, Billy Crain, sitting in his blue Chevy, his door open.

"What *are* you doing?" Gene demanded.

"I flunked deliverance," Billy replied. Years later, they would laugh about the encounter, but it was getting obvious that something wasn't working. Bob Woodson confessed his sins to a deliverance team for an agonizing two days. At the end of that, he was told he had "too many back doors" and they refused to deliver him. However, rebellion was slow to surface, for if anyone protested, that showed they were demonized too. Gene, who knew there were plenty of people who did not assent to community policies, once overheard a shocked Jack Minor say to someone, "You wouldn't want the eldership to hear you saying that, would you?"

Marilyn was also getting warning signals. "I feel the Spirit of God is leaving here," she blurted out at one morning meeting of the counseling staff. They were doing the same things, but He was not there. It was self-criticism—she was at the top of the heap with Jim, in charge of the deliverance ministry. Meanwhile, the Clowes' marriage was noticeably in trouble, with Jane intuiting that her husband was unfaithful. She was even having dreams about it.

To all outward appearances, Redeemer was at the peak of its popularity. Taft Metcalf's wife, Peggy, had finally gotten involved with Redeemer, and had become chair of an altar guild that was more like an ecclesiastical garment factory. Talented seamstresses and tailors sewed a collection of altar frontals, funeral palls (casket covers), Fisherfolk banners, wedding banners, and vestments for each liturgical season; in all, about 50 stoles and 25 chasubles and palliums (tunic-like vestments) for the priests. It was enough to outfit a large cathedral. And the handiwork on the vestments was not only magnificent, but all of it was free.

The beauty of Redeemer attracted Jonathan Goldhor, who dropped out of the University of Illinois Law School to join. When he informed his parents of his impending decision, his father's only question was, "Are they pacifists?" Jonathan replied that people had been known to walk out of Graham's sermons urging young men not to register for the draft, which satisfied his parents. He arrived Christmas of 1975 to find an Anglican paradise: worship, households, sacrifice, strong Christian men in leadership—everything he had been searching for. He stayed with the Minors, who were giving away their best car to someone.

Gradually, he began to notice that not everyone followed the party line, especially in the highest levels of leadership. You did not advance to junior or senior elder by rocking the boat. Instead, Jonathan noticed, being a junior elder was like making partner at a major law firm. There were things going on, he knew, but no one seemed to be speaking out against them. And this was a group that Graham had taught to speak out. That is, their voices might be the only ones God had available, and if they did not speak up, no one else would. But no one wanted to sacrifice their spiritual careers at Redeemer. It was the sort of atmosphere where a strong elder could run amok and the one person who had the authority to reign him in, Jeff Schiffmayer, did not have the backbone for it.

Jonathan found several lawyers had gotten to Redeemer before him, among them Bill Linden, a partner in Houston's largest law firm, Vinson & Elkins. It had hundreds of lawyers and took up much of First City Tower in downtown Houston. Bill's office had a formidable view of Houston's southeastern quadrant and he could glimpse Redeemer's bell tower from his window. His specialty was tax law and the earnings from his practice financed a gorgeous home in Houston's Memorial suburb.

Bill and his wife, Martha Ann, and their four children had been attending St. Christopher's Episcopal Church in west Houston, where they met Audrey Tindall, a woman baptized in the Spirit during Graham's first years at Redeemer. On her recommendation, the Lindens went to a Friday night service to check Redeemer out. It was a renewal weekend in 1973, Graham was teaching, and the church was packed. Bill had never seen anything like it: people praising

God with a fervor and intensity he had never seen before, not even in the charismatic prayer group at St. Christopher's. And this group broke all social barriers.

The Lindens were hooked, and they began transitioning to Redeemer. Bill had an innate way of finding his way to the top people of an organization and The Fishermen, Inc. got wind of him and asked him for some tax advice, which he gave gratis. He and Graham hit it off and Bill visited the various communities with Graham, giving them tax advice and becoming good friends with the Pulkinghams. Bill was the kind of person you wanted to get to know. He had contacts, influence, personality and money he was willing to donate to the church. Redeemer was not exactly the kind of church up-and-coming lawyers would join to get known about town, but Bill saw something real there that no law office could offer him.

O NE December day, Jane Clowe heard a knock at her back door and, when she opened it, found a disconsolate Marilyn Mazak bearing a Christmas gift for Jane—a pair of earrings.

"Jane," said Marilyn, her eyes filling with tears, "no matter what happens, always remember that I love you."

Jane stood there, bewildered by Marilyn's odd statement. Then again, the last three months of her life had been odd, if not bizarre, ever since the elders decided Jane needed major deliverance. Following a Redeemer custom to isolate a person from their normal environment so they can concentrate on the person's problems, Jim moved his own wife into the household of his mistress, for he and Marilyn were at it again. Jane was told she was crazy—living in fantasy—and that she needed to be disciplined at the Mazak's house for awhile. She was assigned to the "laundry ministry" for the huge household, bunked in with several other women, all ostensibly in need of deliverance, and told she could see her children for only three hours a week on Sunday afternoons, and have dinner but once a week with her husband—on Friday nights. The worst thing about that was Marilyn's family had to be present at these dinners, during which Marilyn and Jim would sit and talk with each other. None of this helped Jane's manic depressive state, and she was tortured by the fear that if she disobeyed her counselors, she would be disobeying God.

Then Jim left for England for a few weeks, leaving Jane to the whims of her counselors. When one of the elders informed her they were planning to cut off all contact with her husband, she panicked. Having no other way to access money, she quietly planned to sell her Gibson guitar to get a plane ticket back to

Midland—anything to get away from Redeemer.

She made the mistake of telling her plans to her counselors, who promptly accused her of trying to take control. Terrified, Jane packed her clothes and fled to the home of Ethel Frid, a widow since Earle's death several years before. Jane poured out her story to Ethel, but Ethel, sensing somehow that the winds were soon to change at Redeemer, counseled Jane to stay put.

"If you'll submit, God will deliver you from what's going on," she said.

"Ethel," sobbed Jane, "all I want is the will of the Lord in my life. This is a hard price, but if you think that's right, then I'll do it."

She sadly returned to the Mazaks to await Jim's return from England, then had a disturbing dream that her husband was having an affair with Marilyn. Not knowing she had subconsciously guessed the truth, she dutifully told one of the elders about the dream. That elder, who knew of Jim's dalliances with Marilyn the first time Jim had confessed them, informed Jane her dream was from hell. It was all very much like an old movie where the leading characters connive to make their target think she is crazy so she will die and they can get at the inheritance.

Jim, meanwhile, was tortured by his own conscience. What especially drew him to Marilyn was her relationship with the Lord. Their renewed affair was sporadic and infrequent, because of the long hours they both worked.

Finally, Jim broke down and told Grover, one of the few church leaders he fully trusted. Grover made a desperate phone call to Graham in Scotland.

Graham had had a premonition of the problem. Earlier that fall, he had been in the country for a Community of Communities conference. Jim Clowe's presentation of the deliverance ministry sounded eerie and gnostic to Graham. Jim's references to his "assistant" Marilyn alerted Graham that something fishy was brewing.

Although there was no question of keeping Jim on as an elder this time, Jim had developed quite a following at the church. Unless Graham intervened, things were heading for a split, so it fell to Graham to talk Jim into somehow leaving the East End. Graham came up with an idea: He would invite the Clowes to come to Scotland on the pretext of investigating community. Jim tearfully assented, but did not tell his wife the real reason they were moving. The story put out to the parish was that the elders had had a falling-out and that Jim had to go. Not only did Jim want to confess it all to Jane, but he wanted to go in front of the congregation and tell all. But Graham refused to let him, saying it would shock Jane into a depression she would never recover from, plus it would stir the waters at Redeemer. Jane was too mentally unstable, Graham thought. On top of everything else, he didn't want a suicide on his hands.

Only the administrators of the various ministries were told the real reason for the Clowes' departure. But the rest of the congregation had to be told something, so one cold Tuesday evening in January 1977, 280 people gathered to hear Jack Minor hand down the latest decisions from the elders.

He came to the mike, read a few verses from the Bible, then in his breezy, low-key way informed his listeners that the church planned to downscale its 75-person full-time work force. More people would have jobs in the outer world, he explained. The elders wanted to get back to Scripture.

"There's been ways that we might not have given the emphasis we should have," he said. "We were committed to that a long way back. If we were away from it, we sure want to get back to the Lord's word."

There would be fewer people in households, he announced; less dependency on the church and on counseling "to solve all our problems for us"; a de-emphasis on hierarchy, structures, titles, and organization; a decentralization of households; and the abolition of titles such as "administrators, counselors, heavies, and strong women."

The audience laughed at that last addition, but hereafter, Jack said, leaders would merely be known as "members of the pastor's staff." With counseling suspended at the church, the leaders now wanted "more of an open mind" in regard to medication, therapy, psychiatry, surgery, and doctors outside the community. At one point in his sermon, he mentioned people even having fun in households, a remark that a newcomer named Jackie Kraft did not find funny.

If we're having fun, we're in the wrong place, she thought. She was giving her salary and car to the community, having moved in with a couple named Brian and Mary McCullough. She had next to no money and felt her individual preferences blotted out when it came to household spending. Once, with a quarter in her pocket, she went to a blue jean sale at the resale shop. She had asked one of the women in her household, "Who's going there to buy my pair?" "Well," the woman said, "I'll have to check with Brian and Mary to see if we need another pair of jeans."

Gee, thought Jackie angrily, *I can't even spend a quarter the way I want to.*

Commitments made by people like Jackie never had any expiration date. The assumption was that all those in their early 20s, just out of college, talented, single, and celibate, would stay in a household forever. Instead of investing in careers, they worked at lightweight jobs and poured all the richness of their lives into the household and into the Friday and Sunday services. The Fisherfolk teams were the most bound up, for how does one court, marry, have babies, and buy a home while traveling about the globe trying to renew the

English-speaking world? Graham and many of the other leaders already had children and homes when they got involved with Redeemer, which is why they were slow to realize the growing resentment of those forced to work extra years for such benefits.

As the spring of 1977 glided into view, the large, 150-plus singles population that undergirded Redeemer suffered an enormous crisis of confidence. Careers and schooling that had been lightly discarded in years past now became tremendously important as people realized the church was not going to take care of them for the rest of their lives. No one had thought through what would happen if people left and started dividing up property. But now they were seeing with their own eyes how one couple—the male was the son of a leader—was given a house by the church. When they sold the place, they pocketed the profits, and there was little anyone would do about it.

Some of the singles had already bolted—people like Diane Angel, an artist who lived in Montrose and was a new Christian. She was already living in household when she unexpectedly met Larry Reed in the produce department of Weingarten's, a spiffy food store. After she dropped a bag-load of apples on the floor, Larry, an architecture student with a flaming red Afro, gallantly helped her pick them up, then walked away. They met again in just about every aisle, prompting Larry to make a series of wisecracks. When he ended up behind her in the checkout line, they began to talk, and he offered to carry her groceries to the car. When she helped bag his groceries, he asked for her phone number. Mentioning that she never gave out her phone number, she gave it out nevertheless.

Learning she was also a dancer, he asked her out to the ballet. When he came by her household to pick her up, he noticed all the Christian posters on the walls.

"Well," he said brightly, "who's the Jesus freak here?"

"I guess we all are," she replied sweetly. What a shame she was a fanatic, he thought. But the two became friends and eventually he came to a Redeemer service. Diane gave him a Bible for Christmas, which he read cover to cover, and her mother sent him a copy of one of the decade's bestsellers: *The Late, Great Planet Earth* by Hal Lindsey. He began attending church regularly and dating Diane, and at some point the following spring, became a Christian. There was a no-dating rule in effect in the households—no exclusive relationships were allowed. By the summer of 1976, Larry and Diane were getting serious. While sitting on the back porch of his place, Larry felt an inner voice nudge him to propose.

"Will you marry me?" he blurted out and she, before she knew what she was really saying, responded with, "Well, I'd be delighted." They both turned cartwheels in the street, but the hardest part was yet to come. He offered to move into household. No sooner had he done so than the couple were told to "lay their relationship down." Both were told to quit their jobs. Larry was put on maintenance crew, and Diane ended up substitute teaching. Her household had needed the money she got from her former job, but Diane was told she needed to learn to be submissive and depend on others' decisions so she was not in control of her life. Her household head was particularly abrasive; fortunately the Minors, in whose household Larry lived, gave him a few dollars on Friday nights and told them to spend a little time alone with each other. But that November, they were told to forget their relationship completely—after all, several people in community had been waiting years to marry. Moreover, Larry was to forget his architecture career, despite six years of study.

The elders were soon to learn they could no longer rule by fiat. Larry stood up to them, informing them he and Diane were getting married, which they did that next spring, although they had to leave their households to do so. Other singles followed suit and the church's weekend calendar began to fill up with weddings—about one a month for three years—as fast as the newly liberated singles could arrange them. Many of the married people had to quit their jobs at the church, because there were no longer any singles available as nannies to raise their children.

In May 1977, the story of a bizarre occurrence hit the papers although it had taken place at Redeemer some months before. Controversial deprogrammer Ted Patrick was hired to go after 28-year-old Peter Willis, a co-leader of one of the households. Alarmed at her son's increasing involvement at Redeemer, his mother hired Patrick to kidnap her son and sequester him in a hotel room near Intercontinental Airport. Then the mother lured Peter into the hotel room. Peter knew something was up when he saw Patrick, who is black, standing there—he knew his mother did not like black people. For the next 17 hours, Ted Patrick tried to talk him out of going to Redeemer by making him listen to taped testimonies of people who had left cults. When Peter tried to escape, another man, known only as "Goose," blocked the door. Peter retaliated by talking incessantly at bedtime so that none of his roommates could sleep. The next morning, for some unexplained reason, both the deprogrammer and Peter's mother decided to drop him off at the church. When the *Houston Chronicle*'s new religion writer, Louis Moore, called Bishop Milton Richardson to get his reaction, the bishop merely replied that Redeemer was a *"bona fide* Episcopal church in good standing with the Diocese of Texas."

The following November, Moore again interviewed Patrick, who said he was convinced more than ever that Redeemer was a cult. The headline ran: "Deprogrammer: I will strike at Redeemer Church again," along with a drawing of Redeemer, with Patrick's picture superimposed on it.

Clouds were gathering fast over the troubled church and word of its problems reached Michael Harper in England. People who had read his book and then experienced Redeemer were writing to him to let him know of the discrepancies. Harper could see through Graham, and he counseled at least one member of the Fisherfolk, Tim Whipple, to leave. At one point, Michael wrote an article for a new British charismatic magazine, *Renewal*, on what had gone wrong with Redeemer's original vision. Out of courtesy, he sent copies to Jeff and Graham. They asked him not to run it. He agreed, and so the article never saw the light of day.

But the problems were there. Friday night service attendance dropped to less than 500, half of what it had been two years before. Redeemer's yearly church directory went through so many changes after its December 1976 publication that the church office issued several addendums, then published a revised directory seven months later that was half the size of the old one.

Meanwhile, the Clowes were still in Scotland, seeing very little of Graham. Though he was cathedral provost, Graham was there maybe one week every two months, and when he was there, he was hitting Jim up for money to help support the place. But most times, Graham was off traveling. What they did get to see was the impoverished lifestyle of the Cumbrae community, which ate mostly beans and rice, so scant were the finances. Cumbrae was austere, niggardly even, and the two women in charge while Graham was gone rode herd on the other members. Also there were Grady and Janice Manley, the pentecostals who had attended Redeemer in the 1960s. They had moved to California but kept in touch with Graham. He invited them to join him in Cumbrae, so they moved there in August 1975.

As soon as they had arrived, they noticed a change in their old friend. His emphasis had turned from theological to sociological, as he wanted to make a social statement to Scottish society by identifying with the poor. True, the community lived at the poverty level, but a resort island off the west coast of Scotland was not exactly where the poor hung out. The difference seemed lost on the Millport populace, Grady realized, because the community had little contact with them except during Sunday morning services. He wondered if it was not meant more for worldwide consumption, so the community could *say* it was working with the poor. In reality, the Millport people looked upon the community with some suspicion. The Scottish were very blunt, and they had some pointed questions about why the community was there.

The Manleys noticed how Graham had begun downgrading the charismatic renewal and relating more to the evangelical left, especially *Sojourners*, which was filling its pages with editorials against U.S. foreign policy in Central America. Celebration's Post Green branch was creating *Towards Renewal*, later renamed *Grassroots*, a magazine that was a *Sojourners* lookalike with a British sheen. Despite all the talk of renewal, Graham had lost his delicate balance between charismatic renewal and social action. Grady once heard Graham assert that Indian societies and cultures, through the strength of their family ties, brought about miraculous healings, as if the community dynamic was what healed people. *That has nothing to do with God at all,* Grady thought. *Graham, this doesn't sound like you.*

Meanwhile, the Mazaks ended up in Colorado, running smack dab into John Farra's heavy-handed governing policies. The Mazaks were not allowed to read newspapers, and their children were split up among several different households. "Just keep your mouth shut," Marilyn told her husband, "and I'll get you out of here. I know how the pastors think."

In the end, in order to leave in October 1977, they had to lie. They left their son Robert and the twins Don and Michael there to finish out the semester, giving the community legal guardianship of the kids. Robert returned in January. Then Don came back to Houston and the Mazaks nabbed their son while he was attending a wedding. Bob Mazak called Bert Womack, one of the community elders, to inform him that Don was not coming back to Colorado.

"Well, you're the parent," Womack replied, "but I don't want to sacrifice him on the altar of your paranoia."

The Mazaks kept in contact with their remaining son, Michael, by phone until one day they discovered the community was not allowing him to talk to them. Marilyn got a lawyer, who filed a writ of habeas corpus.

The matter hit the newspapers when they showed up in Harris County Family Court for a hearing to retrieve Michael from Woodland Park. It did not help that reporters bandied about the words "commune" and "sect" in their reporting. The Mazaks admitted in the hearing that they had signed a legal paper granting one of the elders parental authority over Michael, but did so only to allow elders to take care of Michael in case of a medical emergency. Never, they said, did they dream the community would use the document to sequester their son against his will. In fact, they had left the community after discovering that at least one of the elders was whipping their sons without their permission. Then Donald and Robert took the stand to tell their side of the story. After their parents left the community, Robert said, the leaders told him and his brothers that his parents "had a problem" and did not really want them. Leaders told him what to say to his parents on the phone and asked him to turn over letters they wrote him.

As the writ made its way to a court in Colorado, Marilyn's persistent phone calls got her in touch with an aide to Bishop Frey, who assured her he would take care of the problem. But what really caught Frey's attention were nightly broadcasts by Channel 13 KTRK-TV personality Marvin Zindler, a bizarre sort who was famous for his exposés of unclean restaurants and various scandals. Hearing of the Mazak episode, Zindler decided the community was a cult and did a week's worth of broadcasts on the matter. Incensed, Frey called Channel 13 and asked to speak to the news director. The employee on the phone refused.

"We're not used to the Episcopal Church being called a cult," Frey explained.

"I don't know anything about that," the employee replied.

"Fine," said the bishop, who had worked a brief stint as a disk jockey for KATL-AM in Houston in the 1940s. "Maybe you can give me the address of the FCC so I can file a complaint." The employee ran to get a supervisor and the station agreed to fly a hostile Zindler up to investigate. Frey and Bert Womack greeted Zindler as he arrived in a white tie and black suit. The three men had no sooner met on the grounds of the community when Zindler realized he knew them. Zindler, too, had worked at KATL with Frey and in law enforcement with Bert, years before in Houston. He had not realized they were now Episcopal priests. Zindler's attitude took a sharp turn toward the more congenial and later, Frey and Grover flew to Houston to tape another Zindler show.

Michael eventually came home and his parents took him to the adolescent unit of a psychological hospital to be deprogrammed. A few months later, in the closing days of November 1978, all the rhetoric on communes and control would come back to haunt everyone.

Out of the jungles of Guyana came a horror story so profound that for the initial days afterward, few believed it. A Disciples of Christ minister named Jim Jones had formed a cult group, People's Temple, in California. He and his followers moved to the jungles of South America where, upon Jones's command, some 900 of them committed mass suicide by drinking a mixture of cyanide and Kool Aid. Horrifying photos ran in news magazines of the purple Kool Aid vat, the bloated bodies, the cache of arms, and Jones's own body.

Jones called himself "God" and a reincarnation of Jesus who pretended to heal his disciples by drawing forth "cancers" from their bodies that were actually bloody chicken gizzards. Not until early December did some of the grisly details of their deaths—along with the murders of three journalists, plus California Congressman Leo Ryan—become publicized. It was a macabre Christmas present for the religious world, showing when and how religion and insanity merged. Most observers saw little difference between People's Temple and the Mazak lawsuit. The events in Guyana seemed designed to frustrate and confuse the faithful and make all religious commitment odious in the eyes of the world. As questions began ricocheting in the press about communities, the whole community movement gave a collective shudder. Their accountability systems were little better than what Jim Jones had started with, and it could have been them lying dead in the jungles of Guyana.

By then, the Mazak marriage was falling apart and in 1979, Bob and Marilyn divorced.

A s the words of prophecy flowed out over the stadium that warm July evening, 45,000 people dropped to their knees in semi-shock.

"Mourn and weep," the speaker said, "for the body of My Son is broken."

"Mourn and weep," he repeated, "for the body of My Son is broken. Come before Me with broken hearts and contrite spirits, for the body of My Son is broken. Come before Me with sackcloth and ashes. Come before Me with tears and mourning, for the body of My Son is broken.

"I would have made you one new man, but the body of My Son is broken. I would have made you a light on a mountaintop, a city glorious and splendorous that all the world would have seen, but the body of My Son is broken."

All was silent. The voice continued.

"The light is dim, My people are scattered. The body of My Son is broken. I gave all I had, in the body and blood of My Son. It spilled on the earth. The body of My Son is broken.

"Turn from the sins of your fathers and walk in the ways of My Son. Return to the plan of your Father. Return to the purpose of your God. The body of My Son is broken. Mourn and weep, for the body of My Son is broken."

Silence fell for several minutes.

Some called it the making of history, that immense conference of charismatics that overwhelmed Kansas City in July 1977. Except for Billy Graham's Congress on Evangelism in Lausanne, Switzerland, in 1973, it was the largest worldwide Christian event in decades. More than 300 reporters, more than half of them from the secular media, covered it. What partly drew them was the program presence of President Jimmy Carter's sister, Ruth Carter Stapleton. Carter had been elected president the year before on a wave of born-again popularity and on the closing night of the conference telephoned a message, asking for prayer. These charismatic Christians were at the apex of their power, able to ford rivers uncrossed since before the Reformation. They were able to bring together Catholics, Protestants, Orthodox, and even Messianic Jews. This was ecumenism that outdid the National and World Councils of Churches and challenged the mainline churches to come up with something better.

What the press saw were 45,000 people at one big charismatic party, nearby highways filled with cars and campers laden with "Jesus is Lord" bumper stickers. Exuberance ran high. There was a tender presence of the Holy Spirit seemingly everywhere. Destiny was in the air as nearly everyone one saw on the elevators and in the streets had been baptized in the Spirit. For those four days in July, the charismatics took over downtown Kansas City, meeting in the city's Arrowhead Stadium for evening sessions and in the surrounding hotels for morning and afternoon sessions. Undergirding the conference were volunteers from South Bend's People of Praise, which numbered 800 members in 40 households and headed a non-profit corporation, Charismatic Renewal Services. The whole operation had moved to Kansas City for the conference.

Fully half of the registrants were Roman Catholics, a majority that was stunningly apparent the Sunday morning of the conference, as row after row of Catholic priests proceeded into the stadium, forming a sea of white robes, their hands lifted in praise. But the Catholics did not dominate, as some Protestants had feared would happen. Instead, unity stole over the conference like a gentle wind, and several warring factions of the Messianic Jews, and among the shepherding versus non-shepherding groups, somewhat reconciled.

Art Katz, a fiery Jewish charismatic with a bent for making listeners as uncomfortable as possible, broke the spiritual ice at the Messianic Jewish workshop on Saturday afternoon, acidly pointing out that the Jews were responsible for the Holocaust because their first-century leaders had arranged for Jesus's death. He then had the Jews in the audience ask the Gentiles for forgiveness and vice versa; meanwhile, the Jewish leaders on stage were to wash each others' feet because of their disagreements. Katz's ability to tear open the surface politeness at the conference and get to the seething differences underneath brought down the house. A delegation of Catholic priests approached the stage, saying they wanted to wash the Jewish leaders' feet. The Jewish leaders washed the priests' feet, and the affair culminated in a healing service.

During the evening sessions, participants delighted in a black oval scoreboard suspended above the stadium that displayed messages, "hallelujah"s, "praise the Lord"s, and decent line drawings of the speakers. Every so often, the misty sound of singing in the Spirit would fill the stadium. But the true highlights of the conference were the prophecies that blazed through the summer night air. Night after night, the charismatics were reminded to repent of their divisions, their mutual hostility, and their fear and mistrust. Whenever things got bubbly, another prophecy would cut across the crowd, imploring for repentance. There was little time to mull over all this, for another speaker would soon be announced. Organizers had stacked the program with so many speakers so that the plenary speaker often did not get to the podium until after 10 p.m. To some it seemed that what God wanted was not forthcoming, and by the time the conference neared the end of its final full day on Saturday, the wished-for brokenness had not arrived and the prophecies were beginning to sound a mite impatient.

That night, Archbishop Bill Burnett, by now a fixture on the charismatic scene following his baptism in the Spirit five years before in his chapel, spoke on South African apartheid, laying the blame for it on the shoulders of the church. After his message and a song came several prophecies, the first one a biting chastisement of the leaders for serving themselves first and not serving God, in effect accusing the American listeners of committing sins similar to those of the South Africans. Another prophecy begged those present to humble themselves and kneel before God, which the whole stadium did. Finally, Ralph Martin, the 34-year-old Word of God leader who had taken a back seat at the conference, came to the mike to deliver a prophecy he had been mulling for several days. It was the fatal salvo, the "mourn and weep" prophecy. For a few eternal moments, there was no clapping, no singing; like the breaking of the seventh seal, there was silence on earth as in heaven.

Perhaps heaven was waiting to see what the charismatics would do with all this unity, power, and people. Would the reconciliation stick? Would the repentance last? At first, it seemed it would. Ecumenical citywide Pentecost day celebrations took place around the country in 1978, and charismatic clergy groups formed, vowing to work together to take their cities for God. Meanwhile, a new creature of the 1970s, the nondenominational charismatic church, had sprung up and charismatic Methodists, Presbyterians, Catholics, and Episcopalians were waking up to the fact that such churches, plus the Assemblies of God, were siphoning off their best members at top speed. Fearing future losses, the Catholic renewal would turn in on itself, and in a few years undergo a major split between its two powerhouse communities in Ann Arbor and South Bend. It meant a philosophical split as well as a power struggle between the leaders of both communities.

Buoyed by the threatening 1975 prophecies, the Ann Arbor group, led by Ralph Martin and Steve Clark, were more and more talking about battening down the hatches for hard times to come. They set about developing Word of God as almost a nation state with its own customs, lingo, structured male-female relations, authority structure, accepted recreation, and reading material. From their experiences and those of friends at various Catholic universities, they knew pluralism and compromise were eating out the heart of the Gospel in the church. If the recent prophecies about a time of national collapse, followed by severe persecution of Christians, proved true, then Christians, they said, needed to unite in a group of strong communities. They saw such communities as a bulwark against the approaching evil, an army to do effective battle against Satan. They would be prepared, disciplined, and trained because of strong authority in their midst, flowing through the ranks from powerful leaders. The South Bend leaders noted this trend with mounting dismay. South Bend was more comfortable in the culture and saw no need to separate itself from it.

The Protestants had their own struggles and compromises. Some of the charismatic groups, such as those of the Episcopalians and the Presbyterians, tried to broaden their appeal by dropping "charismatic" from their mastheads. Except for the Southern Baptists and the Nazarenes, charismatic clergy were no longer being kicked out of their churches. But neither were large numbers of people being baptized in the Spirit. Something had died. As the years passed, those who attended the Kansas City conference noted with some dismay that instead of being the accelerator for the charismatic movement, Kansas City had proved to be its apex.

ABOVE: The exterior of the Church
of the Redeemer, Houston, Texas
(photo by the author)

RIGHT: The Rev. Graham
Pulkingham, age 43, 1970
(photo by Larry Evans, courtesy
Houston Metropolitan Research Center,
Houston Public Library)

LEFT: A communal meal at
the crowded Eckert
household, early 1970s
(photo by Bill Clough, courtesy
Houston Metropolitan Research
Center, Houston Public Library)

Bob Eckert, early 1970s
(photo by Bill Clough, courtesy Houston Metropolitan
Research Center, Houston Public Library)

The Rev. Dennis Bennett
on the cover of the
October 1960 *Full Gospel
Men's Voice* magazine, at
the dawn of the Episcopal
charismatic renewal

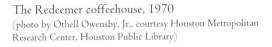

The Redeemer coffeehouse, 1970
(photo by Othell Owensby, Jr., courtesy Houston Metropolitan
Research Center, Houston Public Library)

LEFT: George Mims at
the organ, summer 1980
(photo by Debbie Scott)

RIGHT: A photo of
Graham Pulkingham
that appeared in the
May/June 1976 issue
of *Sojourners* magazine
(photo by Ed Spivey)

©D Scott

The Rev. Jeff Schiffmayer, 1982
(photo by Debbie Scott)

Graham and Betty Pulkingham, with
daughter Martha, at a 1980 church picnic
(photo by Debbie Scott)

The Rev. Ladd
Fields celebrates
Communion during
the Redeemer
reunion in June
1987; the priest
to his left is the
Rev. Paul Felton
(photo by Debbie Scott)

Redeemer's clergy, past and present, gather for a special service
in the late 1980s. From left: Abdias Avalos, Ladd Fields, Graham
Pulkingham, Alan Newton, and Paul Felton
(photo by the author)

Portrayed here is the insignia on the T-shirts made for Redeemer's 1987 church reunion
(photo by the author)

Cliff Wilson with one of his daughters, late 1980s
(photo by the author)

Debbie Scott at a tea for Redeemer members at her home
(photo by the author)

Martha Ann and Bill Linden celebrate New Year's Eve with friends, 1988
(photo by the author)

LEFT: Front of the South
College of the Cathedral of
the Isles, Cumbrae, Scotland
(photo by the author)

RIGHT: North American
Congress on the Holy
Spirit and World
Evangelization, 1987
(photo by Debbie Scott)

Redeemer dancers perform at a Houston street festival, 1988.
From left: Stephanie Sawyer, Linda Myers, and the author
(photo by Debbie Scott)

LEFT: All Saints Episcopal Church
in Aliquippa, Pennsylvania,
in the late 1980s
(photo by the author)

RIGHT: The chapel at Trinity
Episcopal School for Ministry
in Ambridge, Pennsylvania
(photo by the author)

Bishop William Frey, right, poses with
Canon Michael Green at Trinity's 1992
commencement exercises
(photo courtesy Trinity Episcopal School for Ministry)

Pittsburgh Bishop Alden Hathaway presides
at the dedication of a new commons hall at
Trinity Episcopal School for Ministry in
1991. To his left is Trinity professor Steve
Smith and his son, Andrew
(photo by the author)

The Rev. David Wilkerson stands outside of his Times Square Church in Manhattan, September 1989.
(photo by the author)

News clippings from the *Beaver County Times* and the *Pittsburg Post-Gazette* in 1992 and early 1993, telling of Graham Pulkingham's removal from the priesthood and his death
(photo by the author)

CHAPTER 16

The Feast of St. Thomas

"Everliving God, who strengthened your apostle Thomas with firm and certain faith in your Son's resurrection: Grant us so perfectly and without doubt to believe in Jesus Christ, our Lord and our God, that our faith may never be found wanting in your sight. . . ."

—The Book of Common Prayer

O N Memorial Day 1977, Bruce Durst, the son of Pentecostal missionaries and a law school graduate, arrived at Redeemer. Thoughtful, quiet, and dependable, he had grown up in Mali and to him, Redeemer was a strange kettle of fish. When he asked to move into a household, he was told, "There are two guiding principles for moving into a household: You either have a ministry or you need ministry." Thus inspired, Bruce took up residence at the Mims household for three years and three months. After awhile, he could see the community buckling under the strain. Redeemer still had an international reputation, and word had not gotten out yet about the break-up of the households. People were still arriving by the truckload to try household living.

Household living could be quite demanding. Fortunately for Bruce, the Mims household was a continuing fiesta of creative, fun-loving people who would sing around the table and light candles for most evening meals. They were fiercely loyal to their household members, while at the same time possessive about anything that took that person outside the household for a lengthy amount of time. With the Mims, their family was your family; their jokes were your jokes. George and Leslie used their 10-foot-long, cedar dining table as an excuse to celebrate, have guests, and decorate. They did not want to look poor, so they used nice dishes, elegant table settings, and cloth napkins. As many as 20 people at a time lived in their home on McKinney Street. Bruce was a little disenchanted with the teaching—or lack of it—at the church. A reporter from *Texas Monthly* who visited Redeemer at the time also found the sermons less than inspiring.

"Everyone knows Episcopalians can't preach," the reporter wrote, "but this sermon was a pathetic effort, even by Episcopal standards. With a casualness that was initially appealing, the young priest had chosen to walk part way down one of the aisles where, in his white robes, he became a luminous island in the sea of the congregation. Still, none of this informality made up for his lack of formal preparation. He was not at all certain what he wanted to say and tried to obscure that clear fact by a series of Bible readings. 'And then this morning, I thought of this passage,' he would say before rather long hiatuses while he searched through the Bible for his text. After reading, he would offer as interpretation some stupefyingly clichéd homilies or just as often say, 'Well, I don't remember right now why I chose that passage. Anyway,' he would go on, his voice gaining slightly in strength, 'the Lord has just given me another message.' But these messages were only more homilies. 'We all need to love one another.'"

With the households disintegrating, it became no big deal for those who remained to view sexually explicit movies. Word was leaking out about more adulteries. One of the younger men was told by his male counselor that there was no hope for his mental health unless he had sex with him. Two friends told Bruce they had had affairs. Although one had repented, immorality didn't seem to have a stigma anymore. After all, word had leaked out that a top church elder had engaged in adultery, so why shouldn't they?

Some elders bought expensive cars and motorcycles, the married women were buying $90 dresses and gloves and hats at Casual Corner, and the only ones who were not making out well were the singles who moved out of their households with only the things they carried in. Drinking was also acceptable now, a real switch from Redeemer's near-temperance days only a short while before. The world did not present a danger for Redeemer folks now that their disenchantment with the church was so deep. As it veered toward the theologically liberal, it was, Bruce thought, almost as if Redeemer folks believed no one else needed to be saved. Once, a group performing at Redeemer told of their work with street people. As the leader described the urgency of spreading the Gospel, he added, "and I know that is your priority as well."

"No, it isn't," the person next to Bruce muttered under his breath.

Things got more confusing. In the early 1970s, hardly anyone had a TV, for they were seen as distractions to the common life. In fact, one elder had urged everyone to sell their TV sets. Now the leaders were saying that TVs were OK. As more singles abandoned their jobs as nannies or maintenance workers for the careers and schooling they had set aside years before, the full-time people at the church were left in the lurch. No longer could they depend on an underclass of singles to raise their kids.

One household administrator, Harriet Hogle, had seen how the households were getting out of control but felt too intimidated to make a stink about it with the elders. She had some visions of Redeemer, one of which was of a perfect rosebud with a raindrop on it. The raindrop stood for the sin of pride. Another time, she saw Redeemer gutted, as if a bomb had fallen on it. All that remained were jagged sides and rising smoke. As she contemplated the horrible scene, the Lord reminded her that he had put His Spirit and light in that place and no matter what happened there, His Spirit would not leave. She, however, left in 1978 to create a better life for her and her two daughters in Austin.

That year ended on a particularly grim note. Two nights before Christmas, one of the couples from the church was returning late to their home on Jefferson Street, only to find a man hiding in their apartment. Holding a knife to their three-year-old son's throat, the intruder tied up the husband, threw a blanket over his head, and raped his wife—who had recently given birth to a second child—as the boy watched, uncomprehending. The incident sent a deep tremor through the church, as members realized once again the price they, too, could pay for carrying on this social experiment in a dangerous neighborhood. Although news of the rape was carried on the "Redeemer grapevine," it was not addressed publicly, for fear that people would be frightened and move away. Instead, the message conveyed at church was that they should pay any price to live in community. Earlier that year, a single woman was taking out the trash when a man snuck into her unlocked apartment while she was not looking. He surprised her when she walked back in, raped her, then dragged her outside as if to kill her. She created enough noise to attract the neighbors' attention and cause him to drop her.

The one thing that helped people forget their hardships was the exquisite music at the church. It was obvious Betty and Mimi's music was going places, partly due to George Mims, who promoted it, provided orchestrations for it, and performed it all over the world. It was selling extremely well in England, where Jeanne Harper had collaborated with Betty and Mimi on two popular songbooks that set the tone for the entire British renewal. Fisherfolk music conveyed the ambiguities of complex 20th-century life, where no one was wholly bad or wholly good and everything was seen in shades of gray. As the music matured, it talked about people with quirks and neuroses and worries, but it also got harder to sing. Although the choral adaptations and new Mass settings were magnificent, they demanded more sophistication and ability to harmonize; talents way beyond the abilities of smaller churches. Unlike the older days, regular Redeemer members who composed songs now rarely got their music performed. There was no coffeehouse in which to try out their compositions, and all the creativity was assumed to come from England, Scotland, or Colorado.

In 1978, the church got a new organ that required the painting-over of parts of the mural to allow space for the larger pipes. George was commissioned by the Episcopal Standing Commission on Church Music to compile a hymnal supplement of Redeemer music. Immediately, the Redeemer music ministry went into high gear. George's assistants, Charles Mallory and Ruth Newlander—she lived near NASA, and drove 25 miles to the church to work every day for George for no pay—were the worker bees who helped him do most of the work. All of the songs had to be run by an official hymnal text committee in New York, some of whose members got the shivers when confronted by some of the charismatic texts. They were especially repulsed by Brian Howard's "If I Were a Butterfly," a simple song with references to fuzzy wuzzy bears, wriggly worms, giggling fish, and smiling crocodiles, and in their view was totally lacking in Episcopal sophistication. George finally managed to sell the song's intergenerational qualities.

Including Betty's "King of Glory" Mass setting, the supplement, *Songs for Celebration*, had 126 musical pieces and sold more than 100,000 copies. Never before had one Episcopal church created a supplement of its own musical output. Music was becoming big business at Redeemer, and serious singers from around the city, many of them not Episcopalians, joined the 85-member choir just to learn under George. Redeemer was pioneering several concepts, including the idea of the organ and guitar working together. Both Betty and George loved the combination and exploited it to its fullest. These years of fat music budgets were George's best at Redeemer, culminating in 1979 when the choir performed at the Episcopal General Convention in Denver.

With everything else at Redeemer in some disarray, George's highly organized choir became the proverbial tail wagging the dog. Choir members devoted a minimum of five hours a week to practice and were expected to attend all rehearsals, sing at major feast days, and at funerals. Guitarists were expected to take lessons in the classical method.

By now, George was a legend at the church, known for his running commentary during the practices, including such odd sayings as, "I can hear two or three nerds first, then the rest of you," or "You sound like the girl in a pretty dress with spinach between her teeth," all of which was delivered with part dictatorial flair and part wheedle. But it worked, and as spiritual anointing faded from the rest of the church, the music got more extravagant. A perfectionist, George would take choir night practice to early morning hours, just to get the right sound for a recording. Although late rehearsals were hellish, the philosophy reigned that life in community was difficult but worthwhile because all the suffering produced beautiful music. George was such a personality in his own right that choir members Paul Frey and Jeff Wilson took to collecting the "Book of George," a collection of his fractured syntax and weird twists of the English language in a free interchange of verbs, nouns, and adverbs in his puns and jokes. On the down side, he left many burned-out choristers in his trail. Being with George, it was said, was like being in the tail of a comet.

IT was around this time that Kathleen Crow dreamt of a ferris wheel with Jeff Schiffmayer standing beside it. A threat of impending disaster hung in the air if the ferris wheel was allowed to start. She tried to warn Jeff but he turned his back. The ferris wheel started. It began to turn, then spin too fast, and bodies began to fly. Kathleen woke up in terror and, soon afterwards, fled the community.

In late 1978, two couples from Portland came to visit Redeemer. Roger and Barbara Colburn stayed with Bob and Nancy Rodgers. He was an up-and-coming elder burdened with a heavy counseling load. The Rodgers had been there since 1973, finally buying a dilapidated home on Rusk Street near the railroad tracks in Eastwood's grimiest precinct. The church remodeling crew helped transform the house, and 13 people came to live with the Rodgers and their three children.

The Colburns were impressed with the daily noontime Eucharist and the music ministry, but that seemed to be all Redeemer had going for it. They quizzed the Rodgers on church happenings and concluded that Redeemer had had a knee-jerk reaction to its problems on deliverance and authority. Once problems had cropped up in both instances, Redeemer had shelved the whole program rather than work out the kinks. The church had swung from one radical solution to another, burning out parishioners in the process.

The other couple, Bob and Louise Carlson, stayed in another household, likewise picking up on the general disenchantment that hung over Redeemer. To them, the music and teaching were not current and the church was living in the past. To them, it was clear the community was gutted, having given away its leadership, and the only spark to it was coming from its outreach branches. The households seemed disorganized, with no weekly meetings, Bible studies, or consistent meal times. And it was obvious the church was under fire; 280 visitors had come in 1978, many of whom fired back judgments and criticisms.

The Carlsons and the Colburns reported these depressing findings to their own community, a group of households connected to Bethlehem Baptist Church, a charismatic congregation in the Portland suburb of Lake Oswego. Bethlehem had sent the community's two main couples to check out Redeemer, because the Texas church had been a beacon of light to communities for years.

Then one of the Redeemer elders bought himself a BMW, which royally fired up another elder, who understood that Redeemer leaders were to lead simple lives. The fight among the leaders got so tense that Graham had to fly in to resolve it. The scuttlebutt was that Graham was still running the parish from afar, and Jeff was losing his grip fast. Graham's own position was changing as well. There was a new bishop over Cumbrae who did not know what to make of Graham. Plus, other Scottish bishops were trying to make sense of the community and how it would endure after Graham's lifetime. The community had drawn up a constitution chartering itself as an Anglican religious order—essentially, a ruling cadre of chapter members with younger or less mature members as novices and postulants. Sympathizers with the community, some of whom could not relocate to whatever city the community lived in, were to be "companions."

Graham's innate restlessness coincided with crises back home. Jeff asked him to consider returning to Redeemer, which, coincidentally, was the very same time Graham wanted to come back as church clergy. Graham cautioned that his return then was tentative, saying that if the date did not work, he would back off. Jeff, however, had no qualms about working with Graham, and the elders and vestry unanimously decided to bring Graham back to Redeemer.

It was around Christmas 1979 when Jeff broke the news. He began with a meandering announcement about an associate priest coming on and the fact that they had found one, but he couldn't come for several months and, Jeff paused as if waiting for a drum roll, "His name is . . . Graham Pulkingham!"

A stunned silence, then laughter, gasps, and applause greeted his words. Neal Michell, a choir member, broke the tension by blurting out, "But is he qualified?"

Everyone knew Graham would never be content as second-in-command.

1980–1982

CHAPTER 17

Christmas

"Why do you cry out over your wound, your pain that has no cure? Because of your great guilt and many sins I have done these things to you."
                                                    —Jeremiah 30:15

DELL HOFFMAN was in agony. He had been part of Redeemer since the late '60s, but a decade later, he was still wondering if Redeemer would work for him. When he had first come to the church, he saw people moving into the neighborhood, leaving jobs, and giving away houses, all to do the work of the Lord. The Neals bought a house sight unseen, believing it was what the Lord wanted for them. Dell was impressed.

"I wish I could hear the Lord that clearly," he confided wistfully to Ralph Neal.

"How *else* does the Lord speak but clearly?" Ralph replied. So, thought Dell, all these fantastic, faithful people were acting as if the Lord spoke to them in the first person. How could he get in on that?

He never did. By 1972, his marriage was on the rocks. Then his wife became pregnant with their first daughter. The Stringhams' counseling helped Dell unpack his traumatic past, but wasn't the baptism in the Spirit supposed to provide the power to override past hurts? That's what had been advertised. Dell had been prayed over 1,000 times, it seemed, but things had never worked. Why had God not come through for him? He began to wonder if God even wanted him. Then his marriage fell apart.

The Clowes' wedding anniversary date was the same as the Hoffmans' and one day Dell got a call from Jane Clowe, offering him a place to stay if he needed one. No one would condemn him or his wife, Jane said.

"You know how it is," she added. "We have our own sins."

"Well, everyone knows Jim Clowe's sin," Dell retorted.

"Wait a minute. What are you saying?"

"Well, everyone knows how you left Redeemer, Jane," said Dell.

"Spell out for me a little bit more what you're trying to say," Jane pressed him.

"Well, everyone knows about Jim's adultery," Dell responded.

"Wait a minute, Dell. Not Jim's wife."

Dell began to apologize, crying out, "Oh my God! what have I done?" as Jane wheedled details out of him. "Forget it," she finally said. "You've done me a favor."

The next few months were a horror as Jane tried to put together the full story. What a dupe she had been. Everyone had known the true story except her. She confronted Jim right away. "Don't leave me," he begged, reminding her he had been faithful in the intervening years. She caught a flight to Midland to talk with her old friend Sam Hulsey, the bishop of Northwest Texas, who was someone she trusted and far removed from Redeemer.

Finally, one of her friends told her that the hush-up was Graham's idea. "It is not expedient for the body of Christ that Jane should know this," he had said. Once Graham got word that Jane had found out, he flew to see her, which was cold comfort considering how many of the church members had known for years of her husband's duplicity. Now the scene at her back door began to truly haunt her as she remembered Marilyn, standing there with the earrings. "Always remember that I love you," Marilyn had said.

"Always remember that I love you."

A few months before Graham's return—"the Second Coming," some joked— Redeemer chose a theme of exile for their Lenten fast of 1980.

"For three years, we have been responding to a condition we have never come to grips with," a parish letter said, quoting verses from the beginning of Jeremiah 30. Various people had had visions, the letter said, of Redeemer burning to the ground. People from the community stood in the church's ashes, their hands raised, praising God and singing and rejoicing. Parishioners needed to repent, the letter said, of their faulty relationships with the Lord and with each other.

Had they read on further in Jeremiah 30, they would have come to verse 23: "For they have done outrageous things in Israel; they have committed adultery with their neighbors' wives and in My name have spoken lies, which I did not tell them to do. I know it and am a witness to it," declares the Lord.

That March, Wally Braud wrote down a prophecy he did not want or like.

"There is a pride and arrogance in this place," he finally jotted down. "If a place of repentance cannot be found, I must break you because I love you." The elders allowed this to be printed in *The Light* that summer, the same time the Pulkingham household arrived in Houston.

Right away, parishioners could see things were indeed different. Instead of going to one of the predominantly Hispanic local schools, the youngest Pulkingham son, David, was bused across town to a magnet school. Outlooks had changed since the mid-1960s, when his brother Bill was forced to attend Lantrip, where he was regularly beat up. The parish bought the Pulkinghams a house on quiet Altic Street, did $15,000 worth of remodeling on it, and outfitted it with furniture and tools scrounged from around the church, including such niceties as 18 matched iced tea glasses. The Pulkinghams had presented the parish with a list of things they wanted, including a stereo and a TV, and people gave up cherished personal possessions so the alternate rectory would be fully stocked. It was clearly a more comfortable, middle-class existence for the family. Nevertheless, the congregation was excited to get them back, and even presented Betty with the old piano she had left behind years ago.

Graham also announced that Betty, Mimi, and several other members of his household were to share in the worship ministry with George. The household arrived at church during a Redeemer worship conference, and from the Mimses' perspective, they did not wait until it ended to begin criticizing. However, Graham had not reckoned on how huge the leadership vacuum at Redeemer was and how George had stepped into the breach. George, with several albums, a hymnal supplement, and rave reviews from Denver's General Convention under his belt, was far more powerful than when the Pulkinghams had left eight years earlier. Moreover, George and Leslie were furious at the intrusion. That the vagueness of his job's chain of command had never been straightened out 10 years before was coming back to haunt him. Parishioners used the opportunity to complain to Graham about George's autocratic style, and Leslie finally went to see Jeff to complain that the Pulkinghams were kicking her husband around.

"To be honest, I prefer Betty Jane's style," Jeff replied.

"Then why don't you have the guts to fire him?" Leslie flared. She resigned from the worship ministry a week later.

That summer, Grover and John Farra went head-to-head over how the Colorado community should be run, and neither would budge. Grover had noticed how much like a closed order drill their life had become. It took an experienced, mature person to even think of joining that community, which tended to discourage most Christians from approaching them. The relationship became so painful that they finally brought in Graham to arbitrate. Graham asked whose lifestyle the community imitated.

"John's," said Grover.

"It looks like you're insisting on a multiplicity of lifestyles while the bulk of the people are comfortable with the way things are," Graham observed.

So the Newmans returned to Houston, taking with them a vital community support in the community and in John and Margo's marriage. Six years later, the community was dead.

That October, the aspens flashed bright gold against the blue Colorado sky when Graham went to Woodland Park to lead a worship conference along with Margo and John. Leslie Mims went along to do music. The crowd was made up of idealistic people from around the United States and Canada who were interested in community and wanted to see how it was panning out in Colorado. The registrants included two women who had driven from Oregon. One was a police reporter for a small newspaper south of Portland. Having graduated from Lewis and Clark College, she was now living in Bethlehem Community in downtown Portland, the same community that had sent the Carlsons and Colburns to check out Redeemer a few years before. It was one of hundreds of Christian experiments in what many felt would be the cutting edge of Christianity for years to come. These "intentional communities," modeled after Word of God and Redeemer, were often "common purse" affairs where everyone lived hand-to-mouth but were extravagantly hospitable to the many guests who always seemed to show up for the Sunday community meal.

Economy was everything at Bethlehem, where each household had to agree on a common shampoo, because there wasn't money enough to buy two brands. Household members at Redeemer could live mainly in summer clothes because of Houston's humid climate, but living in community in Oregon meant having winter clothes, which were barely affordable considering that one's yearly clothing allowance was all of $75. Wealth in an Oregon community meant being able to afford a $1.50 hamburger, but even that wasn't possible those weeks when everyone's $5 allowances had to be cancelled for lack of funds. Thus, one learned money-saving methods such as buying used clothes, and cutting off the one leg of pantyhose with a run in it and matching it with a similar one-legged pair. Or one grew one's hair long because there was never enough money for a cut. One also found out where to glean food and harvest berries from friends' bushes and resigning oneself to giving away handmade birthday and Christmas gifts. Such a lifestyle was doubly difficult for the reporter, who sometimes had to cover the police beat with holes in her stockings and tattered clothing to the point where one sheriff's deputy growled, "Don't they pay you enough there to get some new gloves?"

Thus, it had been a major financial investment for Bethlehem to scrounge up the money just for the two women to make the three-day drive to Colorado.

But the worship there seemed kind of flat, and Graham, looking quite Texan in his cowboy boots, was wandering about giving hugs to everyone. His theme that week was *chronos* and *kairos*. *Chronos*, he explained, was cause and effect and sequence—the kind of time that marked each day and hour. It was human timing. *Kairos* was being in the right place at the right time; serendipity, or God's timing. The two operated together, indistinguishable from one another, before the Fall. After the Fall, they intersected from time to time, such as when Jesus came from outside of time to be born in the "fullness of time." Those who live in *chronos* cannot bring about *kairos*; they can only cooperate with it or wait for it. They cannot make a thing happen, but they can discern the time and respond.

As the week wore on, the Oregon women developed the disquieting notion that something was very, very wrong with this community. Discerning its nature was another matter, but one disturbing signal was the almost complete lack of prophetic gifts, prayers for healing, or anything remotely charismatic. The Woodland Park attitude, reinforced by Graham's lectures, was that the community had grown beyond such things. Graham implied that renewal had become too institutionalized, that it consisted merely of certain catch phrases, that they were depending too much on a good thing, that true renewal was outreach to the poor and downtrodden, and so on.

Not only was he jaded, but some of the Fisherfolk were aloof, and John Farra looked positively ferocious. The reporter asked Graham about his return from Scotland and what he was doing at Redeemer. She got a curt answer. *Were all Texans this rude*, she wondered.

Finally, one morning at breakfast, she summoned up the courage to sit next to Graham. He hardly looked up, not guessing that his doom was drinking coffee beside him. She asked Graham what he thought of the media.

"No matter what you say, they'll print what they want," he responded. Graham could cut you to ribbons with a look. He could freeze you on the spot. She wilted.

Back at Redeemer, everybody had a different version of what Graham was supposed to be doing in Houston. According to a Graham announcement, he was to obtain another degree at his alma mater, the Episcopal Seminary of the

Southwest, under the tutelage of social ethicist Philip Turner. And he was to assist at Redeemer in his spare time. But Graham had no sooner moved back to Houston than Turner accepted a position at another Episcopal seminary and left the state. Meanwhile, Jeff was obviously snowed under. After Graham arrived, an obviously battered Jeff withdrew even more, staying in his office for hours at a time, reading or talking on the phone. Graham set to work on the parish, confronting some of the more abusive elders, establishing a counseling ministry, and announcing he was available to anyone who wanted to talk to him. With his powerful gift of discernment, he could be a knockout counselor, and it was not long before people were lining up at his door. Often, he was as good as his reputation, and grateful people felt that, at last, their problems would get straightened out, and the good old days were back again. First, Wiley Beveridge, and later, John Farra, made the 1,000-mile trip from Colorado to ask Graham to heal their troubled marriages.

It was as if Redeemer's real pastor had been gone for eight years. Occasionally, while teaching, Graham and Jeff served as perfect sounding boards for each other. Jeff would bounce comments off Graham and Graham would do the same with Jeff.

But Graham was a different person from the man who had left eight years before. His theology was notably different, and he would often end sentences with the question, "Do you know what I mean?" as a way of emphasizing his point. Everyone would murmur "yes."

Bruce Durst noticed how dictatorial Graham now seemed. Twice, when someone complained about what he had said, Graham responded with, "The Lord puts hard words in my mouth," as if those who disagreed with Graham were actually having a problem with the Lord.

Graham tried out some of his new ideas on his counselees. "All relationships are sexual, but they're not necessarily genital," Graham explained to Reid Wightman during one of their counseling sessions. Anyone with discernment realized Graham had not been coming out with stuff like that in the 1960s. Graham's mind had been exploring other avenues, that was plain.

Graham soon developed a string of disciples, most of them handsome young men, whom he would take along with him as escorts during out-of-town trips to serve as aides of a sort and as personal secretaries. A few of these companions began spreading word that Graham had a pricey traveling style, including good hotels and expensive restaurants, a choice unbefitting the founder of an Anglican religious order. Sometime in late 1980, Andrew Franks, a good-looking blond geologist, began coming to Redeemer because of its progressive stance on social issues. He lived in one of the households and was invited to travel with Graham and be his right-hand man. But something was fishy. Andrew knew there was a snare hidden in there somewhere, and he was not about to respond to Graham's overtures. Besides, he had heard that Graham would tire of his companions, then drop them when things did not work out.

Only one of those companions turned the tables on Graham. He was 25-year-old Mark Dyke, who had disturbing dreams and visions and joined Redeemer in hopes of making some sense of them. He began working for a paint business owned by one of the church members. Rising at 5:30 a.m., he would share or pray with his household, cram down breakfast, work eight to 10 hours a day, return home to do chores, attend more meetings, and do more sharing with his household. Perhaps those in the community's inner circle had it better, but for the peons like him, it was a dog's life, he thought. Mark lasted four months, then bolted for his home town, Albuquerque. He returned to Redeemer a few years later, became engaged to one of the women, then was informed by the elders that they had reservations about the planned marital union. His fiancée began to waver.

"You need to decide who will run this marriage or we need to bag it," he told her. Jeff Schiffmayer counseled them to wait a few months and for Mark to come to terms with his anger. The marriage was called off. No one explained what "dealing with your anger" meant, and Mark was at the lowest point of his life when Graham moved back to Houston. Graham spotted the troubled young man, who began to realize he was being courted. If Graham wants you to be his friend, he realized, there is no way to say no. Mark was smoking pot and sexually involved with women at the church. Graham became his confessor. Mark shared every thought and desire with his mentor. Graham never criticized or demeaned down, Mark was relieved to find out. He never called any of Mark's activities a sin. The most he said was that Mark's behavior was "not appropriate."

Meanwhile, having landed a job as a car salesman, Mark began bringing in good money from his commissions. As he began to see more of Graham, he noticed how people at church treated him better. Life with Graham, he realized, was like swimming in an ocean. You could go as deep or as far as you wanted, but there was a constant invitation to dive deeper into the relationship. At the same time, doing so was frightening. With Graham, there was no right or wrong; it was just he and you. And he was there for you, 100 percent of the time, 24 hours a day.

Graham was exceedingly powerful and he knew it. In a rare moment of self-disclosure, he confided to Mark that he was born with an innate power that drew people to him. Mark offered to pay for Graham to return to Scotland for a month, and when Graham did so, he took Mark along. By now, Mark was frightened of the relationship's implications. What if, he wondered, he was in love with this man? He hashed out his fears with people at Cumbrae, who explained that Graham usually did this to people. He would get extremely close, the courted would face their fears, and then it would be over.

One night, things came to a head. Graham would not only share a bedroom with his traveling companion, but even a bed. As the two men talked, Mark lay in Graham's arms, pouring his heart out. Mark realized he wanted love, and if that meant he was a homosexual, then so be it. He kissed Graham and suddenly got a picture of himself jumping off a cliff to his death. When he began to weep, Graham held him, like a father does a small child. Everything became still in Mark's mind and the inner pain stopped. This, he thought, was intimacy. Sex could never approach the depth of what Mark was experiencing.

Later, the two men discussed Mark's catharsis and Graham invited Mark to move into his Houston household. Mark was not homosexual, Graham had reassured him. He was human. But Mark knew it was time to go. He had talked with too many people who had found such a richness in Graham that they ended up milking him far past the time the priest cared about them. What Graham wanted, he realized, was for the person to get healed, attain some threshold of equality, and then move on. Those who hung around, waiting for him to continue fulfilling their needs, would get turned away. Soonafter returning to Houston, Mark left Redeemer for good, moving to Mexico for a time.

Years later, he would think he had outgrown Christianity, or at least the Christianity presented in most churches. Remaining a part of Christianity, he decided, meant lingering at the beginner's level. Every time he attended church, it felt like returning to kindergarten.

CHAPTER 18

The Slaughter of
the Innocents

"Is it nothing to you, all you who pass by? Behold and see if there is any sorrow like my sorrow."   —Lamentations 1:12 (NKJV)

I T was the evening of Good Friday, 1981. Nancy Braud, Wally's brunette wife of two years, was being shaken awake by someone. As she came to, she found, to her shock, a black man with a large kitchen knife standing over her. Dimly, she realized he must have entered through the cracked kitchen window they had never fixed.

He motioned her to wake Wally, who was fast asleep beside her. The man, who was on drugs, demanded money, but Nancy remembered that her purse was in the car. Angered, the assailant tied Wally's hands and feet, then tied Nancy's hands. For both of them, it was like a nightmare underwater—they were groggy and thus not comprehending the danger they were in. Realizing her feet remained unbound, Nancy snapped to alertness, guessing a rape was in the offing. To her horror, the man began to climb atop her.

Meanwhile, Wally had worked free of his bonds and commanded the man to stop in Jesus's name. At the same time, the phone began ringing incessantly. His concentration gone, the robber bolted, dragging Nancy with him outside, then dropping her in a bush. It turned out that another church member had chosen that moment to phone them, not guessing at the disaster about to take place.

News of the attack sent shock waves through the closely knit church, but what really sent the congregation reeling was an attack on another couple inside their home several months later. This couple was not so fortunate, for the woman was raped and both were robbed. What most upset Nancy was that she herself had noticed a latch on this couple's door that could be unlatched by any passerby. With her own near-escape fresh in mind, she begged the couple to fix the latch, but they ignored her.

Graham took the bull by the horns that next Sunday by preaching on the robbery/rape, using an electrical illustration from John Grimmet on what happens when bad things happen to good people. Christians, he said, are called to be like spiritual circuit breakers.

"The love of God," he said, "is like a grounding. When evil comes our way, instead of continuing the circuit, we render love for that evil. We are grounded in the great mass of God's love for us . . . That dissipates the violence and the hatred and the anger. And if we're not grounded in His love, we return it. The circuit is completed."

Graham had little patience with those wanting to leave Eastwood and the church because of the increasing violence.

"And I hear of fears and anxieties among you which could only be that of the roaring lion, seeking something to devour," he chided. " Whoever makes comments like, 'If this is the sort of neighborhood the church is going to be in, I'm not going to live here any more,' should move immediately to wherever God wants you to be, where you can stand safely in that neighborhood and accept the kind of violence you shall surely find there. Because this is a sinful world. And if this isn't your kind of violence, then there is a kind of violence that God will give you the grace to endure. Find that place and live in it."

Christians are going to get persecuted no matter where they live, he added.

"And anything the devil can do to destroy your confidence and trust in Him, he will do it. He'll use your fear, he'll use your anxiety, he'll use your doubts, he'll use everything he can possibly get his hands on to cause you to turn your back and to say that's enough, I want no more.

"And while he's doing that, he'll teach you to get all hung up on the obvious things like sex . . ." Graham let several seconds elapse, "so you spend your time avoiding all that sort of thing while there's an undercurrent of anger, disillusionment and bitterness welling up within your soul because of your fears, because of your anxieties."

Not everyone liked Graham's approach, but at least he dealt with the issues and, for the most part, preached powerful insights from Scripture. Sunday attendance, which had been in the 500s and upper 400s, swung back up over 600.

Meanwhile, Jeff, who had been studying at the Jungian Center in town, was bringing Jung into his sermons. The contrast was painful and it was clear Jeff was out of his league. More than a few people noticed how Jeff would talk about "consciousness" in his sermons and use New Age-sounding terms. When several complained they weren't getting enough Scripture at church, one of the single men, Chris Simpson, began a Bible study class. Chris thought of himself as a fundamentalist Bible thumper, and thought it odd that Redeemerites no longer said that they were Episcopalians who loved the Bible like the Baptists.

Noticing Jeff's weakening state, Graham broached the idea that being rector was a difficult job; too difficult, in fact, for one person. He suggested a "corporate rector," with Jeff as a part of a ruling junta. Basically, the rector would share his pastoral duties with a team, an idea not far removed from how Redeemer was governed by five elders during the 1970s. Redeemer, Graham was saying, lived a "scattered life" of hit-and-miss spirituality that was light years away from the more Spirit-filled days of the late 1960s.

"I am still convinced that the gifts of the Spirit which are in each one of us and which are among us can only really be released and fully developed as we share our lives in common, and the more scattered we are, the less gifted we are," he explained at a Tuesday evening forum in December 1980. "And that means making choices, doesn't it?"

The following March, Graham made his next move, explaining to the vestry how the Society of Celebration had been formed in Scotland and how "corporate rectorship" operates in the Communities of Celebration. He proposed that the Society govern the Redeemer parish much like a religious order does. The Society was to be quite exclusive—one had to be invited to join—and all money and possessions were to go into a common pot. On June 15, 1981, Graham passed out copies of the revised constitution of the proposed "Society of Celebration." The Scottish community had adopted the constitution the year before and now, he implied, it was up to Redeemer, Woodland Park and Post Green communities to follow suit. The charter members of this Society, it was explained, would include members of Graham's household and selected others.

The troops were not happy. A few members of Graham's household had weird personalities, some thought, and if they were to be part of the corporate rector, nobody wanted to submit to them. The Society was also presented as all or nothing; if they rejected the Society, they in effect rejected Graham. People at Redeemer began to suspect that Graham had left Scotland under duress and had ulterior motives for returning to Redeemer. They wondered if establishing the Society at Redeemer's expense, or using Redeemer as a cash cow for the Society, had been his prime agenda the whole time.

Even Jeff was harboring misgivings. Graham had originally said things should evolve naturally at Redeemer, but within a year of Graham's return, this separate entity with bylaws and a constitution was being proposed. It was a major shift in vision, and it was not well-received. There was a feeling in the parish that those who did not join would be second-rate Christians. In addition, the Society had a provision that its leaders could be shipped anywhere, which made some nervous, wondering if they would be dispatched to other communities, much as what had happened in the '70s.

But Jeff gamely went along with the concept. He and Graham met with the newly elected bishop, Maurice "Ben" Benitez, to explain the corporate rector concept. Benitez, who had watched Redeemer from afar as rector of St. John the Divine, said they could not officially have a corporate rector. Too new in the episcopate to want to take on this famous church, Benitez told them what they did internally was their affair, but he wanted to relate to one rector. Privately, he saw through what Graham was doing, and in no way planned to endorse a religious order where Graham would be the abbot.

N EAL MICHELL had been out of law school barely two years when he attended the all-day vestry meeting at the church on Saturday, September 19, to deliberate on whether to recommend the Society to the bishop.

"Neal, use your legally trained mind on that constitution and you'll see a major flaw in it," Bill Linden had told him, but Bill wouldn't say what that flaw was. What Neal did see was how Graham had broken the authority of the elders, transferring it to the vestry. Up until then at Redeemer, the elders had been in control and the vestry had mainly signed the checks. Now, they unanimously voted Graham down. The feeling was that he had vastly underestimated the changes that had taken place at Redeemer and in himself. Although he had kept in touch with some of the leaders, he had not communicated with the grassroots of the parish, and had not correctly assessed the trauma experienced during the eight years he had been gone. People burned by community were terrified of authority and discipline of any kind.

Neal announced the vestry vote the next day at the Sunday morning service, and Graham looked as if a bomb had been detonated directly on him. During the recessional, he walked down the aisle, his head down, dejected and embarrassed. Although heavily medicated for his arthritis and gout, he left for Colorado a month later with one of his aides, Richard Gullen, in tow. While at the airport, he began feeling chest pains and frantically called Joe Wolppman, a doctor at Redeemer, for advice. Wolppman advised him to check with the doctor on call at the airport, but after one glance at Graham's blood pressure, the doctor refused to see him. Graham and Richard headed to the Denver home of Bert and Joanne Womack to spend the night. He woke up a few hours later with even worse pains and had no sooner walked into the hospital when he went into cardiac arrest.

A few hours later, George was meeting in Houston with Betty Jane, Jeff, and a few of the elders to decide who should do music outreaches on behalf of the church. Because these efforts furthered the careers of those who led them, George felt he should be the leader. He had done quite well for eight years without the Fisherfolk, he told them.

"George," said Betty Jane, "I feel you're a little boy wanting acceptance and affirmation."

"Betty," said George, "I am your peer in Christ and not your child." The two continued to argue as they walked outside, then stopped by the flagpole. "Betty," George continued, "my biggest concern about Graham is that in the wake of so many broken and unreconciled relationships, he's headed for a major heart attack."

George had no sooner gotten home than the phone rang. It was Betty Jane, frantic. A call had come in from Colorado saying that Graham had had a heart attack that morning.

Graham stayed at the hospital for over a week, awaiting an operation for a quadruple bypass and grieving over Redeemer. The doctor, guessing Graham's problems stemmed from stress, asked him why he had returned to Redeemer in the first place.

"I was called back there to do some repair work on some pastoral problems," the priest told him.

"Graham," the doctor retorted, "you're a builder, not a repairman."

In the long weeks that followed, Graham lost 40 pounds, went about in a wheelchair, then developed a liver infection from the surgery. His doctor in Denver agreed to release him if he agreed to live apart from his family and stay in a cardiac rehab program near Houston's medical center complex. "That place has broken your heart. Forget it," he told Graham. Thus, Graham got an apartment on the west end of Houston, where he stayed with Richard, who cooked for him and walked with him. He was as good as resigned from the church, which agreed to pay him through July 1982.

Meanwhile, Redeemer had terminated the $800 a month it was sending to the Colorado community. Too many heavy contributors were leaving the parish. Finances at Redeemer were not what they had been. A report given to the vestry the year before showed that 51 percent of the members gave less than $500 a year. Seventy-four percent gave less than $1,200 a year, and three percent contributed more than 26 percent of the budget.

The one bright spot that spring was that Richard Gullen was marrying Jackie Rogers, a young woman who had come to Redeemer in 1979 partly to see what her sister Joyce saw in the place. The two had met while singing in the choir, and there was an attraction, although it seemed to her that Graham sat in on the relationship a lot. Richard was living in Graham's household, and Graham had set rules as to how the household would operate. One of the strangest rules was that any dinner or social invitation to a household member had to be extended to the group en masse because the household did everything as a unit. Because few people could afford to entertain 14-15 people at once, the household didn't go many places.

At first, Graham had wanted them to marry in December. Then he said they couldn't hold hands or kiss, as most engaged couples did. The whole thing drove her batty, even after a wedding date was finally set for June 1982. Graham provided the recipe for their English wedding cake and instructed them as to who their best man and maid of honor should be, namely Wiley Beveridge and 16-year-old Martha Pulkingham, both household members. None of Jackie's family had a part in the wedding, and Richard's parents were told to not bother making the trip from Britain. "What will you do with them for six weeks?" Graham had asked him. Jackie wondered why no one had asked her for her ideas, inasmuch as her parents might have entertained them.

When the day came, Jackie showed up in a spaghetti strap gown and see-through cape wearing a simple circlet with a veil. Richard, who was tall, blond and thin, looked dashing. She was 25 and looking forward to having children and a family, yet during the wedding prayer for children, a thought hit her like a dart from nowhere—that she and Richard would never conceive. They went off to Aspen to stay in a cottage lent by a community friend, but their honeymoon lasted only three days because Richard had a singing engagement in Woodland Park.

Not surprisingly, Graham soon announced he was moving to Colorado. The best light possible was put on the move. "In response to a long-standing invitation from the Bishop of Colorado, and to the need of the Community of Celebration at Woodland Park whose membership has been seriously depleted over the last several months, the Pulkingham household will be moving to Woodland Park," said an announcement in the April 1982 issue of *The Light*. On Graham's last Sunday, July 25, 1982, at Redeemer, he began his sermon by reading all of Ezekiel 2, through the 12th verse of the third chapter. These were the verses God had brought to him 18 years before, soon after his baptism in the Spirit.

"My ministry would change radically," Graham said the Lord warned him, "and I would have as many adversaries as I had friends. That's all right. The Lord warned me."

But Graham's voice was tight and filled with tension. He gazed about the congregation.

"You can look about you now and see the result of what has happened," he said. "Look around you—400 to 500 people. What the Lord promised me at that time was that if I'd be faithful to His Word concerning two things, the unity of the body of Christ and the love of the brethren, that even if at times He would put hard words on my lips, He would yet bring this parish to life . . . And I could say He had done so. He is faithful."

There were no words of apology for the previous two years. Instead, he outlined parish and monastic lifestyles and how he and a few others felt called to bring the two together. The Holy Spirit, he said, was drawing monastic Christians and parish Christians together to prepare the church for whatever was to come. But his dream was not to be realized in Houston or in Colorado. He and his household would wander for another three years. His return to Redeemer had all the trappings of a Christmas gift donated to a weary church. It became a massacre of innocence.

1983–1985

CHAPTER 19

Epiphany

"I am going to prune My church the way man prunes a fruit tree to remove that which is dead and will never bear fruit. . . . I want you to have a great loyalty to one another and to Me because the time when I am going to prune My church is coming much sooner than you think. I want you to have this loyalty so that you can trust that you will not abandon one another under stress."

—prophecy from a 1976 Notre Dame
conference on communities

IN July 1981, Houston surpassed Philadelphia as America's fourth largest city behind New York, Los Angeles, and Chicago. The latter three cities were seaports, with at least a 100-year headstart on Houston, which is on a bayou 50 miles from the sea. By 1981, oil had risen to $40 a barrel, and Houston was adding 1,000 jobs a week. The city was transformed by architects who jumped at the chance to redo the skyline of a major metropolis. At 1,049 feet, the Texas Commerce tower became the world's tallest building outside of New York and Chicago. It was to have been 80 floors high, but the Federal Aviation Administration limited it to 75 because of the proximity of Hobby Airport. The 50-story Texaco Heritage Plaza building was topped by an apex resembling a Mayan temple. The blue-green, 71-story First Interstate Bank Building looked like something out of the Wizard of Oz. Penzoil put its corporate headquarters in two dark bronze trapezoids that looked like large black glass diamonds, and called it Penzoil Place. A window washer's nightmare, the twin buildings ended at pointed peaks outside the 38th floor. Across the street from Penzoil Place, Republic Bank built a neo-Flemish tripartite block with spires that looked like a Dutch guildhall.

Houston in 1981 was an energetic sub-nation of America, a place apart that could define itself brashly and get away with it. Traffic was everywhere, the highways were in gridlock, restaurants were crowded, and developers were going wild. Everything was expanding and ambitious. Texas was the rising region of the country to be in; the oddly shaped land mass with a future.

The city of can-do enthusiasm and verve skidded to a halt in December 1985 when members of the Organization of Petroleum Exporting Countries (OPEC) cartel glutted the oil market. In one month, prices plummeted from $30 to $12 a barrel. Houston companies slashed their payrolls and more than 220,000 workers, mostly from oil and gas and related manufacturing companies, were laid off. The unemployment rate soared to 10.2 percent, the worst since the Great Depression. From 1982 to 1987, the number of companies filing bankruptcy quintupled. The office vacancy rate shot up to 32 percent and housing starts dipped to fewer than 10,000 a year in a city that had vastly overbuilt its suburbs. Home after home was left vacant by homeowners who found it impossible to sell their property or pay the mortgage.

In Houston's East End, it was obvious the neighborhood was going Hispanic in a major way. Neighborhood ministries at Redeemer included persons like Paul Frey, fluent in Spanish from his years in Guatemala, and Tom Herrick, a former Catholic from Cleveland who had been part of the Neal household in 1972. Five years later, he wed his wife Carol in a Hispanic-flavored wedding with tamales, a Mexican hat dance, and a mariachi band. But Redeemer, Tom felt, wasn't listening, especially in regards to Hispanics. By 1981, it was clear that Hispanics were not comfortable with the church's English-language service, nor with using translation earphones. Most Hispanics were not recent immigrants but a Tex-Mex mixture that had been in the country for more than a generation. Their Spanish was not as pure as that of the Central Americans across town, nor were they as highly educated. A Spanish-language service was begun Sunday afternoons and Abdias Avalos, a Hispanic lay pastor and former car mechanic, was recruited to begin studies for the priesthood. Abdias had been part of a Hispanic Bible study group in 1979 with Jackie Krafft, her new husband Greg Davis, Paul Frey, Tom Herrick, and others. There was a little-used provision, Canon 8, that allowed non seminary-educated persons to pursue ordination within a specific congregation. Abdias set his sights on that.

The cost of reaching Hispanics was higher, emotionally, spiritually, and financially than what Graham had faced in the 1960s, for it was a whole

different game with a whole different set of numbers. This time, the requirements weren't spiritual authority; they were how well one could minister in
another language while providing social services at the same time. The population was extremely transient; the people whom you poured into your life today
were apt to move on tomorrow. It was like having your own turf turned into
mission territory; a condition that some Redeemerites adapted to quite well.
The majority did not.

ONCE Ronald Reagan was elected president in 1980, no one paid much
attention to what the Episcopal Church was saying or doing. Whether it
was changing the prayer book, bringing women on as priests, or engaging in
leftist social causes, the feeling around the country was that America's most
prestigious denomination was badly drifting. Baptists such as Jerry Falwell and
Billy Graham, who had sat for years on the sidelines, became respectable and got
invited to the White House. Not so with the presiding bishops of the Episcopal
Church.

But due to Hispanic immigration, the number of Catholics in America was
growing. Stephen Clark had worked out a Christian government of sorts at
Word of God. From 1980-1984, the gigantic community would grow increasingly autocratic. Its elders had complete say over the community activities of
their subordinates, even to the point of seriously disrupting people's lives if
some sort of emergency arose. Clark was thinking in military terms, of crises, of
sieges, and of the coming battle between good and evil in which a worldwide
network of Christian communities would play a decisive role. The foot warriors
in this epic battle had to be whipped into shape through a series of training
courses, the contents of which were highly secret. The courses ended with
participants taking the following pledge:

1. We pledge our loyalty to all who fight with us.
2. We are ready for every sacrifice, even death, if the Lord honors us by
   calling us to die for him or our brothers.
3. We are ready to serve until the Lord indicates that the war has been
   won.
4. We will be loyal to our commanders, knowing that they are committed
   to defend and provide for our homes and families. We will serve where
   they direct us and in the way they direct us.
5. We will keep our plans and movements hidden from the enemy and his
   agents.

But others in the renewal seemed to be suffering a tremendous loss of resolve, part of it stemming from spiritual exhaustion. Some simply chose to move on. One of them was Francis MacNutt, the vibrant white-robed Dominican who thrilled audiences with his electrifying persona. In 1980, he left the priesthood, marrying Judith Sewell, a psychologist 23 years his junior. The National Service Committee of the Catholic Charismatic Renewal released a statement calling his move a "tremendous personal mistake."

In June 1981, another event hit the Catholic renewal like a bombshell: Six teenagers in Yugoslavia claimed to have seen the Virgin Mary in the village of Medjugorje. Unlike the Fatima or Lourdes apparitions, these continued day after day, year after year, as millions of pilgrims began visiting the tiny village to experience some of the alleged miracles happening there. Many of the original European players in this drama were charismatics, and their American counterparts were left grappling with how they would fit Marian apparitions into their theology. Some saw the gap between some of their church's doctrines, the Bible, and this latest incident in Yugoslavia, and defected into nondenominational churches. Others saw Medjugorje as the breath of fresh air their movement needed.

Meanwhile, all the emerging Christian TV networks were being run by charismatics. By the mid-1980s, many charismatic denominational groups had renamed themselves, replacing the word "charismatic" with softer terms like "renewal" in the hopes of mainstreaming their movements. After all, one Anglican bishop, Michael Marshall, had predicted in 1976 that in 10 years, the Episcopal Church would be charismatic or dead. It was time to think of taking over. However, to placate the Protestant evangelicals who still fought charismatic ideology, it was agreed that terms such as "fullness" or "release" could adequately substitute for baptism in the Spirit terminology. "Renewal" could be used by anyone, including those who wouldn't touch a genuine gift of the Spirit with a 10-foot pole. The early blush of the charismatic movement was clearly over, and there were no charts as to where to go from there.

PARISH frustration ran high, especially with Jeff Schiffmayer's annoying habit of rarely answering phone calls. He shirked other duties as well, to the point that the vestry came up with a document on "general duties and obligations for clergy" at their Feb. 21, 1983, meeting. If they defined his duties better, the vestry thought, maybe Jeff would take on more leadership responsibilities. About the same time, Bill Linden had thought up a system of parish councils that would disperse power to various council leaders, which meant things could happen without depending on the moribund rector. Paul Felton was now assistant rector, having returned from several years in Britain with the Fisherfolk. And Ladd Fields, newly ordained, was back in town as parish administrator.

About the same time in early 1983, George made an appointment to confront Jeff on behavior that seemed to him highly inappropriate. It was obvious to George that Jeff was in a crisis of several years' duration and something, George thought, had to change. The whole life of Redeemer was based on the integrity of its leaders, and George was not about to let anything go unchecked. George suggested Jeff confess all to Benitez.

"Can't we just agree and you leave?" Jeff asked George.

"No, we can't agree and I leave," said George, "unless you fire me." George knew he was powerless to change Jeff. Not wanting to go down with a sinking ship, he bided his time until one day in March, when he got a call from St. George's Episcopal Church in Manhattan. It was a huge place not far from Greenwich Village. He used to visit there during his days at Union Theological Seminary and dream of a day when he'd be playing the organ and directing its choir. That day had arrived. He announced his resignation in June, then threw himself a huge good-bye party and farewell service on August 7. Eight hundred people came, some of them out of curiosity after reading his controversial interview in the *Houston Chronicle* the day before. George had let it all hang out, saying that the church was "in a bit of decline," that there was a vacuum in its leadership, and that Redeemer was in a "post-charismatic era." The crowning blow was when he broadly hinted he had outgrown the parish.

That June, Jeff announced that he also would depart Redeemer. This came about after Don Sears, the senior warden, saw the extent to which Redeemer was crumbling. He invited Bill Linden and Bob Kehl, two other former senior wardens, to lunch, where they decided to throw down the gauntlet to Jeff: Either change or wrap things up at Redeemer. The actual meeting in Jeff's office was a lot harder, as the trio hemmed and hawed, hoping Jeff would grasp their point. Faced with an ultimatum from the three most powerful men in the parish, Jeff made it sound as if it was ultimately his decision to leave. He had an asthmatic son, John, who had had several serious attacks and twice had almost died before getting to the hospital. Houston's toxic air was not improving, and Jeff figured that God was not going to protect John forever. He began to talk of redesigning the ministry so another priest could understand it. Then Ladd, who was freshly ordained, came along, needing a place to alight. His wife, June, was dying of ovarian cancer, and Ladd was in no position to strike out into a totally unfamiliar parish.

With Ladd in place, Jeff felt free to go. He called Benitez and asked that he find him a position. Benitez, in turn, asked him to create from scratch St. Francis, an Episcopal mission in College Station near the Brazos River, the home of Texas A&M. At first, Jeff heard jokes about him creating "Redeemer on the Brazos," but when 49 persons signed the charter for the new church, people knew he was serious.

There was some rancor just before he left Redeemer, however. Benitez asked Redeemer to give Jeff $30,000 from the sale of the rectory to help him buy a home in College Station. Unfortunately, the bishop chose Jeff to convey that message, and so the vestry argued and argued for an entire morning over the matter. Some felt that Jeff's lack of leadership and indolence had caused people to leave and others to withhold their tithes. Finances were already tight, you could number the big givers on one hand, and $30,000 would bankrupt the church. Finally, Bill Linden moved that Jeff be given $15,000 from the sale. The motion passed unanimously. On Nov. 27, Jeff's last Sunday, 406 people came.

By then it was clear that June Fields was in the last weeks of her life. Since surgery in September, her body had refused to heal, and she had to be fed through a feeding tube in her leg. She came home from the hospital and Ladd learned to nurse and feed her. The couple had agreed that no extraordinary measures should be taken to prolong her life and, by the end of December, she was comatose.

"We've achieved our goal," the doctor told Ladd December 29. "We kept her alive until Christmas."

It was a dreary day in which June did little else but sleep. The doctor suggested that the feeding tube be removed—June would be a vegetable from then on. Now that the moment had finally come, Ladd was in agony. The tube was her lifeline, and if the doctor removed it, she would starve to death, leaving behind their adopted son, Mark, who was a few weeks shy of his 15th birthday. June had not wanted to die, Ladd knew, but her body had made the choice for her. He removed the tube.

She was still in a coma on New Year's Eve. As the old year waned, Ladd talked to June, telling her he'd miss her, then clasped her hand. It was cold as ice. He had the strange feeling that by saying good-bye, he had permitted her to go. The next morning was Sunday and Essie Avalos, Abdias's wife, came by to relieve him for a few hours. Ladd wandered into the kitchen, noticing it was about 8 a.m. A few minutes later, Essie burst into the room. June had gone.

THE summer before, Esther-Marie Daskalakis, a part-time student at the newest Episcopal seminary, Trinity Episcopal School for Ministry, came to Woodland Park. She found the people defensive and cagey, and the common life fragmented. Many of them had made plans to leave. Margo and John's marriage had ended, and John was a no-show at a conference program he was slated to lead. Margo filled in, first by reading a letter to the conferees of John's decision to move to Houston to get marital counseling from Graham.

"I tried everything I could to make John happy," she confided. "I tried everything, every suggestion. I could be a source of grace in other people's lives; I could not (in mine)."

Margo then sought comfort from other women. One August day, as her best friend left the community with her family, Margo helped them move. The pain of losing this friend was worse than childbirth, Margo thought, and when she returned to her lovely home in Woodland Park, she poured her feelings into a song, "The Sun's Gonna Shine," beginning with, "Helping you go was the hardest thing that I have ever done." The song eventually became the name of an album, but even that did not erase the pain she felt. Eventually, another woman moved into Margo's bedroom with her, to fill the void John had left.

When Esther-Marie arrived in Woodland Park in 1983, she befriended the Pulkinghams, half-hoping there was some way of getting such a community to Pittsburgh. She also knew the new bishop of Pittsburgh, Alden Hathaway, a spellbinding speaker who, though barely 50, had a head of white hair that gave him a dignified air. She talked to Hathaway about community. When Graham mentioned they were looking for a place to move, Esther-Marie quizzed him on specifics. She learned they wanted to be close to a major airport, in a metropolitan area, near a university or a seminary, with a thriving art community, where he could do ministry among the poor. They wanted to be connected to a parish small enough that they weren't lost in it but large enough that they would not be the controlling interest. The 8,200-foot altitude at Woodland Park bothered Graham, and that fall, he and his family moved back to England with several followers. One of them was Steven Plummer and his wife of four years, Anita.

"Is there life after community?" Steven had asked Graham.

"No," Graham replied, "only disappointment."

Esther-Marie reported her findings to Hathaway, and the next spring, she saw Graham and Bill when they came to visit Pittsburgh at the bishop's invitation. Alden had put Esther-Marie in charge of their itinerary, and she took them on a round of poor parishes in ghetto areas. Pittsburgh, which was within a one-day drive of 60 percent of the U.S. population, seemed the right region. The place that clicked most with them was a devastated steel town 23 miles north of Pittsburgh and across the river from the seminary. The city, which encompassed 17,000 in its boom days, was called Aliquippa.

Meanwhile, the Community of Celebration and the Post Green community had parted ways after nine years. It all had come down to who was in control, and when Graham demanded that Tom Lees, the British lord over Post Green, place his ancestral lands into the community pot, Lees refused. Cumbrae was also ready to be shut down, so Graham began raising money to fund the moving of 30-35 persons from Scotland to Pittsburgh sometime in 1985. They needed a major morale boost. That year, they had come out with "A Larger Place," an album where the music was pretty but many of the lyrics were sad and depressing. "Oh, Lord," went one song, "we want to sing to you as we struggle and cry."

So that February, Graham and Betty sent out a fundraising letter asking for $1.1 million in gifts or pledges by April 15. He also wrote a 98-page booklet explaining the ambitious plans they had for their work in Aliquippa, including a conference ministry, a network of companions to the community, and a proposed pilot study with a handful of renewed churches wishing to be restructured along the lines of the community. Graham wrote confidently about their new home parish in Aliquippa, All Saints, and noted that nearby Trinity seminary was being solicited for help in this study.

The booklet also contained Graham's rewrite of the history of Redeemer, stating that the final split of the Fisherfolk and Redeemer took place in 1972, when "Redeemer went its way and we went ours," though Graham's trip to England had been viewed then as only of short duration. Seeing Redeemer vanish from between his fingers a few short years before, Graham had realized that his one legacy was Celebration, and that it was in his interest to create a place for it in Redeemer history much earlier than how the events actually occurred. In fact, it was not until 1979 that Celebration became an entity. It was then that its constitution was submitted to a commission under the provinces of Canterbury and York, whose purpose was to establish and regularize Anglican orders. The commission provisionally approved the constitution and instructed Celebration to live under it for 20 years, after which they could return to the commission for final acceptance as an approved order in the English church.

And so they left Cumbrae. In the years after their leaving, the cathedral took on a pre-community status, with the new provost removing many signs that they had ever been there. Guitars, renewal music, and a platform for the musicians were gone. The service reverted to traditional worship, and there was little mention of the 10-year gap between 1975 and 1985.

Two months after June died, Ladd was elected the new rector of Redeemer. Installed May 3, he had been too smart to "run" for the position, but he had influential supporters. Although some of the vestry worried that he was too inexperienced as a priest to take on the church, Ladd had something no other aspirant had: an indisputed connection with the golden '60s. After all, Ladd had been one of the original five elders, and he was emotionally stable. This was important to a parish whiplashed by the tumult over the Society.

The most important hurdle was Benitez, who had the final authority over a priest selected by a parish. Normally, the bishop did not interfere with such matters, but Redeemer wanted their assistant to succeed their rector, which was against diocesan policy. After a meeting with Bill Linden and Don Sears, Benitez said he would make an exception for Redeemer if overwhelming support for someone was demonstrated. The vestry ran a secret ballot on Ladd, which was unanimous, for after seeing Graham, George, and Jeff depart, parish esteem was so low that people were grateful for someone like Ladd who wanted the position. The vestry returned to Benitez.

"I will make an exception," the bishop said, "and I'll catch flak from every church in the diocese." Other parishes had also wanted their assistants elected rector but had been turned down, while Redeemer twice got its assistant priest promoted to rector. Part of Benitez's reasoning lay in his assessment of charismatics as fiercely independent types and of Redeemer as a hotbed of them. If an outside rector arrived at Redeemer with his own ideas, he'd have his head handed to him on a platter, the bishop thought. Things were too dicey at Redeemer to bring in a stranger, and Ladd, Benitez knew, would not make radical changes.

A few at Redeemer harbored doubts about Ladd taking over. Among them was Ralph Neal, who had known Ladd since the 1960s and viewed Ladd as agonizingly slow to make decisions, always wanting to be meticulous and safe. Greg Davis, who had arrived in 1980 with a divinity degree from Princeton before marrying Jackie Krafft, also saw the potential for disaster. Ladd's gifts were more in counseling, not leading, he thought, plus, Ladd had barely gotten the time to overcome the death of his wife. Except for Greg's, no other voices were publicly raised to question the parish's decision, though one staff member made his way to Benitez's office to privately express his doubts. If you do ordain Ladd, he told the bishop, then do it on a Sunday morning with all the pomp possible to drive home to the congregation that the bishop fully backed Ladd and that Ladd had all the authority as rector, not Graham, and Jeff. Instead, Benitez installed Ladd on a weeknight.

Because Ladd already owned his own home, he had no need for the huge rectory on McKinney Street that Jeff had occupied. The rectory got another occupant: Cliff Wilson, his wife, Dori, and their children. Cliff was another astute businessman who, true to Redeemer style, would make his way quickly up the church hierarchy and become senior warden a few years later. Born in 1951, Cliff was only 33. Younger than a lot of the Redeemer leaders, he already had a thorough grasp of diocesan Episcopal politics and a "who's who" in charismatic renewal circles.

Cliff had first visited Redeemer one Sunday in 1973 on the advice of a friend. Dodging an usher who wanted to hug him, he saw only six people in the church, and this was five minutes before the service was slated to begin. He waited another 25 minutes. The doors then flew open and 600 people surged in from the parish hall. The place filled up in the next five minutes, with chairs placed in the aisles to accommodate the overflow. The opening hymn began, people threw their hands up in the air, and Cliff headed out the door. But he kept coming back throughout the years and by 1983, he and Dori were ready to move to Eastwood. The rectory was up for sale and Cliff, a stockbroker-turned-banker at Chase Manhattan Bank, could afford the lovely, remodeled home.

The rectory was the remodeling crew's proudest achievement and a powerful parish symbol. It had taken 70 people working five nights a week and Saturdays over several months to do about $100,000 worth of remodeling. Because nothing was too good for the rector, they added 1,400 square feet to the 1920s-era house in the form of a new kitchen, several new bedrooms, and two bathrooms. They also added new wiring, new plumbing, new pine flooring, and Mexican tile flooring in the family room, while repairing the porch and adding a new coat of paint throughout. The rectory had been converted into a real showplace. Cliff began building relationships in the parish and, two years later, he was elected to the vestry.

Meanwhile, things were heating up at Redeemer over a controversial deliverance group. Its leader, Chris Simpson, had set up a Bible study that effectively established him as a teacher in the church. He then branched out into his great love: deliverance. For a while, Ladd allowed this and sometimes sent people to Chris. But there was a feeling among the deliverance people that things were becoming more New Age and less biblical at Redeemer, culminating in a tremendous battle in the spring of 1985, when the church conducted conferences on the enneagram, a charting of one's personality rooted in Sufism. Muslim Sufi mystics believe the Divine has nine manifestations to coincide with the nine-sided human personality. This sounded rather occultic to other members, along with another concept, "healing the family tree," that Redeemer was exploring. As a female speaker was explaining these concepts, a picture flashed across Chris's mind of a snake on her head. Impetuously, he stood up and rebuked her for what she was saying. Ladd ordered him to sit down, and later Chris was called up to meet the seven elders.

"Chris," one of his friends said before he left for the meeting, "keep your mouth shut." Once at the meeting, Chris realized that he and the elders were on two different theological tracks. They believed in extra-biblical revelation and he did not, and like IBM and Apple computers, the two systems were not compatible. The elders felt that Chris's group was way too aggressive and at Redeemer, being aggressive got you nowhere. Ladd felt that whenever he approached Chris, he got zapped with Scripture verses, which put him off. It didn't help that Chris had found some supposedly New Age materials in the church bookstore and let everyone know about it, thereby appointing himself the guardian of faith around Redeemer, Ladd thought.

That fall, Ladd gave a sermon that Chris felt legitimized divorce; after all, Ladd's youngest daughter, Jan, had just married Dell Hoffman, a divorced man. This was the last straw for Chris. Thoroughly disenchanted, he left Redeemer, taking with him 35 members, mostly in their 20s and 30s, who were the future leaders of the church. It was a heavy loss for Redeemer, and made worse by the fact that the dissidents continued to criticize the church after they left. Put on the defensive, Ladd gave a sermon in March 1986 based on I John 2:18: "If they had been of us, they would not have gone out from us." Word of Ladd's condemnation soon reached the dissidents, and bitterness between the two groups increased. Eventually, they would reconcile. "It'd been one thing if you all had just left," Ladd told them, "but I get continuing stories of how you tore and wounded this body."

Years later, Chris would admit to being headstrong and immature, but also far more biblically literate than his critics. Redeemer, he felt, was not just caught in the grip of sentimentality, but refused to see evil for what it was. The evil at Redeemer was surrounded by much good, and thus was hard to recognize at first. But now, Redeemer leadership was refusing to see the obvious, he thought. Redeemer's top priority was acting in the name of love, even if it meant not telling the truth.

A strong pastor could have taken him in hand, trained him, and turned him into a powerfully prophetic voice at Redeemer, but after Graham's departure, no such person existed at the church. Chris's group took refuge at the fast-growing, baby-boomer-filled Church in the City in Houston's Heights district. His pastor spoke Chris's language and was willing to disciple him.

I T was a chilly 41 degrees on a January afternoon when the reporter landed at Pittsburgh's grungy, tired airport. The city was due to get a new airport in six years, thus no one really bothered to keep up the 1950s-era terminal. It was seedy and sad.

It had been three years since she had moved from Oregon to Florida. She had taken a few days off from her job at a Florida newspaper to do a story on Trinity Episcopal School for Ministry, which was especially timely because the controversial seminary had just gotten accredited the year before. Esther-Marie, who worked at the seminary and was now married, picked her up at the airport and the two began talking immediately of the Fisherfolk and where they were now.

It was 1986 and most of the community had moved back to the States. Twenty-one of them had snapped up two sets of brick row houses on Franklin Street, the main thoroughfare in downtown Aliquippa, to live in while turning a former funeral home next door into their office. For only $60,000, they had purchased an unused church one block over, an educational building, and a five-bedroom manse, into which Betty and Graham moved. Using the diocese as collateral, the community secured a $324,000 loan.

The community got to work, training four laid-off steel workers and recovered alcoholics to drywall a rowhouse. Buoyed by that success, the quartet went on to get a major construction contract elsewhere. The community was blossoming, lots of people from the seminary were visiting, and NBC had already done a Christmas special on them, with a follow-up slated for 1986. The next year, they would take part in a Palm Sunday march of 1,000 persons through downtown Aliquippa to protest the bankruptcy declaration of LTV Corp., owner of the massive steel factory that ran 6 ½ miles along the Ohio River. LTV had been the city's main employer and the nation's second largest steel company. Then it lost $227 million in 1985 and would file for bankruptcy during the summer of 1986, cutting pensions to several thousand retired workers by at least $400 a month. Such problems were not limited to Aliquippa for, as the steel industry declined nationwide, it could no longer make good on the generous pensions it had promised workers in the much better times of the 1950s. It just seemed as if Aliquippa took the brunt of the industry's decline.

After the Palm Sunday march, both Hathaway and Pulkingham would speak at a follow-up rally, and the Fisherfolk would sing. It was so romantic. Labor disputes, demonstrations, community organizing, worship at All Saints—

this was the kind of stuff Graham relished. Here he could do theology. Here the community could grapple with the gritty inner city, not play ministry games with the poor. Maybe Graham really could repeat his smash hit in Houston here in Aliquippa. After all, what could possibly go wrong? He was 20 years older and wiser, and this time, he had the local bishop openly supporting him.

Aliquippa was not a romantic place, nor was it comparable to Eastwood. The one-industry town that once had boasted 27,000 residents and 15,000 jobs had become a place of empty storefronts for 15,600 citizens and 5,000 jobs. One-third of its population was black, and very few of those folks would attend an Anglicized place like All Saints. Worse, the All Saints rector, whom the Fisherfolk were counting on to help support their ministry, had escaped to another parish not long after the community arrived in town. The church had been doing so well before, that it had founded a mission church in nearby Hopewell, a few miles to the south on the Allegheny County line. Eighty-five percent of All Saints fled to Prince of Peace to worship under the dynamic couple installed to head it. That left 95 members on the books at All Saints. In truth, this actually meant six families, two single persons, and the incoming community. Without wanting it, the community was now in control of the parish. It was the situation that Graham had wanted but had not gotten in Houston—an elite group, or corporate rector, that oversaw the parish. Hathaway asked the community to take pastoral care of All Saints for a three-to-five year period while it got back on its feet. Graham was made the vicar.

The next day, Esther-Marie took the reporter to evening prayer at Celebration, where, for the first time, she saw Mimi and Bill Farra, whom she had only read about before, and Wiley Beveridge, whom she had previously glimpsed at a concert in Florida. Then there was Graham Farra, Mimi and Bill's son, who had been cured of blindness as a child. It was as if legends were coming to life.

Already, people from Redeemer were trekking to Pittsburgh to see their former leader. One of them was Bette Graham, now Bette Graham White, who had been healed in Graham's household on New Year's Eve in 1969.

Now Graham told her, "I want to be healed of a broken heart. Not because of my heart attack, but because of all the pain at Redeemer."

Another visitor was Audrey Tindall, a Redeemerite who had known Graham since pre-renewal days. What struck her now was Graham's luxurious lifestyle, the hot toddies he served, the cocktails every afternoon, the amount of TV he was watching. Twenty-two years before, this man had given up drinking and been on the cutting edge, she thought. Now he no longer was.

1986–1990

CHAPTER 20

Lent

"Who of you is left who saw this house in its former glory? How does it look to you now? Does it not seem to you like nothing? . . . The glory of this present house will be greater than the glory of the former house, says the Lord Almighty. And in this place I will grant peace, declares the Lord Almighty.

. . . The word of the Lord came to the prophet Haggai: "This is what the Lord Almighty says: 'Ask the priests what the law says: If a person carries consecrated meat in the fold of his garment, and that fold touches some bread or stew, some wine, oil or other food, does it become consecrated?' "

The priests answered, "No."

Then Haggai said, "If a person defiled by contact with a dead body touches one of these things, does it become defiled?"

"Yes," the priests replied, "it becomes defiled."

Then Haggai said, " 'So it is with this people and this nation in my sight,' declares the Lord. 'Whatever they do and whatever they offer there is defiled. Now give careful thought to this from this day on— consider how things were before one stone was laid on another in the Lord's temple.' "   —Haggai 2: 3,9–15

THEY stepped into the hushed, dimly lit church, twelve women in flowing white dresses and white ballet shoes. As the oboe poured out a haunting prelude, the dancers slowly swept down the aisle, like graceful swans. Their shoulders were draped with tulle, and white ornaments adorned their hair as they danced to "Let Our Praise to You Be as Incense," an exquisite worship song popularized by the Fisherfolk on their latest album. Based on

Psalm 141:2, it tenderly spoke of God's holiness and the longing to let one's praises be set before God's throne like incense rising in His temple. Each bow, each incline of the head was intended to draw worship from the depths of the viewers' hearts, and each dancer carried bowls holding burning sticks of incense to dramatize the effect.

The procession of white-clad women danced on and on, daintily stepping around the altar, bowing, then circling, their arms creating arcs in the air while others knelt and swayed. A quartet set their bowls on the altar, then formed an inner circle of swaying, and bending princess-like ballerinas. The congregation seemed stunned by this ethereal vision of heavenly worship. As the last notes faded, the people stirred, then began to worship in the Spirit as the dancers hovered like statuettes, their arms lifted in worship.

I was one of these women. Miraculously, while stuck at a sweatshop of a newspaper near Miami, I had gotten a call out of the blue from an editor at the *Houston Chronicle*. It was June 1986, and she asked if I cared to apply for an opening as the religion beat reporter. I got the job and moved to Houston that September. On a muggy Sunday morning a few weeks after arriving in town, some friends took me through a run-down neighborhood to Redeemer, a large, gray-colored stone church that badly needed a sandblasting job. Palm trees flourished in the front of the church, which had glass doors more appropriate for a school or office building. Then there was that famous mural, blazing away behind the altar.

Five years had passed since I'd left the Oregon community, and now here was a community that went further than Bethlehem ever had. Here was the same tenor of breathless commitment, deep worship, use of the gifts, and total trust. When I entered the community, it was partly so that I, always the outsider throughout my short life, might finally find somewhere to belong. Then, forced to make an agonizing choice between my career and the community, I had left Bethlehem and moved to Florida. Now I'd come back home to a pot of gold.

I soon joined Redeemer's large dance ensemble, which included women trained in jazz, ballet, and folk dance. This was no fly-by-night group. Their roots were in the early coffeehouse days, where the first Redeemer dancers got started with folk dances choreographed by Jeff Cothran and Margi Pulkingham. I noticed how large swatches of the congregation knew many of the dances. In fact, when the choir swung into one of the older tunes of the '70s, everyone dashed into the aisles.

Diane Angel Reed, the same woman who had defied convention to marry Larry 10 years before, led the dancers. Although the dance group itself was about as non-political as you could get at Redeemer, you still had to wait in the wings if you wanted a turn to lead. Redeemer lore was that newcomers were expected to take their place at the back of the line, shut up, and stay that way for at least five years. In every church I had been in up until this point, I had led the dance ministry. Here, I was expected to follow Diane. Our philosophies on liturgical dance clashed, to say the least, but I noticed something about Diane that was rare among Christians. She was committed to working out conflicts. One day, when our differences seemed irreconcilable, I mentioned that I had a two-hour gap between the time I finished work at the *Chronicle*'s downtown office and when the dancers met on Monday nights. By the time I commuted 16 miles through rush hour traffic to my townhouse in west Houston, I had to turn right around again and drive another 16 miles to church. It was too exhausting, so I was simply staying at work until dance practice began. Diane, who lived two blocks from Redeemer, offered to let me come dine with her family before practice. I knew she was trying hard to go the extra mile in loving her enemy, and as we talked over dinners at her home, I realized how much of her training in human relationships had come from her days in household. There, one was not allowed to let the sun set on anyone's anger. You simply did not walk away until things were worked out. Years later, Diane was still obeying this precept.

The dance ministry was one of Redeemer's brighter spots. A sleepiness and a malaise hung about the church at large, where congregants seemed casually, sometimes sloppily, dressed. The informality was more than just Texas cowboy; it did not take long for me to discern that at work was a rebellion against institutions and authority that went very high up. Something had clearly happened to these people to sour them forever on being told what to do. Ladd, for instance, often didn't wear clerical collars to work, so I had the odd experience of walking into the church and not knowing who the priest was.

Redeemer was functioning as a typical Episcopal parish, with the slightest of echoes suggesting the fervor of household days, when everyone had lived with everyone else and spent all their free time around the church. Worship in the old days was intense and fiery, and I could detect the romance of people willing to lay down their lives for each other. Many people at Redeemer still thought as if they lived in community, and every time someone left the church, the remaining members felt horribly diminished, as if an arm or leg had been cut off. It was the same community quality I had known at Bethlehem Community in Portland five years earlier. Households had caused it, and households had given the church the openness and transparency that created real community. In the mid-'80s, Redeemer instituted house churches, which were like weekly Bible studies for church members in various parts of the city. But they were a weak substitute for what had been.

Redeemer music was gorgeous, no question about that. With style and grace, the congregation sang four-part harmonies of entire Mass settings that Betty Jane had composed years before. The other songs, mostly composed by the Fisherfolk, were poignant, vulnerable, gentle music of the heart. From time to time during the service, a kind of wistful yearning to touch the Lord or be touched by Him would seep forth from the congregation, but invariably it was squelched by one of the leaders up front. Then I could sense shoulders slumping and eyes dimming around the room.

It was hard to believe this was the same place that had set the pace for charismatic renewal 15 years back. Was community what had made worship really happen? In the Portland community, worship was of a superior timbre to what most churches offered, because Bethlehem members were worshipping from the sense of fellowship they were personally experiencing. Most churches tried to create worship on Sunday mornings from a vacuum, but the Redeemer of the 1960s and 1970s had an ongoing life during the week that set the stage.

At the beginning of Advent, Grover and Bob Warren stood up to give a testimony. Bob Warren was a kind-looking, larger-than-life man with a bushy brown beard and gentle eyes. He was 6-foot-four-inches tall and a building subcontractor. Desperate to revive the glory and power Redeemer had known in the mid-1960s, Grover and Bob realized that one thing the original five elders had done was pray daily, early in the morning. So they too began meeting at 5:30 a.m. each day for Morning Prayer in the chapel. Slowly, more and more people, mostly men, were coming to pray. Praying men were a rarity in most churches, and it impressed me that Grover and Bob were trying to recreate some of the power and beauty of those first early morning prayers with the five elders 22 years earlier.

Bob Warren had stumbled over Redeemer three years before, when, during a summer afternoon, he heard a voice two feet behind his left ear.

"Go to Redeemer," the voice said.

Bob spun around. He was alone in the room. Bob was not predisposed to hear voices—he had not been inside a church for 24 years. He got out the White Pages and looked under "Redeemer, Church of." He first drove to the Lutheran Church of the Redeemer, which was about two miles to the east of the Episcopal version, but for some odd reason, Bob could not make himself get out of the car. Then he tried to find the other Redeemer, which was a real trick because the phone book showed that address on Telephone Road. But Telephone Road stops abruptly several blocks from the church and doesn't pick up until almost at Redeemer's door. Finally, Bob managed to find Redeemer, and made his way to the third floor, where he met Bob Woodson.

"What can you tell me about the Episcopal Church?" Warren asked. Woodson obligingly gave him a booklet, which Warren paged through.

"Look," said Warren, "I really don't want to deal with a bunch of liars and hypocrites."

"This place is filled with liars and hypocrites every Sunday morning and I'm the biggest one," Woodson said.

Impressed, Bob stayed. I began going to these early meetings, and thus got to know Redeemer's most stalwart intercessors. Then we'd head upstairs for coffee while Grover held court in the parish hall, telling entertaining anecdotes about Redeemer history. Grover worked with neighborhood ministries, which meant he handled all the street people who wandered into the parish. He also worked with the Hispanics who filled the parish hall on Thursdays for a program in which they did volunteer work around the neighborhood or church in return for free food. Grover almost always wore suspenders and gold wire-rimmed glasses. He had white hair by now and a *basso profundo* voice. Redeemer fit Grover, who felt out of step with everyone else most of his life, he told us. Here, he was living witness to the fact that you understand Redeemer by intuition, not by logic. The man was childlike, vulnerable, sometimes godly, usually wise, and in a state of perpetual brokenness.

"Sometimes," said Grover during one of those morning coffees, "when I look out and see that congregation seated there like rows of missing teeth, I could just cry."

Grover remembered the golden days when legends walked the parish hall. He was Redeemer incarnate—a suffering soul, a man of sorrows, a just man. According to Jewish legend, the wisdom of the world reposes in 36 "Just Men" who are indistinguishable from other mortals. Often, they are unaware of their own identity, and their calling is to grieve and undergo the world's sorrow in far greater measure than others. If one of them is lacking, the sufferings of mankind poison the world and suffocate humanity. Every place with a destiny is pleased when a Just Man makes his home there, for a prophet has seen fit to rest there and testify, if only by his presence, of how the Messiah suffers even more. Grover was Redeemer's Just Man, a reminder there was more to the church than met the eye.

One of the items the early morning group was praying about concerned Graham's return to Redeemer. Three years into Ladd's rectorship, it was obvious the parish was again at sea. There was no direction as to where they were headed. That October, Bill Linden had proposed to the vestry that Graham do a series of four visits to the parish. Graham, he said, would bring about an anamnesis at Redeemer—a "remembrance of our roots and calling it forth into the present and into the future," is how he put it. The idea was that Graham would be in residence at Redeemer for a week at a time, meeting with various parish groups for "informal discussion and dialogue." Bill then made a motion that the vestry budget $8,000 for four visits in 1987. It passed 8-4, following some bitter arguments. Nevertheless, a vestry memo stated that Graham was invited to act "as a facilitator and a catalyst to enable us to hear the Lord clearly about the direction and the vision of our life together."

Mindful of the bitterness that remained from Graham's previous sojourn at Redeemer and as a condition for his coming, Ladd, Bill Linden and Cliff Wilson, who was senior warden by now, instructed Graham to apologize for his actions in the early 1980s. Still, his detractors were galled by Graham's $2,000 "consulting fee," to be paid for each week of his visitations. To calm things, Bill and Cliff personally footed the bill for the first visit, hoping the vestry would be entranced enough to work Graham's fees into its 1987 budget. The private funding did not show up on the vestry minutes, the duplicity of which outraged one vestryman so much that he resigned.

Graham flew in the first week of December, spending his time with select groups, such as the vestry, house church leaders and a group of younger, potential leaders; in all, about 50 people. The large outer core of Redeemerites, the true grassroots of the parish, was left to speculate as to what took place. Minutes of these meetings were never publicized, if indeed they were ever taken. It was as if Graham did not want his methods tested by the glare of publicity. Some of the Redeemerites who had the clearest perceptions from God about the church and who could have spotted serious, even fatal, flaws in Graham's reasoning, were not invited. Their first glimpse of Graham came during the Friday night service.

The night began with tepid worship and a Graham announcement that he would speak on the church as similar to the temple in the Old Testament. I settled back for a boring speech.

"When I was here in 1980–81, I think I probably said some ill-advised things at times," he said next, "And I ask you to forgive me for those things. I also probably said sometimes things in a harsh way. They may have been advised but not said well. And I would ask you to forgive me for those things, too. The only excuse I can give you is none. The reason is that I really was not well in those days. You knew that, didn't you? I didn't at the time. I don't have a very clear recollection of things that went on in that period of time in terms of details, which is probably an indication of how unwell I was. But it was grievous. It is grievous to me that those things happened and I pray and I hope you pray it will never happen again. Can you say amen to me with that?"

"Amen" the crowd of 330 responded. He preached on his theme for about 20 minutes, then said, "I have the impression that we have, all of us, been going through a rough time. You have felt, many of you, or people that you know, that somehow God's presence has been not so real as it has been in the past. I think you are quite wrong. There's been a different presence of God: A presence for cleansing, for healing, for strengthening, for maturing, for stabilizing, for pruning, but it's been God's powerful presence. And I believe in witnessing the leadership of this church—and that's really all I've seen in this last week, I believe in witnessing the leadership of this church in the last week that God is going to open up once again with mighty power among us here."

Now this is what we wanted to hear; that at the corner of Eastwood and Telephone roads, things would start happening again for the faithful who had hung in there. The glory would come back. God had not forsaken us. In fact, He had sent Graham as an elder statesman to tell us what to do. Best of all, Graham was his old charismatic self again, especially when he exhorted everyone to praise the Lord continually. He had caught onto this truth in a new way only three days before, "and you know," he confided, "I found myself praying in tongues incessantly."

There was a silence.

"Do we all pray in tongues here?" Graham asked mischievously.

"Yeeeeess," the crowd responded with some hesitation.

"Yes, I found myself literally praying in tongues," Graham continued, and he went on in that vein, continuing to urge people to pray in the Spirit. It had been ages since anyone had heard Graham wax eloquent on the gift of tongues.

By the time Communion began, people were so keyed up, so yearning for God's power, that they sang and sang in the Spirit. Then came a prophecy with a mysterious yet bracing quality.

"In the past, you heard about the gentle spirit come into this place," said a parishioner named Ward Schmidt. "Now I am sending a very strong spirit through here. I'm laying before you a choice: to be carried along with this spirit or be knocked down by it. I ask for you to really look at the choice I'm laying before you."

Graham returned in March for more discussions and, to no one's surprise,

Redeemer that spring loaned Celebration $30,000, without interest, to purchase the manse and church in Aliquippa. No deadline was set as to when the loan would be repaid. A few weeks later, Leo Alard preached at Redeemer. Leo was a sleeper. He was a hefty Hispanic man with delightfully earthy metaphors, piercing sermons and no fear of calling things as he saw them. The Cuban-born Leo and his first wife, Irma, had come to Redeemer years before when she was dying of cancer and he never forgot the kindness he was shown there. He had since moved to Austin, Texas, as director of the Hispanic office for Province VII. Hispanic priests were quite the rage in Episcopal circles. Leo was leadership material, and eight years later, he would be elected a suffragan bishop.

Leo had barely been preaching 10 minutes when he began talking about racial prejudice based on the John 4 text on Jesus and the Samaritan woman.

"Everyone here, especially at Redeemer, is Christian," he said. "You're doing a good job in the community, but have you, as a disciple of Christ, allowed Him to take away your deep-rooted prejudice against them Mexicans, against them blacks, against them whatever?"

He joked that this might be the last time he would be allowed to preach at Redeemer, then said, "You have been a light in the darkness for more than 25 years. You have permeated and saturated the Episcopal Church with the love of Jesus, but are you going to remain by the waters of Babylon contemplating the glories of the past, or are you going to be open to see what Jesus wants of the Christian community of Redeemer today? In this present moment, where is He moving you to move the Episcopal Church to?

"You have infiltrated the Episcopal Church, and there is no place in the province or in the country where I travel where an element of the beauty of the music or the spirit of Redeemer has not been carried out. Redeemer has been a center of training, of missionaries, all over this nation. Are you going to remain, or am I to say to you . . . return to your first love? Return to Jesus. Forget the past, as glorious as it may be and look at the present and to the future. Where is Jesus wanting you as a community to move forth? What is He challenging you as individuals, as groups, as a community? What is He challenging you today? Hear the Lord challenging us to forget the glories of the past and to look at Him."

People applauded but Leo had been right. It was many years before he was invited back to Redeemer.

IN the U.S., 1987 was turning into the "year of the bimbo," thanks to Jessica Hahn, Jim Bakker, and the PTL TV network. It was a year of uncertainty as heroes fell, fortunes took a dive on Wall Street, and reputations waned amid press reports of scandal after scandal. It was a religion writer's heaven—so much was happening on our beat that our articles were frequently on our newspapers' front page.

The scandals began in January, when Richard Roberts warned that his father, famed evangelist Oral Roberts, might die if supporters didn't pony up a few million dollars. Then in March came the PTL scandal. Each successive revelation got weirder and weirder. After a while, sources quit calling back with comments. They were too numbed to talk. It got so that nothing could shock us; no one's reputation was inviolable, no sexual misconduct among men of God unheard of. The news was so bizarre that Pope John Paul II's 10-day swing through the country in September proved to be an anti-climax by comparison.

Texas was especially hard hit by scandal. That April 22, 38-year-old Peggy Railey, wife of the senior pastor of First United Methodist Church in Dallas, was found strangled and beaten in their garage. She ended up permanently comatose. Her husband, Walker, 39, had an alibi that didn't quite match up to where he was supposed to have been. Then he tried to commit suicide from a drug overdose. *The Dallas Morning News* began publishing accounts of Railey's liaisons with another woman, the daughter of a deceased bishop.

That was still making headlines a month later when Methodist Bishop Finis Crutchfield, the same bishop who had brought Oral Roberts into the Methodist Church, died in Houston of AIDS. We had been tracking rumors about his homosexuality during the months before he died, and my co-writer and I were even thinking of patronizing Houston's gay bars to see if we could locate the bishop's acquaintances. When he died, the family insisted they did not know how he had contracted the disease, which set off a furor among the local gays, who knew perfectly well why he had died.

Compared to that, my new house church, headed by Bill and Martha Ann Linden, was a refuge. Not including children, there were 33 of us in what was reputed to be Redeemer's most dynamic home group. Bill's hope was that somehow we could regain the closeness of community without living next door to each other as in the old days. His house church was certainly a test of that, because we were scattered all over west and northwest Houston. One of the women, Cindy Engle, was a violin teacher who had these odd prophetic dreams about Redeemer. I had been there but a few months when she offered her latest: a dream about Redeemer's famous mural turning monochrome, a teal color, with two women performing on instruments in front of it. It was, she said, symptomatic of how Redeemer was in imminent danger of losing its distinctiveness and merely becoming a performance.

Other people were also having disturbing dreams that hinted at judgment coming Redeemer's way. I had made friends with Mary Johnson, one of the members of the dance group, who told me of an odd dream she had of some sort of divine deadline set for Redeemer. Redeemer, she said, had from the Advent of 1986, when Graham first came, to the Advent a year later to get its act together. Not long afterwards, Martha Ann told of a dream she had, also involving some sort of deadline the church was under, and stating that 1987 was the final year. Its similarity to Mary's was astonishing, considering the two women moved in different church circles and lived in different parts of town.

In May, Ward Schmidt handed Ladd another prophecy. "I am serious about this matter of confessing your sins," it began. ". . . To go further, you must have an honest and forthright relationship with Me. To do that, you must be aware of and acknowledge your sin."

It was obvious to this newcomer that something was wrong at the church. The grassroots people talked openly about why they did not trust the leaders, and I noticed some people were in eldership because they were friends with Ladd, not because of any consent by the congregation. Because of people's innate suspicions, it was difficult to get the whole congregation moving in one direction, and it was light years from when the church could command dozens of people to show up at Lantrip within a half hour and they'd be there.

It did not help that church offices were on the third floor, making it difficult for a newcomer to find them and giving the impression that "the leadership" was up there thinking things out. People sometimes joked about "the myth of the third floor," because when you actually mounted the two flights of steps, sometimes no one was there. The bookstore, the real heartbeat of the parish, was tucked into one corner of the parish hall. There were no signs near the entrances of the church informing visitors where anything was. The whole construction of the place was built on an assumption that there were plenty of people present to show you around, tell you where to go, and give you directions. Redeemer was a shell by now, and anyone hanging out in the parish hall tended to speak only Spanish. The place seemed aimless and lost, and no one knew what lay at the top of the steps.

I realized this was Redeemer's Lent, the season of the cross and the bleakest of the liturgical seasons. Most Lents end after 40-odd days, but Redeemer's travails seemed to go on and on and on. Even oldtimers like Camp Huntington, the hippie-turned-household-member, was amazed at how visibly downhill things were going. The teaching was a lot less solid, and even Graham's preaching seemed more geared to cleverness than to the cross. Graham had done what he said not to do years ago, Camp thought: Make an idol out of what gives life. People were not confronted from the pulpit as they once were. Love and comfort were preached; repentance was not. As he worked in his favorite hang-out, the sound room, Camp figured God had given Redeemer what members wanted—a world-famous community—but something had happened along the way that was not what He wanted. So, like the children of Israel, He had sent leanness to their souls. Of course, for the spiritually hungry out there, Redeemer was certainly better than nothing. But Camp had tasted what a real steak dinner was like. This was definitely the leftovers. Had he been on his way to catch his freighter today, nothing at the present Redeemer would have prevented him from going.

That spring, I was researching a story on the Fisherfolk and I assigned a *Chronicle* photographer to take Graham's photo. Graham happily posed in his clerical shirt while friends joked about his vanity. That evening, I saw him smiling at me in church. Surely, I thought, it must be at someone behind me, for hadn't I tried to approach him last December about his fantastic sermon and gotten rebuffed? I had not forgotten his rude remark about newspaper reporters years before in Woodland Park. But no, he was motioning to *me* and saying something polite about the photographer, and would it be possible to get some promo pictures out of it? I said I would see what I could do and he smiled again, nodded, then turned back to Ladd. He could sure turn on the charm, I thought, and sure enough, as I was talking after the service with two men from my house church, Graham walked by, brushed aside the two men, gave me a hug, and walked off. Graham seemed to feel that whatever he wanted to express took priority over anyone else's conversation.

I was less charmed by the mysterious "group of 10," the handpicked leaders who met with Ladd and decided the direction of the parish. It was the sort of eldership system that Graham had tried to kill off upon arriving in 1980, yet it had sprung up again as Ladd's kitchen cabinet. I had a run-in with two women in the group who were in charge of devising programs for all the house churches. I asked if the house churches could see a half-hour video promoting an upcoming national charismatic conference in New Orleans that was supposed to follow up the 1977 Kansas City conference. It seemed tailor-made for Redeemerites, because several major Episcopal speakers would be there and it was only a seven-hour drive east.

"I don't want our house churches to take up their time showing it," one of the women said abruptly. "Redeemer really isn't involved in the national charismatic renewal."

"I really disliked the video," the other woman said. "It was way too happy-clappy and I'd never think of telling someone to spend their vacation there."

That was my first encounter with Redeemer's isolationist mentality and its in-bred leadership. Unlike other churches I had attended, these folks didn't read national Christian magazines such as *Christianity Today* or *Charisma*. They were too fundamentalist for them. The reading material in the church office was more *Sojourners* and its ilk, all throwbacks to the community days. Redeemer had everything to do with getting the charismatic renewal started in this country, I thought, but now they wanted nothing to do with it.

I expressed my disgust to Judy Berno, another member of the Linden house church. She thought I had better lie low.

"Ladd says you're a gift to the church," she added, laughing. "But you could also be Pandora's box."

CHAPTER 21

The Feast of St. Polycarp

"Strengthen the things that remain, that are ready to die. . . ."
—Revelation 3:2

I didn't lie low for long. Redeemer had organized a reunion of all its former members for the second week of June and more than 200 out-of-town people were showing up, plus scores more who lived in the Houston area. Everyone was thrilled. Here it was, 1987, and for one weekend, we would have the chance to go back 15 years to the Spirit-anointed era. My Fisherfolk article, which was splashed over the front of the religion section the weekend before, generated more interest. The reunion began on a Thursday, with speeches by a Redeemer old-timer and a Redeemer newcomer. Ladd asked me to say something as the newcomer. I put together the most radical speech I could, showed up at Bill's law firm to rehearse it before him and Judy, who was his secretary, and later before my roommate Karin. I showed up that Thursday morning feeling frightened, for Redeemer was such a maze of subtleties that one misstep could earn one unmistakable scorn. No one would ever say anything, but I would know.

I began with a list of Redeemer's good points, then quotes from Graham's first visit, Leo Alard's sermon, some things Paul Felton and Ladd had said, and a few sentences from Carol Anderson, the priest who had led a renewal weekend at Redeemer in late May. All this was to build on my premise that Redeemer needed to act now to save itself from oblivion. The Lord takes what Redeemer does so seriously that He sent two women dreams last December, I said. And now, the deadline was only six months away.

"God wants to do more mighty works among us. It's up to us whether we'll let Him," I concluded, leaving the stage to rush back to work. I was late and Thursdays were our day to lay out the religion section. Before I could get out the

235

door, nearly a dozen people rushed me, thanking me for saying something about the church's failing state. Paul Felton was beaming and thanking me, Graham gave me a hug and Betty Jane said I had courage. The gamble had paid off.

For the next two days, people bearing name tags from Redeemer's past floated about, the most visible, of course, being Graham and Betty Jane. The original five elders were under one roof for the first time in years and Bob Eckert had a vision in his mind's eye. It was of the original five elders standing in front of the congregation in a show of unity that had not happened since the late 1960s. He had talked with Grover about this, and both men felt that Redeemer would be spiritually stalled until the original "parents" of its renewal visibly reunited, if only to repent the lack of love that had pushed them apart.

But making up for past wrongs was not the zeitgeist here. Bishop Frey flew in and preached about not dwelling on the past, and Jeff Schiffmayer celebrated Eucharist before more than 600 people. That Sunday, when Graham preached, 813 people packed the church. That morning proved to be emotion-packed, egged on by Graham, who began his sermon by having Wiley Beveridge play his new song, "O How Good, O How Wonderful," about life shared in community. "Do you remember the first time you came?" Wiley sang, and everyone did remember the pain, the joy, and something precious that was lost forever. Facing the misty-eyed congregation, Graham reminded them of the Ezekiel passage God had given him 23 years ago, back in the chapel, calling him to renew the Episcopal Church and be a light to the denominations. Those two prophecies have come to pass, he said. Then he called Bill Linden to the lectern.

"There is a story that I am told is true," Bill began in his precise legal fashion, "about the hundredth monkey. Some of you know it. But it goes like this: there is an island somewhere south of Japan and near China where a tribe of monkeys live. Some sociologists went there to study those monkeys. And quite by accident, they found that the monkeys liked peeled bananas. They would peel bananas and throw them down on the beach. The monkeys grew quite fond of them, but they didn't like the sand that was on them. So they tried to brush them all off, but sand grains have a way of sticking to bananas, and they had a difficult time doing it. They would eat the bananas, because they liked them so much they would put up with the sand.

"But one day, one monkey learned something very new: how to wash the banana in the stream of fresh water coming down the mountain. And that one monkey taught her baby monkey to wash the banana in the stream and the next day, that baby monkey taught one of his friend baby monkeys to wash the bananas in the stream, and that baby monkey the next day taught his mother to wash the bananas in the stream, and so, one by one, more and more of the monkeys began to wash their bananas in the stream to get the sand off. The rest of the monkeys, all this time, had been brushing the sand away and eating the sandy bananas."

The congregation began to chortle. Bill continued.

"And so, one day, finally, a strange and very unique thing happened. At dawn, 99 monkeys were washing their bananas in the stream, and all the rest were eating their sandy bananas. It was on that particular day that the 100th monkey learned to wash his bananas in the stream. And a startling thing happened. By the end of that day, the entire tribe was washing the bananas in the stream.

"There is a critical point at which enough monkeys—or people—begin to conform to a certain pattern of behavior that it is a socially accepted pattern of behavior that the entire tribe does it. They don't need to learn one by one any more. It's us. It's what we do. It's who we are."

In terms of churches, Redeemer was "monkey number one," insofar as beginning renewal among Anglicans, Graham explained. Those at Redeemer had not yet reached that critical number for there to be a new beginning, he said, adding that Redeemerites had fallen down in recent years in wanting God to be everything in their lives.

"And I don't know what the critical number is, who are the monkeys restored to that place," he said, "of wanting God to be the only thing in his or her life, but you need to pray diligently for God to raise that number quickly because you have six . . . months . . . left!"

Silence.

"You have no time to waste," he added. There was a pause. "And I know that this denomination of ours, the Anglican Communion . . . until the critical point has been reached in congregations around the world, will, one by one by one, come alive to that spirit of communalism of the kind we have experienced here, until finally, the entire Anglican Communion will have reached the place where it is socially acceptable. And I think that's the pattern of renewal in this communion of ours."

He went on for a few more sentences, then paused.

"Graham?" piped up Ward Schmidt, "Could you explain more about our having six months left? I think a lot of people weren't here."

"I'm sorry," said Graham. "There have been prophecies here which I think have been generally accepted, have they not?"

"We don't know," several people said.

"Well, those who don't know, don't answer me!" Graham ordered, as the congregation laughed. "Those who do know, who have heard the prophecies and have had them affirmed through some of the teachings here on Friday, yes, they have been generally accepted. They were referred to in some of our meetings on Friday, which apparently you were not present at. And those prophecies said that this church had one year to get its act together. And those prophecies have been generally accepted by the prophets in this place and I believe it's true. And you have six months left."

"Is that view professed by the church leadership: Ladd or Grover?" a voice asked.

"I think so, is it not? I took it to be so." Graham turned to Ladd.

"I think so," Ladd said.

"Well, Ladd says yes. And Grover? Are you here?"

"Yes," came a deeper voice.

"Is it true?"

"Yes," said Grover.

"I had not heard that," the voice said half apologetically.

"I see," said Graham smoothly. "Well, I am not originating a new thought. I'm sorry. I thought that was generally known. Maybe this is symptomatic of the problem you're going to have to face." The congregation laughed ruefully.

"Because surely, in a congregation of God's intense love, peace, shared life, and ministry, that kind of thing could not go unnoticed by a significant segment of the community," Graham chided. "Do you know how much I love you?" he concluded. "Any notion? It's unspeakable."

In return, they sang a song, "Graham, Jesus Loves You," and the service floated on like a party bubble. But Bob Eckert wept. The restoration of fellowship among the five elders, for which he had desperately hoped, had never happened.

Graham's announcement hit the rest of the congregation like a bomb. The next night, the vestry demanded an explanation. Ladd gave his version of what had happened and why he and Grover had assented to Graham when put on the spot. No one at that vestry meeting felt that Redeemer had only six months left, nor accepted Ladd's explanation that it had all sprung from a prophecy given last December at a small prayer meeting in the chapel. The first time anything public had been said about the "six months" was during my speech the Thursday before. Graham had heard that and had run with the ball. The furor around the parish did not subside until the following Sunday, when Ladd explained the origin of the "prophecy," then demolished any notion that Redeemer was on a six-month deadline.

Bill Linden was furious at the explanation. Despite the mess-up in communication, he felt that there could be some sort of divine warning in it all; after all, his wife had had the original dream. If Ladd had only run with a message of repentance, Bill Linden mourned, it would have spurred the parish to seek God more fervently. Wasn't 1987 the year of suspended judgment, the year for people to repent? As time went on, I began to see Bill was right.

IT looked like any other American suburb, only a bit more leafy. So this was Ann Arbor, the promised land for charismatic Catholics. Word of God's book arm, Servant Publications, was putting out my first book, and I was in town for some interviews. Early one rainy summer morning, Barbara, a publicist for Servant, and I snuck into the back of an all-men's meeting in one of the houses belonging to the "brotherhood," a celibate men's group within Word of God to which Steve Clark, among others, belonged. The men at this meeting were mostly University of Michigan summer students sampling the brotherhood lifestyle.

As it turned out, their worship was no-holds barred: loud, boisterous, adoring. Everyone sat in rows facing one wall, singing, kneeling, standing, praying in the Spirit; somewhat like a corporate devotional time. The bare-faced intimacy these men exhibited before God, and the ruthless adoration in their singing, was so intense I was geared up for the rest of the day. This was the renewal at its best.

It prepared me for a strange interview I had later on with Ralph Martin. I was working on an article on Catholic televangelists for the *Chronicle* and Ralph certainly fit the bill with his new show, *The Choices We Face*. This was a man who helped found and lead a sweeping renewal movement, had met several times with Popes Paul VI and John Paul II, while at the same time fathering a large family. Now, Ralph was subdued and pensive. He was 44, about my height, with luminous gray-blue eyes he rarely fixed on me; thus, I had this disconcerting experience of interviewing someone who continually stared down at the corner of his desk.

Nevertheless, the interview was informative, more for what Ralph did not say than what he did say. Word of God seemed to be doing well, but Ralph, the man who 10 years before had given the famous "mourn and weep" prophecy, seemed to have lost his fire. He was telling me that the charismatic renewal was one small part of what God was doing, perhaps because a 1980 split between Word of God and People of Praise had demolished the Catholic renewal's strength. The only thing people were excited about now was Medjugorje. Ralph had indeed given the prophecy, but a decade later, he had to come to terms with the fact that even he could not obey it.

Most of the people I met at Ann Arbor were not present at the New Orleans charismatic congress a few weeks later for the simple reason that they were not invited. Most of the Catholic representatives were from the People of Praise. This omission hurt the congress badly, for I had been there only two days when those of us in the press box began admitting how bored we were and how different it all was from Kansas City. The crowd topped off at 35,000, 10,000 less than Kansas City. The most exciting event was a 17-block parade of Christian floats and marchers, yet even that seemed flip and showy; something that would not have even been considered in Kansas City. And though it was the year of the PTL scandals, there was no mention of repentance during the general sessions, mainly because the real prophets of the renewal had not been asked to come. Instead, German evangelist Reinhard Bonnke, famous for his mass healings in Africa, was reduced to pacing back and forth on the red-carpeted stage one night, calling out healings and urging the crowd to sing in tongues so as to bring down the power faster. Obviously, God was not too impressed, for only three people were visibly healed that night, and those of us in the press box leaned back in disgust.

Besides the journalists, the only ones there with any clue as to why things were wrong were the messianic Jewish speakers. Art Katz, in a packed afternoon session, jabbed at the listlessness of the renewal.

"No wonder we've had to turn the amplifiers up to create the sense of excitement and activity," he said. "If we pulled the plug out to see the reality of who we really are, it'd be very disappointing."

In another session, Jews for Jesus founder Moishe Rosen castigated listeners for rejoicing while at the same time much of New Orleans, not to mention the world, was going to hell. Something was wrong, he said, with a rally that could not attract more people than Kansas City.

"I think the day of the big conference is past," he said. I asked him why he, a non-charismatic, came to these meetings. "I love these people," he said. "They are the activists." The saving grace of the conference was a sobering prophecy delivered near the end by Francis Martin, a Catholic priest.

"I have something to say to you leaders among my people. I have chosen you. You did not choose Me," it said in part. "I have placed you to care for My people. I have committed Myself to you and My blood to you but I have this against you. You compete with one another. You rely on human resources. You are attached to money. I tell you this: I have chosen you and because you preach

My name, I will not count you as being against Me. But unless you seek My will, unless you pour out your life before Me, unless you tremble at My Word, I cannot stand by what you do."

Back at Redeemer the following Sunday, a group of us who had been to the conference described our impressions to the congregation. I used my allotted time to simply read the prophecy. After I was done, the congregation was silent. Even when one of the lay readers followed with the Prayers of the People, no one responded.

O UTSIDE, the July evening was bathtub warm; the air still and tender. Inside the church, dozens of persons filled the pews, heads bowed in prayer. "There will be no small groups tonight," the bulletin board in the narthex proclaimed. I and Rob Blain, a friend from the early morning prayer group, looked at each other quizzically.

"Why not?" Rob asked Cliff Wilson, stationed by the entrance to the sanctuary.

"We're waiting until when people can talk about other than themselves," Cliff replied.

"God is still dealing with individuals?" Rob asked.

"Yes, we're getting overwhelming feedback about that," Cliff said. Rob and I entered the cool church, where some sat and a few stood, their arms raised skyward for several minutes. Paul Felton was standing in one pew, his arms outspread in the form of a cross. Redeemer had entered two weeks of a corporate vigil, an idea suggested by Carol Anderson, a visiting female priest, as a way of fine-tuning the parish's vision. Especially after the six months warning, a vigil for listening to God seemed appropriate. By Wednesday of the first week, close to 200 persons were in church: praying, reading, listening, standing, kneeling, and squirming to stay comfortable for two silent hours on hard pews in the dim light. Only a church that knew it has a destiny would have put up with this. All parish events had been cancelled and, as the week wore on, we began meeting in small groups to share our impressions. This continued throughout the second week. By the final Friday night, the tensions of all that accumulated quiet time burst forth in one of the most blazing worship sessions I'd ever witnessed at Redeemer.

It then fell to the leaders of the parish to wade through 58 pages of thoughts, prophecies, warnings, and messages compiled by the congregation in the hope of seeing a pattern. What emerged sounded ominous. One of the men wrote of a vision in which a man's hand holds a crumbling beige brick. In spite of its poor condition, the bricklayer wished to lay it on a nearby wall, but even as he lifted it, brick dust and particles kept on slipping through. In fact, only the bricklayer's hand kept it from falling apart. The vision ended before the bricklayer succeeded in laying the brick atop the wall, and it was by no means certain that the brick would not crumble before it made it to safety.

"A number of nights ago, I was given a dream," someone else wrote, "in which I was driving over a causeway above a large body of water. Off to the left, out in the dark of the night, was a large ship with a hole in it, already leaning far to one side. An enormous stream of water was being pumped out of it, and another ship was out there, assisting. A helicopter was overhead, keeping an eye on the rescue, as work was being poured into making the repair. Pray for this ship and pray for the workers making the repair. For if the repair is made, the ship will be stronger than before, but if it sinks, it will sink to the bottom."

Yet another woman dreamt that she and her family were inside a house being moved off its foundation because they had failed to meet some criterion or deadline. The people inside were intact, but the house had been tossed aside. Repentance, unity, and forgiveness were big themes, and some, like Bill Linden, tracked the vigil notes in great detail, noting how much attention was being paid to major topics such as healing, spiritual gifts, the Bible, and obedience. But underlying it all was a note of warning that went unheeded. For other than a general letter issued by the group of 10 on September 6, nothing further was ever heard about the vigil. All the repentance it called for, all the confession, all of the accountability, came to nothing.

Slowly, death began to invade the church. Graham returned that September for more discussions with the leaders. Redeemer was shaping up to be led by a super-committed group of 60 or so who would set direction for the church. It was very similar to what he had proposed for the Society in 1981. What was quite disconcerting was how those 60 were supposed to pledge they'd remain at Redeemer for life, a maneuver that cut out those of us with growing careers or families in other parts of the country which made remaining in Houston a huge sacrifice. It favored the older set with established careers and families in town. How these chosen 60 were going to agree on anything was beyond most of us, for the 10 existing leaders—whose number was expanded to 15 after Graham left—were obviously working at cross purposes. Bill Linden began preaching every third Sunday on the need for community. Grover would preach on the poor or the Hispanics, getting so wrought up in the pulpit he could barely choke out his message. Finally, he stopped preaching. Ladd never sounded a clear note on anything. It was obvious that Redeemer's powerbrokers were jockeying for secure positions to withstand the deluge.

Further proof of the dangerous spiritual waters came in October, when a well-known woman in the parish was raped. Afraid to stay home alone, she showed up in church Sunday morning on the verge of collapse, weeping throughout the service.

Ten days later, Oct. 19, was Black Monday, when the stock market fell 500 points, 600 million shares were traded, and $500 billion disappeared into nowhere. Newspapers were calling it a "financial meltdown" and a "bloodbath." New York saw the bold black headlines late that Monday afternoon. Later, I learned that David Wilkerson, who had moved back to New York that year to start a church on Times Square, had been wandering about Wall Street only a few days before, burdened with a premonition of something dreadful looming.

Also while in the Big Apple, I visited George and Leslie Mims's new parish, St. George's. Scattered about the pews were Fisherfolk songbooks. In five years, George had done a lot of work. The music was a mélange of folk guitars and drums and traditional organ music that Betty and George had pioneered at Redeemer. Although the music was charismatic, the preaching was not, for the rector was not known as sympathetic to renewal. It was as if all the sets were in the right place, but the drama was taking place elsewhere. Still, it was better than nothing, and attendance had jumped from 40 on Sunday mornings to 225. George was living in a beautifully decorated five-bedroom apartment, spacious by New York standards, and staging Christmas candlelight extravaganzas with a $17,000 budget to pay for all manner of liturgical dancers and renewal music. His reward was that 1,400 persons waited two hours to get in.

Graham did not come to Redeemer that December, for his meetings had been put off for another month by the group of 15. Six months had come and gone since his sermon and nothing was ever mentioned again of that strange, mixed-up prophecy. A child untimely born was allowed to die.

CHAPTER 22

The Feast of Saints
Perpetua and Felicity

"Then she named the child 'Ichabod' saying, 'The glory has departed from Israel!'"

—I Samuel 4:20

O NE January morning, the old stone church with the red door was so frigid that some 80 of us huddled on the oak pews and shivered in our coats at All Saints. I was visiting the Community of Celebration to research an article for *Christianity Today*. It was great grist for *CT*'s mill: evangelicals rolling up their shirtsleeves and doing good deeds for the poor in a run-down steel town on the banks of the Ohio River. The Community of Celebration was nowhere near what *CT* would rate as a truly evangelical group, but I was in no mood to highlight that. That winter wonderland Sunday at All Saints, Graham, dressed in white vestments, was preaching on the Magi. It felt magical, for Graham appeared not to have lost any of his homiletic powers. He was also speaking on his favorite topic: the poor. "And I really mean the poor," he said. "The Gospel was first preached to the poor so they may love one another, which they don't naturally do. Usually they fight over the few scraps they have."

Graham exuded confidence, quoting the many Scriptures he was obviously steeped in and lending credence to the sense that this was a man who expected to be obeyed.

"Are we the star that can attract people to us?" he asked, comparing the church to the star of Bethlehem. "It won't start by preaching the gospel to the rich. But it will start when we preach the gospel to the poor. But we'll have to embrace them, laugh with them, weep with them, and suffer with them. We may not see the fruit of it for 10 years!"

We all sat rapt.

"We are this star in this part of God's heaven," Graham concluded with a flourish. People were clearly moved. We joined in with the Prayers for the People. "Give us grace to this church in Aliquippa to catch the vision of being that star," Bill Farra pleaded to God.

Nevertheless, in this first month of 1988, it seemed as if the church was barely reaching Aliquippa. Perhaps one-third of those attending that Sunday were the 26 community members and their 13 companions. One third were students or faculty at the seminary, and the rest were residents of Aliquippa. The community had seemingly swept in like a ruling family while the old-timers found themselves outmaneuvered and no longer needed. Bit by bit, they had fled to other churches, not wishing to take on the monastic lifestyle offered to the parish. Those who remained were often illiterate or had less than a sixth-grade reading level. The community clearly outclassed everyone else there. Though they included some of the same cast of Eastwood characters from 20 years before, they were completely different people. As in the community in Colorado, there was a reticence about charismatic gifts and evangelism, as if those were for a bygone age.

I spent hours interviewing Bill and Graham, both of whom were upbeat about plans to use their brick worship center as a place to host retreats, sabbaticals, and internships for worship leaders. The idea was that church leaders would be invited to experience the community for up to a year and "do theology with us," Bill explained. He chaired the board of directors for the Aliquippa Alliance for Unity and Development, an ambitious organization trying to start local business in the depressed city. It was housed in a cheery office on Franklin Avenue. He was the community point man around the drab, boarded-up city, for he was personable and didn't mind hobnobbing with the locals. With things so depressed, it was not hard for the community to help better things, if only by their presence, energy, and new ideas. They sponsored the Food Share program, whereby people could pay $12 monthly, do two hours of community service, and receive $40 worth of food. It was all modeled after Graham's old dream of social action, before his baptism in the Spirit had interfered. Now, the sky was the limit. Here was Graham's opportunity to put the failure of the early 1980s behind him and emerge as an elder statesman of the renewal.

"We're starting from scratch," he told me. "I don't like all that much the direction the charismatic renewal has gone; people getting their jollies once or twice a year at a meeting but ignoring their local church."

"Then how do we keep the renewal alive?" I asked.

"Not by mega-meetings," he replied. "Only one thing will do it and that, people don't want to hear. It has to do with authority in the church."

What was he suggesting, I wondered. A return to the bad old days of shepherding and discipleship? Later, I had dinner with Graham and Betty in their spacious, green-walled manse with the grand piano in the living room. We talked about her efforts to start a choir of neighborhood kids, but when I asked her about bringing them to Christ, she gave me a blank look.

Winter blew into spring and Bill Cox, an Episcopal bishop, led a renewal weekend for us. He had walked into a Friday night service in February 1973 and was blown away by the testimonies, the Scriptures expounded, the way the entire congregation sang in harmony, and the spiritual energy that poured out. He was especially amazed to see, when someone entered a pew, the whole row stand and hug that person.

That Sunday afternoon, a few of us took him and his wife, Betty, to Galveston and on the way there, he reminded us that Redeemer, to thousands of people, symbolized the fountainhead of charismatic renewal. We looked at each other. Us? But now, he added, Redeemer needed a vision of where it was going and a game plan on how to get there.

But, one of my companions interjected, wasn't the Hispanic ministry the vision?

No, the bishop replied. That was a ministry, a component, an end. The vision had to be an idea; who are we and what has God called us to? I tried to hide my devastation. After four visits by Graham, the vigil, and the reunion, this bishop could walk in and say that essentially nothing had changed.

The center was not holding and people kept on leaving. That spring, there was a blowup at church when the teachers of the parish Montessori preschool decided they had had it with parish and clergy indifference toward ministry to children. Clergy visits to their classrooms were non-existent and the teachers found, to their shock, that they were not considered a ministry of the parish despite the fact that the school took up part of the ground floor on weekdays. Their 72 students, half of whom did not speak English and many of whom were unchurched, were a ready-made mission field that the church refused to take on. Late that spring, Grover praised the preschool teachers from the pulpit. Theresa Wilson, who taught the two-year-olds, got nervous.

"At Redeemer, we give the eulogy before we bury people," Theresa reminded another teacher sitting beside her. "I've been here 17 years and I begin to see patterns in what happens to people."

She had been around during the early days when people were urged to "lay down their children for the Lord." Leaders tried to beg out of the constant late-night meetings, saying they wanted to read to their young ones. "You need to trust your children to the Lord," they were told, "and come to the meeting." A whole cadre of children in the church was embittered because their parents were never there for them.

One day, Theresa was standing in line, making her way through the church foyer. The plumbing at Redeemer had broken down once again. As she contemplated the removed tiles and the dirt, the Lord informed her: *This plumbing is a picture of the church and the corruption here goes under the foundation.*

Then I need to get the children out, Theresa thought. *You don't leave children inside a burning house.* She realized that God had already declared judgment, not only on the situation but on the church itself.

Meanwhile, another parishioner was hearing odd things come out of the mouth of her three-year-old son. How, she wondered, did he know of such topics? When the talk continued, she and her husband began suspecting the worst; that a man they knew from church was abusing their son and a small girl for whom he babysat while the parents worked. When the parents of the girl came to see this couple with identical suspicions, they all knew some sort of sexual perversion was happening. The news seeped out to some of the preschool teachers, who noticed similar symptoms in several children they knew.

The two couples went to see Ladd, because the man they suspected taught Sunday School at Redeemer. The man had come to Redeemer from another church, they knew, and their question was: Had this man been run out of his former church for the same misconduct? Because Ladd, as a priest, was privy to the secrecy of the confessional, had he known of this man's predilections? When the other couple filed criminal charges and had the man arrested, the Redeemer grapevine buzzed for weeks, especially because Ladd had asked the couples involved to say nothing about the matter. It was like trying to douse a fire with gasoline, for both couples wanted justice, not secrecy. So this was why the preschool was not considered a ministry of the parish. If it was, then Redeemer was liable for whatever had happened there.

The other couple then filed a civil suit against the diocese and Redeemer, and the pressure was on Ladd to do something or at least make a statement. But nothing was ever done, nothing was said in the house churches, the criminal suit was dismissed because the children wouldn't testify, and the civil suit petered out after the couple who filed it left the church. The parents of the three year old remained at Redeemer, but the mother was shocked to find out that people would refuse to babysit her son or invite him to play with their children, as if he had some infectious disease.

Finally, the preschool closed and its $25,000 inventory was given away. The preschool staff destroyed their letterhead and their parish connections, most of them leaving Redeemer within the year. All were baby boomers who were Redeemer's future leaders.

> *Turning and turning in the widening gyre*
> *The falcon cannot hear the falconer*

ESSIE AVALOS was in Austin that summer, taking a Spanish course and trying not to pay attention to the knot in her stomach. She could not get her eldest son, Basil, out of her mind. Thirty-year-old Basil had been baptized in the Spirit at age four, only to get started on drugs by a high school teacher. She knew he was now drinking heavily, and she suspected he was also on drugs. She had begged him to read the Bible, hoping that would help somehow. She prayed fervently for her son, and she could have sworn God told her He would turn Basil around.

She called her husband, Abdias, pleading with him to check Basil's apartment. The horrible feeling in her stomach was getting worse and worse.

Then the phone call came. Basil's body had been found, a Bible on the table beside him. It was clearly a suicide, and to make things worse, Basil had left a brief message on their answering machine, simply saying, "Happy Father's Day . . . and goodbye."

She went into spiritual shock, demanding of God how this could have happened to a child of one of Redeemer's priests.

"You gave him into My hands," the Lord reminded her. *"He's still there. You know how much you love him. Do you think I love him less?"*

It would be two years before Essie would even begin to recover. Eventually, she and Abdias would leave Redeemer to work with Hispanics in Los Angeles.

> *Things fall apart; the centre cannot hold,*
> *Mere anarchy is loosed upon the world,*

MARTHA ANN LINDEN was depressed. No matter what happened at church, nothing ever got done or healed.

Her husband, Bill, had been preaching for months now on community; in fact, nearly every sermon touched on it. After a while, Bill himself would kid about it. Searching for something that redefined community for the 1980s, he discovered pop psychologist M. Scott Peck's latest book, *The Different Drum*. In this 334-page work, Peck had seemingly discovered the very thing Redeemer nearly had the patent on in the 1970s, but packaged in a quicker, less painful way than living in households with other people and putting up with their problems day and night. Peck had perfected a method of creating community in a two-day period, especially over a convenient weekend. The simple recipe required little overt prompting from the leaders. Put a group of people together for a while, and the first byproduct is pseudo-community, during which everyone is as pleasant and non-confrontational as possible. Most Christian groups never get beyond this point because everyone feels pressured to skirt any kind of disagreement.

If the group is fortunate, they may advance to the next step, which Peck termed "chaos." This is when people begin to argue about their differences or try to convert others to their point of view. This can go on for hours, or until the group slides into the third stage, which is emptiness. Members of the group begin to admit doubts, inadequacies, failures, and sins, and the group goes through a kind of death together. The fourth stage, which is real community, comes without warning or planning. The group finds it is at peace and that people are talking about things that really matter. It was community by catharsis—precisely Bill's cup of tea.

For a while, he and the group of 15 were avidly reading Peck's book in the hopes of discovering that missing something Redeemer needed to recreate the community it once enjoyed. Everyone seemed to know what made Redeemer so special: the love people had for each other. And that, they thought, was attained through community. In fact, Redeemer's original community had come as a result of other things, such as ministry and the spiritual revival of the times. It was a means to an end, but Bill saw it as an end that could be partly created through some drawn-out group dynamics.

Long after the leaders had dropped Peck's book and moved on to other things, Bill continued thinking about it. Every so often, Peck and his associates would stage one of their controversial weekends in Houston. Bill made sure he went and got some of the Redeemer leaders to go with him. Peck had come along at an apt time in history when the psychologizing of religion had become quite acceptable. Religion was becoming therapy, and some people were more devoted to their 12-step groups than to church.

The book's key word was "experience." It was central to Peck's first book,

The Road Less Traveled, a best seller and a bridge between a religious culture of sin and salvation and a psychological culture of experience, love, and fulfillment. Peck and others like him were recasting theological language into something more accessible, and sounded the same, yet was vastly different in its implications. What was now most important was the self and its needs. Instead of the self needing to be crucified with Christ, its needs had to be met. Rooted in the philosophy of Alcoholics Anonymous and the co-dependency movement, a string of self-help books flooded secular and religious markets in the late 1980s, redefining the way one saw oneself and God. Instead of being corrupted by sin, the focus now was on imperfections, and it now seemed possible to get healed and become perfect. One way to feel healed was through community.

> *The blood-dimmed tide is loosed, and everywhere*
> *The ceremony of innocence is drowned;*

"SOMETHING is very wrong with Redeemer," Eugenia Rust was telling me. We were sitting one April morning in the 11th Street Cafe, a charming hideout in Houston's Heights district. I ate an omelette and biscuit while Eugenia munched on a patty melt. Eugenia was closer to my mother's age than mine. Years before, she and her husband David had moved to Redeemer from another lively charismatic Episcopal church: St. Paul's in Darien, Connecticut. She was normally thoughtful but upbeat and the kind of woman who would take multi-day retreats at Villa de Matel to get closer to the Lord. So I was not used to seeing Eugenia in despair, but that morning she confessed total hopelessness. She'd had some sort of dream or vision about Redeemer perishing in fire. What was coming was death. The parish was staring it in the face, yet no one was talking about it. Ladd would have to go, she was telling me. It was a mistake to have selected him as rector in the first place, yet few people realized that in the early 1980s.

"I think you're right," I told her. "We are going to die."

"We'll die in many ways," she responded, "but what I saw coming out of the fire were gorgeous roses. So, I mean to stick around for the finale."

I remembered that Cindy Engle had had a dream about fire, too; a fire that jumped continents and eventually engulfed us all. Then there was Karen Frerck's dream. Karen was a tall, quiet woman in my house church who was growing increasingly restless with the doctrinal fogginess there. She would go to leaders with her concerns, laboriously climbing the steps to the third floor office, only to be dismissed—pleasantly, of course, but dismissed all the same. Her nagging doubts persisted. Things at Redeemer were definitely on the wrong track. She liked the Linden house church, and she liked the worship but after she had her dream one night, she knew she had to leave.

The dream had an urgent quality to it, as if someone was signaling that she needed to pay attention. She saw a building that looked very much like Redeemer, but its trademark glass front doors looked more like a storefront. As she stood outside, she saw people from off the street entering the church because of all the music and activity inside. She got the overwhelming feeling that people were going in for the wrong reason, to be entertained. A great sadness hit her, for the people inside looked happy, but the place seemed more like a club than a church.

Someone unseen approached her—someone she could not see when she turned around. But she knew who it was, and he told her, "Come with me and I will show you the real Redeemer."

She followed him as they walked through a garden of thick vines and trees to the side of the church. They entered a building, going deeper and deeper inside. She felt sadder and sadder that they would never find the office. Then the building disappeared and all was gray and black. She continued on, then she and her companion walked out onto a balcony overlooking a traditional church with stained glass windows. There was peace, joy, and warmth. The original Redeemer did not have windows. What church was this?

W E stood around the altar, worshipping after Communion and after Art Katz had given his testimony. So much planning and politicking had had to happen before Ladd would consent to inviting him, and it was such a gamble to have this livewire here to conduct a renewal weekend. Yet, here the man himself stood beside me, worship pouring out of him.

Katz fulfilled everyone's hopes, even the skeptics in our group of 15. He was coming from outside the accepted boundaries of Redeemerspeak, but he had experienced so many of the same things that he pleased the most finicky of the insiders. He had lived in a community in Minnesota that had failed, a predicament those at Redeemer could understand. He understood the theory of shared economics, and of merged lifestyles, and as the weekend wore on, I was amazed at his ability to handle some of the toughest questions thrown at him. The church, he would say, is not a Sunday afterthought; in fact, it is a place reserved by God for the most exquisite suffering. But, he explained, we'd lost our sense of the glory of the church, which is why we were not attractive to the Jews. He went on at length about the church's commission to make the Jews "jealous," as the Apostle Paul had said, of the excellent quality of our life together.

While ruminating about the Minnesota community, he described their decision that the quality of their prayers and singing could not exceed the quality of their lives together. That is, it was easy to be spiritual while worshiping, but with worship came the false impression that the beauty of the music conveyed a health far beyond what the church deserved. I could hear the bells going off. This was the same deception going on at Redeemer—that one could walk into a Sunday service and fall in love with the music, and rave about how alive the church was, but the music did not reflect reality. No one at Redeemer could fail to miss the parallel.

There was little doubt that Art was the prophet Redeemer had been looking for to help us. When parishioners Gordon and Briann Butler hosted a potluck supper on Saturday night, we asked Art to comment further on community life. The Butlers' living room was packed with people eager to listen.

"Community is such an intensification of Christian life that one year there is like 10 years elsewhere," he said. "People who've left can't find anything similar in other charismatic fellowships. There's a quality of life that can't be duplicated." Everyone was nodding their heads in agreement.

"That kind of tension isn't available in our private lives," he continued, "where we rub against no one. Life together raises issues that we'd otherwise not face, that a million Sundays couldn't make us face. Community demands sacrifice."

Grover was sitting in the crowd. "Is prosperity the enemy of the church?" he asked. Art first explained how the poverty of his 55-person community considerably improved their life together.

"Poverty is a revealer of the secret heart," he said. "So many vital Christian questions, like faith, don't arise in affluence. You can't just make out a check so that the problem will go away. And faith is not mere subscription to correct doctrine. It is pulling out all the stops, which means you'll taste death if it isn't true."

But who wanted such suffering? Few of us did, yet he had been through what some of us guessed Redeemer might go through.

"We had to relinquish what we held so dear," he said. "We had to eat the death. It is necessary for those of us who have a calling to the Jews to experience desolation at God's hand, then resurrection. The God of our death is also the God of our resurrection. We shouldn't be taken by surprise. We must taste death, not just agree with it academically.

"What is truly death is when something successful is brought to the grave," he continued. "Why should we think this a strange thing? We must let go. We'll see another form of community in its resurrected life that will be more glorious than before."

> *The best lack all conviction, while the worst*
> *Are full of passionate intensity.*

FROM then on, the signs of Redeemer's death appeared faster and faster. Look at the content of June's sermons, Art had warned Gordon. If there is a watering down of the message, the church was headed for death. Sure enough, there was an initial burst of enthusiasm after Art had left—extra prayer meetings, for example—but eventually those got institutionalized into Compline, a 15-minute Episcopal liturgy recited at 9:30 p.m. Only the most committed could make it to church at that hour. I noticed people slowly drifting away. Leo Alard had warned me that when people outside the neighborhood decide that what's available at Redeemer was not worth the distance, time, and effort needed to get there, death would be in the air. That devastated my house church group, which was in Houston's western outskirts. Bit by bit, people began leaving for other churches, and our numbers began to dwindle.

Then there was the late night conversation with Diane Reed. She and Larry were moving to Tennessee, and she was talking about how inertia gripped Redeemer's leaders and how dead the center was.

"Yes," I said, "but the grassroots people at the edge will bring in the life."

"But," she said, making circular motions with her hands, "if only the outer part is moving and the core is not, then all the outer part can do is go in circles. It's the grassroots people who are leaving, and the Lord keeps on bringing in more grassroots and they keep on saying the same things."

A few weeks later, I was in England, sent there by the *Chronicle* to cover the once-every-10-years Lambeth conference of Anglican bishops. After watching several days of the splintering of the Anglican Communion over women's ordination, I needed a weekend off. I had arranged to visit the British Community of Celebration's center in Bletchingley, a small town south of London. On a Friday afternoon, I took the train from London to the nearby town of Redhill, but did not find Susan Abbott waiting for me as we had planned. She had forgotten to come—an omen.

The main house of the community, Berry House, was on busy High Street, which ran the length of the town. The Abbotts and a couple named Lorna and Steve Ball lived there, and Phil Bradshaw, a member studying for the priesthood, lived down the street with his wife. Lots of former community members had settled in the area, and several of them showed up for evening prayer at Berry House. When the community had made it known they were leaving Post Green, bishops from Liverpool, Southwark, and Birmingham vied for them. The Liverpool and Southwark situations called for social action ministries, whereas Birmingham's was more aimed at charismatic renewal. Gordon Abbott explained how the community had evolved from charismatic involvements to social out-reach, a pattern that all the Communities of Celebration had taken. Just like its American counterparts, the British community lost something immensely valu-able in the transition.

Though it was July, I was shivering in Berry House, and so I drank endless cups of tea to keep warm. The ground floor had red brick flooring, not the greatest heat conductor, so I spent much of my time in the kitchen, which was warmer and offered plenty of places to sit around a large trestle-style table. The lounge on the ground floor was colder and sparsely furnished with dingy and somewhat tattered furniture. A motley collection of community books and games were along one wall. Nevertheless, the place was comfortable, welcoming, and definitely lived in.

Threadbare steps led up to the second and third floor, where I was en-sconced for the night in the community office, an attic room filled with Fisherfolk materials. Lining the wall was a gallery of photos from Redeemer, some of them probably brought to England by the Abbotts when they first arrived in the 1970s. In the alcove was a bookshelf of socio-political-feminist material along with some evangelical offerings and of course "The Post Green Training Manual."

I had hoped to spend some time during my short stay there talking with Susan Abbott about the old days, and had written her beforehand, saying so. My hopes were dashed when I learned she had a line of counseling appointments for the rest of Friday and all of Saturday morning, as if she never had any intention of granting my request. A friend at Redeemer had told me that Susan lived most of her life totally booked up with appointments. Her husband Gordon was not of much help, for after our brief preliminary conversation, he retreated to the TV room for the rest of the evening and I was left alone.

At noon on Saturday, nearly everyone announced they were going to a football game at Wembley Stadium, leaving me there with Lorna. She was my saving grace, for she was friendly and answered questions, made sure I got lunch, and got me back to Redhill to catch the train to London. My short stay was quite revealing for if I, who was from Redeemer and knew my way about the ethos there, got lost in the shuffle, what about the stranger? Gordon had said they had no pretensions of being anything like what they had been in the early '80s because they were too few in numbers. Only the shell was left.

That October, another speaker arrived for a weekend at Redeemer. Philip Weeks, the Florida priest who years before had tried to replicate Redeemer's experiment in Miami, was there to speak on healing. He had some pungent observations on Redeemer, namely that we were too comfortable. The early charismatics depended on miracles for their survival, he reminded us, because they had been so persecuted. These days, we still wanted the same fruits of the radical lifestyle, but we were no longer willing to pay the price.

I could barely listen to him as I spent the weekend in tears. That Friday, just before I went to the airport to pick Philip up, I was informed by an assistant managing editor that a writer junior to me would be my new supervisor. Inasmuch as the *Chronicle* had earned a religion section award that year partly because of my work, the demotion came as a shock. And I had been around stab-in-the-back newsrooms long enough to know that the sheer nastiness with which this editor communicated this development to me meant the job I adored hung by a thread.

From whence came this body blow? Earlier in 1988, my first book, on sexual purity, was published. Soon afterwards, I got the oddest call from Bishop Frey. A reporter friend had given him a copy. The bishop had liked the book, he said, but he warned me, "You're going to be under attack from within and without" as a result. I foresaw some kind of death approaching my own life. I was being brought face to face with it, and with the employees who had planned the betrayal. These were people I had trusted. Like King Belshazzar watching the handwriting on the wall, I saw my doom being written out before me, and like Redeemer, my hour glass was running out.

CHAPTER 23

Annunciation

·"For with God, nothing will be impossible."   —Luke 1:37

Six months later, Phil Reiser arrived. A number of us had been following the teachings of a Dallas evangelist, Larry Lea, and his insistence that Christians could and should spend an hour daily praying through the Lord's Prayer. The way he taught it, the Lord's Prayer covered every need imaginable. Some of us had contacted Larry Lea's Church on the Rock, asking them to send us a weekend speaker to better explain this method. The would-be speaker cancelled at the last minute and Phil Reiser, a young evangelist, came instead. He was not at all a "name" speaker, and many Redeemerites, after having seen what little came of the Art Katz weekend, stayed home.

It was their loss. Reiser's teachings touched a chord with many of us. Some with extra-high Episcopal sensibilities, though, took offense at Phil's insistence that we repeat certain words or phrases as a way of cementing various truths in our minds. They began whispering that he was manipulative. This was typical of the way many non-denominational charismatic leaders taught, so I dismissed the mutterings as inbred ignorance. Phil, it turned out, was quite sensitive to the Episcopal nature of the parish and didn't comment on the liturgy, even to the extent that Art Katz had. Katz had witheringly told the group of 15 how deadening the Prayers of the People were and had walked out on that part of the service. But Katz had 30 years on Reiser and had passed the litmus test of living in community. After Phil's very presentable sermon Sunday morning, the congregation exploded in worship and adoration similar to the golden days. More than $1,600 was put in the offering plates as a thank-you to Phil and he left for

Dallas, promising to return. A number of unlikely parishioners were saying how unexpectedly good the weekend had been.

The next morning, we began holding 5:30–6:30 a.m. prayer meetings at which we followed the Lord's Prayer formula he had taught us. We added some things, such as facing to the east, west, north, and south; praying over the evil spiritual forces in the neighborhood; and commanding the four directions to give up to Jesus the souls destined for him. We prayed for the city of Houston, we prayed for our spiritual leaders. It was something refreshingly different from the Morning Prayer rite.

As the months wore on, we changed our prayer meetings to early Sunday mornings, and the spiritual atmosphere brightened noticeably during the main services. But the changes came too late. On July 30, Gordon Butler, who co-led the early morning meetings with me, announced he was leaving Redeemer. He was one of the church's major intercessors, even moving to a place across the street from the parish to better pray for it. Like many of Redeemer's baby boomers, Gordon was an entrepreneur and visionary who would not tolerate being processed to death while it took the older parish leaders years to make up their minds what was acceptable at church. He, too, had approached parish leaders again and again with prophecies and warnings about Redeemer. It seemed that if you cannot kill your prophets, the next best thing is to ignore them. The leaders had been innovators in their 20s, 30s, and 40s, but had become resistant to change in their 50s and 60s. They lacked the mental agility of their predecessors, and their most obvious characteristic was a reluctance to take risks. From what I could gather, their conversations were like so much inbreeding, and eventually such weaknesses came to the fore and became dominant.

I spilled out my anguish to Bill Linden over lunch.

"The anointing is gone," he agreed, "and people are leaving in droves." And they were—a family of four in my house church had just pulled out. There were many other decent charismatic churches in town where more was going on than what was allowed at Redeemer.

One day in mid-August, Cliff Wilson called to tell me the house church leaders had cancelled Phil Reiser's scheduled October return and declared a moratorium on future speakers. With disbelief, I heard Cliff use words like "negative impact of the weekend" and "the way he presented it was presumptive" to describe the house leaders' reactions. These were the same people who had worshipped so fervently the weekend Phil had come; who had contributed to the overflowing offering plate towards his compensation for the weekend. I asked more questions and learned that grassroots parishioners had taken Phil's words seriously, in fact, too seriously and they were asking why the moribund leadership had not responded. Instead of crafting a decent response, these leaders decided to do away with the problem altogether by getting rid of the man who caused too many disturbing questions to be raised.

I spilled out my frustrations to a member of the dance group.

"The craziness of the system never occurs to you until you smack up against it," she told me, "until you encounter in person its monolithic force and presence. It's like meeting the devil himself—most people flee right then and there. Why did you get into this mess? Because you were a leader. Had you taken no initiative at all, you would have stayed safe on the bottom. We all were on the bottom once, buffered by other leaders on the top who took the pressure for us. Then those leaders left, and suddenly it was in *our* faces. We were on the top and we had to confront it. We could retreat, whimpering, and from then on play it safe, or we could fight it and get crushed. Or leave. Those who leave got tired of never being heard; of seeing our efforts being killed and never bearing fruit in such bitter soil."

As those of us in the early morning prayer group prayed for the church, the mental picture that came up again and again was of an impregnable fortress, encrusted with years of slime and indifference, caked with sin and rebellion. Praying against it was like hitting a wall with a feather. It was like existing in a half-life. Sometimes, even the very air seemed twisted. For when Ladd, who communicated well enough as an individual, took to the pulpit, his words turned convoluted and confused. What needed to be said never got said. Words faltered and we were dumb. It was as if some reigning spirit bound our communication.

T HAT September of 1989, Graham and Betty's youngest daughter, Martha, got married at All Saints. At least one broken heart attended the church ceremony, for Bill and Margi Pulkingham were getting divorced. In her mind, it was because of Bill's spiritual questioning that began when they moved back to the States in 1982. It seemed to her that their marriage had been one long replay of all the hurts between him and his father.

Margi felt that the problem was not their marriage; the problem was Bill and his feelings. He never got a chance to grow up normally, never got to date normally, or be a normal teenager. So now he wanted his freedom. She traveled to Aliquippa to talk to the community. She could no longer pray for her marriage to be saved, she told them, but for healing them both personally. Bill's idea of healing was to leave her.

Anxious not to lose her completely, the Pulkingham family insisted she dance at Martha's wedding and be in all their family pictures. She performed her swan song for them, then drifted out of their lives to live in Galveston, eventually to remarry and bear twins, the kind of fruit she had longed for all her life.

That same month, I was back in New York, on my way to catch the flight to Israel that landed me in that meadow overlooking the Sea of Galilee. I snagged an interview with David Wilkerson in his two-year-old Times Square Church in the former Mark Hellinger Theater at 51st and Broadway. He was definitely not the showbiz type. He did not like being interviewed, he was uncomfortable posing for photos, and he was low on media savvy. This artlessness made him easier to talk with, especially about his warnings to Jimmy Swaggart before the evangelist's well-publicized fall in 1988.

"I don't think sex brings any man down," he mused. "I think it's pride." I asked him what had kept him away from sexual sin. Suffering, he replied. He looked a bit gaunt and obviously tired from having been up since early that morning leading Sunday services. I tried to pry something out of him about Redeemer and Graham. I had heard rumors that he was most unhappy with the turn that events had taken, especially because he was so publicly linked with Graham's spiritual baptism. Wilkerson replied vaguely, as if he had long since lost touch with both Graham and Redeemer. As I was packing away my notes, he looked at me.

"Graham came to me with a problem, you know," he said. "He didn't only come for power." And as far as he knew, Wilkerson added, Graham had achieved victory over his problem.

"The only way to stay righteous," he said, "is to expose your heart to God every day."

What was he hinting at? I wondered. *It's either money or sex.*

Two months later, I flew to Pittsburgh to talk with Graham about the Redeemer book idea. Fallen red and gold leaves were everywhere and the wind was cold. Graham, I found, was still reinterpreting charismatic renewal to fit into his life's love: Community. He had a new word for it: Commonality. The power of the charismatic renewal, he told me solemnly, was the principle of commonality. Just read the end of Acts 2 about how they shared everything in common.

I disagreed. Community was a result of the pouring out of the Spirit, but not the power behind it, I said. But Graham believed the renewal was really nothing without community. It was the community factor that made the difference in Houston; after all, there had always been lots of charismatic churches and social action groups. But community was the fire that ignited the charismatic and social action. What the charismatic renewal ultimately leads to, he added, was liturgy, because liturgy was worship that people did together. And whatever people did together was communal, he reasoned.

As for the book idea, Graham suggested I'd do well to get some theological training before attempting it. My thoughts sprang to Trinity Episcopal School for Ministry just across the Ohio River. I'd been wanting to get a master's degree there for years, but how was I to break loose from a full-time job 1,400 miles away?

T HE 1990s arrived and that following spring, Graham was invited to speak at a clergy conference in Virginia. Afterwards, a group of priests prayed over him and a vision came to one of them, retired Navy admiral-turned-priest Bruce Newell, who was assisting at Truro. Bruce saw Graham standing on an island surrounded by water. He had two images; the first one of Graham only needing to make a tiny movement on the island, and instantly ripples would speed outward. The second image showed Graham's feet so mired in the island that he could not move—hence, no ripples. In real life, Graham's vision was in pieces, the community was in trouble, and people were talking behind his back. When Bruce told Graham of this prophecy, Graham burst into tears. A month later, Bruce accepted the job as administrative dean at Trinity.

There were other troubles. One cool, sunny morning that February, I sat in my living room after prayers, sipping coffee before going to work. A thought hit me like a dart: This was the calm before the storm. I brushed the idea aside. That was my last peaceful moment of the day. Within an hour of the time I walked into my office, the handwriting on the wall sprang to life and twisted its coils about me. The betrayal I had seen 16 months before had fully flowered. Summoned to the office of the managing editor, I was told I was fired. He would not say why. A personnel officer escorted me to the front door.

I landed on the streets of Houston dazed. How could God have let such demented people win? I walked at least 10 blocks to the closest lawyer's office. Bill Linden was out of town, but as Judy listened sympathetically, I sat and cried. Outside the huge glass windows of his office, the grassy treetops of the East End stretched for miles, stopping only at the refineries in the distance. Peeking out of one tree was Redeemer's bell tower, a legacy of Tom Tellepsen's ambitious construction. That experience they could never take from me. I had moved near Eastwood the year before, and so I drove through the neighborhood and collapsed in the same living room where I had so peacefully rocked my chair that morning. Once again, there was peace and quiet, and I realized that good might yet come of this evil.

So I picked up the phone and dialed the seminary.

1991–1993

CHAPTER 24

Palm Sunday

"Blessed is the King who comes in the name of the Lord! Peace in heaven and glory in the highest."　　　　—Luke 19:38 (NKJV)

E VENING was falling that August 5 as Chris Hughes and I arrived in Aliquippa. My good-natured friend from Redeemer had agreed to help me drive a large rental truck from Houston to Pittsburgh a few weeks before my classes at the seminary were to begin. The Community of Celebration was going to loan us their guesthouse while Chris helped around the community and I searched for a place to live.

We had not been there an hour that warm August evening when it became obvious that something had gone terribly wrong with the community. Two of its members were forlornly standing on a corner, visibly upset at recent goings on. One, who had been inducted as a community novice, had put his process on hold because of the control he felt from the community. The other, who had transferred to Prince of Peace, the next closest Episcopal church, explained how All Saints had little or no Sunday School, Bible studies, prayer, or praise. He described how he set up a Bible study class in his home, which was successful until Graham undermined it by scheduling other events at the same time. When he and his wife confronted Graham, he said *they*, not the scheduling, were the problem.

Life in those rowhouses was like Hiroshima after the atomic bomb. Six adults had left or were leaving the community that summer, including two of the priests. Bob Morris was one of them, and his leave-taking had been the messiest and most bitter, because he had been with the Pulkinghams since the early 1970s. His wife, Cathleen, had been nanny to their children, and she and

Betty had been close friends all those years in England, then Scotland.

But by the time they moved to Pittsburgh, the Morrises were smelling a rat. Cathleen especially noticed how Graham had the best of everything: clothes and meals and medical help. The Pulkinghams often got to have liquor and good food in their home during times when the Morrises could not afford a Coke. She also noticed how those who traveled on the Fisherfolk teams got the flashier wardrobes, whereas the community members who remained at home in the office made do with clothes that were 10 or 15 years old.

But Cathleen was loyal, and fiercely so, and these rebellious thoughts did not come easily to her. She began reading the Rule of St. Benedict, noting the role of the abbot, which is what Graham fancied himself to be. But Graham, she thought, wasn't the servant-abbot at all. In fact, Graham had never sincerely repented for anything, so far as she knew. He might feel sorry, but it was more the kind of sorry one feels upon getting caught or causing pain but not in the sense of offending God. She had protected Graham from detection for years, padding his schedule and making excuses for him. He had become almost legendary for canceling or forgetting his appointments and generally not following up on things. The legend had died in Scotland, where Graham was merely painting by the numbers.

Between his trips to the "Y" and time spent in front of the television watching game shows, Graham was still vicar of All Saints. He disliked how the church's stone altar and pulpit were in the way, and had asked the vestry for permission to move them. Although they had not given him the go-ahead by the time Palm Sunday rolled around, Graham took matters into his own hands. A few days later, while the Good Friday service was in progress, two strangers entered the church. Graham had them wait outside and then, after everyone was gone, the two stonemasons hacked away the altar and one of the pulpits. One of the community members dashed in to to see the wreckage. "That's a consecrated altar, for God's sake!" he exploded.

Cathleen was appalled at the damage. Henceforth, the altar would be a simple table covered with a cloth. She could just imagine the expressions on people's faces when they walked in Easter morning and saw the major changes in the church. Clergy lore held that no major changes should ever be made on Easter; that is, if the pastor wants to stay employed. Graham had been priest enough years to know this.

"How dare you?" Cathleen asked Graham. "How can you do this to the people in this church? Graham, it'll take years to put the pastoral pieces together."

"I can do anything I want," was his serene response.

Parishioners continued to flee from All Saints to its daughter church, Prince of Peace, which by now had a new sanctuary. Another crisis arose. It was obvious that Clare Morris, a high school sophomore, was wilting in the poorly equipped Aliquippa school system. Often, she would leave her classes in tears and finally, in the spring of 1990, Bob and Cathleen had had enough. Having aided the Pulkingham children for so many years, Cathleen was well aware of the special exceptions some of them had gotten and the scholarship that sent David to a private school in Boca Raton. They asked for money to send Clare to a private school.

Their plea was rejected. That June, community leaders informed the Morrises that Clare was to be moved to another household, as if Bob and Cathleen were failures as parents. As they mulled over how to react, up came the community's annual companion conference. Such conferences, which drew dozens of people and helped bring in financial support, could be nightmarish, because Graham did not prepare for them even when he was the main speaker. Bob had been with Graham just before one spring companion conference when Graham turned to him and said, "Bob, what should I teach on?"

Thinking Graham was joking, Bob replied, "Well, Graham, I guess whatever the Lord had you prepare for them."

"No, Bob," said Graham, "really, what should I say?"

The 1990 conference proved to be the worst yet, for Graham was in some sort of funk. Finally, one week before the conference, community members persuaded him to get some material together. Bob was up the entire night before the conference's beginning, copying study sheets for the notebooks. Even as people were registering that Friday afternoon, he and one of the community women were madly stapling pages together.

"Why," he asked her, "do we keep doing this for this man?"

Even more bizarre was that Saturday night, when Graham broke down in tears while describing his longing for a brother he never got, saying that God had provided him Bill Farra as his best friend. All this was said with Betty Jane sitting right there. Most people thought this terribly odd, but perhaps Betty Jane was used to it or had cut herself off so completely from it that she was deadened to Graham's weirdness. Then Graham repeated that same theme about his love for Bill the following morning in church. Sitting in the back, Cathleen saw Betty Jane rise, walk to a back pew, sit down, and weep.

It was all getting too insane and the Morrises knew their time was up. They crafted a letter to be read to the community on the morning of July 2, as community members gathered for the daily time set aside for confessing their sins to each other. When the Morrises said they had been advised by outside people, Graham turned beet red.

"How dare you talk to people on the outside?" he exploded. The Morrises negotiated their terms of leaving through a lawyer. By the time I arrived, they were still living in one of the rowhouses, which they would leave a month later, taking with them $467, a beat-up car, the stipend Bob was getting from working at Celebration, and an unexpected cash gift from someone in the community. Although their meetings with Bishop Hathaway had gotten them nowhere, they still sent him a letter, dated Sept.24, warning him of "an evil in the community." That October, Cathleen landed a job at the seminary, assisting Bruce Newell, the new dean of administration and the same Virginia priest who had prophesied over Graham a few months before.

B Y the time I began attending All Saints, Graham was sporting a tiny, diamond-like earring in his left ear lobe, a white beard, and hair tied back in a ponytail. Every so often, his sermons would show traces of the old fire. He would still throw his arms around total strangers in the parish hall, but the magic seemed gone. I had only been there a few weeks when he announced he was resigning at the end of December, putting in four years as the vicar instead of the expected five. All Saints had not grown much since my last visit, even though Prince of Peace, a few miles away, was packing them in. One factor, I decided, were the Fisherfolk, who reserved the task of worship-leading to themselves. Anyone who wished to join them had to be present for several hours on Wednesday evenings to learn how to play the guitar just so. Even then, it was not a sure thing one would get to lead for they controlled their fiefdom tightly. Most of the congregation, however, was content to let the more gifted lead the worship for them.

One of the most gifted was Betty Jane, with her clear soprano voice and a presence that filled the room. She had a grace and private majesty all to herself. She also did not allow mistakes. Betty could carry off flawless holiday productions that were mind-boggling in the complexity of music sung and in the excellence of the children who took part. She had reached the culmination of her career, having been named to the Episcopal Standing Commission for Church Music, replacing George Mims, who had rotated off. She had published an awesome body of music in the past 20 years: 120 original songs, 106 arrangements of existing songs and hymns, and 31 descants and musical responsorial settings for the psalms read each Sunday during three-year cycles in the Episcopal liturgy. She especially loved composing descants because elaborating on hymns only beautified them more and, she believed, produced intense pleasure for God.

The community still envisioned itself as a group of poor believers, living in the neighborhood and challenging the larger political and social structure for change, but it was questionable whether such laudable things had made a dent in Aliquippa. After five years there, they had not made nearly the impact that Redeemer had made in Houston in the five years after Graham's baptism in the Spirit. Instead, the community seemed more shell-shocked by Aliquippa's daunting challenges and the need to constantly protect themselves. Graham and his community, I realized, did not have the spiritual power to make changes. They were the same actors with a similar script, but 25 years had made all the difference in the world.

As the months crept into winter, I noticed how passive the congregation seemed, and realized that it did not matter whether we came to church or not. The coffee hour after the service was agony, for the community people mostly talked with each other, leaving only seminarians or elderly ladies for me to talk to. I began skipping that hour altogether. The townspeople, picking up on the atmosphere of exclusivity, ventured in tiny numbers inside All Saints. It was too odd and too different. Most of the churches in Aliquippa were either all black or Roman Catholic, and the idea of joining an Episcopal religious order for twice-daily prayer wasn't selling. The majority of the seminarians couldn't tolerate the place, either, and although All Saints was a mere three miles from Trinity, they opted for more distant parishes.

Sunshine poured in through the windows of the restaurant in downtown Indianapolis and waitresses rushed back and forth as one of my Redeemer friends, Debbie Scott, and I ate breakfast with two women from the Word of God. They were describing some imminent disaster hanging over the large group. Because whatever happened at Word of God tended to affect the larger charismatic renewal, I listened intently.

By 1984, Word of God had dropped its strict training course, but directives from the prior time remained community policy. Some of the rules verged on the unbelievable, such as the requirement that married men make up a weekly schedule for their wives to follow at home that included all the cleaning, raising of children, and housecleaning, including dishwashing and diaper changing. Wives were never supposed to refuse sex to their husbands and vice versa; the result was a lot of exhausted, angry wives. When Word of God leaders asked one of the single women in 1990 to conduct a poll about community life, the woman was aghast at the horrors her married compatriots were enduring. Twenty percent of the community's women were in some sort of counseling. More wanted therapy, but their husbands would not allow it.

Meanwhile, the relationships were crumbling between Word of God senior coordinator Ralph Martin and Steve Clark, who headed Sword of the Spirit, an international charismatic organization of 51 communities. By 1989, the two men could not work together, and by the spring of 1990, Sword of the Spirit agreed to allow Word of God to switch to "allied" status, which was a looser form of affiliation with Sword of the Spirit. Word of God officially voted that September for this near-separation, and things began to unravel quickly after that. One memorable October evening, Ralph Martin delivered a lengthy speech to the community, outlining a system that had become a charismatic bureaucracy, with numerous committees, rules, and procedures. It had started well, he said, with prophecies at the community's founding in 1970, when the Lord stated, "You are My word to the whole face of the earth. I haven't poured out My Spirit on anybody like I'm pouring it out on you."

That, Ralph was now admitting, was "prophetic hyperbole," adding, "We thought it was us. We were number one. We had it all together. We were the best. We were special."

So was the prophecy false or true? That question was not addressed. Ralph had decided that if he was going to repent, he might as well do it right, and thus, throughout a painful evening, he provided a litany of the community's failures. Some of them sounded hauntingly like Redeemer's.

"We began to withdraw from participating in the wider charismatic renewal," he said. "We began to feel that unless what we did was adding to our thing—people or money and resources through commitment and covenant—it really wasn't that worth doing."

He ended by asking the crowd's forgiveness. When they responded with applause, he said ruefully, "I almost feel like I'm in recovery, like I'm getting reprogrammed or deprogrammed or whatever. I'm seeing things in a way I haven't seen before."

That was not the end of it, for two months later, the community had another evening session to officially dismantle the nefarious training course. After one of the leaders read a numbing list of "we repents," several coordinators came to the microphone, weeping, as they begged forgiveness for their part in prolonging the system. After that, Word of God leaders set about making amends, going out of their way to search out people they had shunned or excommunicated during the preceding 20 years. They freely talked to any publication willing to interview them, though they knew the articles would be critical. Much like Reba Place elders who, 10 years before, got on their knees and, before their community, repented the abuse of their authority, the Word of God leaders pragmatically figured that honesty was the best policy. Although messy in the short term, it left far less residue than did abuses at Redeemer that no one had ever repented for.

It was clear that what was left of the community movement had hit the skids. In December 1990, *Sojourners* magazine published an essay by co-foundress Joyce Hollyday describing how their group, too, was coming apart at the seams. From a high of 45 adults, their membership was now down to 12 after people had left for a variety of reasons. Some were weary of life in the inner city. Others wanted to go in more radical directions than Sojourners wanted to allow. "Each of us," Hollyday wrote, "asked ourselves if the pursuit of shared life was worth the energy and risk. We knew only too well that this same struggle had gripped all the communities with which we had shared friendship over the years—and most had not survived it." Neither had her marriage to Jim Wallis, the leader of Sojourners.

The national charismatic renewal, such as it was, seemed blithely unaware of these communities' agonies. Perhaps the communities were closer to the front lines of spiritual warfare, as well as the first to realize that whatever God had poured out in the 1960s and early 1970s had gotten cut off by the late 1970s. We had been coasting on the echoes for a decade now. My trip to Indianapolis that August had been to cover the 1990 North American Congress on the Holy Spirit and World Evangelization, a follow-up to the New Orleans conference. Although conference organizers expected 30,000-40,000 attendees, and said so publicly, it was plain by the first night that maybe half that number were attending. Obviously, charismatic renewal was no longer selling the way it had, because everything that needed to be said had already been said. The conference opened with former Olympian Jim Ryan running in with a torch, followed by 45 minutes of lively but over-amplified music danced to by a troupe of bouncy young missionaries known as the King's Kids. It was such crass entertainment that dozens in the crowd registered their boredom by walking out before many of the night's speakers got to talk.

The next day, I hit the exhibit hall, walking by a booth for the Jimmy Swaggart Bible College and Seminary. No one was there. Crowds mobbed the Discount Bibles stand across the aisle. Debbie and I had managed to get an invitation to sit in on the nightly prayer meeting that all the charismatic speakers had to attend one hour before the evening session. She and I slunk into the room and sat next to a wall. Someone announced that the Holy Spirit would fall during that night's session. Congress organizer Vinson Synan recounted a vision from someone in the Word Gifts group who watched as one of the night's scheduled speakers, a man, received a message from God over the phone. But, according to the vision, the speaker decided to give his prepared message instead, throwing the phone into the wastebasket. The observer tried to redial the number, hoping to reach God, but all the lines were busy. The next thing she saw was a vacant building.

The assembled group spent no time mulling over this sobering message. They spent more time discussing whether to move up the offering to earlier in the program, because so many people were walking out early. Only $66,000 in donations had come in the first night, and one of the conference organizers said that, to break even, they would need $50 from all wage earners present among the 21,500 attendees. They gathered the four main speakers in the middle of the room and prayed over them loudly in tongues for a few minutes, especially for Bill Beatty, the man making that night's funding pitch. Beatty, it turned out, did well. Introducing himself as a "born-again, Holy Ghost-baptized, tongues-speaking Catholic," he got a roar of applause and $134,000 in the plate. Still, the evening session went late and by 9:30, people were filtering out the doors with several speakers still left.

The next morning found hundreds of us packed into an auditorium where a group loosely known as the "Kansas City prophets" were to speak alongside John Wimber, the charismatic apostle to baby boomers from southern California. Wimber, who headed 300 churches with 500 ordained pastors, was so laid back that he didn't even lift his hands during the worship portion of the meeting. He matter-of-factly talked of a longstanding disagreement one of his churches had with a certain pastor and described how his denomination had to deal with instances of sexual immorality in the ranks of its clergy. He was direct, mellow, and willing to air his group's dirty laundry. One of his pastors, Mike Bickel of Kansas City, was next, speaking on the purpose of the prophetic. His rapid-fire delivery was tremendously gripping and he stuck to his 20-minute limit even though other speakers went over theirs. Everyone was madly taking down notes; no one was walking out. Last to speak was Paul Cain, whom some people were proclaiming a prophet. Cain languidly announced there would be some healings, and pointed a finger at David Collins, the charismatic former dean of St. Philip's Episcopal Cathedral in Atlanta. Yes, Collins said later with some amazement, he was healed right then and there of a problem with his ankle.

That evening, Bill and Gloria Gaither performed a high-decibel, 60-minute act before a largely passive crowd. Next, organizers hit up the crowd with a sock-it-to-them offering pitch, but attendees had been fed nothing spiritually and donated only $55,000. Five thousand people walked out before the final speeches. The conference was like a slow motion dream, running against tremendous resistance. Those of us sitting in the press box were comparing it to swimming underwater and missing the boat, or like biking uphill and being in the wrong gear. Everything worthwhile was missing. There was no sense of awe, of God's holiness. And no one believed God was talking at all. Even the singing in the Spirit was insipid and, like a plane heading down the runway too slowly to take off, all human effort seemed to crash and burn.

By the next day, conference organizers were plainly desperate, for they had to somehow raise $300,000 by the end of the evening. They pulled out every stop that night; Synan even asked for those who wished to give $1,000 to stand for special recognition. Some rose to their feet. Chuck Irish made an Episcopal-style low-key-but urgent plea, which brought in $160,000. Later, a Catholic participant approached Synan with a $150,000 check, saving the shirts of the individual organizers. The evening ended with another light show extravaganza by the King's Kids, Jim Ryan ran out with the torch, and everyone was commissioned to be evangelists. The show was over.

Learning little from the American fiasco, British charismatics led by Michael Harper staged "Brighton '91" the following summer, pegged as the "greatest gathering of charismatic leaders in world history." Organizers had hoped to get 25,000 to attend, but the opening night crowd was less than 2,100. Relatively few Americans attended, because advertising had portrayed the conference as an invitation-only event for leaders. Later, when it became apparent that far fewer people were attending than projected, organizers Larry Christenson and Vinson Synan appeared at charismatic gatherings to ask people to attend. Few did.

Although he was dying of cancer, charismatic author Jamie Buckingham was one of the leaders who did go. He stayed for only part of the conference and later wrote it up as a "backyard pony show," in his magazine *Ministries Today*. Despite the fact that some excellent speakers were present, the organizers once again misjudged people's desire to attend one more conference on evangelizing the world, Buckingham said. Like Indianapolis, it was a financial failure that showed once more that leaders were out of touch with realities such as the recession, travel costs, and people's awareness that such conferences offered the same old fare.

"Future planners will do well to seek God for clear direction before planning conferences," Buckingham sermonized. Undoubtedly, Harper and his co-planners felt they had listened to the Lord when, years before, they got the idea for Brighton '91. But those of us who sat in the press box at the 1987 and 1990 conferences could have enlightened them on the mood of the grassroots, who have an odd way of hearing the voice of the Lord.

MARGO FARRA died of cancer in the fall of 1990, and on a cold Monday night in November, 40 of us gathered at All Saints for a memorial service. Daphne Grimes, a priest from Wyoming who had known community members since their days at Yeldall, led the service, which featured Colorado-inspired Fisherfolk tunes. People shared their memories of the vivacious, playful Margo, who was leprechaun-like in so many ways, until towards the end of her life. After the Colorado community collapsed around her in 1986, she had taken up with various women, and rumors abounded about her sexuality. In her later years, she seemed like a lost soul, and her song, "The Sun's Gonna Shine," played at the end of the service, expressed her forlorn hope that somehow, life would get better.

Those of us gathered there were an odd mixture, beginning with Daphne, a universalist who liked theological mavericks such as Bishop Spong and Matthew Fox, wrote poetry decorated with yin and yang symbols, and detested Trinity's conservatism. And she was Celebration's new spiritual director. Bishop Frey and his wife were also at the service as they had just moved to Ambridge a few months back when he was named Trinity's dean. Their eldest son, Paul, was a student at seminary. My relationship with the elder Freys was a bit frayed because I had not stopped my freelance writing work when I entered seminary because I needed the income. Barbara and I had gotten into an argument over this, particularly when Bill said something delightfully cutting in chapel about a particular bishop. Thinking like a journalist, I figured that the chapel service was a public meeting, and thus the quote was on the record for an article I was writing. Barbara insisted I check with her husband to make sure I could use the quote. I balked, whereupon she asked if I was a student or a reporter.

"Well, a student of course," I replied automatically, at which point she said Bill's remarks had been in-house for students only. I had had conversations like that before. The real questions were left unsaid: Are you with them or with us? Are you a reporter or a Christian? It was always my spirituality that got called on the carpet, never theirs.

Meanwhile, Bill was charming students and faculty with his new role as bishop-turned-college professor. When he co-taught spirituality classes for first-year students, he took off his reading glasses, leaned against the podium, and preached, waving his right arm and reeling off pithy quotes.

"Seminary," he informed us, "is painful because you're dealing with the core of your identity. But the church is a battleship, not Love Boat."

That got a laugh, but the bishop could utter profundities as well. In the midst of a discussion about C.S. Lewis, Frey informed us that erotic, sexual imagery in the Bible tied to God shows a passionate desire for Him.

"Spirituality is a quasi-erotic relationship to God," he informed us. "It's like lovers. It's where God turns you on and you hope to turn Him on. God is passionate for us." And on he went. Never a dull moment.

That January, Bruce Newell took over All Saints for an 18-month stint as vicar. It was a formidable task. Bishop Alden Hathaway had asked him to take on the mission, which was not the most rewarding of posts and especially for a man new to the seminary and new to his second marriage. Moreover, Bruce had left the Diocese of Virginia after a scandal involving him and female counselees at the Falls Church, the largest parish in the diocese. But the matter was kept under wraps and away from the media—at least for a time. No one I knew of at Trinity or All Saints was aware of Bruce's past.

Hathaway was quite aware, but discerned that Bruce was someone who could out-eyeball Graham. As spring wore on, it was plain that the parish was stabilizing under Bruce's basic, organized, Bible-centered preaching. A former naval officer, he used naval metaphors in his preaching and decorated his stole (the scarf-like garment priests wear) with anchors. It was almost comic for the generally pacifistic community.

"Come, Holy Spirit," he would pray before his sermons, "be my pilot, for my ship is so small and the sea is so great." No one murmured about these small ironies. The community had been choking the parish, and Bruce tried to infuse new blood by bringing in preachers from the seminary. In spite of his truly determined efforts, the surroundings did not fit him and everyone sensed it. Graham was acting a lot more chastened these days. After all of the departures the previous summer, Alden had brought in Benedict Reed, the abbot of St. Gregory's Abbey in Three Rivers, Michigan, who could see through Graham as well as anyone. Graham had been made to face the reasons for people's unhappiness with him. He had moped after the confrontations, but everyone hoped he might change for the better.

Since retirement, Graham could do a lot of spiritual direction, which he was especially gifted at given his ability to cut through people's evasions. His top customer was none other than the bishop of Pittsburgh, who found in Graham a breadth, discernment, and knowledge of Anglicanism no one else within driving distance possessed. But Hathaway was the community's Visitor, the only person with any power to discipline the community and Graham. There were lots of raised eyebrows around the diocese about this arrangement, but both men pleaded innocent of any conflict of interest.

One thing Alden tipped off Graham about was a series by British novelist Susan Howatch. During the 1980s, Howatch, better known for her gothic tales of scandalous liaisons and steamy romances in colorful English settings, had turned her formidable talents onto the Anglican Church. Her first book, *Glittering Images*, was about an English clergyman who had daunting powers of discernment, but whose spiritual powers nearly brought him to ruin. What made the series so intriguing to Graham was Howatch's extensive research on past bishops of Canterbury and her inclusion of charismatic spiritual gifts in her narrative. No one before had even tried to include such things in bestselling, swashbuckling prose, but Howatch pulled it off with a flourish. Graham had urged me to read *Glittering Images*, and when I did, it seemed plain that Graham identified with Jon Darrow, the tormented hero of the saga who had God-like "glamorous powers" of healing, and who was simultaneously an abbot, clergyman, and exorcist. Before Darrow had joined his religious order, he had been married to a woman named Betty, who later died. But in Howatch's second book, *Glamorous Powers*, Darrow misused his powers, left his religious order, and suffered a spiritual breakdown.

CHAPTER 25

Maundy Thursday

"Verily, verily, I say unto you, except a corn of wheat fall into the ground and die, it abideth alone: But if it die, it bringeth forth much fruit. He that loveth his life shall lose it; and he that hateth his life in this world shall keep it unto life eternal." —John 12: 24–25

DAVID LENZO had a gentle, hesitant demeanor about him as he surveyed the group of Redeemer notables gathered to hear his message. A man of medium height, short brown hair, wire-rimmed glasses, and a sparse mustache, Lenzo had been Ladd's best man at Ladd's wedding the year before. He had wept through a message he had given to the congregation, but this time he had requested to return for a series of meetings with Redeemer leaders. He had discerned that, at last, the times were shifting in the church's favor, and that anyone involved in a major way in Redeemer's story might want to listen to a series of prophecies and thoughts he had on the church. In 1974, he got impressions of the church entering a long period of exile, much like the Israelites who were sent to Babylon for 70 years. He had moved with Ladd's household to Rhode Island and afterwards linked up with a Christian community in Maryland. Seventeen years later, he thought he could finally deliver his message to the church, for there was no question now that Redeemer was very much in exile. Four of the original elders—John, Jerry, Ladd, and Bob—were there. Graham was in England, and Jeff had not been invited.

The weekend had begun with a Friday night meeting, where the worship sounded tired and tentative. One of the women shared a vision about a stone wall. People were taking stones from it and placing them in nearby places, making the wall longer but weaker. God, she said, wants these stones picked up and put back in the wall so that while the kingdom of God is being spread, the wall will have a strong base. No one had to add what the weakened wall stood for.

A man spoke up, "The Lord spoke to me at the beginning of the service," he explained, "and said, 'Your desolation is ended.'"

"Marvelous," murmured Ladd. "I'm going to accept that."

For much of the weekend, Lenzo hammered home the "your-years-of-exile-are-over" message, saying God had woken him up to say Redeemer would be given a "new name," but that he did not know what it would be called. The church would have to seek out the name. But the church was embarking on a new path, he said, and the future was bright. With so many luminaries from Redeemer's past sitting there, it all seemed possible somehow that things had turned a bend and would swing upwards at last. Finally, Redeemer would be able to fulfill its destiny and complete the work God had called it to. In great contrast to their rejection of Phil Reiser, who had been an outsider, these parish leaders readily accepted what Lenzo, an insider from way back, had to say. The idea had been that these leaders would distill something from this weekend to take to the rest of the parish, which was not included in their deliberations. Although the grassroots possessed the horse sense to shift through what was true and what was wishful thinking, leaders kept on shutting them out.

Nevertheless, the more astute could discern the cloak of despair settling about Redeemer that June. Paul Felton preached about the unspoken question that hung about the place.

"We've been wondering for years, Lord, what are You going to do here?" he said. "We mean, we're a small church now with all the problems, the lack of money, and we don't have the resources we used to have in man and woman power. What is happening? Will the church just wind down in a few years and then must I go find some other place to live?"

Felton concluded the sermon with a burst of faith, declaring that he felt the Lord's presence at Redeemer and for him, that would always be enough. But in less than two years, he would be moving to another job under a younger, more energetic rector in southwest Houston.

Lenzo returned to Redeemer in April 1991 to lead a workshop on his vision for the church. This time, the grassroots were allowed to attend, for it was during another of Redeemer's reunions. After he had said his piece, Reid Wightman's wife Jeanette spoke up.

"I wish I could believe your prophecies," she said, "but I don't."

One product of Lenzo's 1991 visit was a "litany of penance" that was read by the congregation about a month after his visit. The leaders had realized that they had to make some amends for Redeemer's spotty past and so produced this litany, largely drawn up by Cliff Wilson. Surprisingly honest phrases like "the abuse of leadership that controlled, coerced, or manipulated," "the abuse of leadership that unnecessarily wounded and hurt," "the abuse of authority that prevented followers from being responsible to You," and so on were read aloud, with the congregation each time murmuring, "Forgive us, dear Lord." However, the vast majority of those hurt by Redeemer had long since left the church and did not get to hear these admissions. Although it was suggested that Ladd mail out copies of the litany to a large list of former Redeemerites, he did not.

Cliff, at least, heard the message about repentance, for one Sunday morning five months later, he was before the congregation with a message no one expected to hear. It was an auspicious morning, which began with a reading from Isaiah 59: "Behold the Lord's hand is not shortened that it cannot save, or his ear dull that it cannot hear. But your iniquities have made a separation between you and your God, and your sins have hidden His face from you so that He *does* not hear."

Cliff began his sermon by explaining he would speak about "the darkest, deepest sin that I have had to live with the past five years." He was a little vague on details, but somehow he had falsified his net worth while trying to negotiate a transaction. When he saw he could not repay the money, he admitted it all to the federal authorities. He was indicted by a federal grand jury on one count of filing a false financial statement, arraigned that May, and sentenced that fall. The next day, he told his stunned listeners, he was off to a federal prison for five months. "It's the most liberating, freeing experience in your life," he said, "to get your sin into the light."

After he finished, people clapped, as if confession was so novel a thing at the church that it deserved special commendation. But other parishioners were infuriated, realizing that Ladd and other leaders had known about this situation for a long time, yet had allowed Cliff to remain in leadership until his last Sunday there. A lower-level person might not have gotten the same gracious treatment and support. Cliff had come to Redeemer at a time when there were fewer leaders and had moved up too fast.

That December, Ladd sent out a letter inviting several hundred of us to Redeemer's second reunion in June 1992. With some candor, he admitted that "painful memories and a bitter aftertaste" from Redeemer's past years had been enough to bar some from attending the 1987 reunion. He also used a haunting phrase, saying, in effect, that Redeemerites were bewildered because, after having committed their lives to the Lord, He had somehow let them down. Ladd then described the litany of penitence and said he hoped that even those who were not there would receive it in the spirit it was given. Like so much at Redeemer, Ladd's nuanced letter was too little, too late. Nevertheless, former member Wilson Trigg got the letter at his parish in Falls Church, Virginia—he was now an Episcopal priest. *Why it's been 20 years since I lived in household,* he thought, *and back then the leaders were busy reading Watchman Nee and being perfect. Finally they're admitting they might have been wrong.*

SUL ROSS, one of Redeemer's leaders, stood at a microphone facing a cluster of parishioners during a parish gathering one February evening in early 1992. As spokesman for a four-person "rector's council," he had the job to tell parishioners where the church was headed.

"We still see ourselves as a renewal church," he said, "and in that sense, we continue to see ourselves as a light to other churches." Sul was a bit flowery, with his description of Redeemer's "ongoing traditions" that its members were "custodians" of, and his sense that everything was going swimmingly at the parish.

Custodians? Was Redeemer a museum? When several parishioners asked questions, Camp Huntington spoke up.

"I have a little trouble with the idea that we're called to be a 'light to the churches,'" he said. "I think that certainly we were at one time, but I'm not sure that we still are. I feel that for a number of years, we've been in a place of spiritual pride, and it bothers me. I think that maybe the Lord is calling us to a place of repentance."

Then Mac MacNeil, another parish leader, came to the microphone with the sobering news that Redeemer was too broke to pay the diocese the yearly fee it levied. Redeemer also had to cut in half its gifts to seminaries, and decrease contributions to a diocesan mission fund by $100 a month. Despite all the spoken optimism about Redeemer's future, it was clear that parishioners' departures had brought financial hardship to the church. In a troubled church, the disenchanted first withdraw their labor, then their funds and finally, themselves. Redeemer was well into the second and third stages.

Though Camp's words on repentance seemed to be brushed aside, the matter was not laid to rest. Next came shock therapy, beginning that Easter, when Chris Caros strode up to the front to deliver a prophecy.

"What I'm telling you took 21 days to get, so please listen," he began, explaining that he had just finished a 21-day fast and that his message related to Ladd's Easter sermon. As they sang the Nicene Creed at the service, "Just as clear as I can see anyone in this room, I saw Jesus Christ take the first step toward the throne of God," he said. "The Lord told me that you're going to have to die yourself to experience a true Easter revelation of the new Christ in all of us. . . If a handful—12, 14 people in this church—would be willing to truly die, maybe this church would truly be revived. If reading the Bible doesn't work anymore— "

"Excuse me, Chris," Dell Hoffman broke in, "I'm not very comfortable with what you're saying. This is not an addendum to Ladd's sermon."

"OK, now will you sit down and let me finish?"

"Well, maybe I will, but I'd appreciate you stopping."

"OK, I will stop, then. Bless your heart," Chris responded.

The congregation began to murmur agitatedly, and several people shouted at Chris to continue. As the rector, Ladd was responsible for regulating prophecies, but he sat silent during the dispute, offering no word of rebuke to his son-in-law. Chris returned to the microphone.

"I hadn't gotten anywhere in three and a half years," he said. "My prayers weren't going anywhere, and the Bible became so dry it was like parchment paper, because I couldn't read it any more. That is the thing that happened 20 years ago here. Dead people met dead people and Christ met our needs."

THE sun was setting as I drove west on Highway 22/30 towards West Virginia, reaching Ohio a few miles further. Sitting on the Ohio state line was Steubenville, the college town that boasted Franciscan University and a twin community of 350 adult members strong called Servants of Christ the King. The community was in deep trouble because of the cataclysms at its sister community, Word of God. By the fall of 1990, 29 community members, led by a pastoral theologian at the university, compiled a document listing pastoral abuses. No changes occurred in the leadership, so the dissidents approached their bishop, Albert Ottenweller, with the community's financial records in hand. Although the community was a quasi-parish, dissidents pointed out it was not pulling its weight in the diocese. While it was contributing $60,000 to Sword of the Spirit, it was contributing a meager $2,000 to the diocese.

Ottenweller predictably launched an investigation into the community in February 1991, ordering the group to split from Sword of the Spirit. Still no changes were forthcoming, so the dissidents next approached the media. Michael Scanlan, president of the university and leader of the community, resigned his community post two days before the *Pittsburgh Press* ran an article about the problems. The next day, I was in Steubenville, driving about a leafy plateau combed with tree-shaded streets and large, gracious homes where most of the community members lived.

I stopped by the home of a writer and her husband. Somehow, in-between having four children, this woman had managed to earn a master's degree in theology and keep up a brisk freelancing business. Her latest project was on women in community, an oppressed group if ever there was one. Women were not allowed to wear pants to community gatherings, display hoop earrings, or have short hair. Men, in turn, were not to wear pastel colors, especially pink because of its effeminate connotations. They even had teachings on hugs, which were to be a shoulder-to-shoulder squeeze—none of this frontal stuff—especially between men and women.

Next, I dropped by the home of a dissenting couple, who seemed a bit disorganized with several kids running around. Being a Catholic community, Servants encouraged its members to have large families. These people were tired.

"I've a real problem with the charismatic renewal and the church's lack of pastoring us," the husband complained. "In the charismatic renewal, you strive for perfection but never attain it. Then it becomes a theology of guilt."

Afterwards, I went for a walk with Kevin Flynn, a friend from my days at the Florida newspaper. He had moved to Steubenville five years before with so much hope that this might be the Christian family he was longing for. Bitter and disappointed, he was laying plans for an escape route via law school.

"Some husbands and wives were not allowed to hold hands at community gatherings—too familiar," he said. "Women cannot ask men for dates; men have to take the initiative. We've been a cult, and a low-level one at that."

As I followed Kevin's account of the past year, I learned that although the community was hemorrhaging members right and left, there never was an all-out statement of repentance by the community leaders, as there had been at Word of God. As a result, bitterness continued to fester and therapists along the Ohio River Valley enjoyed a surge in business.

As the fortunes of communities nationwide continued to tumble, Celebration attempted to firm up the commitment of those whom they knew to still be with them. In April 1991, it sent out a letter to supporters, asking them to become a "companion" of Celebration, which meant they would contribute money, wear a Celebration medallion, and obey a "rule of life" modeled after the Benedictine Rule. I read the specifications: poverty (simplicity in material possessions), obedience (obeying one's baptismal and other sacramental vows), and chastity, which read "loving faithfulness to the nature of relationships with others."

Whoa! What on earth did *that* mean? The topic of sexuality in the Episcopal Church was a hot one, General Convention was coming up in a few months, and an all-out war against pro- and anti-homosexual forces was expected to rage.

Faithfulness in relationships? Why, that could mean straight *or* gay, or even with one's pet or child. It was filled with holes. I buttonholed Bill Farra in the parish hall, telling him so. My remarks did not sway them, for their revised statement put out for General Convention was not much different.

Months later, while all of us were at Convention in Phoenix, I stood at their booth, arguing with several of them over the wording. I asked what was wrong with simply defining chastity as abstinence from sex outside of marriage and faithfulness to one's spouse within marriage. That was the way everyone else worded it. They were in the midst of informing me how judgmental that sounded when up walked Bishop Jack Spong, the undisputed leader of liberal bishops whom I had long wanted to interview. When I took off with him, the conversation remained unresolved. But it came to mind again one Sunday in September, when I heard Graham, in the midst of a sermon on Mark 7, define fornication as "being excessively concerned about sexuality."

That Christmas, I had a long talk with a friend who, like myself, had lived in a charismatic community in the Northwest. She had no sooner entered the charismatic movement during high school than she and her boyfriend had sex for the first time. They married within the year, she gave up going to college to have children, and years later, they divorced. Her community, she said, was full of people who were dallying with drugs, had slept together before marriage, and had affairs during their marriages. There were even some abortions. Sex was never discussed among them, but female submission was. Now living with another man, my friend informed me she had had it with Christianity.

Sex was never openly discussed in my Portland community either, but there was no hanky-panky going on that I knew of. Still, there were rumors about some of the individuals at Celebration, so one Shrove Tuesday evening, the day before the onset of Lent, I flat out asked one of the men if he was gay.

The man exploded with anger and obscenities, which continued for the next 90 minutes as I tried to explain that instead of talking behind his back, I was asking him to his face. He quoted me verses from Romans I to say that those who condemn sexual sin should condemn gossip and slander as well. Although he pled innocent to homosexual acts, he showed a thorough knowledge of how they were done.

A few days later, I got a call from one of his roommates, who sounded a bit apologetic about his friend's explosive reaction.

"We do try to live up to our vow of celibacy," the roommate said. "We're not always perfect, but at least we try."

We're not always perfect. In what ways were they lapsing?

DURING Lent of 1992, Graham was appointed to teach a basic catechism class at All Saints on Sunday mornings. It was billed as Graham lecturing on the basics. One person in that class, a working class man named Larry, was scheduled to be baptized. The class was really for him, with the rest of us listening in.

On a week when Bruce was out of town, Graham began the class by insisting that people could question him for clarification but not for disputation. He then launched into his latest theological insight: There must be femaleness in the Godhead, or women would not be saved because man and woman are created in God's image.

My mind rapidly shifted back to what I had learned in theology class at the seminary. I didn't remember being in God's image as having anything to do with salvation. Graham was ignoring I Cor. 11:7, which states that man is the image and glory of God but woman is the image of man. Also, I recalled Jesus's intention to save all the human race, not just one gender.

While we were digesting that, Graham showed us his college graduation picture—it was of a young man with platinum blond hair, sensitive features, and an intense expression. This was to illustrate his "image of God" point. Yet he went on to say that he did not believe we were, by nature, sinful and that being in God's image meant our capacity for fellowship with God was not tarnished. However, he continued, because we were tarnished by sin in the womb, sin is thus hereditary. He then suggested that if a child was born of perfect parents, he or she would be perfect.

By then, I figured Larry must be totally lost, for I could see puzzled looks darting about the room, especially on the faces of 5 of us seminarians. Graham went on to say how he disagreed with the concept of original sin; that sin was actually alienation between self and God. It all sounded vaguely heretical and not at all material for a catechism class.

Our spiritual life unites us with God, Graham continued, and though our spirits are not tarnished by sin, our bodies are. It was all reworked Watchman Nee. Someone asked if sin was the result of our environment rather than human nature. Well, yes, Graham explained. Our bodies are our psychological and physical nature, but our spiritual nature is not sinful. Our spirit got stained through life experiences beginning in the womb. Recognizing this as akin to one of the heresies I had been taught about in church history class, I looked around and spotted Bruce's wife, Theresa, scribbling like mad. What sort of fool is Graham, I wondered, to think that, with Bruce gone, he could teach like this and get away with it?

Bruce did hear about it and made his displeasure known at a vestry meeting. Word got back to Graham that he was in the doghouse. The next Sunday, he spent the entire catechism lesson retracting. It was so unlike Graham, who at one time had been an excellent theologian. Graham's erratic theology was a major component of the master's thesis I completed that spring. My topic was why charismatic Christian communities so quickly turn authoritarian. I had spent hours listening to tapes from the mid-1960s, when Graham was afire with the Holy Spirit and preaching in the Redeemer basement, and those of the late 1970s and early '80s, when his lackluster sermons were laced with social action admonitions. I'd covered enough religion scandals to know that when one's theology goes south, start looking also for sins of the flesh. I was not totally sure what was going on with Graham, but I had completed 130 interviews for the book at this point and certain disturbing patterns had come up again and again in these conversations.

My thesis adviser was Stephen Noll, the assistant at Truro who was now Trinity's academic dean. As he mulled over the thesis, he thought back to how some of his charismatic friends from the late 1960s and early 1970s had fared. One priest had committed suicide. At least two others had come out of the closet as homosexuals, then divorced their wives. What accounted for the different behavior, I wondered. The only difference between a charismatic and a liberal, he told me, is that charismatics should be Bible-based. Remove the Bible and the two are equal, because they *both* have experience.

That June, Redeemer had its second reunion and the mood was markedly different than the meeting five years before. Church attendance was back to 1967 levels. The Easter 1967 service brought in 422 persons; the Easter 1992 service brought in 427. Attendance in the first half of 1967 was in the 200s; the same was true for attendance in the first half of 1992. The difference was that attendance crossed the 300 barrier during the fall of 1967 and kept on climbing. Seventy out-of-towners came to the reunion, one-third as many as had showed up in 1987. Organizers asked Jeff to be the special speaker, but he didn't even respond to the written request. The Pulkinghams were conspicuous by their absence. Graham was in Texas that week, but he spent the time visiting his children in various parts of the state.

I graduated from Trinity in May 1992 and, no newspaper job having immediately presented itself, I drove to Houston for a few more weeks of book sleuthing. My interviews were winding down, as I had compiled the basics of Redeemer's history. But there were so many rumors about Graham that I knew my research would not be complete until I could find out more. I spent several weeks wrapping up loose ends and praying that somehow I would bump into someone who had the smoking gun, or knew who had it. Several key people around Redeemer, who knew the truth, refused to be interviewed. I prayed that God would reveal to me the right person to talk to, wherever he was on this planet. It was obvious that Graham had been sexually active with several men. I needed to find only one.

I ended up on a couch in Debbie Scott's tiny apartment, venting my frustrations about the high personal cost of this impossible manuscript. She had left Redeemer for a far more welcoming church, but she was keenly interested in all the information I was digging up. And she had a prophecy: I would indeed complete the manuscript, but I would lose most of my friends doing so.

A few days later, I was at a reception in the new parish hall of Christ Church Cathedral downtown. I wanted to buttonhole Jeff Schiffmayer for an interview, but while munching on refreshments, I saw a friend, Carl Wheeler. He was one of the men at the early morning prayer meetings I had attended at Redeemer six years before. He invited me to have dinner with him and his wife, Joyce, at their home on the way to Galveston.

Not suspecting they would have anything unusual to say, I dawdled getting there, arriving at 9 p.m. We finally ate at midnight. I remembered Joyce as Jackie Gullen's sister, and so I asked them how Jackie was doing. When they told me, I sat there, numb. Here was my smoking gun.

A few days later, on a warm, moist summer Alabama evening, I was on my way back to Pittsburgh, stopping for the night at the house of a friend in Birmingham. The friends were not home, which was just as well, because I needed to phone Jackie in Kansas.

Jackie began by detailing the story of her marriage to Richard 10 years before. Richard had been Graham's aide-de-camp for several years, staying by his side during the heart attack in Colorado and acting as his nurse for months afterwards. Graham had officiated at their wedding ceremony, and when he asked for an offering for the bride and the groom, the congregation gave $800. After the ceremony, Graham suggested the newlyweds use the money to help his household move to Colorado. This stifled the Gullens' spending during their honeymoon, which greatly irritated Jackie. When they returned, the bulk of the money went to help move the Pulkingham household to Woodland Park, which is how Jackie learned firsthand of Graham's talent for talking people out of extra funds.

Things improved when the Gullens, at Jackie's insistence, managed to move out of the Pulkingham household and into their own place, but they disintegrated when the whole group moved back to Post Green, then to Scotland. The two of them would get into horrible fights. Jackie sensed Richard was not truly with her, for when push came to shove, he would always choose Graham. Richard had learned too much from Graham, namely that women did not count. Oh, Graham paid lip service to women, and if there were an especially powerful one around, he'd modify his behavior to suit her. But men were what mattered to Graham.

Then Jackie dropped her bomb: Before the marriage, during a time when he had lots of questions about his sexuality, Richard had lived at Cumbrae. He wondered if he was gay, but fantasized about women. During a counseling session, he confided to Graham about a sexual problem he was experiencing. In response, Graham made a contract with him so that together, they would "explore" his sexuality.

"If you give me total power in your life, I will make you well," Graham told him. Graham had enormous confidence in his abilities, and Richard had been on drugs and was drifting when he saw the CBS program and showed up at Coventry in the early 1970s. Richard had no idea where this experiment would lead, but he found out during a trip he took to Sweden with Graham in 1978. Graham kept Richard up late one night, talking to him in a dark room and criticizing him for various things. Richard thereafter was putty in Graham's hands. The next night, Graham approached him to have sex. When Richard recoiled, Graham said, "What? Don't you like me?"

Richard could not say "no," so the two men became lovers. He was irresistibly drawn to this compelling man, while at the same time fearing the priest who was so obviously in control. And Richard was not in control. Sometimes, prior to a liaison, he would tell Graham how uncomfortable the sex made him feel, and asked what God thought of it? But that did not stop Graham. The liaisons were very easy to pull off, because Richard was Graham's traveling companion on various trips where there were no prying eyes.

The physical part ended with Graham's heart attack. And once Richard got up the courage to say how oppressed he felt by Graham, Graham apologized and asked his forgiveness. That one admission did not undo the extensive damage done to Richard who, to his chagrin, discovered on his honeymoon that all his encounters with Graham had not changed his original sexual problems one whit.

The Gullens split from the community in 1985, staying in England while the rest moved to Aliquippa. Their marriage continued to disintegrate, with Richard complaining that he had an unspecified monkey on his back. Jackie did not suspect who the "monkey" was, but she knew the two were not bonding as a couple. If he spilled the beans about Graham, Graham would bury him, Richard thought.

In desperation, Jackie sought out the Bletchingley community and counseling from Susan Abbott. At the end of 1990, she left her husband and flew back to the safety of her parents and brother in Topeka. It was clear their marriage was on the rocks, and Richard went into therapy in a last-ditch effort to get himself healed. During those sessions, he admitted that a powerful priest had seduced him more than a decade earlier. He also learned that he had not exactly been a consenting adult with Graham. He had been in his early 20s and had complied with Graham's desires because he was desperate for healing, which Graham said came through sexual contact with him. His whole life became Graham, and Graham influenced what he wore, what he ate, and with whom he spent time. Finally, in September 1991, he told his wife that his relationship with Graham had been sexual. "That was child abuse," Jackie cried out.

Richard flew to the States the following July to make one last try at saving his marriage. This time he was out for blood and willing to tell anyone who would listen the truth about Graham, including one of Graham's daughters. The daughter had not seemed overly shocked, and her husband told him he had intuited the truth during some of his visits to the community. Next, Richard headed to Kansas to make peace with his wife. Just before he arrived, I called Jackie from Birmingham.

A few days later, I was back in Ambridge, the small town where Trinity was located. I called Graham to set up an appointment, at the same time learning he was leaving for a six-month sabbatical on August 11. In our talk on July 15, we ranged over several subjects: How he had handled Jim Clowe's exit from Redeemer, his heart attack in Denver, and his recovery in Houston. I remembered that Richard and Graham had been nearly inseparable during that recovery period, and knew that here was my chance to learn the truth about their relationship.

"He was the most blessed gift to me," Graham was saying. "The doctors in Denver said they would not release me to go back to Houston unless I'd agree to live apart from my family . . ." He went to describe the west Houston apartment he and Richard stayed in for three months while Richard cooked and helped Graham exercise.

I told Graham that Richard had been in therapy and was now saying his relationship with Graham had been sexual. Was it?

"No," said Graham quickly. "Richard always had questions about his sexuality. We discussed it a lot. Richard is talking, you said?"

Then Graham launched into a recap of the '60s, when people were embracing each other with full frontal body hugs. He knew there had been rumors about him, he said, but all were misconceptions based on the parishioners' general closeness.

"The intimacy and openness of our relationships were entirely foreign to people," he insisted. "If I were to hug a woman, you'd think nothing of it. If I were to hug a man, you'd think of it."

But Graham, I thought, the people who have told me the rumors haven't said a word about any hugs. Graham then began talking irritatedly about people questioning the implications of his relationships. It was none of anyone's business, he said, except for someone like Bishop Hathaway, the community's Visitor.

As if Alden would ever ask, I thought.

In fact, in May, Bob Morris had confronted his bishop at a diocesan clergy meeting. Hathaway had summoned all 80 clergy to the meeting to hear a spokesman from the Episcopal Church's Pension Fund, which served as the multi-million-dollar repository of pension monies for thousands of priests, sort of like an ecclesiastical Social Security fund. It was also the payee on lawsuits targeted at clergy. Complaints of clergy sexual abuse and harassment were becoming so numerous that the Pension Fund hired two staff members just to handle them. After a whole day of listening to stories of emotional and sexual abuse by dominant clergy figures, Bob was bouncing off the walls, for it had brought up memories of everything Graham had been doing. Afterwards, he came up to Alden, insisting that community members were in danger, and it all had to do with Graham.

But Alden was not computing. *What was Bob alluding to?* he wondered. When Alden appeared unalarmed, Bob exploded in anger.

"You," he said to Hathaway, "will answer to God for this."

CHAPTER 26

Good Friday

"On Good Friday, we enter, the clergy prostrate themselves on the floor and the lay leaders for a considerable long period and I can tell you for a church that has a lot of Protestant evangelicals in it, nothing has spoken more deeply to help us get the message of what it means to be on our faces before God. You need some symbol somewhere where you honestly see somebody who lies prostrate to get the sense that it ever means anything."

—George Mims explaining Redeemer's
Holy Week observances at a 1983 conference of
charismatic Episcopal clergy in Denton, Texas.

T HE night of August 10, 1992, was a sultry, hot Monday in Ambridge. Jackie Gullen's letter arrived that afternoon. She had had a productive time with Richard, she wrote. On July 31, the day before Richard flew back to London, she finished a 10-page, single-spaced formal complaint against Graham, alleging sexual misconduct, lies, deceit, and pastoral misconduct when she and Richard were his parishioners from 1980-82. The letter went to William Smalley, the bishop of Kansas, detailing everything: how Jackie had met Richard, and how she had trusted his priestly advice that she and Richard would make a good couple. After all, Graham was internationally known in the charismatic renewal, she reasoned. He had to be right.

Obviously, the hitherto hidden factor in their bad marriage was Graham's sexual relationship with Richard, she wrote, and she was furious that Graham, knowing that Richard was damaged goods, foisted him on her. So much water had gone under the bridge and now Jackie wanted vengeance.

Smalley was fairly new in the episcopate, but he knew a hot topic when he saw one. He faxed a copy of the letter to national church headquarters in New York City, then wrote several letters, one to Hathaway, one to Benitez, and one to Frey, all of them bishops whom Graham had served under. He also asked Richard to provide a statement. A few weeks beforehand, Richard would have wavered at such a request. But Jackie had gotten a note from me, detailing my July 15 meeting with Graham, during which he denied a sexual relationship with Richard. Richard also seethed when he heard of this. His wife was leaving him, he was racking up thousands of dollars in counseling costs, and Graham was acting as if nothing had happened. Someone needed to bring this man to account, not to mention the Episcopal bishops who knew of Graham's predilections and had done nothing to warn anyone. So when Smalley called, Richard was ready to talk.

The bishop of Pittsburgh, on vacation on an island off the Maine coast for a week, had just sat down with some friends and a glass of wine when his phone rang. It was Graham. He had gotten word of Jackie's charges and he wanted to tell Alden of the horrors to come before someone else got to him.

A half hour later, the phone rang in my hot, sticky apartment. It was Graham. He was calling to ask my forgiveness. "You know the question you asked me about Richard? Well, there's truth in that. Richard is talking and I need not pretend."

He had lied to me when I asked him the month before if his relationship with Richard had been sexual, he continued. The truth was, he said, it had been.

I froze. Rarely in my career had I ever heard a source implicate himself like this.

He began describing how he had been tormented by homosexual inclinations since his teens. He told me that Bishop Clinton Quin had asked him if such inclinations were "a problem" when Graham applied for seminary in 1951. I grabbed a notepad and was scribbling like mad. I didn't need to be told twice that Graham would never spill the beans like this again. I had caught him in a rare moment of remorse. The fish, as it were, had swum right into my net.

Do you know what this is like, he asked me, to be so tormented? I had to admit I did not.

"It came from an almost total failure of male identity in my early life," he said. "There were a lot of things I did to compensate for that. I took very personally what I did that first year at Redeemer," alluding to his 100 percent failure rate until he went to New York.

"When I was baptized in the Spirit," he continued, "I was set free from that torment. I began to live and walk in that freedom and the torment was gone."

I asked him if he had confided these lusts to David Wilkerson. He said, of course he had, that very first day when he was sitting in Wilkerson's office.

"I walked in that freedom for a long time," he said. "Later on, I took liberties with some persons that were sexual in nature. It was a free choice. That's what makes it so shameful. It did involve someone who trusted me. This thing with Richard happened 12 years ago. I am deeply ashamed and entirely guilty of what I did." A few years ago, he asked Richard's forgiveness, and Richard had said yes, he added. Obviously, I thought, Richard must have felt he had no other choice at the time.

"It may have caused my heart attack," he now said. Graham must have been under terrible stress in 1981, not only from a faltering heart and all the drugs he was taking, but from the guilt he was carrying. I pointed out how he had already excused his bizarre actions that year by saying how sick he was.

"Well, I *was* sick in 1981," he said, "but what I did with Richard was sin, not sickness. For it to be tied up with the baptism in the Spirit is so wonderful, yet so shameful," he mused. "It was the personal torment. I felt not only dirty, but most of my life and in my early teens, I felt driven to be what I was. It is deeply ingrained within me."

He kept on repeating the word "torment." Graham was 65 years old. Assuming this hell had begun about the time he was 15, he had been carrying this burden for five decades. He had been a marvelous actor, and having six kids threw off a lot of people as to his sexuality. This also explained Graham's bizarre father-son theology, his reluctance to take Betty on trips, his having no concept as to the love of a woman and no clue as to how a true marriage worked.

"Since the surgery thing, it's not been going on," he said, then hesitated. "Well. . . " he added, "in the last three years, there *was* an incident I regret."

"If you had to relive this whole time, what would you do differently?" I asked.

He would have used the help of a confessor, someone to talk to, someone to whom he would be accountable, he said. The irony of it was too much: Here was a man who had surrounded himself with a community. He was spiritual adviser to the bishop of the diocese. Yet, he was as lonely and tormented as could be.

Graham, I said, I'm writing a book on you. This has to be part of it. Well, he conceded, by the time it got published, the story would be old anyway. One reason he had called, he said, was out of remorse over lying to me during that July 15 conversation. When he had denied any extra-marital sexual involvements, the way I had simply believed him had dug into his conscience.

He concluded the call with a prayer request. Betty had known of Bishop Quin's questions, but he had never told her of the other things he had done. Perhaps she had intuited the truth all these years anyway, he said, and silently bore the pain of his rejection. If not, then tomorrow, as he and Betty drove nine hours to North Carolina for their sabbatical, he would have to tell her.

O N Tuesday, the community was told the news during a meeting that went late into the night. People were bouncing off the walls. I heard that one community member collapsed and had to be put to bed. Another community member vomited for two days. Their whole rationale for existing was gone, for they wondered if Graham had founded community just to meet some of his darkest needs for power? This was the man who did things like telling one of the community women that her beloved dog was interfering with her spiritual life. Unable to find a home for it, she had obediently put it to sleep.

Now they had to deal with the fact that their founder had been living a lie, and that they had helped him live it. Even if he truly repented, the severity and effect of his sin were enough to defrock him forever. Here was the missing piece to why Redeemer had struggled with sexual sin all these years. Defilement flowed from the top on down, Graham was at the apex of Redeemer's spiritual pyramid, and from him, sin had crept through all facets of the church. The bad apple had triumphed.

That same day, Alden suspended Graham from the priesthood. Canonically, this was known as "inhibition," meaning that a priest is suspended from performing all priestly or pastoral functions until the bishop either restores the priest to good standing or deposes him. All that week, Alden was on the phone to the community or to Graham, who was to be sent to a clinic in Florida for psychiatric counseling. Alden was also on the phone to Bill Frey, one of the few fellow bishops he trusted to help him handle the mess.

At the time, I knew nothing of all this, because the community was in a kind of lockdown, and no news was seeping out. I had told only one person of my discovery, a fellow seminarian, Mario Bergner, whom I had dated once or twice. He was writing his first book on his transformation from homosexual activist to heterosexual male. In fact, he ran an informal counseling service around campus to help other seminarians with their sexual issues. Mario and I were also in the same seminary advisee group—a small weekly gathering of seminarians overseen by a faculty member—and Mario kept us laughing with his tales of how neurotic Trinity seminarians were. A lot of us were struggling with issues, that was true, but Mario was the only person most of us knew who understood how gay people thought. Even the faculty asked Mario's advice on how to deal with the gay issue, which was already threatening to become a hot potato in denominational politics. And Mario was like Graham in one important aspect; he, too, had been delivered from a lust for men when prayed over for the baptism in the Spirit. Mario hated visiting All Saints, because he felt men there were eyeballing him.

The next Sunday morning, an innocuous announcement was made during an All Saints service that a "representative of the bishop" would be at a parish meeting that night. Nothing was said as to what the meeting was about. It seemed like a normal service. Wiley even sang "O How Good, O How Wonderful," and Bill Farra preached on faith.

But that night it was a stony-faced group of 40-50 parishioners who gathered. Because Alden was not yet back from vacation, Austin Hurd, a priest who chaired the standing committee, read out loud a short statement. Graham, he said, had been inhibited of his priestly duties and position in the community because of alleged sexual misconduct with various men. The diocese was going to investigate. He asked for questions. He asked for reaction. Parishioners just sat there, some dabbing their eyes. The meeting lasted barely a half hour.

I stayed up until 4 a.m. pondering this media ethics nightmare. Now that the diocese had initiated an investigation, Graham's scandal was public record. The community might not feel that way, but I knew that the public announcement by the diocese had altered the equation. Since graduation, I had gone back to freelancing full-time, and I had the ability to contact several media outlets immediately. But my conversation with Graham was more his plea for forgiveness and at most, something he had in mind for the book. The possibility of any of it going into a newspaper story had not occurred to me at the time, and probably not to him, either. Since then, he had been suspended from the priesthood and, as a public figure, his suspension had become the stuff of news. Most diocesan clergy would probably know of the bishop's action by the next day. Would it be better for me, who knew what the facts were, to do the first story, or to let a local newspaper or TV station stumble onto it? Was I compromised because I had so many friends who were part of this mess? Or was it simply time to blow the whistle on a man whose friends and followers had protected him for years? I felt as if I were in the middle of a Susan Howatch novel.

I remembered a conversation I had had two years before with Chuck Irish, head of ERM, about the charismatic clergy's proclivities toward sexual sin.

"We used to say when someone was baptized in the Spirit, watch out," Irish said, "especially kids or teenagers. We had to really watch them, or else they'd be getting into bed with each other. There was such a high after the baptism that people would take on soul mates early. They'd embrace each other at improper times. There was an intimacy of sharing. At St. Luke's [his former parish], we wouldn't allow a man and woman not married to each other to minister together, or let a man be a spiritual director over a woman. We saw a potential explosion there. It's amazing how many good, solid, renewal clergy have fallen into sexual sin."

But why? It seemed that God had closely connected our sexual and spiritual selves, which is why Graham's baptism in the Spirit had healed his twisted sexuality, at least for a while. With his anointing to lead Redeemer, Graham had ended up in the middle of a spiritual web, and any move he made would affect the entire work. If the pastor was morally pure, the church prospered under him. But this fault in Graham's psyche had created major problems for his spiritual children. Small wonder so many leaders at Redeemer committed adultery, or that All Saints had the patina of sexual weirdness about it. The root malignancy had never been brought to light.

With my decision held in abeyance, I fell asleep for a few hours. Then, at 8 a.m., the phone rang. It was Deanie and Reid, two seminary friends calling from Louisiana, seemingly out of the blue. We had attended All Saints together.

"Have you heard the news?" I asked them. They had not, so I brought them up to date, then described my dilemma. They encouraged me to jump on it. Taking this unexpected call as a sign, I contacted the Religion News Service, which is a wire service, and *Christianity Today*. Just as I had thought, both organizations wanted stories from me that day. After I faxed my story to RNS a few hours later, the staff there saw it and gasped, an editor later told me.

After both deadlines were past, I called Rebekah Scott Schreffler, a friend at the nearby *Beaver County Times*, who was taking classes at the seminary. Because Rebekah covered religion, this story was in her own back yard.

She, too, jumped on the story, which was published the next afternoon, atop the front page, a few hours before Hathaway, now home from vacation, was to address the parish. Unfortunately, I was listed in the story as a member of the community, which I was not. I had given Rebekah a quote from my conversation with Graham that got worded in the story to sound as if it was from a speech he had delivered to the community. I drove to Aliquippa for the Eucharist at which

Alden was speaking. His secretary had called me that morning, saying he wanted to make sure I would be there. He had seen the RNS article and wanted to talk with me about it.

The Epistle they chose for the Eucharist were the first few verses of Galatians 6, beginning with, "Brothers, if someone is caught in a sin, you who are spiritual should restore him gently." Alden preached that, despite this sin, we not disallow everything Graham had ever done, and he urged those there to reach out to Betty and Graham and to those who had been offended. After we passed the peace, Alden again said he needed to talk with me. After the Eucharist was over, people chatted for awhile and I struck up a conversation with a woman in green who was new to the parish and bewildered by the events. The parishioners then sat back down for a parish meeting led by Alden and Austin Hurd. At first, Alden's questions were greeted with the same stony-faced silence as at the Austin announcement two days earlier.

Two people finally shared their thoughts, and then one of the community members stood up. "I don't really feel I can say anything," he said, "as long as Julia Duin is in the room."

All eyes turned to me. I explained I was not planning to write any more articles in the near future, and that my observations from this meeting would go into a book. This would all be water under the bridge by the time it came out. There was a chorus of no's and several people refuted me, including Daphne Grimes, who had flown in from Wyoming to advise the community. The woman in green remarked, totally from left field, that I asked too many questions. Ruth Wieting stood up to clarify why they all disagreed with me; they had taken umbrage, she said, at the *Beaver County Times* article. I explained that I had been misquoted—how odd for a reporter to have the tables turned around on her like that—but that assertion made no difference to them. My name was in that article in the third paragraph, which meant that I had been spilling secrets about the community. This, in their eyes, was betrayal. They assumed I had lied to the newspaper and would lie again in any book I'd write. Moreover, it seemed obvious to them that I cared more about the story than I did about the parish.

Alden interjected that I was interested in revealing the truth. Someone objected to that, and I declared it was time the truth was told because there had already been so much denial within the community. Could, Alden suggested, I simply be present, listen, and write merely that a meeting took place? I could not promise that. I could forego the use of names, but what if someone said something incredibly important?

Someone asked what I was: a reporter or a parishioner? My mind flashed back to Barbara Frey's query. It was the same questioning of loyalties: Was I a journalist or one of them?

"I am both," I replied. "I cannot separate the two."

This was getting ridiculous. Alden had invited me to this crazy meeting, and now I was getting ripped to shreds by folks who could not take their frustrations out on Graham. I posed a question to them: Did they want the truth, or did they want a lie? But I was outnumbered, and the meeting was dead in the water as long as I remained. No one spoke up on my behalf. I opened my mouth to say I would leave rather than compromise, but Alden beat me to it. Having invited me to be there, he now had to disinvite me. Would I leave? he asked.

I was on my feet with a parting shot. "Some of you may respect me as a reporter," I said, "but you do not respect me as a Christian."

"Oh, but I do," Alden said quickly. "I do respect you as a sister in Christ."

I dashed out the door. The woman in green overtook me as I neared the street. She seemed confused, and wondered if her remark had hurt me. Yes, it had, I said. We talked helplessly for a few minutes, groping for what could not be expressed. Trying not to break down, I walked to the car, climbed in, and drove away.

ALDEN called the next day to see how I was and to apologetically suggest I attend another church. I asked him about the chronology of his involvement in this mess, what could happen to Graham, and so on. I waited for all the questions he had planned to ask me the previous night. There were none. We talked a bit about the book. Finally, I asked him if he had any questions. No, he said. I had told him everything he needed to know. But as I hung up, I realized I had told him nothing at all.

I called Richard in England. He had never confronted Graham face-to-face about their sexual relationship, he said, and no, he had not forgiven him. Nor had Graham asked for his forgiveness, except for once, when Richard simply said he felt "oppressed" by Graham.

"Graham's a really smart man," he said. "I can't believe anything he says to me. He'll cover his ass." And, he added, he had ditched his Christianity in the past 12 months.

The week dragged on, the pain from Graham's revelations creeping east from Aliquippa across the Ohio River and flowing south to Houston. The RNS story quickly made its way to *The New York Times*. Bishop Frey was likewise quick to broadcast the news about Graham. He announced it to some students a few hours before word had come out in the newspaper, then called Rebekah at her home the night the article ran, congratulating her.

Bishop Hathaway put out an all-points bulletin, asking to hear from men who had been sexually involved with Graham.

In Houston, at a parish meeting, Ladd and Grover informed 100 parishioners of the action taken against Graham. People knew something was up that morning when they read a statement in the bulletin about the suspension. The matter was incomprehensible to the 50 percent of the parish who did not know who Graham was. During the meeting, bare details were offered on what had happened, and the Gullens' names were not mentioned. People asked polite questions, and prayers were said for all involved. Joyce Wheeler came to listen, but most of the time, she sat there and cried. Everyone else was too traumatized by years of disappointments to react much. Death was staring them in the face, and they could only gaze back, mute.

I remembered back to 1980 and Woodland Park, when I had listened to Graham talk about *kairos* and *chronos*, the two different sets of time. Chronos, he said, was cause, effect, and sequence; in short, our timing. Kairos was more related to being in the right place at the right time or God's timing. When the Bible speaks of something happening in the "fullness of time," it means kairos, and means that the event happened when God chose it to take place. God gives the moment once, then gives us ample opportunity to respond. We cannot make something happen, but we can be alert and ready when things do happen. Chronological time can be controlled by us. Kairos cannot.

What had happened to Graham was simply the arrival of kairos. It was finally God's timing for his sin to be revealed that summer of 1992, though some had wished it had been revealed years earlier. Graham's time had finally run out. In the end, it was three women who had brought this about. Jackie filed her charges in July, when many bishops were on vacation. It was an inconvenient time, and people were caught up short. I decided to publicize the fact before many people thought it was the right time, yet I sensed it was the right time. When is it ever the right time? If the community or Redeemer leaders had had their way, it never would have been the right time to divulge the secrets. Finally, Rebekah wrote her story before even I thought it was time. On our own, all three of us had decided it was time. Kairos had arrived.

K AIROS also arrived that summer for Jeff Cothran, who attended the reunion carrying a cushion to sit on the hard pews. He was a skeleton of his former self. AIDS had devastated his body, and he died shortly after learning the circumstances of Graham's disgrace.

By the time the *Christianity Today* article came out in September, all sorts of Christian publications had picked up the RNS story. After years of avoiding Redeemer, Benitez finally entered the act in November, inviting parishioners to his turf at the diocesan center for a meeting about *l'affaire Graham*. He set out enough chairs for a crowd, but fewer than two dozen people showed up, some of whom had left the church years before. Benitez was assiduously neutral, reassuring everyone that the revelations in no way negated the good Redeemer had done throughout the years. He was in somewhat of a quandary—Graham and Betty Jane were now living in his diocese. After spending a few months in North Carolina, they were now in Austin getting therapy and living with one of their daughters.

About a week after that meeting, Jackie called. She had decided to file for divorce. What was most upsetting her was that Bishop Smalley had suddenly told her he could not afford to pay any more of her bills or counseling or antidepressants. He had paid out only $600 so far, but Richard had submitted a bill for 4,000 British pounds for *his* counseling, in addition to another 450-pound bill for his trans-Atlantic calls, with the understanding that some of the American bishops would help them out. Alden especially had given him that impression in an open letter sent around the diocese. In it, the bishop stated he would "see to the psychological needs and pastoral care of the abused individual and his family." But reimbursement was not forthcoming. Jackie was still being supported by her retired parents and her brother.

"If they would just pay for my expenses," she said, "I'll go away in a year or two."

Chronos time slid into 1993 and Bill Clinton was sworn in as president of the United States. The media continued its reports on sexually erring priests of all denominations, with Graham but one in a long litany of men. More revelations came out about Catholic priests who had manhandled children years ago and about a womanizing archbishop who had to resign his see in Santa Fe. By February, Alden's advisory committee had handed down its verdict that Graham be deposed. Eight men had contacted Alden about abuse, much of it sexual, suffered at Graham's hands. Sometimes, there was no word to describe it. One man wrote a letter detailing how he had confided to Graham some memories that were haunting him. Graham invited him to his room, then commanded the man to take off his clothes and join him in bed. The man obeyed, then was shocked to discover that Graham, too, was naked under the covers.

Graham simply held the man in his arms for about a half hour, then informed him he had another appointment to keep. The man noted that neither he nor Graham had been sexually aroused, but "I also knew that what had happened was not conventional Christian sex therapy."

Despite Alden's broad hints that Graham had acquiesced, Graham was refusing to be deposed. The bishop was at an impasse, for canonically there was a five-year statute of limitations on Graham's crimes. The charges Jackie was filing concerned actions that had happened 11 or more years before. To be deposed, a priest must have a trial. But to have a trial, there must be charges, and for the charges to stick, they must be brought within the statute of limitations. Richard and Jackie had spoken up too late, and Alden could not force Graham to attend a deposition. He wrote Jackie and Richard, informing them that the church could not help them because many of the offenses occurred outside the U.S.; here, he said, the statute of limitations had run out, and there was no proof of long-term harm.

Looking at the smoking ruins of her marriage, Jackie wondered how any ecclesiastical official could say Graham's dallying had not ruined her husband for life. She put her divorce proceedings on hold to concentrate on another legal matter: a civil suit against Graham and the Episcopal Church because, she said, some of the offenses had taken place within U.S. borders, specifically Texas. Letters were going out from her attorney to several bishops, the community and church headquarters with a May 1 deadline for payment, "or other action" would be taken.

I called Alden. The church's insurance company believed there were no grounds for a lawsuit, he told me. As for helping the Gullens purely out of kindness, funds were limited and the Gullens were no one's specific responsibility. Plus, to hand them money would imply liability, and no diocese was about to do that.

Far different was the way the Vineyard had treated one of its fallen leaders a year before. After this leader had been found guilty of "sexual misconduct" with two women, the Vineyard had sent out a press release to Christian magazines explaining that the church's disciplinary actions were to be at a level commensurate with the leader's visibility and ministry. Thus, the man, who had been active in the prophetic ministry, had to write out detailed statements of confession and repentance, undergo extensive counseling, withdraw from all public ministry, and seal himself from contact with all but a few close friends during his "restoration process," which was to take place over an undefined period of time. The sentence was thorough and almost ruthless in its intensity, but at least it was being dealt with in the open. By contrast, the problems with

Graham continued to fester. I warned Alden of legal repercussions, and asked him if he weren't risking a lot.

"What would it cost to buy off a lawsuit?" he wondered out loud. I reminded him of his letter to the diocese, promising that the Gullens would be taken care of. In addition, the national church had spared no expense at getting psychological evaluations and consultations for Graham. Well, he replied, after the final decision is made about Graham, he prayed that the Gullen matter, too, would be decided, but "a lot of opinions need to be considered." Apparently, one of those opinions was not Graham's, for I called him in Austin. He sounded as if he did not know and did not care about any ecclesiastical proceedings against him.

"I'm in the midst of reevaluating everything I've ever thought or ever did," he declared, and had given himself until September 1993 to get his thoughts together. He was staying with his daughter Martha, living on Social Security, a small pension, and gifts from friends. And, yes, they had gotten dozens of letters from well-wishers. But, no, he didn't want to answer any of my questions until at least September. He was not sure how he would define his past now, he said. We made small talk for a few minutes. I wished him well and prepared to hang up.

"Thank you for calling," he said.

A thank you? From Graham? That wasn't like him at all. He had always seemed indifferent to the research I was doing on him. His August 10 confession had been a fluke, and I suspected he never would answer any more of my questions.

SITTING dejectedly in Austin, Graham remembered there was someone in town who could help him. Bishop William Cox, the man with whom some of us had walked on the Galveston beach several years before, had been made an assistant bishop to Benitez, and sent to minister the portion of the diocese in Austin. Graham reached for the phone.

Although well familiar with Redeemer, the bishop had never met Graham. And now here was this man, like a tired lion, begging for help. Would the bishop hear his confession, Graham asked.

Cox wanted to meet a few times first, just to get a feel for everything that had transpired. This man, he thought, was definitely washed up. He had no steam left. When the bishop heard all he wanted to know, he suggested they go inside a church. They both knelt and Graham made his confession. Cox then gave him absolution, then held a private Communion service for the Pulkingham family. It had been months since Graham had received the Eucharist.

Some of Graham's victims were not as fortunate. In late March, Steven Plummer was in Florida, preparing to take his life. With all the scandal out about Graham, was there any hope for him? he wondered. No, there was not. Neither could he bear what he was doing to his wife, Anita.

Anita had known for years that Steven struggled with homosexuality. It had not helped being sexually abused as a child and having an alcoholic father. He had counseled endlessly with Graham about his sexual problems, and now he understood why Graham had told him he would never be healed. Graham had obviously been in despair over his own desires. Then there had been those horrible episodes in Graham's office when Graham had instructed him to remove all his clothes, and to "bare your fears in front of me." It had been so degrading. Then Steven learned he was not the only counselee Graham had done this to. The shame of it all was realizing how much power they had allowed Graham to have over them. It was more shameful than the sexual part; indeed, it was not a sexual issue. It was a power issue.

How could so much wickedness and holiness co-exist in the same person? Steven had done some reading on personality disorders, concluding that whatever Graham's problem was, it caused him no guilt. Emotionally vulnerable younger men had gotten hit by someone with no boundaries. Graham had hooked him, then a Houston teenager, the very first time they had met.

His drug overdose did not take and Steven found himself recuperating in a nearby hospital on April 1, the night my phone rang. The caller was Jackie Gullen, describing the letters her lawyer was drawing up to demand 35 percent of Graham's pension funds or a $95,000 lump sum. We talked about her wedding day in 1982, when she had not allowed her father to give her away because Graham did not think it was right. Eleven years later, she was still mad about that, feeling that something had been robbed from her.

"And you know that part in the wedding ceremony when, if anyone knows any cause why these two persons should not be married, they should 'speak now or forever hold their peace?'" she asked. "Well, Graham married us. He was the officiating priest. He *knew* that we shouldn't marry, and he knew why. But he said nothing. Nothing!"

An hour later, the phone rang again. It was Elizabeth Barry, a friend from the seminary.

"Julia," she said, "there's a request on the prayer chain about Graham. He's had a heart attack."

"When?"

"Sometime today. There was a shoot-out at some store and he collapsed."

"This is his third attack," I told her. "He had a quadruple bypass after the first one in 1981."

"I didn't know that," she said. "They just called us and asked us to pray. I think Bruce knows more details."

Bruce Newell did have more details: It had happened in Burlington, while Graham and Betty were visiting her mother, Bey. They were caring for a sick aunt when someone arrived to give them an hour's reprieve. Their first thought was to go shopping for food at a nearby Winn Dixie store.

Just before 3 p.m., Graham and Betty were near the back of the store when in walked Gerald Howard Snead, a supermarket employee and manic depressive who had been acting strangely during the past month. He had a crush on Pamela Pike, a woman who worked in the supermarket's deli, but Pamela was engaged to someone else with whom she had been living for seven years. Pamela had just finished baking a meatless pizza and was passing around samples to co-workers.

Snead made a bee line for the deli, pistol in hand. He fired three or four shots at Pamela, and she collapsed in a pool of blood. Then Snead aimed his gun at another female employee, shooting her in the leg. That woman scurried into a walk-in freezer, locking it from the inside. Snead next trained his sights on another employee, shooting her in the arm. Hearing the shots, terrified customers scrambled for the exits, leaving half-filled carts in the aisles. The supervisors tried to help them get out, fleeing from they knew not what or whom.

Two customers were not running. Graham, who was in one of the aisles, felt a familiar but frightening pain in his chest before dropping to the floor. Betty tried to give him CPR, a tough assignment for a 64-year-old woman. The shots continued and a store employee stopped to help her. Meanwhile, two off-duty policemen, who were in the store, had rushed out to their car to get a shotgun. They re-entered the store to find Snead reloading his gun. When they ordered him to drop the gun, he raised the rifle at them and fired. Officers returned fire, killing him. Two people were wounded, two were dead, and Graham lay dying. Precious minutes had gone by as this exchange went on. Betty was terrified, for Graham had been without oxygen far too long. The medics broke down a back door to enter, and by the time they raced to his side, Graham was in a coma. They restarted his heart and raced him to the hospital, hoping against hope that he could recover.

That night, Nancy Newman appeared at a Redeemer service to tell everyone the dire straits Graham was in. As the days went on, the prognosis grew grimmer. Graham's brain tissue had begun to swell, a sure sign of oxygen deprivation, and people began to say the dreaded word "brain-dead." Shoot-outs don't happen in grocery stores. They happen in banks, in ghettos, in domestic disputes. Why was it that Graham and Betty were in the market during that fateful hour? Why had Graham been cut off in the middle of his spiritual recovery? And why had this happened during Lent, keeping Graham from making it to Easter? Kairos and chronos had collided, and his hour had arrived.

The angel of death was at hand. The family hastened to his side in North Carolina. The six children, several of whom Graham had once told me were forever turned off to Christianity because of him, arrived. They would wash him and shave him and sing hymns in his presence, and sometimes his eyes would flutter open, but it was clear he was gone. Easter came and went; Jerry Barker flew in for a few days, then left. Funeral arrangements hung in the air. On April 16, a Friday morning, the hour glass ran out. At 7:48 a.m., while Betty Jane and Bill Farra were singing "Rock of Ages" to him, Graham slipped into the next world.

The Present

CHAPTER 27

Holy Saturday

"Sing, my tongue, the glorious battle,
Sing the winning of the fray;
Now above the cross the trophy,
Sounds the high triumphal lay:
Tell how Christ, the world's Redeemer,
As a victim won the day."

—6th-century Lenten plainsong

IN the year before Graham died, we had an Easter vigil early one April morning. The moon was still out in the cold Pennsylvania sky, and the streets filled with shadows, as we arrived at All Saints. The vigil service dates back to at least 215 AD, and the earliest Christians may have observed it as a way of remembering how the tomb was suddenly emptied that first dawn. Betty Pulkingham closed the vigil service, using the Book of Common Prayer and her loveliest music, the Exultet.

"Dear friends in Christ," the priest begins, "On this most holy night, in which our Lord Jesus passed over from death to life, the Church invites her members, dispersed throughout the world, to gather in vigil and prayer. For this is the Passover of the Lord, in which, by hearing His Word and celebrating His Sacraments, we share in His victory over death."

It was cold in the church, but the interior blazed with candles held by the choir. Standing by the altar were Bruce, Graham, and Alden Hathaway, who loved coming to All Saints before dawn, then heading back to Trinity Cathedral to oversee the Easter services there. Betty was poised in front of the choir, ready to conduct. The best musician of the three priests, Graham was chanting the part of the priest. None of us knew this would be the last Exultet Graham would sing. A year later, he would be in disgrace and near death hundreds of miles away, and many of the people in that brightly lit church would have scattered.

"Grant that in the Paschal feast, we may so burn with heavenly desires that, with pure minds, we may attain to the festival of everlasting light; through Jesus Christ our Lord," Graham prayed.

The large Easter Vigil candle was lit, and the congregants approached it to light their own candles. The choir was already standing in place, their candles shining golden lights on their faces. Bishop Hathaway was wearing his miter, and a long golden cope that swirled about his feet.

A T some point during my four-year sojourn in Pittsburgh, Alden had spoken on renewal. "Sin," he had informed us, "is always the last word on a movement." Two years later, he would announce his retirement. Certainly he was weary of the unending battle between the forces of good and evil in the Episcopal Church. The 1994 General Convention in Indianapolis would be particularly draining, with a sally by the conservative bishops met by a nearly equal challenge from the liberal bishops over gay ordinations, same-sex blessings, and other sex-related issues. Subsequent General Conventions would be more depressing, with greater setbacks, culminating in the election of V. Gene Robinson in 2003 as the first openly gay bishop in the Anglican Communion.

By then, the stalwarts were already beginning to flee the denomination. Many charismatics were finally giving up on Dennis Bennett's admonition to stay in the church at all costs, preferring to leave for what seemed to be the best lifeboat available.

In 2000, two Episcopal priests—one of them John Rodgers, a former dean of Trinity seminary—would fly halfway around the world to be consecrated "missionary bishops" in Singapore by a handful of Third World archbishops and American bishops. The two men were vilified by Anglicans around the world, including the archbishop of Canterbury, for seeking to minister to beleaguered conservative Episcopalians. But, as the years passed, dozens of parishes kept joining them and other breakaway groups, as it became clear the

Episcopal Church was in a free fall. Finally at the end of 2008, all these new Anglican groups would collectively cut their ties to the Episcopal Church and form their own Anglican province.

"Rejoice and be glad now, Mother Church," the choir sang in achingly beautiful harmony, "and let your holy courts, in radiant light, resound with the praises of your people."

Iɴ the year Graham died, a curious sort of revival, known for its propensity to send people into gales of helpless laughter, surfaced in North America. Then in the spring of 1994, I was sent to Orlando to interview the man credited with starting it: South African Rodney Howard-Browne. He was six feet tall, built like a football tackle and wore an expensive-looking suit with his initials monogrammed on his cuffs. He was flanked by two pentecostal pastors dressed in nearly identical suits, shirts, brightly colored ties, and expensive cufflinks.

Howard-Browne kept dodging my questions about his finances and offering a version of American church history that squared with the weird manifestations of his meetings. I never could ascertain just whom he was accountable to.

"I'm surrounding myself with pastors from major ministries around the world," he explained, "and I'm accountable to them." "Major ministries" in his parlance meant churches of at least 3,000 members. His friends included Oral and Richard Roberts, whom he had met when he visited Oral Roberts University in the fall of 1993. After he prayed over nearly 4,000 students and faculty, most got slain in the Spirit, as did members of the Roberts family.

Deeply impressed, Oral Roberts was proclaiming Howard-Browne's ministry as the beginning of "another level in the Holy Spirit." More than three decades had passed since the dawn of the charismatic movement, and people were desperate for something new. It had been a long time since pentecostals had experienced power. But here was a leader making the same mistake as Graham had—operating in the big time with little true accountability.

A few hours later, Howard-Browne was explaining to U.S. charismatic leaders what he was doing. Francis MacNutt, Vinson Synan, and other familiar leaders, who had nourished the renewal through so many tumultuous years, were there. No one had anything substantial of a theological or doctrinal nature to ask Howard-Browne, who began encouraging us to lift our hands and "let that river of joy come out of your belly." One side of the room began howling with laughter while the rest of us simply stared. Laughter, Howard-Browne was saying, needs to "bubble up" from where the gift of tongues originates. It was all in some deep spiritual reservoir that needed to be tapped the same way, by faith, he explained.

In terms of being non-biblical, this was off the charts. Then Howard-Browne called us all up for prayer, basically to get slain in the Spirit. A few people fled at that point, including a Catholic bishop. Was this what the renewal had come to?

Unexpectedly, it was my turn. After laying 20–30 people on the floor, Howard-Browne and his two friends asked if I'd like to be prayed over. I hesitated. As a reporter, should I maintain an objective distance or "enter in?" I finally assented to be prayed over and the trio instructed me to lift my hands. I had been around long enough to know that lifting one's hands can put you off balance enough for someone to smack you on the forehead to make sure you got "slain." No, I thought, if it happens, the Lord is going to have to work at it. I leaned forward, folding my hands near my waist.

Undaunted, the three men prayed over me, one or the other claiming he could feel joy rising up in me like a bubble that I only needed to release by laughing. I felt nothing and the Lord wasn't talking. Then Howard-Browne began instructing me to pray loudly in tongues to help out the Holy Spirit, I guessed. I compromised by praying very softly. The three men asked me to pray louder.

What? I thought. Am I praying to them? They did not need to hear me. I looked up into Howard-Browne's blue eyes and felt a tremendous letdown. This was becoming a farce.

"Sorry," I said and walked away.

"This is the night," they sang, "when you brought our fathers, the children of Israel, out of bondage in Egypt, and led them through the Red Sea on dry land. This is the night when all who believe in Christ are delivered from the gloom of sin, and are restored to grace and holiness of life."

WITHIN four months of Graham's death, Betty would survive a six-way heart bypass, the accumulated tension and sorrow having finally caught up with her. She remained in North Carolina, and to everyone's shock, remarried a few years later. Then her second husband died. Community members began scattering to the four corners of the globe as All Saints ran lower and lower on money and people. Redeemer's financial crisis would peak in 1993, forcing Benitez to intervene and to order Ladd to retire at the age of 67.

Relief was already on the way from a parish in Speedway, a suburb of

Indianapolis. It had begun 11 years earlier when Steve Capper, the Texas A&M student who had visited Redeemer back in 1973, was back in Texas at a charismatic Episcopal event in Denton, not far from Dallas. He had long since married his girlfriend, Karen, and become an Episcopal priest. Redeemer's choir was performing at the same event and Steve Capper noticed a couple from the choir making a beeline for him.

"God wants you to know that He wants to use you in significant ways in the church," they said.

"Where?" he asked them. "In the wider church?"

"We don't know," they replied, "but maybe it's at Redeemer." Weird, he thought, and tucked that information away in his memory. In the fall of 1993, he turned 40 years old, had been six years in Indianapolis, and was looking to move. A friend had put his name in as a possible Redeemer rector, and in early 1994, the church contacted him. He was impressed by the stark honesty of the church's self-profile. Particularly striking was the overwhelming distrust parishioners felt for their leaders. He could see why. He and Karen had visited All Saints in Aliquippa in the late 1980s and felt it to be unhealthy. When he reported his findings to Chuck Irish, Chuck asked, "Is Graham still wearing his earring?"

As Redeemer's choices for a rector got narrowed to fewer and fewer people, Karen and Steve prayed all the more. What, they wondered, was the redemptive thread through all this? This was the church that had had it all: creative worship, sacrificial living, a calling to be a light to the world—they had thrown it all away. They knew from the New Testament that the gifts and calling of God are irreversible. These parishioners still had the calling in their hearts—he could see that. Something was pre-existing in these people—something that said the past could still be redeemed.

He also noticed among many the brokenness and hunger for God. *I can be a broken person with these people*, he thought. He gave the search committee three conditions: that the vestry and search committee not leave for two years; that for the first year, they would meet weekly with him for an hour of prayer; and that they would match the insurance, salary, and benefits package he had at St. John's, Speedway. Even in its weakened condition, Redeemer was still a larger parish than Speedway, and his conditions were not unreasonable. The search committee, with a gulp, promised to meet all three conditions, although most had no idea where the money would come from.

He got the call in early July, and on the eve of General Convention in late August, their dining room table was heaped with odds and ends and parishioners were constantly dropping by the rectory to say good-bye. Karen was a wreck. They had just sent off a daughter to Ecuador for a year of studying abroad, and it didn't look as if the house was ever going to get packed for the movers the next day. Nevertheless, she had already bonded with Redeemer. She had not chosen some of the churches to which they had gone. Redeemer was one she wanted very much. It all seemed to be a beautiful fairy tale, and she was scared to move too fast for fear it might not come true.

Her hour came two days later when, on a hot summer morning, the family climbed into their overburdened car and headed south to Houston.

The Cappers had not been in Houston many months when attendance began shooting up and enough money was coming in not only to pay his salary but to renovate the fading mural. When he requested parishioners to show up once a week at 5:30 a.m. for prayer, 100 people came for the first meeting. The hunger was there. The parish loved his meaty sermons, and he was quick to publicly reconcile with people like Chris Simpson, who had parted ways with the parish years before.

But not everyone took to the new rector. An introvert, he often stayed for hours in his office with his door closed. It was a far cry from the open office policy Ladd had followed, and a universe away from Redeemer's dictum to share one's life at any cost. The older parishioners, who had lived through the golden era, saw irreversible changes in the offing and prepared to leave the city and retire elsewhere. Many of them had never liked Houston anyway, and with the death of a vision, they saw no reason to stay.

Steve also removed from the pews all the books containing Redeemer music of the past three decades and had the words to the day's songs printed on the bulletin. Although this fit with the way growing churches were handling their lyrics, it strangled Redeemer's trademark harmonies, because there was no music to read. Instead, the choir had to present the new Vineyard-style music, which was all the rage in non-denominational churches. As parts of the liturgy were removed to make way for freer-form services, Graham's dream of Redeemer as a showcase for Episcopal renewal faded and the beautiful music, which reminded everyone of what was and what still could be, died. The parish struggled, dipping to 150 people each Sunday morning for the English language service. Eventually, Steve went part-time, dividing his hours between Redeemer and another ministry. A few blocks away, the local Catholic diocese constructed a huge, beautiful church tailored for charismatic worship, causing many people in the neighborhood to head there instead.

"This is the night when Christ broke the bonds of death and hell, and rose victorious from the grave! How wonderful and beyond our knowing, O God, is Your mercy and loving kindness to us, that to redeem a slave, You gave a Son."

IN the spring of 2001, I covered a prophecy conference in Kansas City where each powerful worship session lasted at least 90 minutes and singers, dancers, and instrumentalists with prophetic gifts were welcomed onstage. Worship leaders came up with sung prophecies at the drop of a hat, the conference bookstore stocked a CD of Middle Eastern-style worship music that included a long aria in tongues, and one could make an appointment with a prayer team to come up with a "word of knowledge" about one's personal life.

This was night and day from how spiritual gifts were being referred to in most churches. Now very popular was the "spiritual gifts inventory," a handy form used heavily by churches that treated supernatural gifts as similar to such natural talents as hospitality or administration. It was a deadly invention that very efficiently substituted something else for what remained of the renewal movement.

I asked Mike Bickel, the pastor of the sponsoring ministry, how his people had come to be so creative in an era when few churches were doing anything new.

"In theory," he said, "people go out and do what we do at their home churches, but in reality, this is an oasis in the desert."

A co-worker chimed in that several visitors at the conference were from a group of churches that had started out as charismatic. Now their pastors were all concerned about control. I could hardly blame some of them, because what got loosed during a spiritual outpouring was often way too powerful. Any church that became in the least bit involved in the charismatic renewal soon found itself deep in battle against an entrenched principality that hates worship, priests, and marriages, and that delights in disobedience, deceit, and perverse sexuality. It was deeper, more horrible, archangelic spiritual warfare against the dragon in the basement, and it consumed everyone who tried to minister there.

I had to pity certain pastors who knew they were not up to moving the gates of hell; who decided it was better to retrench back to pre-1960s spirituality rather than crash on the shoals of the renewal. At this point, it was clear that nearly everyone was crashing. No one had counted on how lengthy the battle would be, nor how high the price would soar. Mike Bickel had formed around himself a 24-hour prayer force called the International House of Prayer. It served as a community to provide the needed reinforcements for the lengthy battle.

What impressed me about Mike was how he stayed in the background, only moving to center stage when it was clearly time for direction or instruction.

"There's enough people watching what we are doing here," he mused, "and there's a million or two out there who see us raising the flag."

"How holy is this night," the choir sang in the hushed sanctuary, "when wickedness is put to flight, and sin is washed away. It restores innocence to the fallen, and joy to those who mourn. It casts out pride and hatred, and brings peace and concord."

ONE warm September evening in 2002, I was in Oregon, strolling down the streets of southeast Portland with a young couple who headed a community household. It was called Madison House, and it was a grand mansion with a sweeping fireplace, stained glass windows, a majestic staircase, and a welcoming front veranda. I was taking Aron and Yvonne Noll, the couple, on a tour of the old community households in the area. First, we walked about Madison House, the centerpiece of the old Bethlehem Community I'd lived in 20 years before. I told them of all the parties and dinners we had there when we were young Christians in our 20s and out to change the world. Two blocks away was my old household: House of Jubilee and Covenant House. Less than a mile away was a fourth household: Christening House.

All manner of people lived there: tired people, the depressed, the unmarriageable, the chaste but gay singles, and the rest of us who wanted a grand experiment that was bigger than ourselves. How, asked Aron and Yvonne, had you done it? Where were the blueprints? How had you managed to put up with each other? How did you keep on loving?

We then drove across the Hawthorne Bridge into the city, nearing what used to be Bethlehem's "downtown cluster" of community households, situated near Portland State University to better attract would-be student converts. We walked slowly by my old household on Fifth Avenue, Shekinah House, now a dilapidated apartment. We then meandered up the street past other former households: Abba's Way, Beth El, Inn on the Way, and Way Inn, all of which were now frat houses or shops. All of them had witnessed the passionate Christianity we lived then, where no sacrifice was too big, if it added to the kingdom of God.

Best of all were the worship times, which were preceded by a half-hour of silence so we could hear the Lord and bring what He had showed us to the group. We knew each other so well that we could risk failure. People would share dances, visions, exhortations, and prophecies. By the end of two hours, everyone

316

had heard the Lord speak to them personally or through another in a rich tapestry of Scripture, songs, and words from God. Community had provided the natural cradle to nurture the riskier gifts. When community faded, so did the gifts. The two were connected.

Yet, community was so hard. Diaries chronicling my two years there were full of yearnings for escape. Yet I stayed, hoping for a change in the core of my being, so I could be a more powerful, Spirit-filled Christian. Looming above us in the near distance was a steep hillside of homes rising hundreds of feet above downtown. Surmounting it all was an edifice known as "the castle," a private home on Buckingham Avenue built like a medieval battlement, reached by a hidden stairway that snaked up, through the woods, from Broadway Avenue. I often climbed it to get away from household life. I remember gazing at it through the window of my room at Shekinah House. Living in community, I thought, was like climbing up the stairway to the castle. It was the fast road to mature Christianity. I was in a hurry, so I climbed the steps. Others, I reasoned, might take the easier route via paved road. They'd get to the same point eventually, but it would take them so much longer.

However, the cost would be staggering. A few months after the Nolls and I walked the streets of Portland, there was another death. Bob Carlson, the man chiefly responsible for founding the Bethlehem community, was 76 when he died in near poverty, having felt forced to leave the covenant community years earlier. Bethlehem would split his own family down the middle and break his heart, much as it did to a lonely Episcopal priest whose own heart gave out on the floor of a North Carolina supermarket.

"How blessed is this night, when earth and heaven are joined and man is reconciled to God," the choir sang with sweetness and power.

I was 33 when I started this book project. With the publishing houses I queried, it was controversial, to say the least. And the 33rd publisher I approached gave me a contract. Twenty years had passed; 20 years when all the people who had promised to pray for the writing of this book had long since tired and moved on. But I did not give up. I could not give up. I was forbidden to give up.

"Holy Father, accept our evening sacrifice, the offering of this candle in your honor. May it shine continually to drive away all darkness. May Christ, the Morning Star who knows no setting, find it ever burning—He who gives His light to all creation, and who lives and reigns for ever and ever. Amen."

GRAHAM was right. It was community that made Redeemer and other powerful charismatic fellowships across the country what they were; it was community that allowed the Holy Spirit to move so quickly; it was community that birthed the music and the worship, that encouraged the spiritual gifts, that created an undefinable quality of love that drew thousands to Houston, that caused millions to read the books and listen to the music.

People there gave generously because they had been loved generously by God, so much like the Christians who, 2000 years earlier, gave away all they had to gain Christ. It was a sacrificing community that made love so real to so many, that rescued the neighborhood for a brief few decades, that drew in the lost and unwanted. This is not the conclusion I expected to find, but a reporter's job is to tell the truth. My task is done, and here you see it complete.

Holy Saturday is but a day in the liturgical calendar, yet it has been unnaturally stretched into a season of lessons in the dark. We wait, with Christ, for Easter and a resurrection to a church more charismatic than before and much closer to suffering; a place of God's power and desire.

Someday, the vision before us will be so bright, we will no longer have to look back. The city on a plain gleams and shines at sunrise, its sparkling jewels set against a glowing Texas sky. The amber light races across the plain, over houses and trees and freeways to catch fire on the glass skyscrapers, a range of glittering man-made mountains. They shimmer in the saffron light like a heavenly city awaiting a king's arrival.

He is coming in majesty, and we have been warned. Art Katz foretold it.

"The God of death is also the God of our resurrection," he said. "We shouldn't be taken by surprise. We must taste death, not just agree with it academically. What is truly death is when something successful is brought to the grave.

"Why should we think this a strange thing? We must let go. We'll see another form of community in its resurrected life that will be more glorious than before."

LIST OF

INTERVIEWS

The warp and woof of this detailed and lengthy book is due to the help of so many people who let me interview them, some of them multiple times. Although I could not fit all of their names into the manuscript, I want to acknowledge the wealth of their combined insights, anecdotes, assessments, memories and, in some cases, confessions. Several bishops and many clergy are included on this list and families (parents, children, siblings and spouses) are all grouped under one listing.

I counted at least 182 separate interviews for this book and there are 204 people on this list alone. Some of the people named below were not so much interviewed as they were available for me to bounce ideas and questions off of. Undoubtedly, several worthy names may have inadvertently been left out. I am thankful to everyone who helped me in this 20-year project.

My interviewees included:

1. Leonard and Sue Abbott
2. Susan Abbott
3. Bob and Diane Davis Andrew
4. Gene Antill
5. Bill and Johnna Appenbrink
6. Helen Appleberg
7. Gwenyth Arnold
8. Essie Avalos
9. Bruce and Barbara Baker
10. Ed Baggett
11. Jerry, Owen and Alison Barker
12. Lyn Bazemore
13. Maurice "Ben" Benitez
14. Rita Bennett
15. Wiley Beveridge
16. Dick and Ivis Bird
17. Rob and Martha Blain
18. Jack Bradshaw
19. Wallace and Nancy Braud

20. Larry Brown
21. Norma and Bob Burlingame
22. Gordon Butler
23. Steve and Karen Capper
24. James Cappleman
25. Chris Caros
26. Jim Carr
27. Barbara Christman
28. Jim and Jane Clowe
29. Winnie Compton
30. Elizabeth Constantian
31. Jeff Cothran
32. William Cox
33. Jennifer and Billy Crain
34. Mary Cromwell
35. Chopin "Choppy" and Carol Lee Evans Cusachs
36. Jackie and Greg Davis
37. David Davis

38. Raymond Davis	84. Don and Glenna McLane
39. Bruce Durst	85. Charles Meisgeier
40. Mark Dyke	86. Taft and Peggy Metcalf
41. Max Dyer	87. Neal Michell
42. Bob and Nancy Eckert	88. Gary Miles
43. Cindy Engle	89. Leslie and George Mims
44. Bob and Mary Ella Evans	90. Jack and Delores Minor
45. Margaret Farra	91. Cathleen and Bob Morris
46. Carl and Beverly Faught	92. George and Holly Moses
47. Paul and Mary Felton	93. Esther-Marie Daskalakis Nagiel
48. Jan, Ladd and Linda Fields	94. Sue and Ralph Neal
49. Charlie and Gwen Foss	95. Bob and Ruth Newlander
50. Martha and Andrew Franks	96. Grover Newman
51. Paul, Anne, Bill and Barbara Frey	97. Steve Noll
52. Ruth Newell Garmony	98. Suzie and Paul Patton
53. Pat Beall Gavigan	99. Mary and Marty Pearsall
54. Alison and Jonathan Goldhor	100. Steve Peklenk
55. John and Edith Grimmet	101. Karen Frerck Peterson
56. Jackie and Richard Gullen	102. Wanda, Steven and Anita Plummer
57. Kevin Hackett	103. Graham, Betty, Nathan
58. Marie Haeffner	and Margi Pulkingham
59. Linda Newton Harbove	104. Bonnie Ramirez
60. Michael Harper	105. Larry and Diane Reed
61. Alden Hathaway	106. Don Richardson
62. Elise Hazel	107. Nancy Rodgers
63. Tom Herrick	108. Ann and Al Rountree
64. John Hines	109. David and Eugenia Rust
65. Dell Hoffman	110. Jeff Schiffmayer
66. Donna Hollis	111. Debbie Scott
67. Elaine Holway	112. Rebekah Scott Schreffler
68. Brian and Ruth Gordon Howard	113. Sandy and Kathleen Scott
69. Camp Huntington	114. Don and Mary Sears
70. Mary Johnson	115. Ron Seeger
71. Jim Kearney	116. Carolyn Shaver
72. Nona Keene	117. Jon Shuler
73. Carol and Mikel Kennedy	118. Chris Simpson
74. David Knight	119. Sister Kathleen Smith
75. Ken "Kino" Langoria	120. Jim Stringham
76. Nancy Lawshae	121. Tom Sumners
77. Bill and Martha Ann Linden	122. Howard Tellepsen
78. Grady and Janice Manley	123. Jack Tench
79. Betty Masquelette	124. Kathleen Thomerson
80. Kevin Martin	125. Audrey Tindall
81. Frank and Marie Marzullo	126. Jane and G. Wilson Trigg
82. Marilyn Mazak	127. Janet and Steve Troy
83. Jeanne McGranahan	128. James von Minden

129. Dick Wall
130. Dick and Rose Marie Wallace
131. Bob Warren
132. Beau Weaver
133. Philip Weeks
134. Ruth Weiting
135. Joyce and Carl Wheeler
136. Tim Whipple
137. Bette Graham White
138. Reid and Jeanette Wightman
139. Mike and Sharon Wilkens

140. David Wilkerson
141. Jon and Sylvia Wilkes
142. Martha and David Williams
143. Cliff Wilson
144. Jeff Wilson
145. Victor and Theresa Wilson
146. Oressa Wise
147. Bert Womack
148. Bob and Topsy Woodson
149. Jill Lokey Youmans

ENDNOTES

Although the majority of my 182 interviews occurred in the Houston area, others were conducted in Aliquippa and Ambridge, Pennsylvania, and at points around the country stretching from Seattle to Pensacola. Most were conducted in person. A number of people, such as Redeemer's original five elders, did multiple interviews.

Chapter 1—Pentecost

Information in this chapter is drawn heavily from Graham Pulkingham's first autobiography: *Gathered for Power* (Morehouse-Barlow Co., New York, 1972). Additional details were furnished in interviews on Oct. 17-18, 1990, with Graham and Betty Pulkingham in Aliquippa, Pa.

The Pentecostalism did not go down well: This episode is described in Catherine Marshall LeSourd's *Something More: In Search of a Deeper Faith* (McGraw Hill, 1974) pp. 281-282.

The two clicked as Graham described: From a December 1998 interview of David Wilkerson in New York.

Chapter 2—Trinity

Information in this chapter is taken mainly from interviews of Graham and Betty Pulkingham on Oct. 17-18 and Dec. 13, 1990, in Aliquippa and of Graham on Aug. 10, 1992. Background on Houston came from articles by Douglas Milburn, "Houston, Designed for the 20th Century," and "Speaking of Texas," *Texas Highways*, June 1990, pp. 2-9, 23.

Its much ballyhooed builder: From *Tom Tellepsen: Builder and Believer*, by Andrea Flynn (Anson Jones Press, Salado, Tex., 1956). Other details were furnished in a June 24, 1991, interview of Howard Tellepsen in Houston.

Afterwards a woman approached him: From an interview of Wanda Plummer, July 4-6, 1990.

John and Edith Grimmet: July 2, 1991, interview.

Things remained at an impasse: July 7, 1992, interview of Bishop John Hines at a retirement home near Asheville, N.C.

Years later: From a sermon Graham preached Nov. 4, 1990, at All Saints Church, Aliquippa.

After Houston Chronicle: Steakley, Melvin, "Eastwood Episcopal Priest Seeks 'Community' Role," *Houston Chronicle*, Oct. 12, 1963.

One of the 12-year-olds: July 7, 1991, interview of Ken Langoria.

Chapter 3—Mary Magdalene

Betty Jane was wondering: From a Dec. 13-14, 1990, interview of Graham and Betty Pulkingham and from Betty's 1977 book *Little Things in the Hands of a Big God* (Word Books, Waco, Texas).

On Maundy Thursday: From an April 9, 1990, interview of Grover Newman.

Betty Masquelette, a laywoman: July 2, 1991, interview of Betty Masquelette.

Graham continued his sojourns: This material is taken from *Gathered for Power* plus Graham's second book, *They Left Their Nets* (Morehouse-Barlow Co., New York, 1973). Graham furnished extra details during interviews.

When he heard: From a June 13, 1992, interview of Ann and Al Rountree.

Word spread: Don Richardson, interviewed Aug 12, 1991, provided the anecdote about the retreat, which he had attended as a layman from elsewhere in the diocese.

Graham had another test of his sanity: This and all other material in this chapter about Bob and Nancy Eckert came from three days of interviews on July 4-6, 1990.

One of the couples: Interview of Jerry Barker, April 28, 1990.

At the mens' prayer group: Interview of Ladd Fields, July 18, 1990.

Chapter 4—Transfiguration

Richardson privately contacted: From a May 22, 1990, interview of Bob and Mary Ella Evans.

One of the earlier tests: This incident, recorded on p. 129 of *Gathered for Power*, was confirmed in a March 15, 1993, interview of Nathan Pulkingham.

The scattered elders: From interviews of Bob Eckert and Ladd Fields in July 1990, Jerry Barker in April 1990.

The Grimmets left: From a July 30, 1991, interview of John and Edith Grimmet.

That summer: From a June 26, 1991, interview of Susan Abbott.

Some friends of theirs: From a June 20, 1992, interview of Ralph and Sue Neal.

All the same: The material from here to the end of the chapter came from a Dec. 14, 1990, interview of Graham Pulkingham.

The eleventh person: From a June 20, 1992, interview of Helen Appelberg and a July 18, 1990, interview of Ladd Fields.

Chapter 5—Holy Cross

One day Graham: Material in this section is from *Gathered for Power* and a June 24, 1992, interview of Kathleen Thomerson.

Another visitor: From an Aug. 17, 1990, interview of Michael Harper. Nearly the same version of this incident is recorded in his book, *A New Way of Living* (Logos International, Plainfield, N.J., 1973).

"There are many in this fellowship": from the sermon "Love the Brethren, Sacrifice Yourself," given Nov. 1, 1966, by Graham Pulkingham. Other material from this chapter came from the sermon "Wilderness," preached by Graham on June 7, 1966.

On September 14: From a May 1, 1990, interview of Bette Graham White.

This bowled over: From a June 14, 1992, interview of Grady and Janice Manley.

One August evening: From the sermon "Our Ministry to God," given Aug. 23, 1966, by Graham Pulkingham.

Graham needed: From a July 7, 1991, interview of Ken "Kino" Langoria.

In 1967, two events: This short history of the Catholic charismatic renewal was previously reported by the author in "Catholics on the Pentecostal Trail," in *Christianity Today*, June 22, 1992, pp 25-27. Another source was "The Night We First Prayed in Tongues," an article by Bert Ghezzi in *Charisma*, March 1987, pp. 30-31.

Chapter 6—St. Matthew

Background information for this chapter was taken from these issues of the church magazine *The Light*: July 18, 1967, June 14, 1967, and Feb. 14, 1968.

It was a warm evening: This anecdote came from a July 15, 1992, interview of Graham Pulkingham.

Marie Marzullo, a transplant: From a May 28, 1990, interview of Frank and Marie Marzullo.

Bob and Mary-Ella Evans's college-age daughter: Material in this chapter comes from a July 9, 1991, interview of Carol Lee Evans Cusachs.

Ed Baggett was a thoughtful: From an Aug. 2, 1991, interview of Ed Baggett.

Some of them: From a May 10, 1990, interview of Norma and Bob Burlingame.

Once at the church: From interview of John and Edith Grimmet, July 2, 1991.

One day in the spring: From a June 27, 1992, interview of Jeff Schiffmayer.

Wayne Hightower was: Anecdotes in this chapter were collected during a Redeemer ushers' reunion in the spring of 1990.

Chapter 7—St. Michael and All Angels

The material from Stephen Noll came from conversations with him while he was advising the author in 1991-92 on her master's thesis on authoritarian trends in charismatic Christian communities.

A car pulled up: Anecdotes about the North Main house and the naming of the Way In come from Betty Pulkingham's 1977 book *Little Things in the Hands of a Big God*, (Word Books).

Some were either getting off drugs: April 24, 1990, interview of Carolyn Shaver.

"Worship is horizontal...": Feb. 22, 1992, interview of Wiley Beveridge.

Victor Wilson, a backslidden: July 14, 1990, interview of Victor Wilson.

Jeff was 21: June 28, 1991, interview of Jeff Cothran.

Several hundred students: Dec. 27, 1991, interview of Mikel and Carol Kennedy.

However, placing a handful: July 21, 1991, interview of Owen Barker.

One of the Way In visitors: Sept. 1, 1993, interview of Raymond Davis.

Graham was in fact: Graham's theology of the family was spelled out in "Walking in the Authority of our Sonship in Christ," circa 1974, a series of talks to a conference of community leaders and in "God's Authority: A Gift to His Family," a four-part sermon series given during the same era.

Chapter 8—St. Francis

The meeting in Ft. Lauderdale was described in Don Basham's 1972 book *Deliver Us From Evil* (Fleming H. Revell Co., Old Tappan, N.J.). The material from *Look Magazine* was written by Brian Vachon in "The Jesus Movement is Upon Us," published Feb. 9, 1971, pp. 15-21. The *Time* magazine article was written by Richard Ostling, in "The New Rebel Cry: Jesus is Coming!" on June 21, 1971, pp. 56-63.

Jim had bushy eyebrows: All material in this book describing the Clowes comes from interviews with Jim and Jane Clowe on Aug. 13-14, 1991, in Pensacola.

Also at Redeemer: From an Aug. 9, 1991, interview of Paul and Mary Felton.

That same spring: Interview of Ruth Newell Garmony on July 14, 1990.

Another newcomer was Taft: From a June 12, 1990, interview of Taft and Peggy Metcalf.

Redeemer's fervor deeply: Interview of Camp Huntington on July 24, 1991.

By the fall of 1970: Interview of Sister Kathleen Smith, June 20, 1990.

There were charismatic stirrings: July 31, 1992, interview of Tom Sumners.

Redeemer attracted people: June 11, 1990, interview of Chris Caros.

Bob Eckert's life: Interviews with Bob and Nancy Eckert from July 4-6, 1990.

One visitor to the Eckert household: June 11, 1990, interview of Charles Meisgeier.

One day Betty: From an April 13, 1991, interview of Betty Pulkingham.

Chapter 9—St. Luke

Much of the material in this chapter came from interviews with George and Leslie Mims from Aug. 19-21, 1991, in South Carolina. Material on the history of the Catholic charismatic renewal was taken from these issues of *New Covenant* magazine: May 1974, Sept. 1973, Oct. 1973, June 1973 and August 1974.

Mikel Kennedy married: From a May 14, 1990, interview of Carol Kennedy.

Two University of Houston: Interview of Carl Wheeler on June 30, 1992, and Max Dyer, June 29, 1992.

Bob Burlingame's new wife: From a May 10, 1990, interview of Norma and Bob Burlingame.

It was New Year's Eve: This episode was recounted in a May 1, 1990, interview of Bette Graham White and in an Oct. 18, 1990, interview of Cathleen Gillis Morris.

Jane Clowe noticed: From an Aug. 13-14, 1991, interview.

Around the time Bill: From interviews with Graham Pulkingham, Sept. 25, 1991, and Margi Pulkingham, July 25, 1991.

Having left home: Dec. 27, 1991, interview of Tim Whipple.

On Christmas Eve, 1971: From an Aug. 18, 1991, interview of Ruth Gordon Howard.

Seventeen-year-old Bonnie: From a July 17, 1990, interview of Bonnie Ramirez.

One night: From a Nov. 28, 1992, interview of Donna Hollis.

Little did: From a June 20, 1992, interview of Ralph and Sue Neal.

When one young woman: From a July 27, 1991, interview of Kathleen Crow.

Every so often: From a July 31, 1991, interview of Jeanette Harrington Wightman.

Jeff Cothran noticed: From a June 28, 1991, interview of Jeff Cothran.

Jon and Sylvia Wilkes noticed: From a June 14, 1991, interview of the Wilkes.

Chapter 10—St. James

She stood outside: From interviews with Bob and Diane Andrew Davis, Nov. 24, 1990, and Gary Miles, May 20, 1990.

Using Arabella: From "The Christian Community," a four-part lecture series apparently given to a British audience in 1974.

Elaine Holway was 22: From a June 16, 1991, interview of Elaine Holway.

The singles were instrumental: Some of the information about Lantrip comes from a piece by Jeff Schiffmayer: "Is that your school across the street?" pp. 14-16, *New Covenant*, January, 1974 and from a Nov. 5, 1990, interview of Charlie and Gwen Foss.

A social worker named Ivis Good: From a July 21, 1991, interview of Dick and Ivis Good Bird.

Many of the gracious: Descriptions of the community in Evanston came from the author's visit there in 1979 and the following books by Dave and Neta Jackson: *Coming Together: All those communities and what they're up to* (Bethany Fellowship, Minneapolis, 1978).

Living Together in a World Falling Apart (Creation House, Carol Stream, Illinois, 1974).

Glimpses of Glory (Brethren Press, Elgin, Illinois, 1987).

Listening in, George: From interviews with George and Leslie Mims on Aug. 19-21, 1991.

Underneath her: Much of this material was taken from a series recorded by Margo Farra, called "The Sun's Gonna Shine: Hope," Fisherfolk/Woodland Park conference, date circa 1982, Tapes 1-3.

One day that woman: From an interview of the victim.

Other women: From a July 3, 1992, interview of Pat Beall Gavigan.

Other forces: Much of the information for this section came from Michael Harper's book *Bishops' Move* (Hodder and Stoughton, London, 1978).

By the summer of 1972: From an Aug. 5, 1972, sermon by Graham Pulkingham.

A few weeks later: From an Aug. 26, 1972, sermon by Jeff Schiffmayer.

Chapter 11—Sts. Simon and Jude

On Sept. 5, 1972: Interview of Graham Pulkingham, Sept. 25, 1991.

Just before Graham left: From an April 22, 1992, interview of G. Wilson Trigg and an April 12, 1991, interview of Jane Trigg Teschner.

The central factor: June 27, 1992, interview of Jeff Schiffmayer.

"There are laws...": From a sermon given Aug. 16, 1972, by Jeff Schiffmayer.

Likewise, Jerry Barker: From a June 1, 1991, interview of Jerry and Allison Barker and a June 20, 1992, interview of Ralph and Sue Neal.

By 1971: Many of the statistics come from James E. Clark's doctoral dissertation on Redeemer titled, "Joy, healing and power: The Prophet's Work in the Modern World," University of Houston, 1981.

The airport: From a Sept. 27, 1991, interview of Bill and Barbara Frey and a March 8, 1991, interview of Paul Frey.

At a gathering of 300 Episcopal clergy: Memories of this meeting were furnished by Jack Tench, rector of St. Luke's, Ballard (Seattle), in December 1992.

Chapter 12—Thanksgiving

The details at the beginning of this chapter were furnished through interviews with Graham and Betty Pulkingham, Michael Harper, Aug. 17, 1990, Max Dyer, June 29, 1992, and other former Fisherfolk members.

General Convention time: From a June 30, 1992, interview of Joyce Rogers Wheeler and a Dec. 15, 1990, interview of Jeff Wilson.

One of them: From a June 29, 1991, interview of Bob and Topsy Woodson.

When the white-haired: The Suenens' anecdote came from Jeff Schiffmayer, June 27, 1992.

These were the salad days: Redeemer statistics were supplied by James E. Clark, in his doctoral dissertation on Redeemer titled, "Joy, healing and power: The prophet's work in the modern world," University of Houston, 1981.

It was around that time: From an interview of Billy and Jennifer Crain, June 3, 1991.

Charlotte and Jim Stringham: From a June 23, 1990, interview of Jim Stringham.

One of his listeners: Ibid, Jeff Wilson.

Steve Capper, a tall: From an Aug. 23, 1994, interview of Steve and Karen Capper.

There were other: Norma Burlingham, May 10, 1990.

In December 1973: From *'God is my Buddy' and other Charismatic Misnomers*, by Philip Weeks (Barnabas Publications, Maitland, Fla., 1988).

This unwelcome advice: Bill Frey, Sept 27, 1991.

They may have been: Chris Caros, June 11, 1990.

Chapter 13—Advent

But some remembered: David Wilkerson had a vision in April 1973 of America's eventual collapse. He preached about it the following August. Much of it is recorded in his 1974 book *The Vision*, (New York: Pyramid Books).

The Swedish sky: From interviews with Ed Baggett, Aug. 2, 1991, and Max Dyer, June 29, 1992.

Other marriages: From a June 1, 1991, interview of Jerry and Alison Barker.

Margi was tiny: From a July 25, 1991, interview of Margi Pulkingham.

Redeemer hit: From an Aug. 2, 1991, interview of Jack and Delores Minor in Austin.

The fourth elder: From a May 22, 1991, interview of George and Holly Moses.

Chapter 14—St. Andrew

That October: From an Aug. 1, 1991, interview of Reid Wightman.

The new community: From a March 26, 1990, interview of Mary and Marty Pearsall in Colorado Springs and a July 27, 1991, interview of Kathleen Crow in Houston.

Paul was a distant: From a June 9, 1992, interview of Paul and Suzie Patton.

The rest of the team: June 28, 1991, interview of Jeff Cothran.

Some members: From a Sept. 27, 1991, interview of Bill and Barbara Frey.

Meanwhile the charismatic renewal: Details about this time period are also described in Richard Quebedeaux' 1983 book, *The New Charismatics II* (Harper & Row Publishers, San Francisco), pp 140-141. Other charismatic history was recounted in *One Lord, One Spirit, One Body*, by Peter Hocken, (The Word Among Us Press, Gaithersburg, Md., 1987).

Elders, Graham said: From "Walking in the authority of our Sonship in Christ," a series of talks given around 1974.

Listening to this: From an Aug. 2, 1991, interview of Jack and Delores Minor.

In the fall of 1975: The doctoral dissertation by James E. Clark that would emerge from this is "Joy, healing and power: The prophet's work in the modern world," University of Houston, 1981.

One of those: See Steve Clark's *Man and Woman in Christ* (Servant Publications, Ann Arbor, Mich., 1980).

To drive the point home: Taken from David Crumm's profile: "Word of God: The Rise and Fall of a Heavenly Empire," *Detroit Free Press Magazine*, Sept. 20, 1992, pp. 6-19.

Chapter 15—St. Clement

Much of the information in this chapter was taken from an Aug. 11, 1991, interview of Marilyn Mazak in Houston and Aug. 13-14, 1991, interviews of Jim and Jane Clowe in Pensacola.

Perhaps the person most damaged: From a July 1, 1991, interview of Don and Mary Sears.

One night: From a June 29, 1992, interview of Gene Antill and a June 29, 1991, interview of Bob Woodson.

To all outward: From a June 12, 1990, interview of Peggy Metcalf.

The beauty of it all: From an April 18, 1990, interview of Jonathan Goldhor.

The Lindens were hooked: From a June 22, 1992, interview of Bill and Martha Ann Linden.

Graham had had a premonition: From a July 15, 1992, interview of Graham.

He came to the mike: Quotes are taken from "Changes," a tape of a speech made by Jack Minor on Jan. 25, 1977. The tape "Trip to England" from a speech to the church given by Jim Clowe Dec. 7, 1976, also provided background.

If we're having fun: From a July 1, 1990, interview of Jackie Krafft Davis.

Some of the singles: From an Aug. 4, 1990, interview of Larry and Diane Angel Reed near Chattanooga.

In May 1977: Information was taken from these articles by Louis Moore: "Deprogramming attempt is made on member, 28, of Houston's Episcopal Church of the Redeemer," *Houston Chronicle*, May 7, 1977, and "Deprogrammer: I will strike at Redeemer Church again," *Houston Chronicle*, Nov. 12, 1977.

Also Rick Barrs piece, "Religion tug-of-war, Couple gains writ for son's return from sect's commune in Colorado," *Houston Post*, Aug. 2, 1978, and Nene Foxhall's article, "Commune leader to appeal order requiring boy's return to parents," *Houston Chronicle*, Aug. 2, 1978.

They had moved to California: From a June 14, 1992, interview of Grady and Janice Manley.

Well, you're the parent: from a Dec. 4, 1993, interview of Bert Womack.

As the writ: From a Sept. 27, 1991, interview of Bill Frey.

Out of the jungles: Taken from Donald Neff's "Nightmare in Jonestown," *Time*, Dec. 4, 1978, pp. 16-30.

As the words of prophecy: From David Manuel's *Like a Mighty River* (Rock Harbor Press, Orleans, Mass., 1977). Also see James Jones's "The Charismatic Renewal after Kansas City," *Sojourners*, Sept. 1977, pp. 11-13.

Perhaps heaven was waiting: J. David Pawson's "Whatever happened to the baptism in the Spirit?" *Renewal* magazine, unspecified 1993 issue, pp 25-28, helped provide background.

Chapter 16—St. Thomas

The descriptions of the musical output by the Fisherfolk and Redeemer were taken from interviews with George Mims, Betty Pulkingham and Ruth Newlander. Credit is due to Jeff Wilson for showing me the "Book of George."

On Memorial Day: From a June 24, 1990, interview of Bruce Durst.

"Everyone knows": From an article by Gregory Curtis, "They Found It!" *Texas Monthly*, p. 144, December 1977.

One household administrator: From an Aug. 1, 1991, interview of Harriet Hogle.

Earlier that year: Nancy Braud (who was not the woman attacked here) mentioned this event in a May 23, 1991, interview. The couple described in the previous passage talked with the author on July 28, 1991.

In 1978: From an Oct. 20, 1992, interview of Nancy Rodgers. The information on visitors from Portland came from a memo they wrote to the Bethlehem Church community in the fall of 1979.

It was around: From a May 28, 1992, interview of Neal Michell.

Chapter 17—Christmas

Information in this chapter was taken from previously cited interviews with Graham Pulkingham, George and Leslie Mims, Grover Newman, Bruce Durst, Reid Wightman and Jane Clowe.

Chris Simpson and Eugenia Rust also provided insights about Redeemer during this time period. Material was also taken from Redeemer vestry minutes beginning in 1979; however, large swatches of material are missing from these minutes. Parish directories beginning in 1963 were also examined. The years 1971-1973 were missing.

Descriptions of Woodland Park come from extensive notes taken by the author in October 1980.

Dell Hoffman was: From a June 19, 1992, interview.

That March: From an Aug. 4, 1990, interview of Wallace and Nancy Braud.

Right away: Several former parishioners provided information for this segment, including Barbara Baker, interviewed June 21, 1992.

Graham soon: From interviews with Andrew Franks on April 30 and June 19, 1990.

Only one of the companions: From a June 28, 1990, interview of Mark Dyke.

Chapter 19– Epiphany

The city of can-do: From David Ivanovich's "City's 'go-go years' went," *Houston Chronicle*, July 8, 1990.

But Redeemer, Tom felt: From an April 21, 1992, interview of Tom Herrick.

That June: From a July 1, 1991, interview of Don Sears.

About the same time: From previously cited interviews with George Mims. Also see a piece by Charles Ward "Departing Redeemer choir director: Congregation 'in post-charismatic era,' " *Houston Chronicle*, Aug. 6, 1983.

Faced by an ultimatum: From a June 27, 1992, interview of Jeff Schiffmayer.

By then it was clear: From a June 17, 1991, interview of Ladd Fields.

Margo filled in: From an undated tape "The Sun's Gonna Shine" made at Woodland Park, Colo.

The booklet also contained: See *The Story of Celebration and Its Rationale*, 1985.

If any outside rector: See above interview of Ladd Fields.

A few at Redeemer: Taken from interviews with Greg Davis, July 1, 1990, and Ralph Neal, June 20, 1992.

Cliff had first: From a June 29, 1991, interview of Cliff Wilson.

Meanwhile things were heating up: From a June 24, 1991, interview of Chris Simpson.

Another visitor: From a July 28, 1990, interview of Audrey Tindall.

Chaper 20—Lent

Bob Warren had stumbled: From an interview on July 15, 1990.

Mindful of the bitterness: From a June 29, 1991, interview of Cliff Wilson.

The night began: From a tape of "We are the Body of Christ," a sermon Graham Pulkingham gave Dec. 5, 1986, at Redeemer.

Leo had barely been: From a March 22, 1987, sermon at Redeemer given by Leo Alard.

Even oldtimers: From a July 24, 1991, interview of Camp Huntington.

Chapter 21—St. Polycarp

All the quotes from Graham's sermon, "A New Beginning," come from a June 14, 1987, tape of the service provided by Church of the Redeemer.

The saving grace: The Rev. Francis Martin gave this prophecy on July 25, 1987, in New Orleans.

Chapter 22—Sts. Perpetua and Felicity

One day, Theresa: From a July 28, 1991, interview of Theresa and Victor Wilson.

Turning and turning in the widening gyre: The eight lines of the poem sprinkled throughout the chapter come from the opening stanza of William Butler Yeats's "The Second Coming," published in 1921 in his collection of poems *Michael Robartes and the Dancer.*

Essie Avalos was: From a June 18, 1991, interview of Essie Avalos.

We were sitting: From interviews with David and Eugenia Rust on June 20 and 24, 1990.

Karen was a tall: From a June 19, 1990, interview of Karen Frerck Peterson.

Chapter 23—The Annunciation

In her mind: From a July 25, 1991, interview of Margi Pulkingham.

Chapter 24—Palm Sunday

By the time they moved: From a Jan. 25, 1992, interview of Bob and Cathleen Morris.

Word of God had dropped: Much of this information was taken from various Word of God tapes, including "Comments on Allied Status" by Ralph Martin, Oct. 21, 1990; also "Training Course Report," taped by Ken Wilson, Dec. 16, 1990.

It was clear that: Taken from a piece by Joyce Hollyday: "The Vision That Sustains Us," *Sojourners,* Dec. 1990, p. 28.

Although he was dying: See the Buckingham Report in the Sept./Oct. 1991 issue of *Ministries Today.*

Chapter 25—Maundy Thursday

Information for the beginning of this chapter was taken from tapes of David Lenzo's talks to Redeemer leaders, April 6-7, 1991.

Paul Felton preached: From a June 24, 1990, sermon.

Cliff began: From an Oct. 27, 1991, sermon.

Sul Ross: From a Feb. 27, 1992, parish gathering.

Next came: From Chris Caros's prophecy during the Easter 1992 service at Redeemer.

The sun was setting: See Ann Rodgers-Melnick's piece "Catholic Bishop of Steubenville to Probe Charismatic Community" which ran May 5, 1991, in the *Pittsburgh Press.*

Jackie began: From a July 5, 1992, interview of her, bolstered by details from an Aug. 19 interview of Richard Gullen.

For in May: From an Aug.16, 1992, interview of Bob Morris and a March 30, 1994, interview of Alden Hathaway.

Chapter 26—Good Friday

The beginning of the chapter was drawn from conversations with Jackie Gullen on Aug. 10, 1992, and Richard Gullen on Aug. 19 and Alden Hathaway on Feb. 15, 1994.

Unfortunately I was listed: From "Priest 'sorry' for misconduct," by Rebekah Schreffler, *Beaver County Times,* Aug. 18, 1992.

The RNS story: From "Religion Notes" by Peter Steinfels, *New York Times,* Aug. 22, 1992.

One man wrote a letter: From "Eulogies, Confessions and Apologies," an unpublished manuscript released by John G. Wilkes in 1996.

Sitting dejectedly: From a Jan. 26, 2009, interview of Bishop Cox.

In late March, Steven: From an April 7, 1994, interview of Steven Plummer.

It had happened in Burlington: From "Gunman kills 1 in busy grocery," *Greensboro News and Record*, April 2, 1993, by Peter Khoury and Donald Patterson. Jim Carr, a member of the family, supplied extra details in an April 11, 1993, interview.

Chapter 27—Holy Saturday

The Easter Vigil service is taken from the *1979 Episcopal Book of Common Prayer* (Seabury Press, New York).

ACKNOWLEDGMENTS

The author would like to thank Margaret and Scott Hornbostel for their hospitality and generosity in allowing her to stay at their Eastwood home during the many weeks over two summers that it took to do the bulk of the interviews for this book. She also wishes to cite Bill Newcott, formerly of *National Geographic*, who was so helpful in putting together a proposal for this book at a time when very few people were willing to help her on this project. She also is thankful to the Rev. G. Wilson Trigg for his interest and comments over the years, to Paul Frey for steering her in the right direction, to Roberta Kenney for her encouragement, to Joel Kneedler for his support and advice, and to the folks at Crossland Foundation for taking a chance on me.

INDEX